More praise

for *Change and Continuity*

"*Change and Continuity* is the preeminent text on American elections and voting behavior. The book utilizes the context of the most recent presidential and congressional elections to introduce students to the core concepts and theories needed for studying voting behavior. It draws on survey and historical data to answer questions about voter participation, electoral choice, and the changing nature of political parties in contemporary American politics. Perhaps most important, Abramson, Aldrich, and Rohde do a wonderful job of weaving all of these lessons of electoral scholarship into a substantive narrative that captures students' interest. I use *Change and Continuity* every time I teach elections and voting behavior, and I cannot imagine teaching the course without it."

—Brad Gomez, *Florida State University*

"When I have taught voting and elections, or related courses in the past, I have routinely used the *Change and Continuity* books by Abramson, Aldrich, and Rohde. The textbook successfully blends theoretical discussion of political behavior with accessible, compelling narratives of recent presidential and congressional campaigns and current findings from the venerable American National Election Studies series, helping students understand the ways in which political scientists study elections and voting. Perhaps most important, the authors also place recent elections in a rich historical context, illustrating the key trends in the public mood, party allegiances, and voting patterns over time."

—Chris Lawrence, *Texas A&M International University*

CHANGE AND CONTINUITY IN THE 2008 ELECTIONS

CHANGE AND CONTINUITY IN THE 2008 ELECTIONS

Paul R. Abramson
MICHIGAN STATE UNIVERSITY

John H. Aldrich
DUKE UNIVERSITY

David W. Rohde
DUKE UNIVERSITY

CQ PRESS

A Division of SAGE
Washington, D.C.

CQ Press
2300 N Street, NW, Suite 800
Washington, DC 20037

Phone: 202-729-1900; toll-free, 1-866-4CQ-PRESS (1-866-427-7737)

Web: www.cqpress.com

Cover design: Auburn Associates, Inc.
Typesetting: C&M Digitals (P) Ltd.

♾ The paper used in this publication exceeds the requirements of the American National Standard for Information Sciences—Permanence of Paper for Printed Library Materials, ANSI Z39.48-1992.

Printed and bound in the United States of America

13   12   11   10   09   1   2   3   4   5

Library of Congress Cataloging-in-Publication Data

Abramson, Paul R.
  Change and continuity in the 2008 elections / Paul R. Abramson, John H. Aldrich, David W. Rohde.
       p. cm.
  Includes bibliographical references and index.
  ISBN 978-1-60426-520-0 (pbk. : alk. paper) 1. Presidents—United States—Election—2008. 2. United States—Politics and government—2001-2009. I. Aldrich, John Herbert II. Rohde, David W. III. Title.

  JK5262008 .A27 2010
  324.973'0931—dc22

                                                        2009040944

To Lee J. Abramson

Contents

Tables and Figures

Tables

Figures

About the Authors

Paul R. Abramson is a professor of political science at Michigan State University. He is coauthor of *Value Change in Global Perspective* (1995) and author of *Political Attitudes in America* (1983), *The Political Socialization of Black Americans* (1977), and *Generational Change in American Politics* (1975). Along with John H. Aldrich and David W. Rohde, he is the coauthor of fourteen additional books in the *Change and Continuity* series, all of which were published by CQ Press.

John H. Aldrich is Pfizer-Pratt University Professor of Political Science at Duke University. He is coeditor of *Positive Changes in Political Science* (2007) and author of *Why Parties?* (1995) and *Before the Convention* (1980). He is past president of the Southern Political Science Association and the Midwest Political Science Association. In 2001 he was elected a fellow of the American Academy of Arts and Sciences.

David W. Rohde is Ernestine Friedl Professor of Political Science and director of the Political Institutions and Public Choice Program at Duke University. He is coeditor of *Why Not Parties?* (2008), author of *Parties and Leaders in the Post-reform House* (1991), coeditor of *Home Style and Washington Work* (1989), and coauthor of *Supreme Court Decision Making* (1976).

The authors, from left to right: David W. Rohde, John H. Aldrich, and Paul R. Abramson

Preface

On November 4, 2008, Democrat Barack Obama was elected president. In addition, the Democrats made substantial gains in the congressional elections. Having already won in 2006 a net thirty seats in the U.S. House of Representatives and six seats in the Senate, as well as control of both chambers, the Democrats added another twenty-one House seats and eight Senate seats in 2008.

Only four years earlier, some pundits had called the 2004 Republican victory a signal that the GOP had consolidated a long-term majority, whereas by 2009 some were pronouncing the Republicans nearly defunct. In our view, it is fairly easy to explain why the Republicans lost. We provide substantial evidence that the Democratic victory largely resulted from negative evaluations of George W. Bush and the Republican Party. Granted, this is not a novel explanation, but we believe it to be correct and we support it with a great deal of evidence.

OUR ANALYSIS

In our study of the 2008 elections, we rely on a wide variety of evidence. We begin by analyzing the election results of both the presidential and the congressional elections. Our investigation of the nomination process in Chapter 1, coauthored with Brian Pearson, includes new material examining alternative models that predict the probability of success. In our study of both the nomination contest and the general election campaign, we examine polls, especially those conducted by the Gallup Organization.

Throughout much of our book, we refer extensively to surveys from four sources. In studying voter turnout, we employ the Current Population Survey (CPS) conducted by the U.S. Census Bureau. The CPS provides information on the registration and voting of nearly 133,000 individuals from over eighty thousand households. In examining voting patterns, we rely heavily on a survey of over twenty thousand voters interviewed as they exited the voting polls and conducted by Edison Media Research/Mitofsky International for a consortium of news organizations, commonly referred to as the "pool poll." And in studying the party loyalties of the American electorate, we analyze the General Social Surveys conducted by the National Opinion Research Center at the University of Chicago, which measured party identification twenty-seven times between 1972 and 2008, usually relying on about 1,500 respondents.

Our main source of survey data is the 2008 American National Election Studies (ANES) survey based on 2,323 face-to-face interviews conducted before the 2008 election and 2,102 interviews conducted after the election, using the version of the data released for analysis in May 2009. This study is part of an ongoing series funded mainly by the National Science Foundation. These surveys, carried out by a team of scholars at the University of Michigan, began with a small study of the 1948 election; the first major study was in 1952. They have studied every subsequent presidential election, as well as all thirteen midterm elections from 1954 to 2002. In the course of our book, we use data from all twenty-nine surveys conducted between 1948 and 2008.

The ANES data are available to scholars throughout the world. Although we are not responsible for the data collection, we are responsible for our analyses. The scholars and staff at the ANES are responsible for neither our analyses nor our interpretation of these data.

ACKNOWLEDGMENTS

Many people assisted us with this study. We would like to begin by thanking our research assistants, Michael C. Brady and Melanie S. Freeze at Duke University and Tae-Eun Song at Michigan State University.

Lee J. Abramson, to whom we dedicate this book, helped us calculate the issue preferences of the electorate and also commented on several of the chapters.

Jack Citrin of the University of California at Berkeley made helpful suggestions for our discussion of presidential politics in California. In our study of turnout, we were greatly assisted by Michael P. McDonald of George Mason University, who provided us with information about the Current Population Survey. Russell J. Dalton of the University of California at Irvine and Robert W. Jackman late of the University of California at Davis helped us locate information about cross-national estimates of voter turnout. Abraham Diskin of the Hebrew University of Jerusalem helped us locate turnout data for Israel; Lawrence LeDuc at the University of Toronto helped us find turnout results for Canada; Michael Mintrom of the University of Auckland helped us find turnout results from New Zealand; and Dennis Patterson of Texas Tech University helped us locate turnout results from Japan. William Claggett at Florida State University read our chapter on turnout and provided several suggestions. We owe special thanks to Corwin D. Smidt at Michigan State University for his assistance in constructing our measure of religious tradition.

Abraham Diskin made helpful suggestions on our discussion of Israeli politics, as did Michal Shamir of Tel Aviv University. Martin J. Bull of the University of Salford and Joseph LaPalombara of Yale University made suggestions for our discussion of Italian politics. Finally, Kaare Strøm of the University of California at San Diego contributed suggestions to our summary of Swedish politics, and Dennis Patterson commented on our summary of Japanese politics.

We are especially grateful to Janet C. Abramson for copyediting our manuscript before we submitted it to CQ Press.

At CQ Press we are grateful to Charisse Kiino for encouragement and Allison McKay for help in the early editorial stages. We are especially grateful to them for finding reviewers who had assigned our book in the past, thereby allowing us to receive input from instructors and, indirectly, from students. The reviewers were Craig Brians, Virginia Tech University; Dennis Chong, Northwestern University; Helen Abbie Erler, Kenyon College; Brad Gomez, Florida State University; Kay Schlozman, Boston College; and Sean Theriault, University of Texas at Austin. We are grateful to Gwenda Larsen, our production editor. Sabra Bissette Ledent did an excellent job of copyediting the manuscript.

This book continues a series of fourteen books that we began with a study of the 1980 elections. In many places we refer to our earlier books, all of which were published by CQ Press. Some of this material is available online through the CQ Voting and Elections Collection, which can be accessed through many academic and public libraries.

Like our earlier books, this one was a collective enterprise in which we divided the labor. Paul Abramson had primary responsibility for Chapters 3, 4, 5, and 11, John Aldrich for Chapters 1, 6, 7, and 8, and David Rohde for Chapters 2, 9, and 10.

We appreciate feedback from our readers. Please contact us if you disagree with our interpretations, find factual errors, or want further clarification about our methods or our conclusions.

Paul R. Abramson
Michigan State University
abramson@msu.edu

John H. Aldrich
Duke University
aldrich@duke.edu

David W. Rohde
Duke University
david.rohde@duke.edu

PART I

The 2008 Presidential Election

On November 4, 2008, Barack Obama, the freshman Democratic senator from Illinois, was elected president. The son of a white mother from Kansas and a black father from Kenya became the first African American to win the nation's presidency. As Adam Nagourney wrote in the lead story in the next day's *New York Times*, "Barack Hussein Obama was elected the 44th president of the United States on Tuesday, sweeping away the last racial barrier in American politics with ease as the country chose him as its first black chief executive."[1] According to *The Economist*, Obama's victory rally "was a suitably exhilarating end to the most thrilling presidential race in a generation.... A sense of history in the making hung over the election: a country that has been torn apart by race peacefully elected a black man to the highest office in the land."[2]

Presidential elections in the United States are partly a ritual reaffirmation of its democratic values, a major reason why Obama's election was so important. But presidential elections are far more than rituals. The presidency confers a great deal of power, and those powers have expanded during most of the twentieth century as well as the early twenty-first century. Moreover, at times presidential elections have played a major role in determining public policy, and in some cases have shaped the course of American history.

The 1860 election, which brought Abraham Lincoln and the Republicans to power and ousted a divided Democratic Party, focused on whether slavery should be extended to the western territories. After Lincoln's election, eleven southern states attempted to secede from the Union, the Civil War broke out, and the U.S. government abolished slavery completely. Thus an antislavery plurality (Lincoln received only 40 percent of the popular vote) set in motion a chain of events that freed some four million black Americans.

In the 1896 election, Republican William McKinley defeated the Democrat and Populist William Jennings Bryan, thereby beating back the challenge of western and agricultural interests to the prevailing financial and industrial power of the East. Although Bryan mounted a strong campaign, winning 47 percent of the popular vote to McKinley's 51 percent, the election set a clear course for a policy of high tariffs and the continuation of the gold standard for American money.

Lyndon B. Johnson's 1964 landslide over Republican Barry M. Goldwater provided the clearest set of policy alternatives of any election in the twentieth century.[3] Goldwater offered "a choice, not an echo," advocating far more conservative social and economic policies than Johnson. When Johnson received 61 percent of the popular vote to Goldwater's 38 percent, he saw his victory as a mandate for his Great Society programs, the most far-reaching social legislation since World War II. The election also seemed to offer a clear choice between escalating American involvement in Vietnam and restraint. But America's involvement in Vietnam expanded after Johnson's election, leading to growing opposition to Johnson within the Democratic Party, and four years later he did not seek reelection.

WHAT DID THE 2008 ELECTION MEAN?

Some scholars argue that elections have become less important, and there is some truth to their arguments.[4] Still, elections do offer important choices on public policy, and those choices were sharper in 2008 than in most presidential contests. As we will demonstrate, the 2008 election was not primarily about choosing between the policies offered by Barack Obama and John McCain. Rather, it was more about rendering a judgment on George W. Bush and the Republican Party. But there were sharp policy differences between the major political parties.

Four years earlier, the war in Iraq and domestic security dominated the contest between Bush and Sen. John F. Kerry, and Bush won largely because Americans saw him as better able to protect America against terrorism.[5] In 2008 America was still at war, and the war in Iraq remained controversial. But terrorism was no longer a major issue. Even so, there were policy differences between the two candidates, with Obama promising to close the U.S. detention center at Guantanamo Bay, Cuba. Obama also pledged to order the military to remove U.S. combat forces from Iraq and to send two additional brigades to Afghanistan.[6] Unlike McCain, who opposed tax increases, Obama pledged to raise income taxes on families with incomes of more than $250,000 a year and individuals with incomes of more than $200,000 a year. Obama also promised a major overhaul of the U.S. health care system. And then there was the ailing economy; it was clear that Obama was likely to infuse it with massive financial aid to stimulate growth. Indeed, the long-running slowdown in the economy took a dramatic turn downward during the general election campaign itself, greatly altering campaign strategies and electoral dynamics.

Obama also promised to support reproductive rights, whereas McCain was opposed to such rights. However, both candidates agreed that they would support federal funding of embryonic stem cell research, an issue on which McCain's running mate, Alaska governor Sarah Palin, disagreed. Obama pledged to repeal the "don't ask, don't tell" rules for U.S. military service, under which openly homosexual men and women cannot serve. McCain disagreed. Obama also promised to assure that gay, lesbian, bisexual, and transgendered Americans would have equal rights, but he opposed same-sex marriage. Indeed, both Obama and McCain opposed an amendment to the U.S. Constitution to outlaw same-sex marriage, but for different reasons. Obama was opposed in principle to such bans, whereas McCain believed this was an issue for the states to decide.

Perhaps most important, the candidates clearly differed on the type of person they would nominate to fill vacancies on the U.S. Supreme Court. Obama had voted against the confirmation of both of Bush's Supreme Court appointments, John G. Roberts Jr. to chief justice and Samuel A. Alito Jr. to associate justice. He acknowledged that both were qualified jurists, but he believed their views on the Constitution were wrong. In sharp contrast, McCain praised both appointments. Later, Obama would nominate a Supreme Court replacement with liberal views. When on May 1, 2009, Associate Justice David H. Souter announced his intention to resign from the Court, it was clear that Obama would replace him with another liberal, and by the end of the month he had nominated federal appeals court judge Sonia Sotomayor to replace Souter. Although Sotomayor was viewed as a liberal justice, on the highly charged issue of abortion her position was ambiguous. On August 6, 2009, she was confirmed by the U.S. Senate by a vote of 68–31, with fifty-nine Democratic votes but only nine Republican votes. Two days later, she was sworn in as associate justice, becoming the third woman and the first Latino to serve on the Court. Granted, her seating will probably not greatly affect the liberal–conservative balance of the Court, but a President McCain likely would have nominated a jurist with conservative credentials, thereby changing the tilt of the Court.

The extent to which President Obama will achieve his goals while in office will depend on many factors beyond his control, especially the state of the economy. And foreign policy crises, such as the collapse of the government in Pakistan or Iran's acquisition of nuclear weapons, could force a drastic rethinking of American foreign and military policy. Of his domestic goals, reforming the health care system faced opposition from insurance companies and physicians, as well as congressional Republicans and conservative congressional Democrats.[7] Even so, it seems likely that many reforms will be implemented, although some may be derailed by the state of the economy. In 2008 the Democrats gained twenty-one seats in the House so that as the 111th Congress opened, they held 257 seats to the Republicans' 178. In the Senate, the Democrats eventually gained eight seats.[8] But close to a veto-proof majority was secured when Pennsylvania senator Arlen Specter switched to the Democratic Party in April 2009, giving the Democrats one shy of the sixty votes needed to invoke cloture and end filibusters. With Al Franken's win in Minnesota, they briefly held a precarious sixty to forty-vote margin. But with the death of Sen. Edward M. Kennedy on August 25, they temporarily lost this supermajority.

The 2008 election exhilarated the Democrats, although they did not express as much optimism as the Republicans had displayed after their narrow win four years earlier. All the same, some observers saw the election as a turning point that could lead to future Democratic dominance, restoring Democrats to their status as the majority party, which they had enjoyed between 1932 and 1968. Lanny J. Davis, a former special counsel to President Bill Clinton, wrote: "Tuesday's substantial victory by Barack Obama, together with Democratic gains in the Senate and House, appear to have accomplished a fundamental political realignment. The election is likely to create a new governing majority coalition that could dominate American politics for a generation or more."[9]

Obama was even compared to Franklin D. Roosevelt, under whose presidency (1933–1945) the New Deal coalition was forged. According to *Washington Post* columnist Harold Meyerson, "Even though Obama's victory was nowhere near as lopsided as Franklin Roosevelt's in 1932, his margins among decisive and growing constituencies make clear that this was a genuinely realigning election."[10] And as James W. Ceaser, Andrew E. Busch, and John J. Pitney Jr. point out, "*Time* magazine went so far as to suggest a parallel with Franklin Roosevelt's 1932 victory, printing a morphed Barack Obama's head onto an iconic photo of FDR, sporting his thirties style 'lid' and driving in a convertible."[11]

Four years earlier, scholars had been speculating about a pro-Republican realignment. Indeed, speculation about Republican dominance can be traced back to the late 1960s, when Kevin P. Phillips, in his widely read book *The Emerging Republican Majority*, argued that the Republicans could become the majority party, mainly by winning support in the South.[12] Between 1969, when his book was published, and 1984, the Republicans won three of the four presidential elections, winning by massive landslides in 1972, when Richard M. Nixon triumphed over George S. McGovern, and in 1984, when Ronald Reagan defeated Walter F. Mondale. In 1985 Reagan himself proclaimed that a Republican realignment was at hand. "The other side would like to believe that our victory last November was due to something other than our philosophy," he asserted. "I just hope that they keep believing that. Realignment is real."[13]

Reagan won 59 percent of the popular vote in November 1984, a clear reason for exuberance. George H. W. Bush's victory in 1988, with 53 percent, raised the possibility of continued Republican dominance. But in 1992 Bush won only 37 percent of the vote, a twenty-two-point decline from the GOP's high-water mark.

Obviously, the 1992 and 1996 presidential elections called into question the claims of a pro-Republican realignment. But Bill Clinton won only 43 percent of the popular vote in 1992 and just 49 percent in 1996. Moreover, the Republicans won control of the U.S. House of Representatives in the 1994 midterm elections, breaking a forty-year winning streak for the Democrats, who had won twenty consecutive elections.[14] The Republicans also gained control of the Senate, although this was far less of a shock.[15] They then held control of the House for the next five elections, and, except for a brief period between June 2001 and January 2003, controlled the Senate as well.[16]

The Republicans under George W. Bush regained the presidency in 2000, even though he won only 47.9 percent of the popular vote, while his Democratic opponent, Vice President Al Gore, won half a percentage point more, with 48.4 percent. But Bush won a slim 271–266 electoral vote majority. His victory was the third contest in a row in which the winner had failed to gain a majority of the popular vote. That raised the possibility that loyalties to the major political parties as well as established voting patterns were breaking down, a condition that political scientists have called "dealignment." Despite Bush's narrow reelection victory, some analysts saw the contest as an indication that the Republicans had become the majority party. Ceaser and Busch maintained, "No one would call the 2004 election a landslide, but the Republicans emerged from the election ascendant as the nation's majority party."[17] They argued that realignment had occurred.[18] "A realignment," they write, "can be conceived simply as a major change in the underlying strength of the two political parties during a specific period of time. By this definition, realignment has already taken place in the time period between the 1960s or 1979, when the Democratic Party was in the clear majority, and today, when the Republican Party holds an edge."[19] Moreover, according to Fred Barnes, Karl Rove, Bush's chief strategist, believed that whether the GOP would become the majority party would be decided by the 2004 elections. Rove argued that under Bush there has been a "rolling realignment" favoring the Republican Party.[20]

What do the terms *realignment* and *dealignment* mean? Political scientists define *realignment* in different ways, but they are all influenced by V. O. Key Jr., who developed a theory of "critical elections" in which "new and durable electoral groupings are formed."[21] Elections like that in 1860 in which Lincoln's victory brought the Republicans to power, in 1896 in which McKinley's victory solidified Republican dominance, and in 1932 in which the Democrats came to power under FDR are obvious candidates for such a label.

But later Key argued that partisan shifts could also take place over a series of elections—a pattern he called "secular realignment." During these periods, "shifts in the partisan balance of power" occur.[22] In this view, the realignment that first brought the Republicans to power might have begun in 1856, when the Republicans displaced the Whigs as the major competitor to the Democrats, and might have been consolidated by Lincoln's reelection in 1864 and Ulysses S. Grant's election in 1868. The realignment that consolidated Republican dominance in the late nineteenth century may well have begun in 1892, when Democrat Grover Cleveland won the election but the Populist Party, headed by James D. Weaver, attracted 8.5 percent of the popular vote, winning four states and electoral votes in two others. In 1896 the Populists supported William Jennings Bryan and were co-opted by the Democrats, but the electorate shifted to the Republican Party. The pro-Republican realignment might have been consolidated by McKinley's win over Bryan in 1900 and by Theodore Roosevelt's victory in 1904.

Though the term *New Deal* was not coined until 1932, the New Deal realignment may have begun with Herbert C. Hoover's triumph over Democrat

Al Smith, the first Roman Catholic to be nominated by a major political party. Although badly defeated, Smith carried two New England states, Massachusetts and Rhode Island, which later became the most Democratic states in the nation.[23] As Key points out, the beginnings of a shift toward the Democrats was detectable in Smith's defeat.[24] However, the New Deal coalition was not created by the 1932 election but after it, and it was consolidated by Roosevelt's 1936 landslide over Alfred M. Landon and his 1940 defeat of Wendell Willkie.

Although scholars disagree about how long it takes to create a partisan alignment, they all agree that durability is an essential element of any realignment. As James L. Sundquist writes, "Those who analyze alignment and realignment are probing beneath the immediate and transitory ups and downs of daily politics and periodic elections to discover fundamental shifts in the structure of the party system."[25] According to Lawrence G. McMichael and Richard J. Trilling, realignment is "a significant and durable change in the distribution of party support over relevant groups within the electorate."[26]

Not all scholars believe that the concept of realignment is useful. In 1991 Byron E. Shafer edited a volume in which several chapters questioned its utility.[27] More recently, David R. Mayhew published a monograph critiquing scholarship on realignment, and his book has received widespread critical acclaim.[28] Mayhew cites fifteen claims made by scholars of realignment and then empirically tests these claims. He disputes the widely argued thesis that the 1896 McKinley-Brian contest marked a realignment. He argues that the claims made by scholars of realignment do not stand up, and that the concept of realignment should be abandoned.

Although we disagree with many of Mayhew's arguments, this is not the place for an extensive discussion. We would, however, like to make four points. First, although Mayhew discusses fifteen claims made by scholars of realignments, he mentions only two that guide our discussion.[29] Second, we believe that there is substantial evidence that the 1896 election was critical in establishing Republican dominance.[30] Third, we disagree with the arguments that increases in turnout are not related to past realignments. Finally, there has been excellent research that employs the concept of realignment, such as the work of David W. Brady, Peter F. Nardulli, and Gary Miller and Norman Schofield.[31]

In our view, partisan realignments in the United States have had five basic characteristics: (1) changes in the regional bases of party support; (2) changes in the social bases of party support; (3) the mobilization of new groups into the electorate; (4) the emergence of divisive issues; and (5) changes not just in voting patterns but also in how voters think about the political parties.

1. *Changes in the regional bases of party support.* For example, compare the Republican Party with the Whigs, who were the major opposition to the Democrats between 1836 and 1852. Between 1836 (when the Whigs opposed Democrat Martin van Buren) and 1852, the Whigs drew at least some of their support from the South. The last Whig candidate to be

elected, Zachary Taylor in 1848, won sixty-six of his electoral votes from the fifteen slave states.[32] In his 1860 victory, Lincoln did not win a single electoral vote from the fifteen slave states[33] But he did win all the electoral votes from seventeen of the eighteen free states, as well as a majority of the electoral votes in New Jersey. Subsequent realignments have not involved this degree of regional polarization, but they all have displayed regional shifts in party support.

2. *Changes in the social bases of party support.* Even during a period when one party is becoming dominant, some social groups may be moving to the losing party. During the 1930s, for example, Roosevelt gained the support of industrial workers, but at the same time he lost support among business owners and professionals.

3. *Mobilization of new groups into the electorate.* Between Calvin Coolidge's Republican landslide in 1924 and Roosevelt's third-term victory in 1940, turnout among the voting-age population rose from 44 percent to 59 percent. Although some long-term forces were pushing turnout upward, the sharp increase between 1924 and 1928 and again between 1932 and 1936 resulted at least in part from the mobilization of new social groups into the electorate. Ethnic groups that were predominantly Catholic were mobilized to support Al Smith in 1928, and industrial workers were mobilized to support Franklin Roosevelt in 1936.

4. *Emergence of new issues that divide the electorate.* In the 1850s, the Republican Party reformulated the controversy over slavery to form a winning coalition. By opposing the expansion of slavery into the territories, the Republicans contributed to divisions within the Democratic Party. No issue since slavery has divided America as deeply, and subsequent realignments have never brought a new political party to power. But those realignments have always been based on the division of the electorate over new issues.

5. *Changes not in just how voters vote but also in how they think about the political parties.* During the Great Depression in 1932, many voters who thought of themselves as Republicans voted against Hoover. Later, many of these voters returned to the Republican side, but others began to think of themselves as Democrats. Likewise, in 1936 some voters who thought of themselves as Democrats disliked FDR's policies and voted against him. Some of these defectors may have returned to the Democratic fold in subsequent elections, but others began to think of themselves as Republicans.

Since World War II, similar changes have occurred. Most obvious are the fundamental shifts in the regional bases of party support. Some groups shifted their voting patterns such as the southern whites who shifted away from the Democratic Party and the New Englanders who moved toward the Democrats. Moreover, there have been changes in party loyalties. After 1964, there was a substantial erosion in party loyalties among whites, and from 1988 to 2004 there was near parity in the percentages of Republicans and Democrats. Despite these changes, the Republicans have never emerged as the majority party among the electorate, whereas, because of the gains in Democratic loyalties between 2004 and 2008, the Democrats have once again emerged as the majority party.

The percentage of Americans who identify with a political party is substantially lower than it was between 1952 and 1964 when party loyalties were first systematically measured. Moreover, a great deal of volatility has emerged in the voting patterns of the electorate. Since the end of World War II, in two elections, 1968 and 1992, a third-party or independent candidate has won a sizable share of the vote.

These changes have led some scholars to use the term *dealignment* to characterize American politics during the last four decades. The term was first used by Ronald Inglehart and Avram Hochstein in 1972.[34] A dealignment is a condition in which old voting patterns break down without being replaced by newer ones. Most scholars who use this term find that a key component is the weakening of party loyalties. As Russell J. Dalton, Paul Allen Beck, and Scott C. Flanagan point out, dealignment was originally viewed as a stage preliminary to a new partisan alignment. But, they argue, dealignment "may be a regular feature of electoral politics."[35] Dalton and Martin P. Wattenberg are more specific: "Whereas realignment involves people changing from one party to another, dealignment concerns people gradually moving away from all parties." The large vote for H. Ross Perot in 1992, they argue, may have come from voters who had few feelings— positive or negative—toward the parties. Many scholars "express concern about potential dealignment trends because they fear the loss of the stabilizing, conserving equilibrium that party attachments provide to electoral systems."[36]

The concept of dealignment applies to other countries as well.[37] Bo Särlvik and Ivor Crewe characterized the 1970s as "the decade of dealignment" in British politics.[38] And Harold D. Clarke and his colleagues suggest that Canadian politics has reached a stage of "permanent dealignment." "A dealigned party system," they write, "is one in which volatility is paramount, where there are frequent changes in electoral outcomes, as well as lots of individual flexibility."[39]

Contemplating questions about the prospects for realignment and dealignment leads to several questions that we will ask throughout this book. Most important, why did the Republicans, who seemed to many to be on the cusp of attaining electoral dominance, lose their majority over a mere four years? Clearly, the congressional losses in 2006 resulted from dissatisfaction with the war in Iraq, and, even more clearly, their losses in 2008 resulted from the economic downturn, which, in turn, contributed to dissatisfaction with Bush's performance as president. But did other forces also undermine Republican prospects? Will the Democrats be able to solidify their majority, and, if so, what will they need to do to improve their prospects? What is the best Republican strategy for regaining power? Most important, why has postwar American politics experienced the highest level of volatility since the Civil War, and is that volatility likely to continue?

SURVEY RESEARCH SAMPLING

Our book relies heavily on surveys of the American electorate. It draws on a massive exit poll conducted by Edison Media Research/Mitofsky International, surveys conducted in people's homes by the National Opinion Research Center and the U.S. Census Bureau, as well as telephone polls. But our main data source for 2008 is a face-to-face survey of 2,323 U.S. citizens conducted in their homes as part of the American National Election Studies (ANES) Time Series Survey.[40] The Survey Research Center (SRC) and Center for Political Studies (CPS) at the University of Michigan have conducted surveys using national samples in every presidential election since 1948 and in every midterm election between 1954 and 2002.[41] Since 1952, the ANES surveys have measured party identification and feelings of political effectiveness. The CPS, founded in 1970, has developed valuable questions for measuring issue preferences. The ANES surveys are the best and most comprehensive for studying the issue preferences and party loyalties of the American electorate.

Readers may question our reliance on the ANES surveys of 2,300 people when some 213 million Americans are eligible to vote. Would we have similar results if all adults eligible to vote had been surveyed?[42] The ANES uses a procedure called multistage probability sampling to select the particular individuals to be interviewed. This procedure ensures that the final sample is likely to represent the entire population of U.S. citizens of voting age, except for Americans living on military bases, in institutions, or abroad.[43]

Because of the probability procedures used to conduct the ANES surveys, we are able to estimate the likelihood that the results represent the entire population of noninstitutionalized citizens living in the United States. Although the 2008 ANES survey sampled only about one in every 92,000 voting-eligible Americans, the representativeness of a sample depends far more on the size of the sample than the size of the population being studied, provided the sample is drawn properly. With samples of this size, we can be fairly confident (to a level of .95) that the results we get will fall within three percentage points of that obtained if the entire population had been surveyed.[44] For example, when we find that 27 percent of respondents approved of the job George W. Bush was doing as president, we can be reasonably confident that between 24 percent (27 − 3) and 30 percent (27 + 3) approved of his performance.[45] The actual results could be less than 24 percent or more than 30 percent. But a confidence level of .95 means that the odds are nineteen to one that the entire electorate falls within this range. The range of confidence becomes somewhat larger when we look at subgroups of the electorate. For example, with subsets of about five hundred (and the results in the 50 percent range) the confidence error rises to plus or minus six percentage points. Because the likelihood of sampling error grows as our subsamples become smaller, we often supplement our analysis with reports of other surveys.

Somewhat more complicated procedures are needed to determine whether the difference between two groups is likely to reflect the relationship found if the entire population were surveyed. The probability that such differences reflect real differences in the population is largely a function of the size of the groups being compared.[46] Generally speaking, when we compare the results of the 2008 sample with an earlier ANES survey, a difference of four percentage points is sufficient to be reasonably confident that the difference is real. For example, in 2004 when George W. Bush was reelected, 24 percent of respondents said that the economy had improved in the last year; in 2008 only 2 percent did. This twenty-two percentage point difference is far more than we would need to conclude that the public's perception of the economy had soured.

When we compare subgroups of the electorate sampled in 2008 (or compare those subgroups with subgroups sampled in earlier years), a larger percentage is usually necessary to conclude that differences are meaningful. For example, 28 percent of men and 26 percent of women approved of Bush's performance as president. Even though 1,029 men and 1,217 women answered this question, a two-point difference is too small to safely conclude that this gender difference was real. Generally speaking, in comparisons of men and women a difference of five percentage points is needed.[47] By contrast, 32 percent of whites approved of Bush's performance as president, whereas only 5 percent of blacks did. Granted, 1,773 whites were interviewed, but only 274 blacks.[48] In general, a difference of nine percentage points is needed to conclude that differences between whites and blacks are meaningful. Here, however, there is a twenty-seven-point difference, and so we can say with extreme confidence that blacks had a more negative evaluation of Bush than whites.

This discussion represents only a ballpark guide to judging whether reported results are likely to represent the total population. Better estimates can be obtained using the formulas presented in many statistics textbooks. To make such calculations or even a rough estimate of the chances of error, the reader must know the size of the groups being compared. For that reason, we always report in our tables and figures either the number of cases on which our percentages are based or the information needed to approximate the number of cases.

THE 2008 CONTEST

In this section on the 2008 presidential election, Chapters 1 and 2 follow the chronology of the campaign itself. As described in Chapter 1, in most contests in which the incumbent president is not running for reelection, a large number of candidates compete. The 2008 contest was no exception: eight Democrats and eight Republicans were running when the election year began. In Chapter 1, we discuss the regularities in the nomination process that explain why some candidates run while others do not. We then examine the rules governing the nomination contests, noting that because of the U.S. federal system there is a great deal of variation among the states. In recent contests, states have tended to move their delegate selection contests—whether state-run primaries or party-run caucuses—to early in the delegate selection season, a phenomenon called front-loading. We also assess the importance of campaign financing and the way in which Barack Obama used the Internet to raise campaign funds.

The dynamics of multicandidate contests and the concept of momentum used by John H. Aldrich to discuss nomination contests in the 1970s are covered in Chapter 1 as well. We also update two academic models used to predict which candidates will succeed—one developed by Randall E. Adkins, Andrew J. Dowdle, and Wayne P. Steger and the other developed by Barbara Norrander. We then turn to the Democratic contest and explain why Obama was able to prevail in a protracted contest with Hillary Rodham Clinton, the former first lady and junior senator from New York. We next turn to the Republican contest to see how John McCain, the senior senator from Arizona, resurrected his seemingly moribund campaign to defeat his seemingly strong rivals, such as Rudy Giuliani, former mayor of New York City, Mitt Romney, the former governor of Massachusetts, and Fred Thompson, a former senator from Tennessee—all of whom seemed to have reasonably good prospects of victory during 2007. And we will see how McCain was able to withstand the challenge from Mike Huckabee, the former governor of Arkansas who became the favorite of the Christian right.

Finally, we discuss why Obama made the fairly conventional choice of Joe Biden, the senior senator from Delaware, as his running mate, and why McCain made the unconventional choice of Sarah Palin, the governor of Alaska. And we take a look at the party nominating conventions because, although they no longer play an important role in selecting the presidential candidate, they are the springboards from which candidates launch their general election campaigns.

Chapter 2 moves to the general election campaign. Because of the rules set forth by the U.S. Constitution for winning presidential elections, candidates must think about how to win enough states to gain a majority (270) of the electoral vote (538 since 1964). We examine the rules by which states allocate their electoral votes as well as their voting patterns over the last five elections. These patterns indicate a relatively close balance between the parties, but conditions as the general election campaign began suggested an advantage for the Democrats. That advantage grew after the financial meltdown that began in mid-September, which in retrospect dealt a fatal blow to the Republican chances.

As for the strategies adopted by the campaigns, Obama's most important decision was to decline the $84 million in federal funding for his campaign that he could have claimed as a major-party candidate, whereas McCain accepted this funding and the spending limits it imposed. Obama's remarkable success at fundraising played a crucial role in his ability to buy media time and to finance his organization. In making their appeals to the voters, McCain, who had supported immigration reform in the past, lost his ability to appeal to Latino voters. Obama hammered away on the weakness of the economy and did his best to link McCain to Bush. Meanwhile, the GOP tried to portray Obama as a liberal who would raise taxes and as someone who lacked the experience to serve as president.

In Chapter 2, we also reexamine the selection of the vice presidential candidates and dissect the roles that Biden and Palin played during the campaign. As the campaign progressed, the public became increasingly concerned about Palin's ability to serve as president, another factor that may have weakened McCain's chances.

Both campaigns focused on the so-called battleground states—that is, those states that both parties had a chance of winning. But as the campaign developed, McCain spent more time defending states that had voted for Bush in both 2000 and 2004, whereas toward the end of the campaign Obama was targeting states that had seldom voted Democratic since Lyndon Johnson's victory in 1964.

As in 1960 and in every election from 1976 onward, debates played a major role in the campaign. There were three presidential debates and one vice presidential debate. We conclude that their effects were not one-sided, but that the Democrats were the moderate beneficiaries.

Last, we turn to the end game of the campaign, the battle over turnout. Getting one's supporters to the polls is largely a "ground game" won through organizational tactics, not by advertising on television and the radio. It is widely argued that the Democrats won these get-out-the-vote efforts, although Part II reveals that the empirical evidence is inconclusive. In 2008 both candidates tried to get their supporters to the polls early, and so the level of early voting was unprecedented. Once again, however, there is mixed evidence about which side benefited from this development.

Chapter 3 turns to the actual election results, relying largely on the official election statistics. In this chapter, we make very little use of survey research data, because we believe that any analysis of elections should begin with the actual results and turn to polling later. We follow this strategy in our analyses of both the presidential election and the congressional elections.

We present the official election results by state in Chapter 3, as well as for Maine's two congressional districts and for Nebraska's three districts. Our look at electoral vote patterns is followed by a discussion of the election rules, noting that the U.S. plurality vote system supports Duverger's law, a proposition developed by the French political scientist Maurice Duverger in the 1950s. We examine the pattern of results during the sixteen postwar elections, as well as those in all forty-five elections between 1832 and 2008. As we point out, since 1948 politics has been characterized by the highest level of volatility since the Civil War.

We then analyze the state-by-state results, paying particular attention to regional shifts in the elections between 1980 and 2008. One finding is that even as recently as 1980 the South was not a distinctively Republican region, although in every presidential election since 1984 the Republicans have fared better in the South than outside the South. Changes in four regions are of particular interest. We focus most of our attention on electoral change in the postwar South, because this region has been the scene of the most dramatic changes in postwar

U.S. politics. Meanwhile, the mountainous West has also shifted to the GOP, whereas New England has moved to the Democrats. And then there is California, which has shifted from leaning Republican to voting strongly Democratic in presidential elections.

Finally, we study the results of the last five presidential elections to assess the electoral vote balance. As we reveal, after 2004 an examination of the five most recent elections suggested an extremely close balance between Republicans and Democrats. But this balance has now clearly shifted toward the Democrats.

Chapter 1

The Nomination Struggle

*With Brian Pearson**

The presidential nomination campaigns of both parties in 2008 were widely regarded as unusually exciting and unpredictable. Many onlookers were stirred because the candidates were particularly popular and offered both thrilling and surprising plot lines. Some candidates expected to be among the strongest contenders failed early. Former senator and TV star Fred Thompson and former New York City mayor Rudy Giuliani failed to show strongly in a single Republican primary, even though they were among the favorites in 2007. Conversely, although he seemed strong early on, Arizona senator John McCain saw his campaign all but collapse in mid-2007, and the media wrote his presidential obituary—rather too early as it happened. On the Democratic side, the emergence of Sen. Barack Obama of Illinois was the surprise story of 2008. The resilience of the campaign of New York senator Hillary Rodham Clinton was also dramatic. If bets had been laid in late 2007, the favorites would have been a long, drawn-out Republican contest and an early end to the Democratic race because of the strength of the Clinton campaign.[1]

Of course, these predictions were dashed, with the media pundits and bettors alike forecasting very badly (although, as we describe, scholarly expectations were closer to the mark). In many respects, however, the presidential nomination contests of 2008 looked similar to all of those fought since 1972. Reforms in the late 1960s and early 1970s had brought about a new form of nomination campaign, one that required public campaigning for resources and votes. The "new nomination system of 1972," as we call it, has shaped many aspects of all contests from 1972 onward, and we examine the similarities that have endured over its thirty-six-year existence. Each contest, of course, differs from all others because of the electoral context at the time (for example, the state of the economy, of war

---

*Brian Pearson, coauthor of this chapter, is a Duke alumnus ('08) currently working in the private sector.

and peace) and because the contenders themselves are different. And in the new nomination system, the rules change to some degree every four years as well. The changes in rules, and the strategies that candidates adopt in light of those rules, combine with the context and contenders to make each campaign unique.

In 2008, as in other recent campaigns, the changes in the rules that had the most impact on candidate strategy and the ultimate outcome of the nomination contest were the dates on which each state held its presidential primary or caucuses. State legislatures (which determine the dates of primaries) and state parties (which determine the dates of caucuses) have increasingly tried to hold their primaries or caucuses as early in the year as possible. This front-loading, as it is now known, became one of the most important forces shaping the campaigns from 1996 to 2008. Learning from the experiences of their predecessors, in 2008 the candidates carefully designed their strategies around the front-loaded campaign. This confluence of circumstances accounts for many of the most striking aspects of the 2008 campaign—its early beginning in both parties, its early conclusion among Republicans, and the convergence to what turned out to be a protracted two-candidate race among the Democrats. This confluence also helps us understand why McCain won and how Obama could emerge from virtually nowhere to challenge and then to defeat the early front-runner, Clinton.

In this chapter, we examine some of the regularities of the campaigns since 1972 and see how they helped shape the 2008 nomination contests. Next, we turn to the first step of the nomination process: the decisions of politicians to become—or not to become—presidential candidates. Then we examine some of the rules of the nomination system they face. Finally, we consider how the candidates ran and why McCain and Obama succeeded in their quests.

WHO RAN

A first important regularity of the nomination campaign is that when incumbents seek renomination, only a very few candidates will contest them, and perhaps no one will at all. In 1972, although President Richard M. Nixon did face two potentially credible challengers to his renomination, they were so ineffective that he was essentially uncontested. Ronald Reagan in 1984, Bill Clinton in 1996, and George W. Bush in 2004 were actually unopposed. They were so, in large part, because even a moderately successful president is virtually undefeatable for renomination. Conversely, Gerald R. Ford in 1976, Jimmy Carter in 1980, and George H. W. Bush in 1992 faced one, or at most two, credible challengers. Although Bush defeated his challenger, Pat Buchanan, rather easily, Ford and Carter had great difficulty defeating their opponents, Reagan and Democratic senator Edward M. Kennedy of Massachusetts, respectively. Those two campaigns, while demonstrating that incumbents are not assured of victory, nevertheless demonstrate the power of presidential incumbency because both incumbents were victorious despite facing the strongest imaginable challengers and despite being relatively weak incumbents.

The second major regularity in the nomination system concerns the other set of contests, those in which the party has no incumbent seeking renomination. In such cases, a relatively large number of candidates run for the nomination. Eight major candidates sought each party's nomination in 2008. Several more in both parties had declared but dropped out of the race by January 1, 2008. There have been ten such campaigns since 1980, and the number of major candidates that were in the race as the year began varied remarkably little: seven in 1980 (R), eight in 1984 (D), eight (D) and six (R) in 1988, eight in 1992 (D), eight in 1996 (R), six in 2000 (R), and nine in 2004 (D), to go along with the two eight-candidate contests in 2008. The major exception to this regularity is that only Vice President Al Gore and former New Jersey senator Bill Bradley sought the Democratic nomination of 2000, even though many others seriously considered doing so.

The Democrats in 2008 were Senators Joe Biden of Delaware, Hillary Clinton of New York, Christopher J. Dodd of Connecticut, and Barack Obama of Illinois; former senators John Edwards of North Carolina and Mike Gravel of Alaska; New Mexico governor Bill Richardson; and Rep. Dennis Kucinich of Ohio. Former governor Tom Vilsack of Iowa had declared his candidacy but dropped out of the campaign in 2007. The Republican candidates were Sen. John McCain of Arizona; former senator Fred Thompson of Tennessee; former governors Mike Huckabee of Arkansas, Mitt Romney of Massachusetts, and Tommy Thompson of Wisconsin; Reps. Duncan Hunter of California and Ron Paul of Texas; and former New York City mayor Rudy Giuliani. Sen. Sam Brownback of Kansas, former Virginia governor Jim Gilmore, and former representative Tom Tancredo of Colorado had declared their candidacies but dropped out before 2008 began.

We have so far illustrated two regularities: few or no candidates will challenge incumbents, but many candidates will seek the nomination when no incumbent is running. A third regularity is that among the candidates who are politicians, most hold, or have recently held, high political office. This regularity follows from "ambition theory," developed originally by Joseph A. Schlesinger to explain how personal ambition and the pattern and prestige of various elected offices lead candidates to emerge from those political offices that have the strongest electoral bases.[2] This base for the presidential candidates includes the offices of vice president, senator, governor, and, of course, the presidency itself. Note that Hunter, Paul, and Kucinich were the only members of the U.S. House to actually run for the presidential nomination. House members do not have a strong electoral base from which to run for the presidency and may forgo a safe House seat to do so. As a result, few run and fewer still are strong contenders.[3]

Most candidates in 2008, as in all earlier campaigns under the new nomination system, emerged from one of the strong electoral bases. Table 1-1 presents the data for 2008 and for all campaigns from 1972 to 2008 combined. Over two-thirds of the presidential candidates had already served as president, vice president, senator, or governor; another one in eight was a member of the U.S. House. Many of the early presidents were chosen from the outgoing president's cabinet (especially the sitting secretary of state), but the cabinet is no longer a serious

TABLE 1-1   Current or Most Recent Office Held by Declared Candidates for President: Two Major Parties, 1972–2008

Office held	Percentage of all candidates who held that office	Number, 1972–2008	Number, 2008
President	6	7	0
Vice president	3	4	0
U.S. senator	39	47	8
U.S. representative	13	15	3
Governor	20	24	4
U.S. cabinet	3	4	0
Other	7	8	1
None	8	10	0
Total	99	119	16

Sources: 1972–1992: Congressional Quarterly's Guide to U.S. Elections, 4th ed. (Washington, D.C.: CQ Press, 2001), 522–525, 562; 1996: Paul R. Abramson, John H. Aldrich, and David W. Rohde, *Change and Continuity in the 1996 and 1998 Elections* (Washington, D.C.: CQ Press, 1999), 13; 2000: *CQ Weekly,* January 1, 2000, 22; 2004: *CQ Weekly,* Fall 2003 Supplement, Vol. 61, Issue 48. The 2008 results were compiled by the authors.

source of presidential candidates. Although mayors rarely run for president, the mayor of New York City is particularly prominent in the media, and Mayor Rudy Giuliani's unique role in the attacks on the United States of September 11, 2001, gave him great national visibility.

A fourth regularity, also consistent with ambition theory, is that of the many who run in nomination contests without incumbents, only a few put their current office at risk to do so. Among the Republicans in 2008, only the members of the House and Sen. McCain were then holding office, and only the House members were up for reelection. Among Democrats, only Biden and Kucinich were up for reelection, and under Delaware law Biden could run simultaneously for both offices. Ultimately, he did run for both vice president and Senate, won both, and then resigned his Senate seat to become vice president.[4]

THE RULES OF THE NOMINATION SYSTEM

The method that the two major parties use for nominating presidential candidates is unique and amazingly complicated. To add to the complication, the various formal rules, laws, and procedures for the nomination are changed, sometimes in large ways and invariably in numerous small ways, every four years. Beyond the formal rules lie informal standards and expectations, often set by the news media or the candidates themselves, that help shape each campaign.

As variable as the rules are, however, the nomination system of 1972 has one pair of overriding characteristics that define it as a system: first, since 1972 the major-party presidential nominees have been selected in public and by the public, and, second, as a result all serious candidates have pursued the nomination by seeking the support of the public through the various communication media.

The complexity of the nomination contests is a consequence of four major factors. The first of these, federalism, or the state as the unit of selection for national nominees, is at least 180 years old. The second factor, the rules on the selection (and perhaps instruction) of delegates to the convention, and the third factor, the rules on financing the campaign, are the often revised products of the reform period. The fourth factor is the way in which candidates react to these rules and to their opponents, and grows out of the keen competition for a highly valued goal. These factors are described in more detail in the sections that follow.

Federalism or State-Based Delegate Selection

National conventions to select presidential nominees were first held for the 1832 election, and for every nomination since then the votes of delegates attending the conventions have determined the nominees.[5] Delegates have always been allocated at the state level; whatever other particulars may apply, each state selects its parties' delegates through procedures adopted by state party organizations (for caucuses), by state law (for primaries), or both. Votes at the convention are cast by state delegation, and in general the state (including the District of Columbia, various territories, and, for the Democrats, even Americans living abroad) is the basic unit of the nomination process. Thus there are really fifty-one separate delegate selection contests in each party (plus procedures for the remaining units). There is no national primary, nor is there serious contemplation of one.

That there are more than fifty separate contests in each campaign creates numerous layers of complexity, two of which are especially consequential. First, each state is free to choose delegates using any method consistent with the general rules of the national party. Many states choose to select delegates via a primary election, which is a state-run election like any other, except that each primary selects delegates for only one party's convention. (It also is often an election to select the party's nominees for the various other elected offices.) The Democratic Party requires that its primaries be open only to registered Democrats.[6] States not holding primaries use a combination of caucuses and conventions, which are designed and run by each political party and not by the state government. Caucuses are simply local meetings of party members. Those attending the caucuses typically report their preferences for the presidential nomination (and must do so on the Democratic side) and choose delegates from their midst to attend higher-level conventions such as the county, congressional district, state, and eventually the national party conventions. In addition to selecting delegates, caucuses and subsequent conventions may endorse platform proposals and usually conduct other party business.

The second major consequence of federalism is that the states are free (within bounds described later) to choose when to hold their primaries or caucuses. These events are thus spread out over time, although both parties now set a time period—the delegate selection "window"—during which primaries and caucuses can be held. New Hampshire has held the first primary in the nation since the state began to hold primaries in 1920, and state law requires that New Hampshire's primary be held before any other state's. A more recent tradition, dating from 1976, is that Iowa holds the first caucuses before the New Hampshire primary, but this "tradition" has been challenged by other states, which have tried from time to time to schedule even earlier caucuses. In 2008 states continued to push their starting dates earlier and earlier. As a result, Iowa held its caucus on January 3, by far the earliest start to the delegate selection phase of the campaign. The Democratic Party sought to ensure that other types of (small) states were among the earliest to select delegates, and thus authorized Nevada to hold its caucus on January 19 and South Carolina to hold its primary on January 26, so that states from various regions, including Nevada, with its considerable Latino population and strong labor unions, and South Carolina, with its significant numbers of African Americans, would be involved early. This development forced New Hampshire back to January 8.

Two large states decided to hold their primaries early—Michigan on January 15 and Florida on January 29—thereby defying the national Democratic Party. The result was conflict over whether the delegates would be given votes or "punished" for intentionally violating party rules. A compromise was eventually reached, but only in the summer before the election, after Obama had secured majority support. The more immediate result of all these changes was that a substantial number of delegates were up for grabs far earlier than even in the most front-loaded primary season, 2004. On the Republican side, Wyoming, New Hampshire, Michigan, South Carolina, and Florida saw their delegate totals cut in half because they held their primary or caucus before the Republicans permitted delegates to be selected; their window opened on February 5.[7]

All this shows just how front-loaded the campaigns have become over the years. In Figure 1-1, we compare the cumulative total of delegates awarded by week of the campaigns in 1976 and 2008.[8] In 1976, 60 percent of the delegates were selected by the seventeenth week of the campaign, but in 2008 that percentage was reached by the fifth week (February 5, three weeks earlier than the New Hampshire primary in 1976)! The 2008 primary season ended on June 3, although caucus procedures continued throughout the month.

The Nomination System of 1972: Delegate Selection

Through 1968, presidential nominations were won by appeals to the party leadership. To be sure, public support and even primary election victories could be

FIGURE 1-1   Front-loading, 1976 and 2008

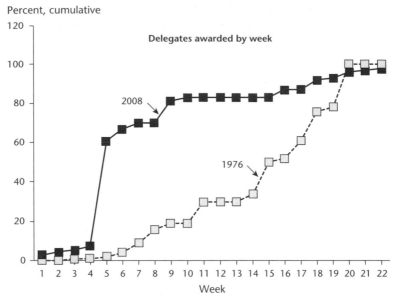

Source: Compiled by the authors.

important in a candidate's campaign, but their importance stemmed from the credibility they would give to the candidacy in the eyes of party leaders. The 1968 Democratic nomination, like so many events that year, was especially tumultuous.[9] The result was that the Democratic Party undertook a series of reforms, led by the McGovern-Fraser Commission and adopted by the party convention in 1972. The reforms were sufficiently radical in changing delegate selection procedures that they, in effect, created a new nomination system. Although it was much less aggressive in reforming its delegate selection procedures, the Republican Party did so to a certain degree. However, the most consequential results of the Democratic reforms for our purposes—the proliferation of presidential primaries and the media's treatment of some (notably the Iowa) caucuses as essentially primary-like—spilled over to the Republican side as well.

In 1968 Democratic senators Eugene J. McCarthy of Minnesota and Robert F. Kennedy of New York ran very public, highly visible, primary-oriented campaigns in opposition to the policies of President Lyndon B. Johnson, especially the conduct of the war in Vietnam. Before the second primary, held in Wisconsin, Johnson surprisingly announced, "I shall not seek and I will not accept the nomination of my party for another term as your President."[10] Vice President Hubert H. Humphrey took Johnson's place in representing the establishment and the policies of the Democratic Party. Humphrey, however, waged no public campaign; he won the nomination without entering a single primary, thereby splitting an already deeply divided party.[11] Would Humphrey have won the nomination had Robert Kennedy not been assassinated the night he defeated McCarthy in California, effectively eliminating McCarthy as a serious contender? No one will ever know. Democrats did know, however, that the chaos and violence that accompanied Humphrey's nomination clearly indicated that the nomination process should be opened to more diverse candidacies and that public participation should be more open and more effective in determining the outcome.

The two most significant consequences of the reforms were the public's greater impact on each state's delegate selection proceedings (delegates would now be bound to vote for the candidate for whom they were chosen) and the proliferation of presidential primaries.[12] Caucus-convention procedures became timelier, were better publicized, and in short, were more primary-like. Today in most elections, including in 2008, the media treat Iowa's caucuses as critical events, and the coverage of them is similar to the coverage of primaries—how many "votes" were "cast" for each candidate, for example.

At the state level, many party officials concluded that the easiest way to conform to the new Democratic rules in 1972 was to hold a primary election. Thus the number of states (including the District of Columbia) holding Democratic primaries increased from fifteen in 1968 to twenty-one in 1972 to twenty-seven in 1976, and the number of Republican primaries increased comparably. By 1988 thirty-six states were holding Republican primaries, and thirty-four were holding Democratic ones. In 2000 forty-three states were conducting Republican primaries, and Democratic primaries were being held in forty states. By 2008 the numbers were forty-one on the Republican side and thirty-nine on the Democratic side. Thus it is fair to say that the parties' new nomination systems have become largely based on primaries.

The only major exception to this conclusion is that about one in five delegates to the Democratic National Convention is chosen because he or she is an elected officeholder or a Democratic Party official. Supporters of this reform of party rules (first used in 1984) wanted to ensure that the Democratic leadership would have a formal role to play at the conventions of the party. These "superdelegates" may have played a decisive role in the 1984 nomination of Walter F. Mondale and again in 2008 when Obama, like Mondale, had a majority of the non-superdelegates, but not a majority of all delegates. Each candidate needed only a relatively small number of additional superdelegates to commit to vote for them to win the nomination. They both received those commitments the day after the regular delegate selection process ended, and, with that, they were assured the nomination.[13]

The delegate selection process has, as noted, become considerably more frontloaded, which has changed nomination politics.[14] The rationale for front-loading is clear enough: the last time California's (actual or near) end-of-season primary had an effect on the nomination process was in the 1964 Republican and the 1972 Democratic nomination contests. Once candidates, the media, and other actors realized, and reacted to, the implications of the reformed nomination system, the action shifted to the earliest events of the season, and nomination contests, especially those involving multiple candidates, were effectively completed well before the end of the primary season. More and more state parties and legislatures (including California's) realized the advantages of front-loading, bringing more attention from the media, more expenditures of time and money by the candidates, and more influence to their states if they held primaries sooner rather than later.

If the rationale for front-loading was clear by 1996, when it first became controversial, the consequences were not. Some argued that long-shot candidates could be propelled to the front of the pack by gathering momentum in Iowa and New Hampshire and could, before the well-known candidates could react, lock up the nomination early. The alternative argument was that increasing front-loading helps those who begin the campaign with the advantages associated with being a front-runner, such as name recognition, support from state and local party or related organizations, and, most of all, money.

Indeed, as the primary season has become more front-loaded, the well-known, well-established, and well-financed candidates have increasingly dominated the primaries. Sen. George S. McGovern of South Dakota and Jimmy Carter won the Democratic nominations in 1972 and 1976, even though they began as little-known and ill-financed contenders. George H. W. Bush, successful in the 1980 Iowa Republican caucuses, climbed from being, in his words, "an asterisk in the polls" (where the asterisk is commonly used to indicate less than 1 percent support) to become Reagan's major contender and eventual vice presidential choice. And Colorado senator Gary Hart nearly defeated former vice president Mondale in 1984. In 1988 the two strongest candidates at the start of the Republican race, George H. W. Bush and Bob Dole, contested vigorously, with Bush winning. Gov. Michael S. Dukakis of Massachusetts, the best-financed and best-organized Democrat, won the nomination surprisingly easily. Clinton's victory in 1992 appeared, then, to be the culmination of the trend toward an insuperable advantage for the strongest and best-financed candidates. Clinton was able to withstand scandal and defeat in the early going and eventually cruise to victory.

The campaign of former Democratic senator Paul Tsongas of Massachusetts illustrates one important reason for Clinton's victory. Tsongas defeated the field in New Hampshire, and, as usual, the victory and the media attention it drew opened doors to fund-raising possibilities unavailable to him even days earlier. Yet Tsongas faced the dilemma of whether to take time out of daily campaigning for the public's votes so that he could spend time on fund-raising or to continue campaigning in the upcoming primaries. If he campaigned in those primaries, he would not have the opportunity to raise and direct the funds he needed to be an effective competitor. Front-loading had simply squeezed too much into too short a post–New Hampshire time frame for a candidate to be able to capitalize on early victories as, say, Carter had done in winning the nomination and election in 1976. The events of 1996 supported the alternative argument—that increased front-loading benefits the front-runner—even though it took nearly all of Dole's resources to achieve his early victory.[15]

This lesson was not lost on the candidates for 2000, especially George W. Bush. In particular, he began his quest in 1999 (or earlier!) as a reasonably well-regarded governor, but one not particularly well known to the public outside of Texas (although, of course, sharing his father's name made him instantly recognizable). He was at that point only one of several plausible contenders, but he worked hard to receive early endorsements from party leaders and raised a great deal of money well ahead of his competition. When others sought to match Bush's early successes in this "invisible primary," they found that he had sewn up a great deal of support. Many, in fact, withdrew before the first vote was cast, suddenly realizing just how Bush's actions had lengthened the odds against them. Bush was therefore able to win the nomination at the very opening of the primary season. Incumbent vice president Al Gore, on the other side, also benefited from the same dynamics of the invisible primary, although in the more classical role of one who began the nomination season as the odds-on favorite and therefore the one most able to shut the door on his opposition well before any voters cast their ballots.[16]

The pre-primary period on the Republican side in 2008 was, as noted earlier, quite variable, with first McCain, then Giuliani, then Romney surging to the front. McCain's campaign was considered all but dead in the water, but it regathered strength before 2007 ended. There was, then, no strong front-runner in the GOP; the campaign was wide open. It was not so wide open, however, that pundits imagined Huckabee had any chance, and so his victory in the Iowa caucuses was a genuine surprise (at least from the perspective of, say, October 2007). On the Democratic side, Hillary Clinton was a clear front-runner. In retrospect, it was also clear that Obama had developed an impressive organization both by mobilizing support across the nation and by fund-raising, especially through adroit use of the Internet. Thus once his organizational strength became publicly visible, it was no surprise that he and Clinton easily defeated their rivals.

The Nomination System of 1972: Campaign Finance

The second aspect of the reform of the presidential nomination process began with the Federal Election Campaign Act of 1971, but it was the amendments to the act of 1974 and 1976 that dramatically altered the nature of campaign financing. The Watergate scandal during the Nixon administration included revelations of substantial abuse in raising and spending money in the 1972 presidential election (facts discovered in part in implementing the 1971 act). The resulting regulations limited contributions by individuals and groups, virtually ending the power of individual "fat cats" and requiring presidential candidates to raise money in a broad-based campaign. Small donations for the nomination could be matched by the federal government, and candidates who accepted matching funds would be bound by limits on what they could spend (a provision that effectively limited Massachusetts senator John Kerry's campaign efforts in 2004, after he had won the primaries but before the nominating conventions).

These provisions, created by the Federal Election Commission to monitor campaign financing and regulate campaign practices, altered the way nomination campaigns were funded. Still, just as candidates learned over time how to contest most effectively under the new delegate selection process, they also learned how to campaign under the new financial regulations. Perhaps most important, presidential candidates learned—though it is not as true for them as for congressional candidates—that "early money is like yeast, because it helps to raise the dough."[17] They correctly believed that a great deal of money was necessary to compete effectively.[18]

The costs of running presidential nomination campaigns, indeed campaigns for all major offices, have escalated dramatically since 1972. But a special chain of strategic reactions has spurred the cost of campaigning for the presidential nomination.

When many states complied with the McGovern-Fraser Commission reforms by adopting primaries, media coverage grew, enhancing the effects of momentum, increasing the value of early victories, and raising the costs of early defeat. As we described earlier, these reactions, in turn, led states to create the front-loaded season that candidates faced in 2008. All of these factors created not only a demand for more money, but also a demand for that money to be raised early, ahead of the primary season. The result, using 2000 for illustration, was that only by raising large sums of money in 1999 could candidates hope to compete effectively in the eleven coast-to-coast primaries held on March 7, 2000, known as "Super Tuesday." In 2008 sixteen primaries and six caucuses were held on February 5, making it even more "super" than past Super Tuesdays.

By 2008 very few candidates were accepting federal matching funds, because doing so would bind them to spending limits in individual states and over the campaign as a whole. And the fund-raising was huge. Consider just the itemized contributions, which are useful for securing matching funds if a candidate were so inclined. Among Republicans, only McCain accepted these funds; among Democrats, Biden, Dodd, Edwards, and Gravel accepted such funding. Through the July 5, 2008, reporting date of the Federal Election Commission, Obama had raised $221 million, Clinton $159 million, and McCain $90 million. For all Democrats, the total was $438 million, whereas for the much shorter Republican contest it was $230 million. And these amounts are only about half of the total contributions most candidates received. Through May 2008, thus indicating how much money the three major nomination candidates had on hand for the nomination season itself, the fund-raising totals were $296 million for Obama, $238 million for Clinton, and $122 million for McCain.[19]

The 2008 campaign was also marked by the dramatic expansion in the use of the Internet to raise money, following on the efforts of Democrat Howard Dean, the former governor of Vermont, in 2004. Ron Paul, for example, raised more than $6 million on a single day, December 6, 2007, through the Internet. But it was Obama's successes that are likely to serve as the model for future campaigns, such as the $55 million he raised in February 2008 at a critical moment for the campaign.[20] Indeed, not only may Obama's organizational ability further the demise of federal funding of presidential nominations, but the carryover to the fall may signal its demise in future general elections (see Chapter 2). Finally, Internet fund-raising solved the "Tsongas dilemma" described earlier, because Obama could raise money on the Internet without leaving the campaign trail.

THE DYNAMICS OF MULTICANDIDATE CAMPAIGNS

The most significant feature, from the candidates' perspectives, of the nomination process is its dynamic character. This system was designed to empower the general public, giving it opportunities to participate more fully in the selection of delegates to the national party conventions, and often even instructing them on how to vote. The early state delegate selection contests in Iowa and New Hampshire allowed largely unknown candidates to work a small state or two using the "retail" politics of door-to-door campaigning to achieve a surprising success that would attract media attention and then money, volunteers, and greater popular support. In practice, this was exactly the route Jimmy Carter followed in 1976.

John H. Aldrich developed this account of "momentum" in campaigns, using the 1976 campaigns to illustrate its effect. He first showed that there is no stable balance to this process.[21] In practical terms, he predicted that one candidate will increasingly absorb all the money, media attention, and public support, and thereby defeat all opponents before the convention. He further showed that the tendency for this process to focus rapidly on a single winner increases the *more* candidates there are. This finding was just the opposite of the original theories in this area, and, indeed, what at the time seemed obvious: the greater the number of candidates, the longer it would take to reach victory. But commonsense was not a helpful guide in this case.

There was, however, one exception to this pure "momentum" result: the possibility of an unstable but sustainable balance with two candidates locked in a nearly precise tie. Early campaigns offered two illustrations compatible with two candidates in (unstable) equipoise, the 1976 Republican and 1980 Democratic contests.[22] In both cases, a relatively moderate but unpopular incumbent was challenged by a popular contender who represented the ideological (and thus relatively more extreme) heart of his party. In both cases, the campaigns lasted for a considerable period in this nearly even balance. And in both cases, the incumbents eventually moved ahead, sufficiently so that they achieved a majority of committed delegates by the end of the primary season. It had remained close enough in each contest, however, that the challengers could imagine upsetting that majority through a rules change at their respective conventions. In both cases, these hopes were unsurprisingly dashed—unsurprising because the incumbent actually had majority support and the changes in the rules, no matter how desirable otherwise, were obvious ploys to try to shake loose part of the incumbent's majority support.

A campaign in which an unpopular moderate incumbent is challenged by a popular senior leader in the party who stands as the embodiment of the party's beliefs is a sufficiently rare empirical circumstance that there has not been a comparable case since then. It turns out, however, that there is a second route to a long-lasting two-candidate campaign, a route that has now also appeared twice. Like the first pair of cases, these two cases are also surprisingly similar. In both the 1984 Democratic and 2008 Democratic contests, the campaigns began with a large number of candidates, none of whom was an incumbent president or vice president. There was a strong, well-financed, well-known, well-organized candidate who, it turned out, was challenged strongly by a heretofore little known (to the public) candidate who offered a new direction for the party. The multicandidate contest quickly shrank to just two viable candidates, with the little-known challenger surprising (and even surpassing) the well-known and well-financed front-runner. The front-runner, however, remained very closely competitive and, with great resources, retained sufficient resiliency to be locked in an even contest when all others had dropped by the wayside. This rapid narrowing of the many to the few was, of course, the prediction. Indeed, it is possible, if not common, that every once in a while the narrowing of the field ends with two candidates nearly tied for the lead instead of one candidate ahead.

In any event, there are good reasons to expect the occasional campaign that is reduced to a two-candidate, balanced contest. One of these good reasons is the superdelegates. If in addition to two candidates emerging from a larger pack to be in uncertain equipoise there is a large bloc of uncommitted party elites available to woo, we can easily imagine a competitive opportunity for candidates that goes beyond a primary season selection of delegates bound as the public chose them in nearly even proportions. At least that was what happened in both the 1984 Mondale-Hart contest and the 2008 Obama-Clinton contest.[23]

In the more usual case of momentum yielding one leader who emerges to win, front-loading strengthens the rapidity of the dynamics of momentum. The same basic model applies. This dynamic fits every other campaign in which no incumbent president is seeking renomination. That includes the Republican contest in 2008, and it is therefore true that, even though it was surprising that McCain won, the process by which he won was not at all unusual or unexpected.

In Figure 1-2, we report the length of all campaigns without a presidential incumbent running—that is, the number of weeks between the New Hampshire primary and the end of the campaign.[24] The standard until 1988 was that the campaign lasted until the end of primary season. But beginning with 1988 on the Republican side, and extending with no exceptions until this year's Democratic contest, the campaign has ended shortly after New Hampshire.

FIGURE 1-2   Length of Multicandidate Campaigns, 1976–2008

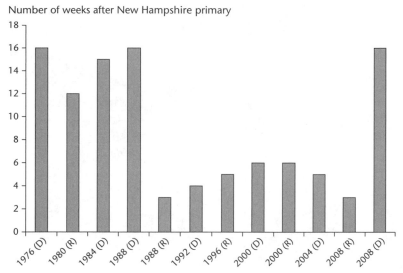

Source: Compiled by the authors.

In 1988 George H. W. Bush had essentially won the nomination by Super Tuesday. Three Democrats—Michael Dukakis, Al Gore, and Jesse Jackson—essentially divided the Super Tuesday events. Dukakis broke this deadlock by defeating his opponents in New York a short time later, prompting Gore to concede defeat. Jackson, however, continued his campaign through the convention, even though Dukakis amassed a clear majority of the delegates. In part, Jackson was able to do so because the proportional allocation of delegates on the Democratic side slowed the accumulation process for Dukakis. More important, however, Jackson was raising issues and attracting attention to his causes rather than seeking to win a simple majority of delegates, a strategy that required continuation of campaigning, even after all hope of victory had ended.

The two special cases of campaigns that began with multiple candidates but settled on two balanced competitors deserve special consideration. In 1984 Mondale had begun the campaign as the front-runner. Hart, the "outsider," became one of the three finalists with early successes and presented a strong challenge the rest of the way. Eventually, though, he fell behind, rather more so than Clinton trailed Obama late in the delegate selection season. After the last primary, however, Mondale was still a few delegates short of a majority. Fortunately, he was able to convince enough additional superdelegates to endorse him that his nomination was assured the day after the last primaries. The 2008 race was even closer. In Figure 1-3, we report the delegate totals won in the primaries and caucuses by Clinton and Obama, as a percentage of the majority needed to win nomination. The point to observe is how these lines diverge little

FIGURE 1-3   Competitiveness of the 2008 Democratic Nomination, Obama
and Clinton

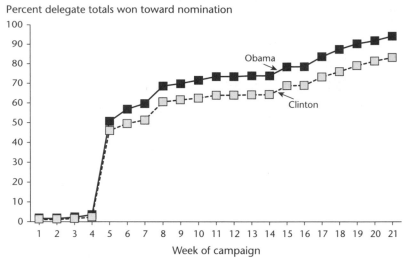

Percent delegate totals won toward nomination

Week of campaign

Source: Compiled by the authors.

from a 50–50 split. That proximity illustrates clearly the role available for the superdelegates.

EXPLAINING WHO WON AND WHO LOST IN 2008

Although the dynamics of campaigns provide insight into the politics of the new nomination system, they do not reveal which of the candidates capture momentum and which do not. For that we turn (as we do in several places in this book) to academics who have developed models to predict who succeeds and who fails. Two such models share some similarities. Most especially, they rely on information: candidates' success in building organizational and resource strength in the pre-primary period and candidates' success in Iowa and New Hampshire. The first of the two models is by Randall E. Adkins, Andrew J. Dowdle, and Wayne P. Steger (shortened here to ADS) who test their model with contests between 1976 and 2000.[25] They have applied their model through 2004, and we update it to 2008. Barbara Norrander developed the second model by examining the 1980–1996 period, and we update it through 2008 as well.[26]

Adkins and his colleagues base their predictions on several considerations. One is popular support, as measured in the last national Gallup poll prior to the Iowa race (for the 2008 contest, this poll was conducted December 14–16, 2007). They also examine financial support—both incoming (for our replication, cash reserves on hand at the end of 2007) and spending (measured as the proportionate share of a candidate's spending). In doing so, they differentiate southern Democrats from all other candidates.[27] Finally, because of the importance of the opening events, they look at who won in Iowa and New Hampshire and the candidate's vote share in each.[28]

Norrander's model is similar. She also includes candidate standing in the last Gallup poll and performances in Iowa and New Hampshire. And she considers financial support, here the amount a candidate raised in the year prior to the campaign as a proportion of that raised by the leading fund-raiser that year. She includes a variety of other considerations as well: whether Democratic and Republican races differ (because of the more heterogeneous Democratic constituency over much of this period), whether the primary is proportional or some version of winner-take-all, the effect of front-loading (measured as the proportion of delegates selected before March 31), and whether the candidate comes with a strong electoral background (including being a member of the U.S. House).

As predicted by the two models, the probability of winning is presented for each candidate from both parties in Table 1-2. On the Republican side, the ADS model predicted accurately McCain's eventual emergence as the nominee and by a comfortable margin. The model also predicted that Huckabee would end up in second place, consistent with his strong showing. The surprises in this model were Romney and Giuliani, but for opposite reasons. Giuliani was predicted to be a top-tier candidate by this model, but perhaps because of his untraditional strategy of pulling out of Iowa and New Hampshire (possibly attributable to unusual strategic reasoning or to anticipated poor performance), he underperformed the position forecast by the model. Romney, by contrast, performed considerably better than expected. Norrander's "attrition" model accurately predicted the two final candidates. It did, however, have a "flatter" prediction, with only modest differences from the first two to the next two candidates (Romney and Giuliani). The original prediction of pundits that the Republican race would be wide open is supported here.

TABLE 1-2   Estimated Probabilities of Candidate Nominations, ADS and Norrander Models, 2008

Republicans	McCain	Romney	Huckabee	Giuliani	Thompson	Paul
ADS	0.40	0.08	0.22	0.20	0.06	0.03
Norrander	0.21	0.17	0.21	0.18	0.13	0.09

Democrats	Obama	Clinton	Edwards	Richardson	Biden	Dodd	Kucinich
ADS	0.27	0.53	0.17	0.003	0.013	0.005	0.001
Norrander	0.23	0.31	0.15	0.08	0.08	0.07	0.08

Source: Calculated by the authors.

Note: Data used in the calculation of these probabilities were at least in principle available before the 2008 campaign began. In particular, polling data are from the Gallup poll of December 14–16, 2007, and financial data are from Federal Election Commission end-of-year reports for 2007 (although these were not released at that time).

For the Democrats, the ADS model predicted the three strongest candidates, but in doing so it made Clinton a much heavier favorite than Obama. However, the model did accurately forecast a well-defined first and second tier of candidates. Norrander's forecasts are very similar in terms of ranking the strongest and weakest candidates. Like the ADS model, Norrander's model predicted that Clinton would have an advantage over Obama. However, her model predicts attrition and not the winner, and it did accurately predict the final two candidates in the race. Like the ADS model, Norrander's model also suggested two well-defined tiers of candidates, with Obama and Clinton on one tier and Biden, Dodd, and Kucinich on the other.

The models, therefore, predicted the set of strong candidates, and the set of less strong candidates, quite accurately. They were weaker, especially on the Democratic side, in assessing which of the stronger candidates would actually win. To understand why these models underestimated Obama's strength and how McCain engineered a quick and decisive victory in the face of his campaign's near collapse in mid-2007, we must look more closely at the individual races.

How Obama Won

Three candidates were serious contenders for the Democratic nomination: Clinton, Edwards, and Obama. Edwards was the longest shot of the three, but he came in second, ahead of Clinton, in Iowa. However, this success was followed by a relatively weak third-place showing in New Hampshire, and two equally weak third-place finishes in the first two southern primaries, South Carolina and Florida. As a result, Edwards withdrew from the race before Super Tuesday (see Tables 1-3 and 1-4 for results of the caucuses and primaries).

We have already noted how strong, well organized, and well financed Clinton's campaign was. The Obama campaign was less obviously so in 2007, but that was partially because the organization's use of the Internet was so novel, effective, and less easily observable.

The Clinton campaign prepared for an early victory. As we have seen, this has been the story of presidential nominations over the last twenty years, and Clinton's apparent advantages over any other rival indicated that an early defeat was extremely improbable. As a result, the campaign organized effectively in the primary states. It did not, however, expend the resources to create the complex organizational efforts needed to win caucus after caucus. As the contest closed, Clinton was able to claim correctly that she had won many primaries, that she had won more delegates from primary states than Obama, and that she had won primaries in states such as Ohio, Pennsylvania, and even Michigan and Florida (Obama did not contest these states because they had violated the national party rules), which a Democrat would have to win in the fall to defeat the Republican nominee.

In the end, though, not only did Obama win at least a few more votes in primary states overall, but he amassed his lead by large victories in caucus states.

TABLE 1-3   Results of Democratic Caucuses, 2008 (percent)

State	Date	Clinton	Obama	Edwards	Other
Iowa	1/3/2008	30.43	34.91	31.20	3.47
Nevada	1/19/2008	50.82	45.09	3.71	0.37
Alaska	2/5/2008	24.71	75.16	0.00	0.14
Colorado	2/5/2008	32.26	66.53	0.08	1.13
Idaho	2/5/2008	17.21	79.54	0.65	2.60
Kansas	2/5/2008	25.76	73.98	0.14	0.12
Minnesota	2/5/2008	32.23	66.39	0.46	0.92
North Dakota	2/5/2008	36.55	61.15	1.49	0.82
American Samoa	2/5/2008	57.19	42.46	0.00	0.35
Nebraska	2/9/2008	32.18	67.56	0.00	0.26
Virgin Islands	2/9/2008	7.56	89.95	0.00	2.49
Washington	2/9/2008	31.15	67.56	0.00	1.28
Maine	2/10/2008	39.85	59.30	0.00	0.86
Hawaii	2/19/2008	23.58	75.77	0.11	0.55
Texas	3/4/2008	43.72	56.18	0.00	0.10
Wyoming	3/8/2008	37.83	61.44	0.00	0.73
Guam	5/3/2008	49.92	50.08	0.00	0.00

Source: Adapted from "Dave Leip's Atlas of U.S. Presidential Elections," www.uselectionatlas.org.

Because the Democratic Party requires proportional allocation of delegates, contested primaries yield victories but relatively small edges in delegates won. Ohio, for example, was a very important victory for Clinton, but that victory gave her only eight more delegates than Obama (out of 141). Proportional representation is used in caucus states as well, but their much more complicated rules tend to reduce the extent of proportionality. Clinton often did not seriously contest those states. For example, Idaho selected only eighteen delegates in its caucus to Ohio's 141, but Obama won fifteen to Clinton's three—a twelve-delegate margin and more than the eight-delegate difference between Clinton and Obama in Ohio. According to our calculations, Obama won 1,429 delegates in the primaries, and Clinton won 1,463. But in the caucus states Obama won 324 delegates, and Clinton won 170—that is, Obama won 49 percent of the delegates the two candidates won in primaries, but he won 66 percent of those selected in caucus states.

Thus Obama and Clinton were able to compete closely, but Obama gained just enough of an edge (see Figure 1-3) that he had nearly a majority when delegate selection ended, and needed but a few superdelegate commitments to go over the top, which he did the next day.

Obama faced three tasks over the summer. The first was to heal the rift caused by a close, hard-fought campaign. Indeed, a good number of Clinton's strongest

TABLE 1-4   Results of Democratic Primaries, 2008 (percent)

State	Date	Clinton	Obama	Edwards	Other
New Hampshire	1/8/2008	39.09	36.45	16.94	7.52
Michigan	1/15/2008	54.61	0.00	0.00	45.39
South Carolina	1/26/2008	26.49	55.42	17.63	0.46
Florida	1/29/2008	49.77	32.93	14.38	2.92
Alabama	2/5/2008	41.57	55.96	1.46	1.00
Arizona	2/5/2008	50.37	42.39	5.18	2.06
Arkansas	2/5/2008	70.05	26.25	1.87	1.83
California	2/5/2008	51.47	43.16	3.82	1.55
Connecticut	2/5/2008	46.66	50.70	0.97	1.68
Delaware	2/5/2008	42.29	53.07	1.29	3.35
Georgia	2/5/2008	31.11	66.39	1.72	0.79
Illinois	2/5/2008	32.76	64.66	1.95	0.62
Massachusetts	2/5/2008	56.01	40.64	1.60	1.74
Missouri	2/5/2008	47.90	49.32	2.03	0.75
New Jersey	2/5/2008	53.76	43.93	1.38	0.93
New Mexico	2/5/2008	48.94	47.80	1.44	1.82
New York	2/5/2008	57.37	40.32	1.18	1.13
Oklahoma	2/5/2008	54.76	31.19	10.24	3.80
Tennessee	2/5/2008	53.82	40.48	4.45	1.25
Utah	2/5/2008	39.07	56.72	2.86	1.35
Louisiana	2/9/2008	35.63	57.40	3.39	3.58
D.C.	2/12/2008	23.77	75.31	0.28	0.64
Maryland	2/12/2008	35.78	60.66	1.20	2.37
Virginia	2/12/2008	35.47	63.66	0.53	0.35
Wisconsin	2/19/2008	40.76	58.08	0.60	0.56
Ohio	3/4/2008	53.49	44.84	1.67	0.00
Rhode Island	3/4/2008	58.37	40.35	0.61	0.67
Texas	3/4/2008	50.88	47.39	1.04	0.69
Vermont	3/4/2008	38.59	59.31	1.25	0.85
Mississippi	3/11/2008	36.67	61.15	0.91	1.27
Pennsylvania	4/22/2008	54.40	45.26	0.00	0.34
Indiana	5/6/2008	50.56	49.44	0.00	0.00
North Carolina	5/6/2008	41.61	56.14	0.00	2.26
West Virginia	5/13/2008	67.00	25.69	7.31	0.00
Kentucky	5/20/2008	65.48	29.92	2.03	2.58
Oregon	5/20/2008	40.50	58.52	0.00	0.98
Puerto Rico	6/1/2008	68.42	31.58	0.00	0.00
Montana	6/3/2008	41.05	56.56	0.00	2.39
South Dakota	6/3/2008	55.35	44.65	0.00	0.00
Democrats Abroad		32.46	65.85	0.69	1.00

Source: Adapted from "Dave Leip's Atlas of U.S. Presidential Elections," www.uselectionatlas.org.

Note: Texas held a caucus as well as a primary.

supporters were offended by the nature of the overall campaign, particularly the coverage of a female candidate in the media. Although Obama did not engage in such tactics, many observers believed he got something of a pass as an African American male that a white female did not, and that perhaps he could have intervened to denounce the worst of the media coverage. But these were only the kinds of hurts felt by all nearly victorious but eventually defeated candidates and their campaigns and activists. Nevertheless, Obama and then Clinton herself had to work hard at the convention to reunite the party in preparation for the fall campaign.

Obama also had to pick a running mate, and he chose Joe Biden. Biden had run a weak campaign in 2008, but he had several attractions as a running mate. First, he was a longtime veteran of the Washington scene and was therefore able to balance the upstart nature of Obama's candidacy. Second, he had a great deal of experience in foreign affairs, something that Obama did not have, and so was valuable to anyone facing two hot wars and a war hero as an opponent. Third, Biden harkened strongly to the traditional working-class, union base of the Democratic Party, balancing Obama's background as an Ivy League–trained law professor and an activist in Chicago's African American community.

Finally, Obama had to make the transition from a candidate seeking the Democratic Party nomination to a candidate seeking support of the whole electorate. His nomination acceptance speech marked the full transition from uniting the party to seeking to unite the nation. Although not as wildly popular as his keynote address at the 2004 national convention, a speech that marked him as a young comer in politics, the speech was highly successful both in its content of appeals to a divided and troubled nation and in its manner of calm assurance. The stage was then half-set for the general election contest to begin in earnest.

How McCain Won

In the Iowa Republican caucuses, Mitt Romney came in second, receiving nearly twice as much support as McCain (see Tables 1-5 and 1-6 for the Republican caucus and primary results). The media story, however, was that Mike Huckabee was the surprising upset winner in Iowa, winning over a third of the "votes" to Romney's one-quarter and McCain's (and Thompson's) one-eighth. Huckabee had little organization and few resources. He was, however, a popular former governor and a favorite of the Christian right. Indeed, caucuses are won as much through organizational effort as through popular support, and Huckabee, having little of either, relied on the organization provided by the Christian churches in Iowa to win.

Five days later, in New Hampshire, the compression from front-loading caught up with Huckabee, and he was unable to translate much of the favorable publicity into popular support. McCain, who had targeted New Hampshire, won the primary (37 percent to Huckabee's 11 percent of the vote), but defeating Huckabee was not what mattered; it was defeating the former

TABLE 1-5   Results of Republican Caucuses, 2008 (percent)

State	Date	McCain	Romney	Huckabee	Paul	Giuliani	Other
Iowa	1/3/2008	13.11	25.23	34.41	9.96	3.45	13.84
Wyoming	1/5/2008	4.17	54.17	0.00	0.00	0.00	41.67
Nevada	1/19/2008	12.75	51.10	8.16	13.73	4.31	9.95
Maine	2/2/2008	21.07	52.04	5.75	18.36	0.06	2.73
Alaska	2/5/2008	15.82	44.58	22.35	17.26	0.00	0.00
Colorado	2/5/2008	18.39	60.11	12.76	8.42	0.08	0.23
Minnesota	2/5/2008	22.01	41.37	19.88	15.68	0.00	1.06
Montana	2/5/2008	21.96	38.34	15.03	24.54	0.00	0.12
North Dakota	2/5/2008	22.73	35.67	19.90	21.28	0.00	0.43
West Virginia	2/5/2008	1.09	47.36	51.55	0.00	0.00	0.00
Kansas	2/9/2008	23.50	3.35	59.58	11.18	0.17	2.22
Washington	2/9/2008	25.90	15.45	23.52	21.64	0.00	13.49

Source: Adapted from "Dave Leip's Atlas of U.S. Presidential Elections," www.uselectionatlas.org.

Note: Hawaii and the Virgin Islands held caucuses, beginning on January 25 and on April 5, respectively, for which no results are reported.

governor of Massachusetts, and McCain did defeat Romney, who received 32 percent of the vote.

McCain followed this victory with wins in South Carolina and Florida, two of the next three primaries (he lost, as expected, to Romney in the Michigan primary, which was now much smaller because of the punishment by the national party). In South Carolina, McCain avenged his loss to George W. Bush in 2000—a defeat that effectively ended the McCain candidacy—and he defeated Romney again by two to one. Huckabee was able to wage a much closer contest in South Carolina, a state open to his appeals and able to provide church-based organizational support. But a close defeat is still a defeat. In Florida, McCain won by defeating Romney by a few points and by defeating not only Huckabee but also Giuliani in his first primary. By this point, McCain had effectively ended the bids of all his rivals. Romney and Huckabee continued to campaign, but by February 7 Romney withdrew, although Huckabee not did not withdraw until March 4, after McCain had won in Texas and Ohio, as well as in Rhode Island and Vermont.

How did McCain win? Recall that the race was wide open, with four candidates—Giuliani, McCain, Romney, and Thompson—rated in late 2007 about even in their chances for victory. All four had some strong credentials, but all four also had weaknesses. Giuliani, for example, was a hero for his handling of the 9/11 attacks, but his policy positions, such as being pro-choice, that were electorally helpful in New York City made him unacceptable to the conservative base of the party. And because he did not enter the electoral fray until

TABLE 1-6   Results of Republican Primaries, 2008 (percent)

State	Date	McCain	Romney	Huckabee	Paul	Giuliani	Other
New Hampshire	1/8/2008	37.00	31.56	11.22	7.65	8.48	4.09
Michigan	1/15/2008	29.68	38.92	16.08	6.27	2.84	6.22
South Carolina	1/19/2008	33.15	15.30	29.84	3.62	2.15	15.94
Florida	1/29/2008	36.00	31.03	13.47	3.23	14.68	1.60
Alabama	2/5/2008	37.10	17.75	41.25	2.68	0.39	0.83
Arizona	2/5/2008	47.17	34.53	9.03	4.19	2.52	2.55
Arkansas	2/5/2008	20.22	13.53	60.46	4.79	0.29	0.70
California	2/5/2008	42.25	34.56	11.62	4.27	4.39	2.92
Connecticut	2/5/2008	52.00	32.91	7.00	4.15	1.63	2.32
Delaware	2/5/2008	45.04	32.53	15.34	4.24	2.50	0.35
Georgia	2/5/2008	31.63	30.17	33.92	2.92	0.74	0.62
Illinois	2/5/2008	47.45	28.60	16.46	5.01	1.32	1.16
Massachusetts	2/5/2008	40.91	51.12	3.82	2.65	0.54	0.96
Missouri	2/5/2008	32.95	29.27	31.53	4.49	0.61	1.15
New Jersey	2/5/2008	55.36	28.33	8.17	4.82	2.74	0.57
New York	2/5/2008	51.60	27.59	10.61	6.22	3.60	0.38
Oklahoma	2/5/2008	36.64	24.78	33.40	3.34	0.72	1.12
Tennessee	2/5/2008	31.80	23.59	34.47	5.60	0.93	3.61
Utah	2/5/2008	5.38	89.49	1.44	2.99	0.33	0.37
Louisiana	2/9/2008	41.91	6.34	43.18	5.33	0.99	2.25
D.C.	2/12/2008	67.59	6.41	16.42	7.95	1.63	0.00
Maryland	2/12/2008	54.84	6.99	28.54	5.98	1.42	2.23
Virginia	2/12/2008	50.04	3.68	40.67	4.50	0.41	0.69
Washington	2/19/2008	49.44	16.24	24.06	7.64	0.97	1.64
Wisconsin	2/19/2008	54.74	1.97	36.95	4.65	0.47	1.23
Ohio	3/4/2008	59.92	3.32	30.59	4.63	0.00	1.55
Rhode Island	3/4/2008	64.18	4.34	21.47	6.52	0.00	3.50
Texas	3/4/2008	51.22	2.00	38.02	4.87	0.44	3.44
Vermont	3/4/2008	71.32	4.54	14.30	6.61	2.34	0.89
Mississippi	3/11/2008	78.98	1.50	12.59	3.83	0.65	2.45
Pennsylvania	4/22/2008	71.21	0.03	11.03	15.49	0.00	2.23
Indiana	5/6/2008	77.62	4.74	9.98	7.66	0.00	0.00
North Carolina	5/6/2008	74.01	0.00	12.18	7.20	0.00	6.61
Nebraska	5/13/2008	85.68	0.00	0.00	12.81	0.00	1.52
West Virginia	5/13/2008	76.04	4.40	10.32	5.01	2.40	1.83
Kentucky	5/20/2008	72.26	4.65	8.29	6.79	1.54	6.47
Oregon	5/20/2008	80.88	0.00	0.00	14.46	0.00	4.67
Idaho	5/27/2008	69.65	0.00	0.00	23.72	0.00	6.63
Montana	6/3/2008	76.04	0.00	0.00	21.53	0.00	2.44
New Mexico	6/3/2008	85.97	0.00	0.00	14.03	0.00	0.00
South Dakota	6/3/2008	70.19	3.26	7.10	16.52	0.00	2.93

Source: Adapted from "Dave Leip's Atlas of U.S. Presidential Elections," www.uselectionatlas.org.

Note: American Samoa (February 23) and Guam (March 3) held primaries for which no results are reported. Washington and West Virginia held caucuses as well as a primary.

Florida, the public had turned its attention to the other candidates in their electoral ups and downs. Giuliani was therefore never able to get his campaign off the ground that late. Romney, as governor of Massachusetts, had been pro-choice and had taken other more liberal positions, especially on social issues, although he worked hard to change his stance and image among the conservative base after he left that office. However, his Mormon faith generated media controversy and apparently affected his support among the Christian right. Thompson proved to be an ineffective campaigner, raising little money, enthusiasm, and support. Huckabee thus emerged as the strongest competitor to McCain, but hit the Tsongas dilemma, which was accelerated by the increased compression of front-loading in 2008 compared even with 2000. Huckabee appealed strongly to the conservative base, making it harder for Romney to convince an originally skeptical party base to embrace him. In a sense, then, McCain won in part because no one else could. But he also won for positive reasons—his abilities to rebuild an organization, gather money, and capitalize on his popularity in the nation at large, and because he was a genuine hero. He also was able to point to the highly public ways in which he broke with the Bush administration, thereby establishing a reputation as a "maverick" that would play a rather different role in the general election.

McCain had accepted federal matching funds, so that once he had vanquished his rivals, he was financially limited in his ability to campaign as the presumptive nominee. Meanwhile, the media and the public were fascinated with the still hotly contested Democratic race, and so McCain found it difficult to attract attention. As a result, his campaign was rather quiet after Huckabee withdrew in early March, thereby delaying any attempt to create a new image as the national party nominee until the convention itself.

Conventions no longer have a decision-making role in choosing a presidential nominee. The public effectively chooses that nominee, who, in turn, effectively chooses the vice presidential nominee.[29] The remaining major decision, the party's platform, is also effectively crafted well before the convention gavel comes down. Thus today's national convention is merely a stage on which the party and its nominees present themselves to the nation. Their acceptance speech provides them the opportunity to speak at length to the entire nation alone on the stage.

In this light, McCain faced two decisions: who his running mate would be and how he would present himself to the nation. These decisions were made in the context of a public that had turned against the Republicans in office. Bush's approval ratings had long been very low. The public now thought that the Iraq War was a mistake and that the nation was on the wrong track in general. The economy was slumping and about to crash. Thus McCain needed to capitalize on one of his strengths, his reputation for standing up against the incumbent, George W. Bush.

His running mate could reinforce that independent stance. He eventually picked Alaska governor Sarah Palin, who literally was, apart from Hawaii's Republican governor, Linda Lingle, as far from Washington as any statewide elected Republican officeholder could be, and figuratively was even more removed from Bush and the entire Washington establishment. Palin had a second attractive attribute: her social conservatism, which allowed her to appeal to the party base in a way that McCain could not. Adding her to the ticket might energize the Republican base, and yet she and McCain could stand as distinctive from the incumbent administration.

The convention did the job the party had hoped. It provided an opportunity to unite the party, attack the recently nominated Obama-Biden team, and allowed first Palin and then McCain to use their acceptance speeches to define their candidacies. Both speeches provided the opportunity to claim maverick status, each in their different ways. The result was that, at least in some polls, the Republican ticket caught up to, if not passed, the Democratic ticket. The question was whether this "convention bounce" in the polls was real or only a temporary burst of enthusiasm.

Chapter 2

The General Election Campaign

Once they have been nominated, candidates choose their general election campaign strategies based on their perceptions of what the electorate wants, their own relative strengths and weaknesses and those of their opponents, and their chances of winning. Candidates who are convinced they have a dependable lead may choose strategies very different from those used by candidates who believe they are seriously behind. A candidate who believes that an opponent has significant weaknesses is more likely to run an aggressive, attacking campaign than one who does not perceive such weaknesses.

After the 2008 conventions, the polls showed a close race. Most observers, and both candidates' organizations, believed that either Barack Obama or John McCain could win (although most also thought that the political context offered the Democrats an advantage), and that the campaign could really make a difference. Part II of this book considers in detail the impact of various factors, including issues and evaluations of George W. Bush's job performance, on the voters' decisions. This chapter provides an overview of the campaign—its course and the context within which strategic decisions were made.

THE STRATEGIC CONTEXT AND CANDIDATES' CHOICES

Within the strategic context, candidates must consider the track records of the parties in recent presidential elections. In presidential races, the past is certainly not entirely prologue, but it is relevant. From this perspective, the picture was slightly more encouraging for the Republicans than for the Democrats in 2008. Of the fourteen presidential elections from 1952 to 2004, the Republicans had won nine of them. Similarly, the GOP had won three of the last five races since 1984, and the biggest Electoral College victory during that period (1988) also belonged to the Republicans. And yet Bill Clinton had won two convincing victories, and George W. Bush's two successful races had been extremely close.

The nature of the American system for electing presidents calls for a closer look at the state-by-state pattern of results. Article II, section 1, of the U.S. Constitution gives states considerable autonomy in how they select their presidential electors; states may appoint electors "in such Manner as the Legislature thereof may direct." U.S. voters do not directly vote for president or vice president. Rather, they vote for a slate of electors pledged to support a presidential and a vice presidential candidate. In every state except Maine and Nebraska, the entire slate of electors that receives the most popular votes is selected. In no state is a majority of the vote required. Since the 1972 election, Maine has used a system in which the winner of the plurality vote in the state as a whole receives two electoral votes. In addition, the winner of the plurality vote in each of Maine's two House districts receives that district's single electoral vote. Beginning in 1992, Nebraska allocated its five electoral votes in a similar manner: the state-wide plurality vote winner gained two votes, and each of the state's three congressional districts awarded one vote on a plurality basis.

If larger states used the district plan employed by Maine and Nebraska, the dynamics of the campaign would be different.[1] For example, candidates might target specific congressional districts and would probably campaign in all large states, regardless of how well they were doing in the statewide polls. But because of the winner-take-all rules employed in forty-eight states and the District of Columbia, candidates cannot safely ignore the pattern of past state results. A state-by-state analysis of the five presidential elections from 1988 to 2004 suggests that the playing field was tilted a little in favor of the Democrats in the effort to win the 270 electoral votes required for victory, a situation that was considerably better for them than those revealed by similar analyses of recent presidential elections.[2]

As Figure 2-1 shows, sixteen states voted Republican in all five of these elections. Only eight states, plus the District of Columbia, were equally loyal to the Democrats.[3] These consistently loyal states provided a prospective balance of 135 electoral votes for the Republicans to only ninety-two for the Democrats. More advantageous for the Democratic candidates were the next groups of states. Five states voted Republican in every election but one, with a total of sixty-four electoral votes. These were offset by twelve states with 168 electoral votes that had supported the Democrats in four of the five contests.[4] Thus if each of these states' political leanings were categorized solely on the basis of the last five elections, one might expect that 199 electoral votes were likely to go to the GOP, while 260 were as likely to go to the Democrats, which would leave the Democrats only ten votes short of victory.

Thus state voting patterns in recent elections indicated a Democratic advantage, but also uncertainty about the likely outcome. Moreover, the pattern of voter inclinations is always in flux, so the candidates and their campaigns were justified somewhat in hoping for better performance in some states than indicated by their past voting patterns. Indeed, there have been some important shifts in the electoral landscape in recent decades. In particular, the Democrats

FIGURE 2-1   States That Voted Republican at Least Four out of Five Elections, 1988–2004, with Number of Electoral Votes

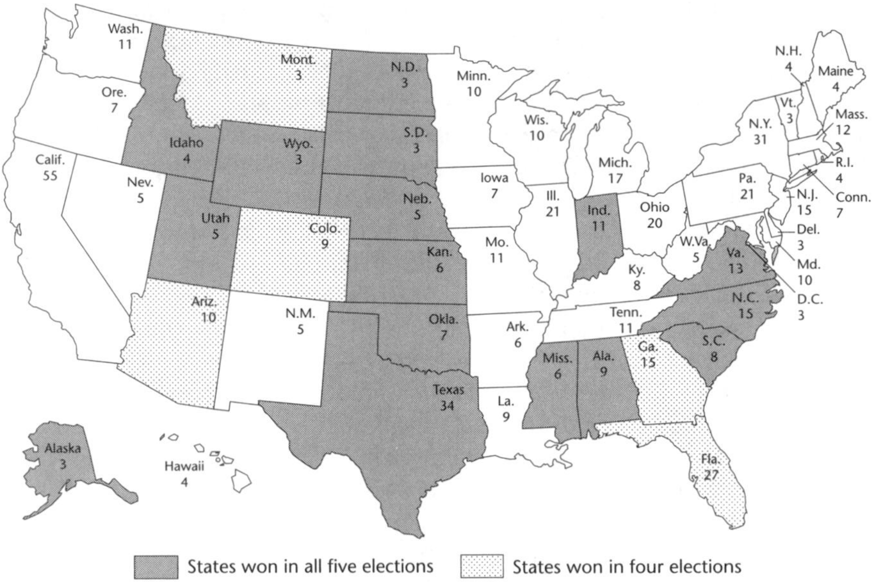

Source: *Presidential Elections, 1789–2004* (Washington, D.C.: CQ Press, 2005), 244–248.

pried the largest state, California—which had once been dependably Republican—away from the GOP. Similarly, in the 1980s Republican presidential candidates performed distinctly better in Florida than their national percentage, but Bill Clinton whittled away this advantage (carrying the state in 1996), and in 2000 Al Gore did slightly better there than his national percentage.

Thus in 2008 either party could win, and both the campaign organizations and the national media had settled on almost the same sets of states as potentially determining the outcome. In these "battleground" states, both campaign organizations would concentrate the lion's share of their time, money, and effort. Those organizations formulated their state campaign strategies while peering through the lens of the Electoral College, and the next section provides some details on those strategies.[5]

POLITICAL CONTEXT, OVERALL STRATEGY, AND OPENING MOVES

In 2004 President Bush's renomination was never in doubt, and Sen. John Kerry had secured the Democratic nomination by the first week in March. Thus the general election contest that year was about eight months long. In 2008 Obama did not clinch the Democratic contest until June 3, substantially shortening the general election phase.[6] On that date, Obama had a slim 1.4 percentage point lead over McCain in the national polls.[7] However, with the internal conflict of the nomination race behind him, the presumptive nominee quickly opened up a 7.5-point lead by June 24.

The Context of the Election

Obama's initial lead reflected the difficult political context facing the Republicans—on a variety of crucial issues they were in trouble. For one thing, Bush had become a very unpopular president. During the summer of 2008, Gallup polls showed that between 61 and 68 percent of Americans disapproved of the job he was doing as president.[8] More generally, the NBC News/*Wall Street Journal* polls indicated that between 67 and 74 percent of the public thought the country was on the "wrong track." In large part, these results stemmed from the dismal state of the economy. The ABC News Consumer Confidence Index (which ranges between +100 and −100) hovered between −41 and −50 during these months. In addition, negative attitudes toward the war in Iraq prevailed. CNN polling data indicated that two-thirds of respondents opposed the war.

Obama also was in better financial shape than McCain. Historically, GOP candidates have had a fund-raising advantage over their opponents. For example, in 2000 George W. Bush raised $95.5 million during the primaries, nearly twice as much as Al Gore's $48 million. Obama, however, had turned this advantage around; in the fifteen months through April 30, 2008, he raised $265 million and had $46 million on hand; McCain, during the same period, had accumulated $96 million and had less than $22 million in cash available.[9]

These circumstances led to one of the most important strategic choices of the campaign: Obama announced on June 19 that, contrary to a previous pledge, he was going to decline public financing in the general election. His campaign claimed he was worried about the millions of dollars being spent by independent conservative groups on attack ads and the expected substantial spending advantage that the Republican National Committee (RNC) would have over its Democratic counterpart. If candidates accept public financing in the general election, their spending is limited to the $84 million received thereby. The candidate's party could spend only an additional $19 million in coordination with the candidate, but it could spend an unlimited amount on uncoordinated activities.[10]

McCain immediately attacked Obama for his decision, saying, "He has completely reversed himself and gone back, not on his word to me, but the commitment he made to the American people." McCain and his staff, however, were worried about the potential funding disadvantage, especially because many former Bush donors were holding back from contributing funds to his campaign.[11] Yet McCain's vigorous fund-raising efforts began to pay dividends, and in June he raised $22 million, the highest monthly total of his campaign.[12] With the public funding McCain would accept in September, plus the money likely to be spent by the RNC, the campaign expected to have access to $210 million from September 4 through election day.[13] Not wanting to lose its financial advantage, the Obama campaign redoubled its efforts, yielding receipts of $51 million in July and an amazing $66 million in August.[14] Exploiting his advantage, Obama spent $53 million in August ($32 million of it on advertising) compared with the $41 million spent by McCain.[15] But campaigns involve more than fund-raising. Central to both campaigns were voter registration and turnout efforts, which we consider at length later in this chapter.

Strategies and Appeals

Some of the candidates' strategies were targeted to specific groups, and none was held to be more important than Latinos. This growing segment of the electorate was a significant portion of the voters in many battleground states such as New Mexico, Florida, Nevada, Colorado, and New Jersey.[16] During the Clinton years, Latinos had tilted strongly to the Democrats, but they accounted for only a small percentage of voters. In the two Bush campaigns, however, their participation grew, and the GOP attracted more support from them. According to the exit polls, Bush received 35 percent of the Latino vote in 2000, and that share increased to 40 percent in 2004.[17] In 2008 analysts predicted that their turnout would further increase.

The Latino vote offered opportunities and concerns for both candidates. Obama had lost this segment of the electorate to Hillary Clinton in the nomination contest, and so some in the Democratic Party worried about his ability to attract the Latino vote. And yet polls in the summer indicated that Obama was running better among Latinos than Kerry had. Initially, McCain had good reason to be hopeful about appealing to this group. He had, after all, cosponsored an immigration bill with Sen. Edward Kennedy in 2007 that had included an opportunity for undocumented immigrants to gain legal status. The rub was that this position had outraged many conservative Republicans, for whom the issue was very salient. Once he began his presidential campaign, McCain took a less visible role in pushing for his bill, and when it failed he said that he would from that point on focus first on securing the nation's borders in dealing with the issue of illegal immigration. This tack was very appealing to conservatives, but led to doubts among Latinos about McCain's views.[18]

Both campaigns pursued tactics designed to build up their candidates and undermine the other party. The Democrats' most prominent message was that an Obama presidency promised change. Indeed, *change* was the word most frequently used in speeches at the party convention.[19] This message took advantage of the unpopularity of the Bush administration, and Democrats sought to tie McCain to the president, claiming that he offered a "third Bush term."[20] As noted, before the campaign season McCain had built a reputation as a maverick who had disagreed with Bush and his party on some important issues such as campaign finance reform, but during the GOP nomination race McCain had touted his high level of support for Bush's policies, and Obama was able to use those claims against McCain.

Another and related line of attack for the Democrats was the economy. In a speech in North Carolina on June 9, Obama contended, "We were promised a fiscal conservative [in George W. Bush]. Instead we got the most fiscally irresponsible administration in history. And now John McCain wants to give us another."[21] Then in mid-September, when the financial crisis hit, McCain's statements gave Obama another opening on the economy. The GOP candidate, speaking at a rally in Florida, repeated a line that he had used frequently in earlier speeches: "The fundamentals of our economy are strong." Obama responded by saying, "It's not that I think that John McCain doesn't care about what's going on in the lives of most Americans, I just think that he doesn't know. Why else would he say, today, of all days, just a few hours ago, that the fundamentals of our economy are strong? Senator, what economy are you talking about?"[22]

The Republican campaign's main line of attack was to claim Obama was liberal, inexperienced, and not ready to be president. On the day the Democrat tied up his nomination, McCain made a speech "casting the Democrat as an out-of-touch liberal who offers a false promise of change."[23] An official of the RNC characterized Obama's views as "very far to the left."[24] Later, in September, the RNC bought time in fourteen states for an advertisement that claimed Obama and congressional Democrats were "ready to tax, ready to spend, but not ready to lead."[25]

Angry about Obama's domination of media attention and wanting to trivialize him, the GOP campaign launched what came to be known as the "celebrity ad." In July, as part of a foreign tour, Obama gave a speech in Berlin that attracted a crowd estimated at 200,000. Images of Obama's speech were alternated with pictures of Britney Spears and Paris Hilton, while an announcer said, "He's the biggest celebrity in the world."[26] The Republicans also sought to couple their claims that Obama was unprepared for the presidency with the public's concerns about national security and terrorism, issues on which the party historically had held an advantage. For example, in a speech at the GOP national convention Rudy Giuliani said, "Tough times require strong leadership, and this is no time for on-the-job-training." He also claimed the Democrats were "in a state of denial" about Islamic terrorism, and he characterized Obama as a "machine politician" who "has never led anything. Nothing. Nada."[27] Earlier, in July, pointing to Obama's opposition to the war in Iraq, McCain had contended that Obama "would rather lose a war in order to win a campaign."[28]

Lurking in the background of these exchanges was another issue and a sensitive one. That issue was race, the most divisive fault line in American politics. Writing in 1840, Alexis de Tocqueville argued that the main threat to American democracy was "the presence of blacks on the soil of the United States."[29] Many observers worried about the passions that were stimulated by the candidacy of a black man who actually had a realistic chance of being elected president. Few believed that the Republican campaigners were racists, but some Democrats thought that the GOP efforts were designed to make Obama appear untrustworthy and different from mainstream Americans. Wanting to head off anything that could undermine his advantage, Obama responded. On the day of the GOP's "celebrity ad" Obama was campaigning in Missouri. There he told a crowd that the Republicans were "going to make you scared of me. You know, he's not patriotic enough. He's got a funny name. You know, he doesn't look like all those other presidents on those dollar bills, you know. He's risky."[30]

McCain's campaign responded quickly, claiming that Obama had "played the race card, and he played it from the bottom of the deck."[31] Of course, this claim itself directly raised the race issue. The Republicans vigorously denied that they wanted to appeal to racist sentiments, but analysts wondered how many voters might react on this basis. Indeed, Dick Armey, the former Republican majority leader in the House, contended in early September, "There's an awful lot of people in America, bless their heart, who simply are not emotionally prepared to vote for a black man. It's deplorable, but it's real."[32]

In addition to deciding what issues to emphasize, another strategic choice that faced both presidential candidates early in the campaign was the vice presidential nominee. As we saw in Chapter 1, because of his lead in the polls and the favorable context, Obama made a "safe" choice by picking Joe Biden. It was thought that Biden's substantial experience and "common touch" demeanor would appeal to the traditional party groups who had supported Hillary Clinton. McCain, by contrast, with his significant disadvantages, did not feel he could play it safe. His choice of Sarah Palin certainly shook up the political landscape. As one of McCain's aides said of the choice: "We just threw long."[33]

The McCain campaign had hoped that Palin would help them with three groups: social conservatives, women, and voters who thought the country was on the wrong track (and who would, it was hoped, see her as a reformer).[34] At first, things appeared to go extremely well. Palin drew large crowds—much larger than McCain had been pulling alone—and polls indicated a generally positive reaction to her. In a *Newsweek* poll conducted September 9–11, 52 percent of respondents had a favorable opinion of Palin (three points better than Biden), and 24 percent of white women said that Palin's presence on the ticket made them more likely to vote for McCain. Perhaps even more important, 71 percent of McCain voters said that they supported the ticket strongly compared with only 39 percent who had said that before the Republican national convention.[35]

Palin also seemed to offer a boost for McCain in the national polls. On September 2, the opening day of the GOP national convention, the average of national polls indicated a 6.4 percentage point lead for Obama, reflecting a bump from his convention. However, a week later McCain had taken the lead by 2.9 points. But the picture also contained the hints of problems to come. The *Newsweek* poll had indicated that only 45 percent of respondents thought that Palin was ready to step in as president (compared with 71 percent for

Biden), and successive national TV interviews with Charles Gibson of ABC and Katie Couric of CBS raised additional doubts about her suitability. Eventually, the Republicans' convention bounce dissipated, and by September 17 the race was tied.

Battleground States

Most campaign activities were directed at the "battleground" states. In early June, the *Washington Post* published a list of sixteen states on which it expected the candidates to concentrate.[36] And they did just that, especially the larger states in the group such as Florida, Michigan, Ohio, and Pennsylvania. Many of the remaining states—even large ones such as California, New York, and Texas—would see little evidence that a presidential campaign was in progress.

One measure of how the general election campaign unfolded was where the presidential and vice presidential candidates made personal appearances. CNN tracked these visits between June 8 and November 4, and the patterns reflect the strategies of the campaigns.[37] In all, John McCain and Sarah Palin made 223 visits, compared with 212 by Barack Obama and Joe Biden. Of the Republican total, 77 percent were allocated to the battleground states listed by the *Washington Post*; the corresponding figure for the Democrats was 67 percent. The top three states for both parties were similar but not identical. For the Republicans, they were Pennsylvania, Ohio, and Missouri (seventy-three visits altogether, almost a third of their total), whereas the Democrats went to Ohio, Virginia, and Pennsylvania (fifty-seven visits, 27 percent).

The pattern of visits also reflected the special aspects of the 2008 race. The centrality of fund-raising was demonstrated by a larger number of visits to states that were uncompetitive. For example, the Democrats made fifteen visits to the District of Columbia and thirteen to Illinois (fourth and fifth on their list), while the GOP candidates went to New York eleven times (the fifth most and the same number as to Florida) and eight times to California (eleventh). These locations were all certain victories for the Democrats, but excellent sources of money for both campaigns.

The data also demonstrate the Obama campaign's decision to use the unfavorable political climate and its money advantage to expand the playing field by focusing on states that had in previous years been dependably Republican. The most obvious example was Virginia, which had voted for a Democrat for president only once between 1952 and 2004 (in Lyndon Johnson's landslide victory in 1964). Obama and Biden made nineteen visits (second most), forcing the Republicans to counter with ten visits (seventh). Other examples were twelve visits by the Democrats to North Carolina and eight to Indiana. The latter was not even expected to be a battleground state, but the Democrats' efforts made it one, and eventually it was their narrowest win. Nebraska's unusual method of allocating electoral votes provided a last unusual battleground (albeit no candidate visits). Reflecting the Democrats' determination to seek every possible vote, the campaign allocated substantial efforts to the second district (Omaha and its suburbs), and succeeded in carrying it on election day.

THREE WEEKS, FOUR DEBATES

Because of the late conventions and the compressed general election period, the four debates (three presidential and one vice presidential) were packed into less than three weeks. Unfortunately for McCain, in the days leading up to the first debate, scheduled for Friday, September 26, the difficult situation he faced got even worse as the weak economy went into a tailspin. Lehman Brothers, the big investment bank, announced it would file for bankruptcy; a major insurance company, American International Group (AIG), had to seek an emergency loan from the Federal Reserve; and the giant broker Merrill Lynch collapsed. There were warnings that unless Congress passed a financial rescue package by Monday, September 29, the whole credit system might collapse.[38] On September 24, Obama called McCain, seeking to make a joint statement on the crisis. When they spoke, McCain indicated that he was thinking of suspending his campaign and asking to postpone the first debate so that he could join the negotiations. Then, almost immediately after the telephone conversation, McCain publicly announced his plans. But when he got to Washington, neither the Democrats nor the Republicans welcomed him. The GOP candidate had asked Bush to invite all the congressional leaders and the candidates to the White House, but this meeting just resulted in angry conflict, particularly when House Republican leader John Boehner indicated that he did not have the votes to pass the financial rescue package bill.

In the wake of the meeting, McCain decided he could participate in the debate after all. The campaigns had agreed that the subject of the first encounter would be foreign policy. (Because this subject was expected to be McCain's strong suit, the Democrats had judged it was best to get this one out of the way.) But because of the financial crisis, it was inevitable that the crisis would be addressed, and the initial questions as well as the lion's share of the time dealt with it. As usual, both candidates had spent a great deal of time preparing for the event, with each engaging in a series of practice debates with stand-ins for their opponents. Obama's staff emphasized the need to use this opportunity to help convince the public that he was prepared to assume the office of president.[39] The day of the debate, the average of national polls showed that Obama had again opened up a lead of 4.2 points.

There was a good deal of conflict between the candidates as the debates proceeded, but to most observers there was no "game changing" moment. In the first debate on Friday evening, September 26, both candidates offered mild support for the "bailout" bill, and they disagreed about the wars in Iraq and Afghanistan. The next day, McCain went back to Washington to try to persuade House Republicans to support the rescue bill, while the two campaigns sought to influence public perceptions of who had won the debate. (McCain's image was not helped by his singular lack of success back on Capitol Hill. He was not able to get even one of the four GOP members from his home state to vote for the bill.) By Monday, the consensus in the polls was that Obama had won. For example, in a *USA Today*/Gallup poll, equal percentages of respondents said they had a more or less favorable opinion of McCain after the debate, whereas the proportion that had a more favorable opinion of Obama was more than twice as large as the unfavorables.[40]

The vice presidential debate was held six days after the first presidential one. Perceptions of Palin had continued to become more negative. For example, a *Washington Post*/ABC News poll indicated that the proportion of respondents who thought she lacked the experience to be president had increased fifteen points, to 60 percent, since the beginning of September. And a Pew Research Center survey showed that she was not attracting women to her ticket; Obama had 54 percent support among women versus McCain's 37 percent.[41] Moreover, the unflattering opinions of her were not confined to Democrats. David Frum, a conservative columnist and former Bush speechwriter, said, "I think she has pretty thoroughly—and probably irretrievably—proven she is not up to the job of being president of the United States."[42]

In the debate, Palin sought to get her message across mainly by evading the questions of the "media elite" as she characterized them (in this case posed by the moderator, Gwen Ifill of PBS). She sought to appeal to the middle class ("Joe six-pack and hockey moms"), and characterized herself and McCain as "mavericks." Biden, who was respectful of Palin, tried to tie the GOP ticket to the Bush administration and "the worst economic policies we have ever had."[43] Again in this debate, most observers saw the outcome as fairly even, but at least two instant polls perceived Biden to be the winner by substantial margins.[44]

Perhaps more telling than the vice presidential debate and its results was a strategic decision the McCain campaign made the same day. It announced that it was pulling resources and staff out of Michigan. The Democrats had carried the state in the last four presidential elections, but McCain had hoped to flip it in 2008, in part because of his large victory over Bush in the 2000 GOP primary there. But his campaign had never gained traction against Obama in Michigan, and the state polls showed the Democrat with a double-digit lead. Even worse from the point of view of the national effort, part of the reason for the Michigan decision was to permit the campaign to shift resources to Indiana, a state that had gone Democratic only once since 1936.[45]

The second presidential debate was held a few days later. It employed a town meeting format that was supposedly advantageous for McCain. Reflecting his lagging position in the polls, McCain and his campaign had stepped up their attacks on Obama's qualifications and record. They also made it clear that this effort was setting the stage for the upcoming debate. (At a campaign rally, Palin told the crowd that she had advised McCain to "take the gloves off."[46]) The GOP candidate did go on the offensive that night, attacking Obama on many fronts.

Among other things, he claimed that Obama intended to raise taxes and that he would not adequately support the development of nuclear power. By contrast, Obama sought to continue to focus on the economy (the Dow Jones Industrial Average had fallen five hundred points that day) and to blame Bush and the Republicans. As in the earlier debates, a CNN poll indicated that respondents believed Obama had performed better by 54 percent to 30 percent for McCain. Moreover, perhaps reflecting the difference in tactics by the candidates, they perceived Obama as more likeable by 65 percent to McCain's 28 percent.[47]

The final debate, which was to focus on the economy and domestic policy, was on Thursday, October 16. The McCain campaign staff wondered whether it was time to tell their candidate that he no longer had a chance. "Not yet" was the consensus, but they knew that he would need a very strong performance to turn things around, which meant going on the attack again.[48] Yet it was far from certain that this tactic would have a positive effect. In recent weeks the GOP campaign had stepped up its attacks on Obama. Almost all its ads were negative, including one that sought to link the Democrat to a former 1960s radical, who had since become involved in Chicago politics. (Reflecting his front-runner status, Obama's ads were a mix of positive and negative.) However, there were indications that the strategy was having detrimental effects on people's opinions of McCain. An Ipsos Public Affairs survey indicated that 53 percent of voters said the Republican candidate engaged in more negative campaigning than Obama, whereas only 30 percent said the opposite.[49] A *New York Times* poll showed an even greater disparity, with McCain seen as more negative by 61 percent compared with Obama's 31 percent. Among respondents who said that their opinions of Obama had changed recently, twice as many indicated that they thought better of him than worse of him. As for those who had changed their opinions about McCain, three times as many said they thought worse of him than better of him.[50]

The subject of the negative tone of the campaign figured prominently in the last debate, with each candidate claiming that the other was mainly responsible for it. McCain tried to raise doubts about Obama's competence, and he continually charged that the Democrat would raise taxes. Obama countered that under his plan only the wealthiest citizens would see an increase, and 90 percent would get a tax cut. When it was over, McCain's performance had failed to produce the big shift in public opinion his campaign needed. On the Tuesday after the debate, Obama led the average of the national polls by 7.2 points, and election day was only two weeks off.

END GAME: THE BATTLE OVER TURNOUT

Over the last few presidential elections, efforts to entice citizens to go to the polls have increased in intensity and expense. Through 2004, the Republicans had an advantage in this area (called "the ground game" by professionals, as opposed to "the air war" waged on television and radio), but it was a shrinking one as Democrats substantially accelerated their turnout operation to catch up. As the official election day for 2008 approached, both campaigns ratcheted up their efforts to rally their supporters and get them to the polls.

Turnout Efforts

In 2004 the Democrats' turnout efforts were largely in the hands of an independent group called "America Coming Together" (ACT). The group was mainly financed by wealthy liberals, who were able (under the campaign finance laws) to contribute what they wished. But the group could not coordinate its activities with the party and its candidate, and it was restricted in mentioning candidates. In 2008, by contrast, the Obama campaign funded its own get-out-the-vote (GOTV) operation, which included pouring $112 million into state party activities. Republican spending on the turnout operation increased only a little over its 2004 level.[51] The scope of the Democratic organization was remarkable. In Florida, for example, Obama had "65 offices, paid staff of 350, active e-mail list of 650,000, [and] 25,000 volunteers on any weekend day."[52]

One aspect of the parties' GOTV effort began early in 2008, especially for Democrats—encouraging voter registration. Obama's nomination campaign made a big effort to register new voters, especially blacks.[53] And that effort continued into the general election. Many states had a significant gap between white and black registration. For example, in Florida in 2004, 71 percent of whites were registered compared with only 53 percent of blacks. The comparable figures in Virginia were 72 percent versus 58 percent.[54] These battleground states were important to Obama's strategy, and so boosting black registrants had the potential to yield a big payoff. But blacks were not the only target of registration efforts, and the Democratic Party apparatus was not the only active player. Nonpartisan groups ran their own registration programs, and often the effect was beneficial to Democrats. For example, in September Spanish-language media launched a major initiative, with financial support from State Farm Insurance Co., to register and turn out Latinos.[55]

Overall, the Democratic registration efforts were very successful. American University's Center for the Study of the American Electorate estimated that 73.5 percent of citizens eighteen and older registered to vote compared with the previous record (in 1964) of 72.1 percent.[56] The October data from eight battleground states that registered voters by party revealed that total registration grew 7 percent compared with 2004, from 32.3 million to 34.7 million. In those states, the Democratic registration plurality nearly doubled, from 1.6 million voters to 3.1 million voters.[57]

Another aspect of the GOTV strategies was litigation. In recent elections, the Republicans have sought to block efforts to make registration easier, and they have also tried to increase voter identification requirements and to purge previously registered voters from the rolls.[58] Enhanced ID requirements adopted in

Indiana were upheld by the U.S. Supreme Court in April 2008,[59] but the GOP had less luck with other strategies as November approached. For example, the GOP sought a court order to require the Ohio secretary of state to provide counties with a list of about 200,000 newly registered voters whose information on forms did not match driver's license or Social Security records.[60] Democrats claimed that this effort could prevent legitimate voters from having their votes counted, while the Republicans claimed it was necessary to prevent fraud. (There was evidence that voters were being misclassified as ineligible in many state databases, and that voter purges in six swing states appeared to violate federal law.[61]) The GOP succeeded in securing an order from an Ohio court, but it was overturned in a unanimous ruling by the U.S. Supreme Court. The Republicans also suffered setbacks in other states, including Wisconsin, Michigan, and Indiana.[62] The Democrats and their supporters also went to court to counter Republican efforts. In a Colorado case, the secretary of state had removed tens of thousands of names from the voter rolls. A coalition of groups sued in federal court, claiming that such purges were generally prohibited by federal law within ninety days of an election. The agreement reached permitted all of the questioned voters to cast a provisional ballot that would be counted unless election officials could prove the voters were ineligible.[63]

Early Voting

One important feature of the GOTV effort in 2008 was the focus on early voting. Early voting has long been held, mainly in the form of absentee ballots that have required some excuse such as a disability that prevented travel. However, until recently the proportion of the electorate that voted early was small (7 percent in 1992) and generally tilted in favor of the Republicans. Then many states began to adopt in-person, no-excuse early voting, and the proportion of votes cast this way has grown substantially, reaching 20 percent in 2004 (in fact, Oregon voters cast all ballots "early" by mail).[64]

By 2008 the number of states permitting early in-person voting had grown to thirty-four, thirty-one of which required no excuse.[65] Some states—among them, Virginia, Georgia, and Michigan—offered the opportunity to vote as early as mid-September. Some votes were thus cast even before the first presidential debate. Because of the Democrats' success in registering new voters and the fact that in the past a larger percentage of registered Democrats had failed to vote, the Obama campaign saw early voting as a great opportunity in their massive turnout effort. Obama visited Tampa, Florida, on October 20, when early voting started, and told a crowd, "You can start voting today, so I want everybody after this rally to go and vote." The same day, Hillary Clinton held some early-voting rallies targeting senior citizens.[66]

One of the key advantages of early voting is that a campaign's late mistake or problem cannot hurt it with people who have already voted. This situation may be particularly beneficial to the front-runner. A late October poll indicated that

59 percent of early voters were supporting Obama versus 40 percent for McCain, as compared with a 60–40 advantage for Bush in 2004.[67] However our analysis of the 2008 American National Election Studies (ANES) survey shows no Democratic advantage: 52 percent of the early voters supported Obama, and 48 percent voted for McCain, which is not much different from the results for the entire electorate.

Not surprisingly, the Democrats focused special attention on the African American community, with substantial success. In 2008 blacks accounted for 21 percent of registered voters in both Florida and North Carolina. However, in North Carolina blacks were 26.5 percent of early voters, and in Florida the percentage was even higher at 34.9.[68] Overall, Michael McDonald calculates that about 30 percent of 2008 voters cast early votes. After Oregon, the top states were Washington (89.2 percent) and Colorado (78.9 percent).[69]

The Final Days

With two weeks to go, Obama led in the average of national polls by 7.2 percent, while for the Republicans almost all the news was bad. For one thing, the public's opinion of Sarah Palin, who had provided such an initial boost to the GOP ticket, continued to decline. In one poll at the end of October, 59 percent of respondents said she was not prepared for the job of vice president, up nine points from the beginning of the month.[70] In addition, 89 percent had a negative perception of the economy, and 85 percent said the country was on the wrong track. Moreover, the respondents' views of which candidate would be more likely to accomplish desirable goals were heavily tilted toward the Democrats. For example, when asked whether a candidate's policies would make the economy better, 54 percent of respondents favored Obama compared with 32 percent for McCain. As for whether the candidate's policies would bring about real change in the way things are done in Washington, 64 percent gave the nod to Obama versus 39 percent for McCain.

Possibly affecting these public perceptions was a series of endorsements of Obama by significant Republican figures. Perhaps most notable was the endorsement by former Bush secretary of state Colin Powell on October 19. Powell called Obama "a transformational figure," and said he "displayed a steadiness, an intellectual curiosity, a depth of knowledge, and an approach to looking at problems … that showed he was ready to be president."[71] Later that week, the Democrat was endorsed by former governor William Weld of Massachusetts and former governor Arne Carlson of Minnesota.

In the campaign's closing days, Obama continued to draw on his financial advantage. In the third week of October, he outspent McCain three to one on TV ads. And on October 29, six days before election day, the Democrats bought half-hour slots for commercials on three networks.[72] Some observers wondered whether people would tune in for such a heavy dose of politics, but they did. The presentation, which also aired on four cable channels, drew 33.6 million viewers, more than the finale for the previous season of *American Idol*.[73] The next day Obama was in Virginia urging supporters to continue their efforts. "Don't believe for a second that this election is over. Don't think for a minute that power concedes," he said. "We have to work like our future depends on it this last week—because it does."[74]

On Monday, the day before campaigning would end, McCain appeared at eight rallies in seven states. Reflecting his disadvantaged situation, all except Pennsylvania were states Bush had carried in 2004. Obama, by contrast, campaigning as the front-runner, spent the day in Florida, North Carolina, and Virginia. It was a remarkable picture to end a remarkable election year: a black northern Democrat from Abraham Lincoln's home state seeking the support of voters in three southern states that had not voted for a candidate of his party in decades. And Obama succeeded in all three.

DID THE CAMPAIGN MAKE A DIFFERENCE IN THE OUTCOME?

The answer to this question depends to a degree on the yardstick used to measure the effects of the campaign. Did it determine the winner? Did it affect the choices of a substantial number of voters? Did it put issues and candidates' positions clearly before the voters? Would a better campaign by one of the candidates have yielded a different result? Did the campaign produce events that will have a lasting impact on American politics? We cannot provide firm answers to all of these questions, but we can shed light on some of them.

Regarding the outcome and voters' decisions, it seems quite clear that the campaign did indeed have an effect.[75] As noted earlier, the relative standing of the candidates ebbed and flowed from June to November, and these changes seemed to be linked in part to events in the campaign. Indeed, McCain had taken a lead in the polls after the GOP convention, but lost it as the public's judgment on Palin turned negative and as Obama was able to focus attention on the declining economic situation. To be sure, the political context was very difficult for the Republicans. Exit poll data show that among actual voters, 71 percent disapproved of Bush's job performance, and 75 percent thought the country was on the wrong track.[76] In those groups, Obama received 67 percent and 62 percent of the vote, respectively.

However, to be successful in that context the Democratic campaign had to make good use of its advantages and counter its disadvantages. This it seemed to do effectively. For example, the Democrats used their financial advantage to enhance turnout and persuade doubters. The exit polls indicate that 6 percent of voters was contacted only by the McCain campaign, whereas 13 percent was contacted only by Obama supporters. (Another 13 percent was contacted by both.) The Obama campaign also succeeded in raising doubts about Palin. Exit polls reveal that 66 percent of respondents thought Biden was qualified to be president if necessary, whereas only 38 percent thought the same about Palin.

Indeed, fully 49 percent said that *only* Biden was qualified, and Obama won 91 percent of the vote from that group.

Obama largely neutralized the main GOP lines of attack. Although McCain had an advantage because of his experience (59 percent said he had the right experience), the Democrat's 50 percent was enough. Obama received 93 percent of the votes from those who thought he had the right experience, while McCain won only 69 percent from those who thought that about him. Republicans emphasized the threat of another terrorist attack as a reason to be concerned about Obama's limited experience. However, even though the public remained concerned, with 70 percent saying they were worried about another attack, McCain carried that group by only 50 percent to 48 percent.

And yet the Obama campaign was persuasive in approaching voters about some of its major campaign themes. For example, when asked which candidate was "in touch with people like you," 26 percent of respondents in exit polls said only McCain, whereas 44 percent said only Obama (and the Democrat carried that latter group 99 percent to 1 percent). Similarly, when asked which candidate "attacked unfairly," only 10 percent said Obama, but 24 percent said McCain. Finally, Obama's cool demeanor and command of details seem to have influenced the voters' evaluations. When asked whether candidates had the "right judgment," respondents divided evenly in evaluating McCain (49 percent to 49 percent), but 57 percent evaluated Obama favorably (and he received 90 percent of their votes).

A final way in which the campaign appears to have made a difference in the 2008 results was the success of the Democrats' turnout operation, not only in safe Democratic states, but also in those that shifted from supporting Bush in 2004 to supporting Obama in 2008. Table 2-1 lists the nine states that moved from the Republican to the Democratic column in 2008, along with their level of turnout in both years and the national change in turnout for comparison. In six of the nine cases, not only did the increase in turnout exceed the national change, but it was about double or more. One cannot say that the Democrats won just because of the successful GOTV effort, but it is certainly fair to say that it was a significant advantage and that without it other aspects of the campaign might have been more difficult than they were.

And what are the implications of the 2008 campaign for the future of American politics? Some commentators have wondered whether it was the beginning of a realignment along the lines of the New Deal.[77] A full analysis of that issue would require far more space than we can allocate here, but we can say with confidence that it is too soon to know. Realignments are enduring changes to electoral patterns, and so we will not know for a while whether the pro-Democratic changes in 2008 will persist or fade away. We can, however, point to some 2008 developments that should surely be of concern to the GOP as it thinks about the future.

First, although there is no indication of a significant ideological shift in the electorate in a liberal direction, there is evidence of an increase in the Democrats'

TABLE 2-1   Changes in Turnout among Voting-Eligible Population between 2004 and 2008, Nationwide and in States that Switched from Republican to Democrat (percent)

	2004	2008	Percent change
Nationwide	60.1	61.7	+1.6
Colorado	66.7	69.8	+3.1
Florida	64.4	67.5	+3.1
Indiana	54.8	59.4	+4.6
Iowa	69.9	69.9	0.0
Nevada	55.3	58.6	+3.3
New Mexico	59.0	60.3	+1.3
North Carolina	57.8	65.8	+8.0
Ohio	66.8	66.7	−0.1
Virginia	60.6	67.7	+7.1

Sources: Michael P. McDonald, "2004 General Election Turnout Rates," http://elections.gmu.edu/Turnout_2004G.html; McDonald, "2008 General Election Turnout Rates," http://elections.gmu.edu/Turnout_2008G.html.

advantage in party identification. We will discuss this matter in detail in Chapter 8, and so we will just note here that in the exit polls in 2008, 39 percent of respondents identified as Democrats compared with 32 percent who said they were Republicans. Of course, this may be just a fleeting shift caused by some disaffected GOP voters staying home, but it may be more than that.

Of greater concern to the Republicans should be some of the demographic patterns in the voting. As we discussed earlier, the growth of the Latino vote over the last two decades placed that group front and center in campaign efforts. The exit polls reveal that Latinos made up a slightly larger share of the electorate in 2008 than in 2004 (9 percent versus 8 percent), but the portion of Latino voters won by Obama increased to 67 percent from 53 percent for Kerry in 2004. Partly reflecting that support, President Obama nominated a Latina, Judge Sonia Sotomayor, as his first appointment to the U.S. Supreme Court, and he indicated early on that immigration reform would be a priority for his administration, although the issue ended up receiving relatively little attention while the health care debate raged. In responding to these initiatives, the GOP will have to tread carefully lest it further alienate this important and growing segment of the electorate.[78]

Another group that concerns the Republicans is the youngest segment of voters. In 2008, 18 percent of voters were under thirty, and they supported Obama over McCain by 66 percent to 32 percent. If this group were to maintain its pro-Democratic tilt as a larger portion of its members begin to participate in elections, it would present a huge political challenge for the GOP.

Whether these trends persist will depend in large measure on the public's reactions to the style and substance of Obama's governance. If the economy turns down again, or if the national security challenges the administration faces appear to make the nation less safe, then the electorate is likely to punish the Democrats and the problems facing the GOP may vanish. Similarly, failure to enact significant health reform to which the public responds positively or a deterioration of the situation in the war in Afghanistan may have a negative impact on Democratic fortunes. But if the electorate perceives that Obama's policies and strategies have improved their situation, or that the Democrats are not at fault for what problems persist, the political difficulties facing the Republicans may intensify and deprive them of control of government for a long time.

Chapter 3

The Election Results

As the general election campaign closed, it was clear that Barack Obama was very likely to prevail. Obama led in all seventy of the publicly reported trial heats of likely voters conducted from September 19 to November 3, and in the sixteen polls conducted during the week before the election he held leads ranging from 7 percentage points to 13 percentage points.[1] Web sites that forecast the election results predicted an Obama victory.[2] Moreover, two gaming Web sites—Intrade. com, a site based in Dublin, Ireland, and the Iowa Electronic Markets (IEM), based at the University of Iowa—also showed the Democratic candidate as the likely presidential winner. By the day before the election, according to Intrade. com, the probability of a Republican presidential victory was pegged at 0.113, and the IEM probability of a GOP popular vote majority was 0.112.[3]

By November 4, election day, it seemed clear that Obama would win unless the polls were fundamentally flawed. If a sizable minority of Americans who said they would vote for Obama were lying to conceal their reluctance to vote for an African American, John McCain might emerge victorious. But the so-called Bradley effect, named for Tom Bradley, the black mayor of Los Angeles who was defeated in the 1982 California gubernatorial election, remained a thin reed on which to base Republican hopes. Whether such effects would materialize was problematic, and there were other instances of blacks winning statewide office in which the actual election results mirrored the pre-election polls.[4] When the first election night returns came in, it was clear that Obama was winning. Shortly after 9 p.m. EST, it appeared he would win more than 270 electoral votes as soon as the polls closed in California, Oregon, and Washington (a total of seventy-three electoral votes) at 11 p.m. EST.[5]

At about 11:15 p.m. McCain made a gracious concession speech, stating: "This is an historic election, and I recognize the special significance it must have for African Americans and for the special pride that must be theirs tonight."[6] At midnight, Obama spoke to a victory rally in Chicago's Grant Park before a crowd of 250,000. Spontaneous street parties broke out in major U.S. cities, including Boston, Atlanta, Philadelphia, and San Francisco, as well as cities abroad such as Berlin, London, Osaka, Rio de Janeiro, and Sydney. And there were celebrations in Nairobi, the capital of Kenya, where Obama's father was born, raised, and died.

In the final tally, Obama won 52.9 percent of the popular vote, becoming the third Democrat since World War II to win a popular vote majority.[7] McCain won 45.7 percent. Obama's 7.2 percentage point margin was solid, but it pales beside Lyndon Johnson's 22.6 percentage point margin in 1964 over Barry Goldwater. Moreover, the Republican candidates won by larger margins in six postwar elections: 1952 (10.5 percentage points), 1956 (15.4 points), 1972 (23.2 points), 1980 (9.7 points), 1984 (18.2 points), and 1988 (7.8 points).[8] In 2008, as in 2004, independent and third-party candidates won only a negligible share of the vote: 1.4 percent, with 0.6 percent for Ralph Nader, an independent, and 0.4 percent for Bob Barr, a Libertarian.

Table 3-1 presents the official election results by states, including those for Maine's two congressional districts and Nebraska's three districts.[9] Obama's total of nearly 69.5 million votes was substantially greater than the previous record of 62 million votes won by George W. Bush four years earlier, and Obama won 10 million more votes than John Kerry, the 2004 Democratic candidate. His overall vote share was 4.6 percentage points more than Kerry's. However, these gains were unequally distributed across the country, and in four states—Arkansas, Louisiana, Oklahoma, and West Virginia—Obama's vote shares declined from those of Kerry.

Obama carried twenty-eight states, as well as the District of Columbia, and McCain carried the other twenty-two states (see Figure 3-1). Obama's electoral vote total was 365 to McCain's 173. Thus Obama's total was very close to Bill Clinton's in 1992 (370) and in 1996 (379). Unlike Bush's disputed win in 2000 in which he won with one more vote than a majority, or even Bush's 286 vote tally in 2004, no serious critic could challenge the legitimacy of Obama's victory. As Figure 3-1 shows, Obama won all nineteen states carried by Kerry. In addition, he won nine states Bush had won in 2004: Colorado, Florida, Indiana, Iowa, New Mexico, Nevada, North Carolina, Ohio, and Virginia. These states, with their total of 112 electoral votes, along with the one vote from Nebraska, added 113 to the Democratic total.[10]

THE ELECTION RULES

In 2008 Obama won a clear majority of both the popular and electoral votes, and one might argue that he would have won under most election rules. But we would argue that the crucial, steady reduction in the independent third-party vote between 1992 and 2004 and the negligible total in 2008 result from U.S. election rules. In 1992 H. Ross Perot won 18.9 percent of the popular vote; in 1996 his support dropped to 8.4 percent. In 2000 Ralph Nader won

TABLE 3-1 Presidential Election Results by State, 2008

State	Total vote	McCain (Rep.)	Obama (Dem.)	Other	Rep.-Dem. plurality		Total vote (%) Rep.	Total vote (%) Dem.
Alabama	2,099,819	1,266,546	813,479	19,794	453,067	R	60.3	38.7
Alaska	326,197	193,841	123,594	8,762	70,247	R	59.4	37.9
Arizona	2,293,475	1,230,111	1,034,707	28,657	195,404	R	53.6	45.1
Arkansas	1,086,617	638,017	422,310	26,290	215,707	R	58.7	38.9
California	13,561,900	5,011,781	8,274,473	275,646	3,262,692	D	37.0	61.0
Colorado	2,401,462	1,073,629	1,288,633	39,200	215,004	D	44.7	53.7
Connecticut	1,646,797	629,428	997,772	19,597	368,344	D	38.2	60.6
Delaware	412,412	152,374	255,459	4,579	103,085	D	36.9	61.9
Florida	8,390,744	4,045,624	4,282,074	63,046	236,450	D	48.2	51.0
Georgia	3,924,486	2,048,759	1,844,123	31,604	204,636	R	52.2	47.0
Hawaii	453,568	120,566	325,871	7,131	205,305	D	26.6	71.8
Idaho	655,122	403,012	236,440	15,670	166,572	R	61.5	36.1
Illinois	5,522,371	2,031,179	3,419,348	71,844	1,388,169	D	36.8	61.9
Indiana	2,751,054	1,345,648	1,374,039	31,367	28,391	D	48.9	49.9
Iowa	1,537,123	682,379	828,940	25,804	146,561	D	44.4	53.9
Kansas	1,235,872	699,655	514,765	21,452	184,890	R	56.6	41.7
Kentucky	1,826,620	1,048,462	751,985	26,173	296,477	R	57.4	41.2
Louisiana	1,960,761	1,148,275	782,989	29,497	365,286	R	58.6	39.9
Maine[a]	731,163	295,273	421,923	13,967	126,650	D	40.4	57.7
Maryland	2,631,596	959,862	1,629,467	42,267	669,605	D	36.5	61.9
Massachusetts	3,080,985	1,108,854	1,904,097	68,034	795,243	D	36.0	61.8
Michigan	5,001,766	2,048,639	2,872,579	80,548	823,940	D	41.0	57.4
Minnesota	2,910,369	1,275,409	1,573,354	61,606	297,945	D	43.8	54.1

| | | McCain | Obama | | Rep.-Dem. | | Total vote (%) | |
State	Total vote	(Rep.)	(Dem.)	Other	plurality		Rep.	Dem.
Mississippi	1,289,865	724,597	554,662	10,606	169,935	R	56.2	43.0
Missouri	2,925,205	1,445,814	1,441,911	37,480	3,903	R	49.4	49.3
Montana	490,302	242,763	231,667	15,872	11,096	R	49.5	47.2
Nebraska[b]	801,281	452,979	333,319	14,983	119,660	R	56.5	41.6
Nevada	967,848	412,827	533,736	21,285	120,909	D	42.7	55.1
New Hampshire	710,970	316,534	384,826	9,610	68,292	D	44.5	54.1
New Jersey	3,868,237	1,613,207	2,215,422	39,608	602,215	D	41.7	57.3
New Mexico	830,158	346,832	472,422	10,904	125,590	D	41.8	56.9
New York	7,640,931	2,752,771	4,804,945	83,215	2,052,174	D	36.0	62.9
North Carolina	4,310,789	2,128,474	2,142,651	39,664	14,177	D	49.4	49.7
North Dakota	316,621	168,601	141,278	6,742	27,323	R	53.3	44.6
Ohio	5,708,350	2,677,820	2,940,044	90,486	262,224	D	46.9	51.5
Oklahoma	1,462,661	960,165	502,496	c	457,669	R	65.6	34.4
Oregon	1,827,864	738,475	1,037,291	52,098	298,816	D	40.4	56.7
Pennsylvania	6,013,272	2,655,885	3,276,363	81,024	620,478	D	44.2	54.5
Rhode Island	471,766	165,391	296,571	9,804	131,180	D	35.1	62.9
South Carolina	1,920,969	1,034,896	862,449	23,624	172,447	R	53.9	44.9
South Dakota	381,975	203,054	170,924	7,997	32,130	R	53.2	44.7
Tennessee	2,599,749	1,479,178	1,087,437	33,134	391,741	R	56.9	41.8
Texas	8,077,795	4,479,328	3,528,633	69,834	950,695	R	55.5	43.7
Utah	952,370	596,030	327,670	28,670	268,360	R	62.6	34.4
Vermont	325,046	98,974	219,262	6,810	120,288	D	30.4	67.5
Virginia	3,723,260	1,725,005	1,959,532	38,723	234,527	D	46.3	52.6

(Continued)

TABLE 3-1   Presidential Election Results by State, 2008 (*continued*)

State	Total vote	McCain (Rep.)	Obama (Dem.)	Other	Rep.-Dem. plurality		Total vote (%) Rep.	Dem.
Washington	3,036,878	1,229,216	1,750,848	56,814	521,632	D	40.5	57.7
West Virginia	713,451	397,466	303,857	12,128	93,609	R	55.7	42.6
Wisconsin	2,983,417	1,262,393	1,677,211	43,813	414,818	D	42.3	56.2
Wyoming	254,658	164,958	82,868	6,832	82,090	R	64.8	32.5
District of Columbia	265,853	17,367	245,800	2,686	228,433	D	6.5	92.5
United States	131,313,820	59,948,323	69,498,516	1,866,981	9,550,193	D	45.7	52.9

Source: Rhodes Cook, Alice V. McGillivray, and Richard M. Scammon, *America Votes 28: Election Returns by State, 2007–2008* (Washington, D.C.: CQ Press, 2010). Based on reports of the secretaries of state of the fifty states and the District of Columbia.

[a] The winner of the plurality vote in each of Maine's two House districts received that district's single electoral vote:

Maine	731,163	295,273	421,923	13,967	126,650	D	40.4	57.7
1st District	383,626	144,604	232,145	6,877	87,541	D	37.7	60.5
2nd District	347,537	150,669	189,778	7,090	39,109	D	43.3	54.6

[b] In Nebraska the statewide plurality vote winner gained two votes, and each of the state's three congressional districts awarded one vote on a plurality basis:

Nebraska	801,281	452,969	333,319	14,983	119,660	R	56.5	41.6
1st District	273,958	148,179	121,468	4,311	26,711	R	54.1	44.3
2nd District	277,744	135,439	138,752	3,313	3,313	D	48.8	50.0
3rd District	246,742	169,361	73,999	4,842	96,262	R	68.6	29.6

[c] For Oklahoma, no results for other candidates were reported.

FIGURE 3-1   Electoral Votes by State, 2008

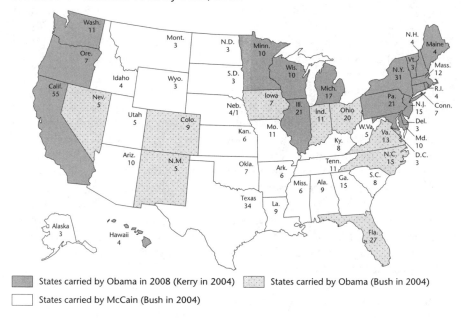

States carried by Obama in 2008 (Kerry in 2004) | States carried by Obama (Bush in 2004)

States carried by McCain (Bush in 2004)

Source: Rhodes Cook, Alice V. McGillivray, and Richard M. Scammon, *America Votes 28: Election Returns by State, 2007–2008* (Washington, D.C.: CQ Press, 2010).

Note: Barack Obama won 365 electoral votes, John McCain 173. We classify Nebraska as being carried by the Republicans in both 2004 and 2008. George W. Bush carried all five of Nebraska's electoral votes. McCain won the statewide race as well as two of Nebraska's three congressional districts, winning four of Nebraska's five electors.

only 2.7 percent of the popular vote, and other minor-party candidates and independents won 0.6 percent. In 2004 minor-party candidates and independents (including Nader) won a bare 1.0 percent of the vote, and in 2008 this share crept up to 1.4 percent. Partly because of these independent and third-party candidates, Clinton was able to win with only 43.0 percent of the popular vote in 1992, and he was still short of a majority when he was reelected in 1996 with 49.2 percent of the popular vote. In 2000 Bush won with only 47.9 percent of the popular vote, even though Al Gore had won 48.4 percent. And in 2004 Bush won with a narrow majority (50.7 percent) of both the popular and electoral votes (286 out of 538).

As we saw in Chapter 2, voters do not vote directly for president. Rather, they vote for a slate of electors pledged to support certain presidential and vice presidential candidates. Moreover, in every state except Maine and Nebraska the slate that receives the most popular votes is elected. In no state is a majority required to win. In two of the states Obama carried (Indiana and North Carolina), he fell just short of a majority, and he would have easily captured an electoral vote majority without their twenty-six electoral votes. In 2004 Bush won a popular vote majority in all but two of the thirty-one states he carried (Iowa and New Mexico) and would have won a narrow electoral vote majority without their twelve votes. But in 2000 he won a majority in only twenty-six of the thirty states he carried (falling short in Florida, Nevada, New Hampshire, and Ohio) and would have won only 217 electoral votes if a popular vote majority had been required.

The plurality vote win, winner-take-all system usually transforms a plurality of the popular vote into a majority of the electoral vote. And it takes a majority of the electoral vote to produce a winner. If there is no majority winner, the House of Representatives, voting by state delegations, chooses among the three candidates with the highest number of electoral votes. But the House has not chosen a winner since 1825, mainly because the plurality vote win system is very likely to produce a winner in the Electoral College as well as a two-party system. In forty-three of the forty-six contests from 1828 to 2008, the candidate with the most popular votes has won a majority of the electoral votes.[11] The three other elections—1876, 1888, and 2000—were all very close.[12] During this period, in fourteen elections a candidate won a plurality of the vote, not a majority, and won a majority of the electoral vote.[13]

The system places a heavy burden on third-party or independent candidates. Even a relatively successful third-party candidate usually receives a far smaller share of the electoral vote than of the popular vote.[14] Here it is useful to review the fates of the four most successful third-party and independent candidacies (in popular vote results) since World War II: George C. Wallace won 13.5 percent of the popular vote in 1968, John B. Anderson won 6.6 percent in 1980, and H. Ross Perot won 18.9 percent in 1992 and 8.4 percent in 1996. In 1980 and 1992, Anderson and Perot, respectively, had some modest regional support. Both fared better in New England than elsewhere, and both fared worst in the South.[15] Perot also did well in the mountain states.[16] He even came in second in two states in 1992: Maine, where he came in ahead of George H. W. Bush, and Utah, where he came in ahead of Clinton.[17] In 1996 Perot fared somewhat better in New England, but regional differences were small. Wallace, by contrast, had a regional base in the South. Even though he won a smaller share of the popular vote than Perot in 1992, Wallace came in first in five states (winning a majority in Alabama and Mississippi) and gaining forty-six electoral votes (including one from a faithless elector from North Carolina).[18] But even Wallace won only 8.5 percent of the electoral vote, less than his popular vote share.[19]

The U.S. plurality vote system is a confirmation of Duverger's law, a proposition advanced by French jurist and political scientist Maurice Duverger in the 1950s. According to Duverger, "the simple-majority single-ballot system favours the two-party system."[20] In other words, a plurality vote win system with no runoffs tends to favor the dominance of two political parties.[21] Indeed, Duverger argued that "the American procedure corresponds to the usual machinery of the simple-majority single-ballot system. The absence of a second ballot and of further polls, particularly in the presidential election, constitutes in fact one of the historical reasons for the emergence and the maintenance of the two-party system."[22]

According to Duverger, this principle applies for two reasons. First, a plurality vote system produces a "mechanical" factor: third parties may earn a large number of votes nationally but fail to gain a plurality of the votes in many electoral units. Scholars agree that this effect is important, except in countries where smaller parties have a geographic base. Second, some voters who prefer a candidate or party they think cannot win will cast their votes for their first choice between the major-party candidates, which Duverger labels the "psychological" factor. This behavior is called "sophisticated" or "strategic" voting, and in Britain is referred to as "tactical" voting. William H. Riker defines strategic voting as "voting contrary to one's immediate tastes in order to obtain an advantage in the long run."[23] Whether strategic voting occurs to any significant extent is controversial, but we have demonstrated that a substantial numbers of voters who preferred a third-party or independent candidate in the 1968, 1980, 1992, 1996, and 2000 elections wound up voting for one of the major-party candidates.[24] A small amount of strategic voting probably occurred in 2004 as well, with some voters who preferred Nader to both Bush and Kerry voting for the major-party candidates.[25] Because the 2008 American National Election Study did not measure "feelings" toward either Nader or Barr, it is impossible to estimate how many voters preferred them to Obama and McCain, but it seems very unlikely that strategic voting affected the general election result.[26]

Even if the rules had no immediate effect on the 2008 election per se, they did help create the conditions that led to major-party dominance. Choosing the president by presidential electors is a central part of these rules, and a strong case can be made for eliminating the Electoral College.[27] But change through a constitutional amendment is unlikely because gaining approval of three-fourths of the states would be difficult in a system that overrepresents the smaller states. As described earlier, Maine and Nebraska both have district systems for choosing electors, and other states could choose that system through legislation. But most states do not want to diminish their potential influence by making it likely that their electoral votes will be split. Opponents of a 2004 Colorado ballot proposition that would have divided the state's electoral vote according to proportional representation made this argument, and the proposal failed by a margin of 65 percent to 35 percent.

One proposed reform would retain the Electoral College, but would eliminate its importance by establishing a compact among states that would guarantee that electors would vote for the national popular vote winner regardless of the outcome within their own state. This compact would come into effect when states with a total of a majority of the electoral votes agreed. As of April 2009, six states with a total of sixty-one electoral votes had agreed to the National Popular Vote Interstate Compact.[28] Because an interstate compact requires congressional approval, there would still be an additional hurdle, but a majority can approve an interstate compact vote, not the two-thirds supermajority to initiate a constitutional amendment.[29] In our view, a reform that moves toward a de facto popular vote election would weaken the two-party system. Whether it should be weakened is another question.

THE PATTERN OF RESULTS

Two fundamental findings emerge from the 2008 election results. First, the election underscores the competitive nature of postwar elections, with a relatively even balance between the two major parties. Second, the election continues a pattern of postwar volatility.

Despite Obama's victory, the Republicans still hold a slight balance over the postwar years. They have won nine of the sixteen elections held since World War II. In doing so, they have won a majority of the popular vote seven times since the war ended (1952, 1956, 1972, 1980, 1984, 1988, and 2004), while the Democrats have had a majority only three times (1964, 1976, and 2008). The average (mean) level of popular support shows a very close balance: the GOP has won 48.9 percent of the vote, the Democrats 46.6 percent. These numbers also reveal the dominance of the two major parties: the average level of support for third-party and independent candidates has been only 4.5 percent.

This even balance of electoral support is closely related to volatility. Table 3-2 presents presidential election results since 1832, the first election in which political parties used national nominating conventions to choose their candidates. From 1832 to 1948 are four periods in which the same party won three or more elections in a row. After 1948 a period of electoral volatility began. From 1952 to 1984, neither party was able to win more than two elections in a row. The Republicans won in 1952 and again in 1956, the Democrats won in 1960 and 1964, and the Republicans won in 1968 and 1972. In all three sets of wins, the second win was by a larger margin than the first (substantially bigger in 1964 and 1984). Volatility increased in 1980, when the Democrats, who had won the White House in 1976, failed to hold it. The 1980 and 1984 elections reverted to the pattern of a win followed by a bigger win, and Ronald Reagan's second win was by a substantially bigger margin than his first. Then in 1988, George H. W. Bush's election gave the Republicans three elections in a row, breaking the pattern of postwar volatility. With Clinton's victory in 1992 volatility returned, and in 1996 he won by a slightly larger margin. George W. Bush's defeat of Al Gore in 2000 continued the postwar volatility, and Bush, who trailed his opponent in 2000, slightly improved his popular vote share in 2004. Obama's 2008 victory once again restored the pattern of postwar volatility. Pundits who predict Democratic dominance should remember that to break this pattern of volatility the Democrats would need to hold the White House not only in 2012 but in 2016 as well.

The 1976 and 1980 elections are the only successive elections in the twentieth century in which two incumbent presidents in a row lost.[30] But two periods in

TABLE 3-2   Presidential Election Results, 1832–2008

Election	Winning candidate	Party of winning candidate	Success of incumbent political party
1832	Andrew Jackson	Democrat	Won
1836	Martin Van Buren	Democrat	Won
1840	William H. Harrison	Whig	Lost
1844	James K. Polk	Democrat	Lost[a]
1848	Zachary Taylor	Whig	Lost
1852	Franklin Pierce	Democrat	Lost
1856	James Buchanan	Democrat	Won
1860	Abraham Lincoln	Republican	Lost
1864	Abraham Lincoln	Republican	Won
1868	Ulysses S. Grant	Republican	Won[b]
1872	Ulysses S. Grant	Republican	Won
1876	Rutherford B. Hayes	Republican	Won
1880	James A. Garfield	Republican	Won
1884	Grover Cleveland	Democrat	Lost
1888	Benjamin Harrison	Republican	Lost
1892	Grover Cleveland	Democrat	Lost
1896	William McKinley	Republican	Lost
1900	William McKinley	Republican	Won
1904	Theodore Roosevelt	Republican	Won
1908	William H. Taft	Republican	Won
1912	Woodrow Wilson	Democrat	Lost
1916	Woodrow Wilson	Democrat	Won
1920	Warren G. Harding	Republican	Lost
1924	Calvin Coolidge	Republican	Won
1928	Herbert C. Hoover	Republican	Won
1932	Franklin D. Roosevelt	Democrat	Lost
1936	Franklin D. Roosevelt	Democrat	Won
1940	Franklin D. Roosevelt	Democrat	Won
1944	Franklin D. Roosevelt	Democrat	Won
1948	Harry S. Truman	Democrat	Won
1952	Dwight D. Eisenhower	Republican	Lost
1956	Dwight D. Eisenhower	Republican	Won
1960	John F. Kennedy	Democrat	Lost
1964	Lyndon B. Johnson	Democrat	Won
1968	Richard M. Nixon	Republican	Lost
1972	Richard M. Nixon	Republican	Won
1976	Jimmy Carter	Democrat	Lost
1980	Ronald Reagan	Republican	Lost

(Continued)

TABLE 3-2   Presidential Election Results, 1832–2008 *(continued)*

Election	Winning candidate	Party of winning candidate	Success of incumbent political party
1984	Ronald Reagan	Republican	Won
1988	George H. W. Bush	Republican	Won
1992	Bill Clinton	Democrat	Lost
1996	Bill Clinton	Democrat	Won
2000	George W. Bush	Republican	Lost
2004	George W. Bush	Republican	Won
2008	Barack Obama	Democrat	Lost

Source: Presidential Elections, 1789–2008 (Washington, D.C.: CQ Press, 2009).

[a] Whigs are classified as the incumbent party because they won the 1840 election. In fact, their presidential candidate, William Henry Harrison, died a month after taking office and his vice president, John Tyler, was expelled from the party in 1841.

[b] Republicans are classified as the incumbent party because they won the 1864 election. (Technically, Lincoln had been elected on a Union ticket.) In fact, after Lincoln's assassination in 1865, Andrew Johnson, a war Democrat, became president.

the nineteenth century were actually more volatile than that in postwar America. The incumbent party lost four elections from 1840 to 1852, a period of volatility between the Democrats and the Whigs, and again between 1884 and 1896, a period of alternation between the Republicans and the Democrats. Both of these periods were followed by party realignments. In 1854, just two years after the decisive defeat of the Whigs, the Republicans were founded, and by the 1856 election their candidate, John C. Fremont, had come in second behind James Buchanan, the Democratic winner.[31] By 1860 the Republicans had captured the presidency and the Whigs were extinct.[32] Although many Whigs, including Abraham Lincoln himself, became Republicans, the Republican Party was not just the Whig Party renamed. The Republicans had transformed the political agenda by capitalizing on opposition to slavery in the territories.[33]

The 1896 contest, the last of four incumbent party losses, is usually considered a critical election because it solidified Republican dominance.[34] Although the Republicans had won five of the seven elections since the end of the Civil War, after Ulysses S. Grant's reelection in 1872 all their victories had been by narrow margins. In 1896 the Republicans emerged as the clearly dominant party, gaining a solid hold in Connecticut, Indiana, New Jersey, and New York, states that they had frequently lost between 1876 and 1892. After William McKinley's defeat of William Jennings Bryan in 1896, the Republicans established a firmer base in the Midwest, New England, and the Mid-Atlantic states. They lost the presidency only in 1912, when the GOP was split, and in 1916, when Woodrow Wilson ran for reelection.

The Great Depression ended Republican dominance. The emergence of the Democrats as the majority party was not preceded by a series of incumbent losses. The Democratic coalition, forged in the 1930s, relied heavily on the emerging working class and the mobilization of new groups into the electorate.

As the emergence of the New Deal coalition demonstrates, a period of electoral volatility is not a necessary condition for a partisan realignment. Nor perhaps is it a sufficient condition. In 1985 Reagan himself proclaimed that realignment had occurred. Political scientists were skeptical about that claim, mainly because the Democrats continued to dominate the U.S. House of Representatives. With George H. W. Bush's victory in 1988, in which the Democrats easily held control of the House, some analysts argued that a "split-level" realignment had occurred.[35]

Although Bush's election suggested that Republican dominance might have arrived, Clinton's 1992 victory called this thesis into question, and his 1996 victory cast further doubts on the idea that a realignment had occurred. And yet the Republicans' capture of the House and Senate in 1994, and their ability to hold both chambers for the next five elections, countered any claim that Democratic dominance had been reestablished. After the 2000 election, the Republicans held control of the House, the Senate, and the presidency for the first time since 1953, although they temporarily lost control of the Senate between June 1991 and January 1993.[36] But the closeness of the election called into question any claim of Republican dominance. The 2004 election was also extremely close, but the Republicans were encouraged by their gains in the Senate, and some saw the election as a major turning point in American politics. But just two years later, in 2006, the Democrats gained six Senate seats, giving them tenuous control, and gained a net thirty seats in the House, wresting control from the GOP after twelve years. The 2008 election handed the Democrats eight more seats in the Senate once Democrat Al Franken prevailed over Republican Norm Coleman in the long, drawn-out legal battle over the 2008 Senate contest in Minnesota. The Democrats also gained an additional twenty-one seats in the House. In April 2009, when Pennsylvania's senator Arlen Specter switched to the Democratic Party, the Democrats controlled fifty-nine seats, only one vote short of the supermajority needed to invoke closure to end filibusters. After Franken joined the Senate in July, the Democrats held a supermajority, although they temporarily lost it with Edward Kennedy's death on August 25.

We will save speculation for Chapters 9 and 11, but it is clear that during the last half-century there has been a great deal of volatility in American politics. Indeed, in reviewing the last 176 years of U.S. presidential elections, the only period of greater volatility was between 1840 and 1860 during which the incumbent party lost five out of six presidential elections and during which a major political party, the Whigs, disappeared. We now turn to the state-by-state results that contributed to this recent volatility.

STATE-BY-STATE RESULTS

Because states deliver the electoral votes necessary to win the presidency, the presidential election is, in effect, fifty-one separate contests, one for each state and one for the District of Columbia.[37] As we saw in Chapter 2, with the exception of Maine and Nebraska, the candidate who wins the most votes in a state wins all of the state's electors. Regardless of how a state decides to allocate its electors, the number of electors is the sum of its senators (two), plus the number of its representatives in the U.S. House.[38] Since 1964, there have been 538 electors and a majority, 270, is required to win. In 2004 and 2008, the number of electors ranged from a low of three in Alaska, Delaware, Montana, North Dakota, South Dakota, Vermont, Wyoming, and the District of Columbia, to a high of fifty-five in California.

Because each state, regardless of population, has two electoral votes for its senators, the smaller states are overrepresented in the Electoral College and the larger states are underrepresented. The twenty smaller states and the District of Columbia were home to 10 percent of the U.S. population in the 2000 census, but they had 16 percent of the electoral votes. The nine largest states, which had 52 percent of the population, had only 45 percent of the electoral vote.

Some critics of the Electoral College have argued that the overrepresentation of the smaller states gives the Republicans an advantage because they tend to do better in those states. For example, in 2000 the thirty states that Bush carried yielded an average of 9 electoral votes, while the twenty states that Gore carried (plus D.C.) yielded an average of 12.7 votes. In 2004 the thirty-one states that Bush carried yielded an average of 9.2 electoral votes, and the nineteen states (plus D.C.) that Kerry carried yielded an average of 12.6 votes. But even in 2000 the tendency of the Republicans to win smaller states played a negligible role in Bush's minority victory.[39] In 2008 the states McCain won yielded an average of 7.9 electoral votes, while the states (plus D.C.) that Obama won yielded an average of 12.6 electoral votes. But McCain's greater "advantage" in winning overrepresented states was lost because he failed to win several of the "underrepresented" states that Bush had carried, most notably Florida and Ohio.

Even though small states are overrepresented in the Electoral College, presidential candidates tend to focus on the larger states unless polls indicate that they are unwinnable. Despite being underrepresented in the Electoral College, California provides one-fifth of the votes necessary to win. Even so, in 1992 George H. W. Bush quit campaigning in California in early September because polls showed that Bill Clinton had a commanding lead. In 2008 Obama's lead in California was so great that McCain did not make a campaign visit during the general election campaign, and made more visits to Ohio (twenty votes) and Pennsylvania (twenty-one votes) than to any other states. Obama made only one campaign trip to California, and made the most trips to Florida (twenty-seven votes) and Virginia (thirteen votes), states that were expected to be close.[40]

States are the building blocks of winning presidential coalitions, but state-by-state results can be overemphasized and may sometimes be misleading for three reasons. First, in forty-three of the forty-six elections between 1828 and 2008 the candidate with the largest number of popular votes also won a majority of the electoral votes. Thus candidates can win by creating a broad-based coalition throughout the nation (although they must consider whether they are more likely to win specific states). Moreover, because of the nature of national television coverage candidates must run national campaigns. They can make specific appeals to states and regions, but the national media broadcast these appeals. And presidential debates, which have been held in every presidential election since 1976, also reach a nationwide audience.

Second, state-by-state results can be misleading, and comparisons may even conceal change. To illustrate this point, we compare the results of two close Democratic victories—John Kennedy's defeat of Richard Nixon in 1960 and Jimmy Carter's defeat of Gerald Ford in 1976—that have many similarities. In both 1960 and 1976, the Republicans did very well in the West, and both Kennedy and Carter needed southern support to win. Kennedy carried six of the eleven states of the old Confederacy—Arkansas, Georgia, Louisiana, North Carolina, South Carolina, and Texas—and gained five of Alabama's eleven electoral votes, for a total of eighty-one electoral votes.[41] Carter carried ten of the eleven southern states (all but Virginia) for a total of 118 electoral votes.

The demographic basis of Carter's support was quite different from Kennedy's, however. In 1960 only 29 percent of African Americans in the South were registered to vote compared with 61 percent of whites. According to our analysis of the American National Election Studies, only about one in fifteen of the Kennedy voters in the South was black. In 1976, 63 percent of African Americans in the South were registered to vote compared with 68 percent of whites.[42] We estimate that about one in three southerners who voted for Carter was black. A simple state-by-state comparison would conceal this massive change in the social composition of the Democratic presidential coalition.

Third, state-by-state comparisons do not tell us why a presidential candidate received support. Of course, such comparisons can lead to interesting speculation, especially when the dominant issues are related to regional differences. They can even lead to hyperbolic comparisons of "red states" versus "blue states."[43] But unless these analyses are conducted with care, such as in the work by Andrew Gelman and his colleagues, they can produce more confusion than clarity.[44] With these qualifications in mind, we now turn to the state-by-state results.

Between 1984 and 2004, the South was clearly the best region for the Republicans, and they won all eleven southern states in 1984, 1988, 2000, and 2004. While not as dominant, the Democrats did best in New England. In 2008 New England was once again the best region for the Democrats (see Figure 3-2, which shows Obama's margin of victory over McCain in all states). As in 2004, they

FIGURE 3-2   Obama's Margin of Victory over McCain, 2008

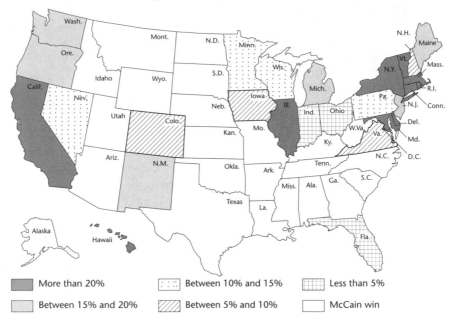

	More than 20%		Between 10% and 15%		Less than 5%
	Between 15% and 20%		Between 5% and 10%		McCain win

Source: Rhodes Cook, Alice V. McGillivray, and Richard M. Scammon, *America Votes 28: Election Returns by State, 2007–2008* (Washington, D.C.: CQ Press, 2010).

carried all six states, and won four of them by twenty points or more. Obama won 60.7 percent of the vote in New England compared with only 37.7 percent for McCain. Obama also carried six states outside of New England by more than twenty points, including the electorally rich states of California, Illinois, and New York. Moreover, he cut deeply into the Republican strength in the South by winning three of the five largest states—Florida, North Carolina, and Virginia— thereby winning fifty-five of the South's 153 electoral votes. Virginia had not voted Democratic since Johnson's 1964 landslide, although it had been inching toward the Democrat column because of the suburban growth from D.C. Like- wise, Indiana had not voted Democratic since 1964, although voters in northern Indiana may have been familiar with Obama because it is in the Chicago media market.

McCain had areas of strength as well. He did best in the South, where he carried Alabama and Arkansas by over twenty percentage points, and Louisiana and Tennessee by between fifteen and twenty points. He won Texas by twelve points. Thus he had a popular vote edge in the South, winning 52.6 percent of the vote to Obama's 46.4 percent. He had strength in the mountain West as well, where he carried five of the eight states and won by over twenty percentage points in Idaho, Utah, and Wyoming. He also won by over twenty points in Alaska and Oklahoma. In the mountain West, McCain won 50.5 percent of the vote compared with Obama's 47.6 percent. But Obama won by more than three million votes in California, so Obama's overall share in the West was 53.9 percent compared with McCain's 44.2 percent.

Ninety-eight of McCain's electoral votes were from the South, just over half of his total. The South has now been transformed into the base of the Republican Party, and this is the most dramatic change in postwar American politics. Obama clearly benefited by cutting into this base, for he would have been reduced to only 310 electoral votes without Florida, North Carolina, and Virginia. However, in all three of the most recent Democratic victories (1992, 1996, and 2008) the Democratic candidate could have been elected with no southern support. But George W. Bush could not have been elected or reelected without southern electoral votes.

An increase in variation among the states was evident between 2004 and 2008. Alan I. Abramowitz points out that the average margin of victory for the winning party increased from 15.8 percentage points to 17.4 points. Moreover, he notes that the number of states in which the winning candidate won by ten or more points increased from thirty to thirty-seven, while the number of states in which the margin of victory was five points or less fell from eleven to six.[45] All the same, the overall pattern since World War II has been a decline in regional differences, which can be demonstrated through statistical analysis. Joseph A. Schlesinger has analyzed the state-by-state variation in the vote in presidential elections from 1832 to 1988, and we have updated his analyses through 2008.[46] Schlesinger's measure is the standard deviation in the percentage of the Democratic vote among the states. The state-by-state variation was 9.54 in 2008, up from the 8.39 deviation for 2004, but well below the state-by-state deviation of 11.96 in the 1964 contest between Johnson and Goldwater, which was the highest deviation of any postwar election.[47] But Schlesinger's analysis clearly reveals the relatively low level of state-by-state variation in postwar elections. According to his analyses (as updated), all sixteen of the presidential elections from 1888 to 1944 displayed more state-by-state variation than any of the sixteen postwar elections. To a large extent, the decline in state-by-state variation results from the transformation of the South.[48]

ELECTORAL CHANGE IN THE POSTWAR SOUTH

The South is a growing region that has undergone dramatic political change. Even though five of the eleven southern states have lost congressional representation since World War II, Florida and Texas have made spectacular gains. In the 1944 and 1948 elections, Florida had only eight electoral votes, but by the 2004 and 2008 elections it had twenty-seven. In 1944 and 1948, Texas had twenty-three electoral votes, but by 2004 it had thirty-four. Since the end of World War II, the South's electoral vote total has grown from 127 to 153. And this number will increase again by the 2012 election.[49]

The political transformation of the South was a complex process, but the major reason for the change was simple. As V. O. Key Jr. brilliantly demonstrated in *Southern Politics in State and Nation* in 1949, the main factor in southern politics is race. "In its grand outlines the politics of the South revolves around the position of the Negro.... Whatever phase of the southern political process one seeks to understand, sooner or later the trail of inquiry leads to the Negro."[50] And it was the Democratic Party's new stance toward African Americans that smashed Democratic dominance in the South.[51]

Between the end of Reconstruction in 1877 and the end of World War II in 1945, the South was a Democratic stronghold. In fifteen of the seventeen elections from 1880 to 1944, all eleven southern states voted Democratic. The only major defections were in 1928, when the Democrats ran Alfred E. Smith, a Roman Catholic. As a result, the Republican candidate, Herbert Hoover, won five southern states. Even then, six of the most solid southern states voted for Smith, although all but Louisiana were overwhelmingly Protestant.[52]

After Reconstruction ended in 1877, many southern blacks were prevented from voting, and in the late nineteenth and early twentieth centuries several southern states changed their voting laws to further disfranchise blacks. The Republicans ceded those states to the Democrats. Although the Republicans had black support in the North, they did not attempt to enforce the Fifteenth Amendment, which bans restrictions on voting on the basis of "race, color, or previous condition of servitude."

In 1932 a majority of African Americans in the North remained loyal to the Republicans, although by 1936 Franklin D. Roosevelt had won the support of northern blacks. But Roosevelt made no effort to win the support of southern blacks, most of whom remained disfranchised. Even as late as 1940, about 70 percent of the nation's blacks lived in the states of the old Confederacy. Roosevelt carried all eleven of these states in each of his four victories. His 1944 reelection, however, was the last contest in which Democrats carried all eleven southern states.

World War II led to massive migration of African Americans from the South. By 1948 President Harry Truman was making explicit appeals to blacks through his Fair Employment Practices Commission and in July 1948 he issued an executive order ending segregation in the armed services.[53] These policies led to defections from the "Dixiecrats" and cost Truman four southern states in the 1948 election, but he still won all seven of the remaining southern states. In 1952 and 1956, the Democratic candidate, Adlai E. Stevenson, de-emphasized appeals to blacks, although his opponent, Dwight Eisenhower, still made inroads in the South. In 1960 Kennedy played down appeals to African Americans. As we saw earlier, southern electoral votes were crucial to a win over Nixon.[54] Kennedy may have also strengthened his campaign in the South by choosing a Texan, Lyndon Johnson, as his running mate. Clearly, Johnson helped Kennedy win Texas, which he carried by only two percentage points.

But if Johnson as running mate aided the Democrats in the South, Johnson as president played a different role. His explicit appeals to African Americans helped end Democratic dominance in the South. Barry Goldwater, the Republican candidate, had voted against the Civil Rights Act in 1964, creating a sharp difference between the two candidates. Goldwater carried all five states in the Deep South, as well as his native Arizona. In 1968 Hubert Humphrey, who had long championed black equality, carried only one southern state, Texas, which he won with only 41 percent of the vote. He was probably aided by George Wallace's third-party candidacy, because Wallace, a segregationist, won 19 percent of the Texas vote. Wallace carried Alabama, Arkansas, Georgia, Louisiana, and Mississippi, while Nixon carried the remaining five southern states. Nixon won every southern state in 1972, and his margin of victory was greater in the South than in the rest of the nation. Although Carter won ten of the eleven southern states in 1976 (all but Virginia), he carried a minority of the vote among white southerners.

In 1980, as noted earlier, Reagan won every southern state except Georgia, Carter's home state. In his 1984 reelection victory, Reagan carried all the southern states and his margin of victory in the South was greater than his margin outside it. In 1988 George H. W. Bush was victorious in all eleven southern states, and the South was his strongest region. Four years later, in 1992, Clinton made some inroads in the South and somewhat greater inroads in 1996. All the same, the South was the only predominantly Republican region in 1992, and in 1996 Bob Dole won a majority of the electoral vote only in the South and mountain states. In 2000 the South was the only region in which Bush carried every state, and over half of his electoral votes came from that region. In 2004 Bush carried every southern state, along with all of the states in the mountain West. Once again, more than half of his electoral votes came from the states of the old Confederacy. Despite slippage in 2008, Republicans have won every southern state in five of the ten elections (1972, 1984, 1988, 2000, and 2004) between 1972 and 2008.

Although the transformation of the South is clearly the most dramatic change in postwar American politics, the 2008 election underscores that the Republicans do not hold the same level of dominance that the Democrats once enjoyed. Florida is highly competitive. Clinton won the Sunshine State in 1996, and in 2000 Bush carried the disputed contest by a negligible margin. And Obama narrowly won Florida in 2008. North Carolina has Democratic pockets such as the Raleigh-Durham Research Triangle, and in 2008 Obama captured the Tar Heel State by a 0.3 percentage point margin. Although Virginia had not voted Democratic since 1964, the growth of the Washington, D.C., suburbs in northern Virginia has made the state more competitive. Even in Georgia, the Democratic vote in Atlanta and its close-in suburbs can make the state competitive. Clinton carried Georgia in 1992, and McCain won by only 5.2 percentage points in 2008. In their analysis of exit poll data from all fifty states, Chuck Todd and Sheldon

Gawiser classify Georgia as an "emerging battleground state." They also place Texas, which McCain carried by 11.8 percentage points, in this category. However, they conclude that it seems likely that these states will remain Republican.[55]

OTHER REGIONAL CHANGE

Although not as dramatic or important as the change in the South, there has also been change in the mountain West. This change has been little studied, in part because these states are sparsely populated and yield few electoral votes.[56] Since World War II, Arizona, Colorado, Nevada, New Mexico, and Utah have all gained at least one electoral vote, and only Montana has lost an electoral vote. After the war, these states contributed thirty-two electoral votes, but even with postwar population growth they still contribute only forty-four.[57] The shift in these states has not been as dramatic as in the South because they never had a long history of voting Democratic. Granted, even as far back as 1892 three of the then-five mountain states voted for James B. Weaver, the Populist candidate, and in 1896 all then-six mountain states supported the Democratic and Populist candidacy of William Jennings Bryan. In 1916 all eight mountain states voted to reelect Woodrow Wilson, perhaps because he seemed more opposed to American entry into the war in Europe than did the Republican candidate, Charles Evans Hughes. These states voted Republican in 1920, 1924, and 1928, although like most states they voted for FDR in 1932 and 1936. Among these states, only Colorado voted Republican in 1940. In 1944 six of the eight mountain states voted to reelect Roosevelt, and only Colorado and Wyoming voted for Thomas Dewey. In 1948 Harry Truman carried all eight mountain states, the last time the Democrats swept this region.

Writing in 1987, Eric R. A. N. Smith and Peverill Squire observed that between 1952 and 1984 the Democratic candidates had won mountain states only twice—in 1960 when Kennedy won Nevada and New Mexico and 1964 when Johnson won every mountain state except Arizona.[58] The Democrats also failed to carry any of the mountain states in 1988. But the Republican hold weakened in 1992 and 1996. In 2000, when Gore did win New Mexico, his 366-vote margin was the smallest of any state. In 2004 Bush carried New Mexico by less than one percentage point, although the Republicans once again swept the region. The Republicans still had an edge in the mountain states in 2008, but Obama cut into their base, winning the only two states that Clinton had carried in both of his elections—Nevada and New Mexico—as well as Colorado, which Clinton had carried in 1992. And some pundits think that Arizona might have been competitive had it not been McCain's home state—even McCain carried the state by only an 8.5 percentage point margin. Todd and Gawiser view Arizona as an "emerging battle-ground state," mainly because of its large Latino population.[59]

Because the mountain states have been little studied, it is difficult to speculate on the reasons for their shift toward the GOP. Arthur H. Miller concludes that "the realignment which has been occurring in the Mountain West reflects a combination of shifting demographics, political attitudes and partisan evaluations."[60] Even though Goldwater carried only a single mountain state in 1964, his candidacy may have led voters to identify the Democratic Party with unpopular welfare policies, and George S. McGovern's candidacy in 1972 may have increased negative views of the Democrats. "In short," Miller writes, "the growth in negative evaluations of Democratic party performance, a dramatic shift toward conservative social welfare policy preferences, and a professionalization of the population of the region ... provide a description of the major forces that produced the Mountain realignment in voting behavior and party identification."[61]

Although the South and mountain West have moved toward the Republicans since World War II, the six New England states have moved toward the Democrats. These states have been losing representation since World War II. After the 1950 census, the New England states had a total of forty electoral votes; by the 2004 election they had only thirty-four.[62] Between the 1960 election and the 2004 election, Massachusetts lost four electoral votes, and Connecticut and Maine each lost one.

From the first time the Republicans contested the presidency in 1856 to William Howard Taft's election in 1908, all six New England states voted Republican. Five of them voted for Wilson in 1912, when the GOP was split. But five of the states voted Republican in 1916, and all voted Republican in the GOP landslides of 1920 and 1924. As noted earlier in the introduction to Part I, in 1928 Massachusetts and Rhode Island voted for Smith, the first Catholic to head a major-party ticket. But in 1932, the first of FDR's four wins, New England was the most Republican region. In 1936 only two states in the nation, Maine and Vermont, voted for the Republican candidate, Alfred Landon, leading James Farley, FDR's campaign manager, to quip, "As Maine goes, so goes Vermont."[63] The Republicans continued to win Maine and Vermont in every election until 1964, but after 1936 they were not the only states in the nation to vote Republican. In Truman's 1948 upset, Massachusetts and Rhode Island were the only New England states to vote Democratic, but Eisenhower carried all six New England states in both of his elections. In 1960, however, Kennedy carried Massachusetts and Rhode Island, as well as Connecticut, another state with a high percentage of Catholics.

In his 1964 landslide, Johnson swept New England, and in his 1968 loss Humphrey still won four of the New England states. In 1972 George McGovern lost forty-nine states; his one win was in Massachusetts. And in his narrow win in 1976, Carter carried Massachusetts and Rhode Island, with Ford winning the remaining New England states.

In 1988 Michael Dukakis, the incumbent Democratic governor of Massachusetts, carried Rhode Island and his home state. But ever since 1992, the Democrats have been extremely successful in New England, carrying all six states in 1992, 1996, 2004, and 2008, and winning every state except New Hampshire in

2000. The decline of the GOP in New England is also seen in the changing partisan composition of its congressional delegation.[64]

The changes in New England may result from the decline of the liberal wing of the Republican Party. As Nicol C. Rae writes, "While liberal Republicanism was disintegrating as a national political force, its position in several state parties was also weakened by the effects of realignment-dealignment and the transformation of the party system. This was true in former liberal Republican strongholds such as in lower New England."[65]

Finally, we turn to California. Granted it is a single state, not a region, and one can even write about regions within California. But its fifty-five electoral votes are more than those of either the mountain West or New England. Although its growth is slowing, California's electoral vote more than doubled from twenty-five after the 1940 census to fifty-five after the 2000 census.[66]

Between 1856 and 1928, California usually voted Republican. It voted Democratic only in 1856, 1892, and 1916, when its thirteen electoral votes were enough to swing the election to Wilson. It voted Democratic for FDR in all four of his victories, and gave Truman a very narrow margin over Dewey in 1948. But then it once again began voting Republican, supporting the GOP presidential candidate in nine of the ten elections between 1952 and 1988. In seven of those elections, the Republican ticket included a resident of California.[67] But in those elections, California did not differ much from the country as a whole: its average level of Republican support was the same as that of the nation as a whole. In 1968 California voted four points more Republican than the country as a whole, but in four elections—1956, 1972, 1984, and 1988—it voted less Republican.[68]

California shifted toward the Democratic Party between 1988 and 1992. Even with Perot winning 21 percent of the vote in California, Clinton defeated Bush by thirteen points. He went on to defeat Bob Dole by the same margin in 1996. In 2000, although Gore defeated Bush by half a percentage point in the nation as a whole, he won by twelve percentage points in California. And although Bush defeated Kerry by 2.4 percent of the national vote in 2004, Kerry won by just under a ten percentage point margin in California. In 2008 Obama carried California by more than twenty percentage points (Figure 3-2) and by over three million votes (Table 3-1). Over a third of Obama's popular vote margin over McCain was cast in this one state.

One reason for this political change is the state's growing Latino population, which increased from 19 percent in 1980 to 36 percent in 2006. However, Latinos are much less likely to be citizens than are non-Latinos, and even those who are citizens are less likely to register and vote. It is difficult to determine the share of actual voters who are Latino. According to Mark Baldassare, based on exit polls in 1990 only 4 percent of California voters were Latinos; by 2000, 14 percent were.[69] According to an exit poll in 2004 conducted by Edison Media Research/ Mitofsky International (usually called the "pool poll" because it is sponsored by a consortium of news organizations), 21 percent of California voters were Latino.[70] The pool poll conducted in 2008 found that 18 percent of California voters were Latino. Of those voters, 74 percent voted for Obama and only 23 percent for McCain.[71]

Baldassare argues that "observers ... speculate that California has become so predictably Democratic and liberal in voting that it has become an irrelevant player in national politics." And yet he writes, "We find the current, popular view that California has become a one-party state off base. In reality, the more significant political trend is the growth and flourishing of the un-party state, which is the result of the public's distrust in its political and governance system."[72]

THE ELECTORAL VOTE BALANCE

The Republicans won five out of six presidential elections between 1968 and 1988. Four years after his narrow win over Humphrey in 1968, Nixon swept forty-nine states. Carter won a narrow victory in 1976, but the Republicans swept most states during the Reagan and Bush elections, with Reagan carrying forty-nine states in his 1984 reelection.[73] Because of these Republican wins some scholars argued that the Republicans had a "lock" on the Electoral College. According to Marjorie Randon Hershey, the Republicans won so many states during that period that they had "a clear and continuing advantage" in presidential elections.[74]

After 1988, however, the Democrats won three of the next five elections. Therefore, it is no longer plausible to claim that there is a Republican Electoral College lock on winning the presidency. One can still argue that the Republicans have an electoral vote edge. After all, they did win the presidency in 2000, even though Gore had more popular votes than Bush. One can also argue, however, that the Democrats have an electoral vote advantage.[75] It seems most reasonable to us to argue that partisan biases caused by the Electoral College, if they exist, are small.[76] Andrew Gelman, Jonathan N. Katz, and Gary King present compelling evidence that since the 1950s partisan biases created by the Electoral College are negligible.[77]

Indeed, electoral vote biases are very unlikely to be important in any election in which one candidate wins by a comfortable popular vote margin. As we have noted, in the three elections in which a popular vote winner was defeated, his popular vote margin was small.

Even though candidates know they will win if they have a substantial popular vote margin, they still must develop electoral vote strategies. As described in Chapter 2, these strategies are guided partly by their knowledge of past voting patterns, but also by statewide pre-election polls. For example, in 2008 Obama devoted extensive resources to winning both Indiana and Virginia, even though they had not voted Democratic in over four decades.

Bearing in mind that past voting patterns are imperfect guides for future elections, let us examine the pattern among the states in the past five presidential elections. As illustrated by comparing Figure 3-3 with a similar figure based on

FIGURE 3-3   Results of the 1992, 1996, 2000, 2004, and 2008
Presidential Elections

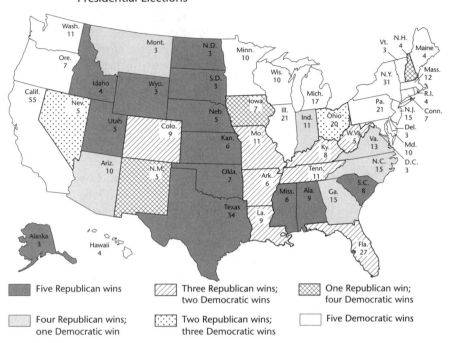

Five Republican wins

Three Republican wins;
two Democratic wins

One Republican win;
four Democratic wins

Four Republican wins;
one Democratic win

Two Republican wins;
three Democratic wins

Five Democratic wins

Sources: Presidential Elections, 1789–2000 (Washington, D.C.: CQ Press, 2002); Rhodes Cook, Alice V.
McGillivray, and Richard M. Scammon, *America Votes 28: Election Returns by State, 2007–2008* (Washington,
D.C.: CQ Press, 2010).

the results between 1988 and 2004, there has clearly been a shift in the electoral
vote balance toward the Democrats.[78] Only thirteen states with a total of ninety-
six electoral votes voted Republican in all five presidential elections between
1992 and 2008. The only large state is Texas, which is likely to gain four electoral
votes by the 2012 election.[79] The GOP won six additional states (with sixty-seven
electoral votes) in four of the last five elections. Although these six states will
probably also gain electoral votes after the 2010 census, two of them did vote for
Obama.[80] And Republicans won eight states (with eighty-six electoral votes) in
three of the last five elections, although the largest of these states, Florida, narrowly voted for Obama.[81]

Also as illustrated in Figure 3-3, on the Democratic side eighteen states and
the District of Columbia with a total of 248 electoral votes have voted Democratic in all five elections. Of these eighteen states, four are large: California,
Illinois, New York, and Pennsylvania. However, three of these large states are
likely to lose an electoral vote after the 2010 census.[82] The Democrats have won
three states (with sixteen electoral votes) in four of the last five contests.[83] And
they have won two states (with twenty-five electoral votes) in three of the last five
elections.[84]

As of 2004, there was an even partisan balance over the course of the last five elections. Between 1988 and 2004, twenty-eight states, yielding 269 electoral votes, voted Republican in a majority of these elections. And twenty-two states (plus the District of Columbia) voted for the Democrats more often than they voted Republican, and they, too, had 269 electoral votes. The Republicans have now won twenty-six states a majority of the time in the last five elections, and they yield 249 electoral votes. The Democrats have won twenty-four states (plus D.C.) in most of these contests, and they yield 289 electoral votes. From this perspective, the Democratic edge is far less impressive, especially when we bear in mind that the Republican-leaning states will gain electoral votes after the 2010 census.[85] All the same, the Democratic edge is likely to exceed the 270 electoral votes needed to win the presidency, even after the next reapportionment.

Despite this close balance over the last five elections, the electoral vote balance may not be as close as these five election totals make them appear. Six of the fourteen states that lean Republican voted Democratic in the 2008 election. All five states that lean Democratic voted for Obama. Moreover, the Democrats are now competitive in all regions of the country, with a Republican advantage only in the South, mountain West, and the prairie states.

To assess the prospects of the major parties, we must go beyond official election statistics; we must understand why some Americans are likely to vote, whereas others are not. To gauge how social coalitions have changed over time, as well as the issue preferences of the electorate, we must turn to surveys. They will reveal the extent to which Obama's victory resulted from negative evaluations of Bush and the Republican Party and the ways in which party loyalties have changed over the postwar years. Thus Part II of our study turns to survey data to examine the prospects for continuity and change in American politics.

Voting Behavior in the 2008
Presidential Election

The national decision made on or before November 4, 2008, was the product of more than 212 million individual decisions.[1] Two questions faced Americans eighteen years and older: whether to vote, and, if they did, how to cast their ballots. How voters make up their minds is one of the most thoroughly studied subjects in political science—and one of the most controversial.[2]

Voting decisions can be studied from at least three theoretical perspectives.[3] In the first approach, voters are viewed primarily as members of social groups. Voters belong to primary groups of family members and peers; secondary groups such as private clubs, trade unions, and voluntary associations; and broader reference groups such as social classes and religious and ethnic groups. Understanding the political behavior of these groups is central to understanding voters, according to Paul F. Lazarsfeld, Bernard R. Berelson, and their colleagues. Using a simple "index of political predisposition," they classified voters according to religion (Catholic or Protestant), socioeconomic level, and residence (rural or urban) to predict how they would vote in the 1940 presidential election. Lazarsfeld and his colleagues maintained that "a person thinks, politically, as he is socially. Social characteristics determine political preferences."[4] This perspective is still popular, although more so among sociologists than political scientists.[5]

A second approach analyzes psychological variables. To explain voting behavior in the 1952 and 1956 presidential elections, Angus Campbell, Philip E. Converse, Warren E. Miller, and Donald E. Stokes, scholars at the University of Michigan Survey Research Center, developed a model of political behavior based on psychological variables, which was presented in their classic book *The American Voter*.[6] They focused on attitudes most likely to have the greatest effect on the vote just before the moment of decision, particularly attitudes toward the candidates, the parties, and the issues. Party identification emerged as the most important social-psychological variable that influences voting behavior. The

Michigan approach is the most prevalent among political scientists, although many de-emphasize its psychological underpinnings.[7] The work of Philip E. Converse is an outstanding example of this tradition.[8] Warren E. Miller and J. Merrill Shanks's excellent work *The New American Voter* embodies this approach and is especially valuable for understanding the long-term forces that have transformed the American electorate.[9] Nearly half a century after its publication, Michael S. Lewis-Beck and his colleagues published an important study attempting to replicate *The American Voter* using the American National Election Studies surveys conducted during the 2000 and 2004 elections.[10]

A third approach draws heavily from the work of economists. According to this perspective, citizens weigh the costs of voting against the expected benefits when deciding whether to vote. And when deciding for whom to vote they calculate which candidate favors policies closest to their own policy preferences. Citizens are thus viewed as rational actors who attempt to maximize their expected utility. Anthony Downs and William H. Riker helped to found this rational choice approach.[11] The writings of Riker, Peter C. Ordeshook, John A. Ferejohn, and Morris P. Fiorina are excellent examples of this point of view.[12]

In our view, however, none of these perspectives provides a complete answer to questions about how voters decide whether to vote and for whom.[13] Although individuals belong to groups, they are not always influenced by their group memberships. Moreover, classifying voters by groups does not explain why they are influenced by social factors. Placing too much emphasis on social-psychological factors can lead scholars away from studying the social forces that shape political behavior. And while the assumptions of economic rationality may lead to clearly testable propositions, the data used to test them are often weak, and the propositions that can be tested are at times of limited importance.[14]

Therefore, we have chosen an eclectic approach that draws on insights from each viewpoint. Where appropriate, we employ sociological variables, but we also employ social-psychological variables such as party identification and feelings of political efficacy. The rational choice approach guides our study of the way issues influence voting behavior.

Chapter 4 analyzes the most important decision of all: whether to vote. One of the most profound changes in postwar U.S. politics has been the decline of electoral participation among the voting-age population. Although turnout grew fairly consistently between 1920 (the year women were enfranchised throughout the United States) and 1960 (the contest between John Kennedy and Richard Nixon), it fell in 1964 and in each of the next four elections. Turnout rose slightly in 1984, but it dropped to a postwar low in 1988, although it rose in the three-way contest in 1992 between Bill Clinton, George H. W. Bush, and Ross Perot. In 1996 turnout fell to its lowest level since 1952. Despite extensive mobilization efforts in 2000, turnout rose only two percentage points compared with 1996. In 2004, with even greater mobilization efforts, turnout among the voting-age population rose four percentage points. In 2008, with the expectation that

Barack Obama would bring many blacks and young Americans to the polls, many observers anticipated a surge in turnout. And turnout did rise, but only about 1.5 percentage points, and the percentage of voting-age Americans who voted was six points lower than in 1960. However, as Michael McDonald shows, turnout has not fallen nearly as far as it appears if one examines the population *eligible* to vote. When the population eligible to vote is used as a base, turnout is only two percentage points lower than it was in the Kennedy-Nixon contest.[15] In Chapter 4 we explain this apparent discrepancy.

Although turnout is low in the United States compared with other advanced democracies, it is not equally low among all social groups, and we will in Chapter 4 also examine these differences in detail, using both the 2008 American National Election Studies survey and the Current Population Survey conducted by the U.S. Census Bureau. We identify those groups in which turnout did rise. And we look at why turnout rose among some groups, but was lower than many expected before the election, especially in view of the widespread phenomenon of early voting (see Chapter 2). Finally, we ask whether low levels of turnout in the United States, as well as the increases in 2004 and 2008, have implications for partisan realignment.

Chapter 5 examines how social forces influenced the vote. We rely mainly on the ANES survey of 1,590 voters, but we also rely on an exit poll of 17,836 voters surveyed at three thousand polling places throughout the nation, supplemented by telephone polls of 2,378 early and absentee voters. As noted in Chapter 3, the exit poll, conducted by Edison Research Media/Mitofsky International, is often referred to as the "pool poll" because it is conducted for a consortium of news organizations.

We then turn to ANES surveys to analyze changing social patterns during the postwar years, and at times we use a survey of the U.S. civilian population conducted in 1944 by the National Opinion Research Center. Support for the Democratic coalition among white southerners has eroded dramatically, and support has dropped as well among working-class whites. During most postwar surveys, support for the Democrats among white union members has been relatively high, but in 2008 union support was only moderately higher than support from whites who were not in a union household. As in all previous elections for which we have data, white Catholics were more likely to vote Democratic than white Protestants. But Barack Obama did little better than split the white Catholic vote with John McCain. It is not surprising that Obama won overwhelming support among African Americans, a mainstay of the New Deal coalition. He also did well among young whites and very well among Latinos, but neither of these groups is traditionally part of the Democratic coalition. Thus, although Obama won a majority of the vote, he did not restore the basic demographic coalition that has usually been drawn together to forge Democratic victories during the postwar years.

In Chapter 6 we look at the attitudes toward the candidates and the issues. We begin by examining feelings toward the candidates using "feeling thermometers."

These feelings are strongly related to the way people voted. We also examine the various traits that respondents associated with the candidates. We find that Obama, a black freshman senator, was generally viewed more favorably than McCain, a war hero who had served in the U.S. Senate for two decades.

Although we are not able to examine the issue concerns of the electorate in 2008, the pool poll strongly suggests it was the economy. We then discuss the electorate's issue preferences, in part to determine whether voters meet the criteria for voting on the basis of issues. We employ seven seven-point issue scales used in 2008 on which respondents were asked to place not only themselves but also Obama and McCain. Most voters could place themselves on the scales, but fewer could place themselves and both candidates. Fewer still saw a difference between the candidates. On average, half were able to place themselves and the candidates on a scale, to see a difference between them, and to perceive that Obama was more "liberal" than McCain. We learned that voters who meet all four conditions for issue voting appear to vote on the basis of the issue, while those who do not meet the conditions do not appear to take the issue into account. We also create a "balance of issues" measure that reveals the electorate was closer to where McCain was perceived to be and that this measure is related to the way people voted.

We explore as well the electorate's opinions about the appropriate policies on abortion, an issue that has divided the public since the 1973 *Roe v. Wade* decision that made abortion legal throughout the United States. Voters were asked where they thought Obama and McCain stood on this issue. Opinions on abortion were clearly related to the vote, with "pro-choice" voters more likely to vote for Obama than "pro-life" voters. But the relationship was much stronger among voters who recognized that Obama was more pro-choice than McCain.

We then turn to how presidential performance influences voting decisions. Recent research suggests that many voters decide to vote on the basis of "retrospective evaluations" of the incumbents. In other words, voters decide mainly on the basis of what the candidates have done in office—not what they promise to do if elected. In Chapter 7 we evaluate the role of retrospective evaluations in past presidential elections. Voters' negative evaluations of Gerald Ford's performance in 1976 played a major role in Jimmy Carter's election, just as, four years later, negative evaluations of Carter helped to elect Ronald Reagan. To a very large extent George H. W. Bush's defeat in 1992 resulted from negative evaluations of his performance as president. And positive evaluations of Clinton's presidency aided his reelection in 1996. The 2000 contest appears to be an exception because positive evaluations of Clinton and the Democrats were nearly as high as they were four years earlier, but the Democratic share of the major-party vote fell from 54.7 percent to 50.3 percent. Perhaps because he did not emphasize the accomplishments of the Clinton administration, Gore was unable to capitalize on the good economic conditions in the fall of 2000. In 2004 retrospective evaluations of President George W. Bush were mixed, which largely accounts for his very narrow reelection victory.

Although we are unable to construct the summary measure of retrospective evaluations we used from 1976 through 2000, or to construct the measure we used in 2004, there is clear evidence that in 2008 evaluations of Bush and the Republican Party were more negative than in any of the elections between 1972 and 2004. Moreover, the summary measure of retrospective evaluations we created with the 2008 ANES survey showed the electorate to be strongly negative toward Bush and the GOP. And respondents with negative evaluations were very likely to vote for Obama. Suffice it to say that no complex explanation is needed to account for the Republican defeat. The electorate was strongly dissatisfied with Bush, negative toward the Republican Party, and thought the Democrats could do better.

As we note in Chapter 7, no one can fully understand the voting decision without examining the factors that shape issue preferences and influence retrospective evaluations. Of all these factors, the most important is party identification, which is a powerful tool in reaching preliminary judgments. How closely do voters identify with a political party? And how does this identification shape issue preferences and evaluations of the incumbent and the incumbent party? In Chapter 8 we explore the impact of party loyalties using the ANES surveys. We find that there was a clear shift toward the Democratic Party between 2004 and 2008, a shift confirmed by other data sources as well. By means of the ANES surveys, we examine partisanship among whites and blacks separately, tracking change from 1952, when party identification was first measured, to 2008. This analysis reveals that the pattern of change among whites and among blacks has been markedly different.

We also take a close look at the role of party loyalties in shaping issue preferences, retrospective evaluations, and voting preferences. The relationship between party identification and retrospective evaluations was very strong in 2008. Moreover, as in every presidential election since 2000, the relationship between party identification and the way whites voted was very high, and, as described in Chapter 10, it was strongly related to the way whites voted for members of Congress as well. The electorate's shift in loyalty toward the Democrats may not indicate that a Democratic realignment is at hand, but it seriously calls into question the claims of scholars only four years ago that America was on the cusp of an era of Republican dominance.

Chapter 4

Who Voted?

Before looking at how people voted in the 2008 presidential election, we must answer an even more basic question: who voted? Turnout is lower in the United States than in any other first-world democracy, with the possible exception of Switzerland. In Table 4-1, we present estimates of postwar turnout in twenty-five democracies, including the United States. Because the International Voter Turnout Database measures turnout by dividing the number of voters by the number of people registered to vote, it is of little use for the United States. In the other countries, the government is responsible for maintaining the registration rolls, whereas in the United States individual citizens are responsible for registering. Therefore, we determined turnout in the United States by dividing the number of voters by the voting-age population.[1]

Of course, there are many differences among these countries. Both Australia and Belgium, which head the list in Table 4-1, enforce some form of compulsory voting, although the sanctions for not voting are scarcely draconian.[2] Some countries have electoral systems that motivate political leaders to mobilize voters. In others, such as the United States and Britain, many electoral units are not competitive and get-out-the-vote efforts are likely to be of little value.[3] And differences among party systems may encourage the lower social classes to vote in some societies and do little to encourage them to vote in others.

Although we are not attempting to account for variation among these twenty-five countries, one central fact remains: the United States clearly ranks last in legislative voting. Granted, midterm elections are not comparable to parliamentary elections in these other democracies. In the United States, the head of government and the cabinet will still govern regardless of the outcome of the midterm elections, whereas even in a semipresidential system such as France the president may be forced to replace his prime minister and cabinet as the result of a National Assembly election. Even so, turnout for U.S. House elections during the sixteen presidential elections since World War II was only 51.6 percent, which

TABLE 4-1   Voter Turnout in National Elections, 1945–2008 (percent)

Country	National parliamentary	Presidential
Australia (26)	94.5	
Belgium (20)	92.4	
Luxembourg (13)	89.9	
Austria (20)	89.6	(11) 89.1
Iceland (19)	89.1	(6) 81.1
Malta (16)	89.0	
Italy (17)	88.9	
New Zealand (22)	86.5	
Netherlands (19)	86.3	
Denmark (25)	86.0	
Sweden (19)	85.5	
Germany (16)	84.5	
Norway (16)	80.2	
Greece (18)	79.4	
Israel (17)	77.0	
Finland (18)	75.9	(10) 74.0
Spain (11)	75.7	
United Kingdom (17)	74.4	
France (17)	74.0	(8) 82.1
Portugal (12)	72.8	(7) 68.2
Ireland (17)	72.3	(6) 57.6
Japan (24)	70.1	
Canada (21)	68.8	
Switzerland (16)	55.4	
United States (32)	44.7	(16) 55.7

Sources: All countries except United States: mean level of turnout computed from results in International Voter Turnout Database, www.idea.int/vt/view_data.cfm. U.S. turnout results, 1946–2002: U.S. Census Bureau, *Statistical Abstract of the United States, 2004–2005* (Washington, D.C.: Government Printing Office, 2004), table 409, 257; U.S. turnout results, 2004, 2006, and 2008: Michael P. McDonald, "2004 General Election Turnout Rates," http://elections.gmu.edu/Turnout_2004G.html; "2006 General Election Turnout Rates," http://elections.gmu.edu/Turnout_2006G.html; "2008 General Election Turnout Rates," http://elections.gmu.edu/Turnout_2008G.html.

Note: For all countries except the United States, turnout is computed by dividing the number of votes cast by the number of people registered to vote. For the United States, turnout is computed by dividing the number of votes cast for the U.S. House of Representatives (or for president) by the voting-age population. Numbers in parentheses are the number of parliamentary or presidential elections. For all countries with bicameral legislatures, we report turnout for the lower house.

is clearly lower than that of any democracy except Switzerland. Moreover, the turnout in U.S. presidential elections ranks lower than those in Austria, Finland, France, Iceland, and Portugal. It is about the same as presidential turnout in Ireland, where the president is largely a figurehead.[4]

In the 2008 U.S. presidential election, Barack Obama won 69.5 million votes and John McCain 59.9 million, so the some 81 million Americans who did *not* vote could easily have elected any presidential candidate.[5] In fact, both parties did a relatively good job of getting their supporters to the polls, although there was more enthusiasm among Obama supporters. Before turning to the 2008 contest, however, it is important to place the election in a broader historical context.[6]

VOTER TURNOUT, 1828–1916

Historical records can be used to determine how many people voted in presidential elections, and we can derive meaningful measures of turnout as early as 1828, the first election in which the vast majority of states chose their presidential electors by popular vote.[7] Turnout in presidential elections is determined by calculating the total number of votes cast for president by the voting-age population.[8] But should the turnout denominator be all people old enough to vote? Or should it include only people who are eligible to vote? The answer to this question will greatly affect our estimates of turnout in all presidential elections through 1916 because women were eligible to vote in only a few states before 1920. Clearly, women should be included in the turnout denominator in the states where they had the right to vote, but including them in the states where they could not vote leads to very low estimates of turnout.

In Table 4-2, we present two sets of estimates of turnout. The first column presents results compiled by Charles E. Johnson Jr., who calculates turnout by dividing the number of votes cast for president by the voting-age population. The second column is based on the calculations of Walter Dean Burnham, who measures turnout by dividing the total number of votes cast for president by the number of Americans eligible to vote (the voting-eligible population). Burnham excludes blacks before the Civil War, and from 1870 on he excludes aliens where they were not able to vote, basing his estimates on what he calls the "politically eligible" population. But the main difference between Burnham's estimates and Johnson's estimates is that Burnham excludes women from the turnout denominator in states where they could not vote.

Most political scientists would consider Burnham's calculations more meaningful than Johnson's. For example, most political scientists argue that turnout was higher in the nineteenth century than it is today. But whichever set of estimates one employs, the pattern of change is the same. There was a large increase in turnout after 1836, when the Democrats and Whigs began to employ popular appeals to mobilize the electorate. Turnout jumped markedly in 1840, the "Log Cabin and Hard Cider" campaign in which William Henry Harrison, the hero of the Battle of Tippecanoe (1811), defeated the incumbent Democrat, Martin van Buren. Turnout waxed and waned after 1840, but it rose substantially after the

TABLE 4-2   Voter Turnout in Presidential Elections, 1828–1916

Election year	Winning candidate	Party of winning candidate	Percentage of voting-age population who voted (Johnson)	Percentage of persons eligible to vote who voted (Burnham)
1828	Andrew Jackson	Democrat	22.2	57.3
1832	Andrew Jackson	Democrat	20.6	56.7
1836	Martin van Buren	Democrat	22.4	56.5
1840	William H. Harrison	Whig	31.9	80.3
1844	James K. Polk	Democrat	30.6	79.0
1848	Zachary Taylor	Whig	28.6	72.8
1852	Franklin Pierce	Democrat	27.3	69.5
1856	James Buchanan	Democrat	30.6	79.4
1860	Abraham Lincoln	Republican	31.5	81.8
1864[a]	Abraham Lincoln	Republican	24.4	76.3
1868	Ulysses S. Grant	Republican	31.7	80.9
1872	Ulysses S. Grant	Republican	32.0	72.1
1876	Rutherford B. Hayes	Republican	37.1	82.6
1880	James A. Garfield	Republican	36.2	80.6
1884	Grover Cleveland	Democrat	35.6	78.3
1888	Benjamin Harrison	Republican	36.3	80.5
1892	Grover Cleveland	Democrat	34.9	78.3
1896	William McKinley	Republican	36.8	79.7
1900	William McKinley	Republican	34.0	73.7
1904	Theodore Roosevelt	Republican	29.7	65.5
1908	William H. Taft	Republican	29.8	65.7
1912	Woodrow Wilson	Democrat	27.9	59.0
1916	Woodrow Wilson	Democrat	32.1	61.8

Sources: Estimates of turnout among the voting-age population based on Charles E. Johnson Jr., *Nonvoting Americans,* series P-23, no. 2, U.S. Department of the Census (Washington, D.C.: Government Printing Office, 1980), 2; estimates of turnout among the population eligible to vote based on calculations by Walter Dean Burnham, "The Turnout Problem," in *Elections American Style,* ed. A. James Reichley (Washington, D.C.: Brookings, 1987), 113–114.

[a] Johnson's estimate is based on the entire U.S. adult population. Burnham's estimate excludes the eleven Confederate states that did not take part in the election.

Republican Party, founded in 1854, polarized the nation by taking a clear stand against slavery in the territories. In Abraham Lincoln's election in 1860, four in five white men went to the polls.

Turnout fell and then rose after the Civil War, peaking in the 1876 contest between Republican Rutherford B. Hayes, the eventual winner, and Democrat

Samuel J. Tilden. To end the controversy over the disputed 1876 election results, the Republicans agreed to end Reconstruction. But once they lost the protection of federal troops, many African Americans were prevented from voting. Although some southern blacks could still vote in 1880, their overall turnout dropped sharply, which reduced southern turnout as a whole. By 1892 turnout had begun to fall nationally, but it rose in the 1896 contest between William Jennings Bryan (Democrat and Populist) and William McKinley, the Republican winner. It dropped again in the 1900 rerun between the two men.

In the late nineteenth century, African Americans were denied the franchise throughout the South, and poor whites often found it difficult to vote as well.[9] Throughout the country, registration requirements, which were in part designed to reduce fraud, were introduced. Because individuals were responsible for placing their names on the registration rolls before the election, the procedure created an obstacle that reduced electoral participation.[10]

Introducing the secret ballot also reduced turnout. Before this innovation, most voting in U.S. elections was public. Because the parties printed their own ballots, which differed in size and color, any observer could see how each person voted. In 1856 two Australian colonies (now states) adopted a secret ballot to be printed and administered by the government. The "Australian ballot" was first used statewide in Massachusetts in 1888. By the 1896 election, nine in ten states had followed Massachusetts's lead.[11] Although the secret ballot was designed to reduce fraud, it also reduced turnout. When voting was public, men could sell their votes, but candidates were less willing to pay for a vote if they could not see it delivered. Ballot stuffing was also more difficult when the state printed and distributed the ballots.

As Table 4-2 shows, turnout trailed off rapidly in the early twentieth century. By the time the three-way contest was held in 1912 between Democrat Woodrow Wilson, Republican William Howard Taft, and Theodore Roosevelt, a Progressive, only three in five politically eligible Americans were going to the polls (column 2). In 1916 turnout rose slightly, but just over three-fifths of eligible Americans voted (column 2), and only one-third of the total adult population went to the polls.

VOTER TURNOUT, 1920–2008

It is easier to calculate turnout from 1920 onward, and we have provided estimates based on both the voting-age population, as well as turnout among the politically eligible population. These two methods lead to fairly similar estimates, although differences have increased since 1972. We prefer focusing on turnout among the voting-age population for three reasons. First, it is difficult to estimate the size of the eligible population. Walter Dean Burnham and coauthors Michael P. McDonald and Samuel L. Popkin have made excellent efforts to provide these estimates.[12] Indeed, McDonald now maintains a Web site (http://elections.gmu.edu) that is the best source for turnout among both the voting-age and the voting-eligible population for the 2004 and 2008 presidential elections. Even so, Burnham's estimates of turnout differ from McDonald and Popkin's, with the latter reporting somewhat higher levels of turnout in all five elections between 1984 and 2000. Second, even though only citizens can vote in U.S. elections, citizenship is not a constitutional requirement for voting. National legislation determines how long it takes to become a citizen, and state laws impose citizenship as a condition of voting. Third, incarceration rates have grown markedly during the last four decades. Only Maine and Vermont allow prisoners to vote, and in ten states felons are permanently disfranchised. According to McDonald, in 2008 over 1.5 million prisoners were ineligible to vote, as were 2.4 million on probation and nearly 600,000 on parole.[13]

Excluding noneligible adults from the turnout denominator may yield misleading estimates, especially when U.S. turnout is compared with turnout levels in other democracies. For example, about one in ten voting-age Americans cannot vote, whereas in Britain only about one in fifty is disfranchised. In the United States, about one in seven black males cannot vote because of a felony conviction. As Thomas E. Patterson writes in a critique of McDonald and Popkin, "To ignore such differences, some analysts say, is to ignore official attempts to control the size and composition of the electorate."[14]

In Table 4-3, we show the percentage of the voting-age population who voted for the Democratic, Republican, and minor-party and independent candidates between 1920 and 2008. The table also shows the percentage that did not vote, as well as the overall size of the voting-age population.

In Figure 4-1, we show the percentage of the voting-age population that voted for president in each of these twenty-three elections, as well as the percentage of the politically eligible population between 1920 and 1944 and the voting-eligible population between 1948 and 2008.[15] The extent to which these trend lines diverge depends on the percentage of the voting-age population that is eligible to vote. In eras when most were eligible, such as between 1940 and 1980, it makes very little difference which turnout denominator one employs. But today there is a much larger noncitizen population, and incarceration rates are high. Back in 1960, when turnout peaked, only 2.2 percent of voting-age Americans were not citizens; as of 2008, 8.6 percent were not. In 1960 only 0.4 percent of Americans were ineligible to vote because of their felony status; in 2008, 1.6 percent were ineligible. Thus as Figure 4-1 shows, in 1960 there was very little difference between turnout among the voting-age population and turnout among the voting-eligible population. In 2008, according to McDonald, 131,304,731 votes were cast for president. Because the voting-age population was 230,917,360, turnout among this population was 56.8 percent. But, according to McDonald, the population eligible to vote was only 212,720,027. Using this total as our denominator,

TABLE 4-3   Percentage of Adults Who Voted for Each of the Major-Party Candidates, 1920–2008

Election year	Democratic candidate		Republican candidate		Other candidates	Did not vote	Total	Voting-age population
1920	14.8	James M. Cox	26.2	Warren G. Harding	2.4	56.6	100	61,639,000
1924	12.7	John W. Davis	23.7	Calvin Coolidge	7.5	56.1	100	66,229,000
1928	21.1	Alfred E. Smith	30.1	Herbert C. Hoover	0.6	48.2	100	71,100,000
1932	30.1	Franklin D. Roosevelt	20.8	Herbert C. Hoover	1.5	47.5	100	75,768,000
1936	34.6	Franklin D. Roosevelt	20.8	Alfred M. Landon	1.5	43.1	100	80,174,000
1940	32.2	Franklin D. Roosevelt	26.4	Wendell Willkie	0.3	41.1	100	84,728,000
1944	29.9	Franklin D. Roosevelt	25.7	Thomas E. Dewey	0.4	44.0	100	85,654,000
1948	25.3	Harry S. Truman	23.0	Thomas E. Dewey	2.7	48.9	100	95,573,000
1952	27.3	Adlai E. Stevenson	34.0	Dwight D. Eisenhower	0.3	38.4	100	99,929,000
1956	24.9	Adlai E. Stevenson	34.1	Dwight D. Eisenhower	0.4	40.7	100	104,515,000
1960	31.2	John F. Kennedy	31.1	Richard M. Nixon	0.5	37.2	100	109,672,000
1964	37.8	Lyndon B. Johnson	23.8	Barry M. Goldwater	0.3	38.1	100	114,090,000
1968	26.0	Hubert H. Humphrey	26.4	Richard M. Nixon	8.4	39.1	100	120,285,000
1972	20.7	George S. McGovern	33.5	Richard M. Nixon	1.0	44.8	100	140,777,000
1976	26.8	Jimmy Carter	25.7	Gerald R. Ford	1.0	46.5	100	152,308,000
1980	21.6	Jimmy Carter	26.8	Ronald Reagan	4.3	47.2	100	163,945,000
1984	21.6	Walter F. Mondale	31.3	Ronald Reagan	0.4	46.7	100	173,995,000
1988	23.0	Michael S. Dukakis	26.9	George H. W. Bush	0.5	49.7	100	181,956,000
1992	23.7	Bill Clinton	20.6	George H. W. Bush	10.8	44.9	100	189,493,000
1996	24.1	Bill Clinton	19.9	Bob Dole	4.9	51.1	100	196,789,000
2000	24.8	Al Gore	24.5	George W. Bush	1.9	48.8	100	205,813,000
2004	26.7	John F. Kerry	28.1	George W. Bush	0.6	44.6	100	220,804,000
2008	30.0	Barack Obama	26.0	John McCain	0.8	43.2	100	230,917,000

Sources: Voting-age population, 1920–1928: U.S. Census Bureau, Statistical Abstract of the United States, 1972, 92nd ed. (Washington, D.C.: Government Printing Office, 1972), table 597, 373; voting-age population, 1932–2000: U.S. Census Bureau, Statistical Abstract of the United States, 2004–2005, 124th ed. (Washington, D.C.: Government Printing Office, 2004), table 409, 257; voting-age population, 2004: Michael P. McDonald, "2004 General Election Turnout Rates," http://elections.gmu.edu/Turnout_2004G.html; voting-age population, 2008: Michael P. McDonald, "2008 General Election Turnout Rates," http://elections.gmu.edu/Turnout_2008G.html; number of votes cast for each presidential candidate and the total number of votes cast for president: Presidential Elections, 1789–2008 (Washington, D.C.: CQ Press, 2009).

Note: The names of the winning candidates are italicized.

FIGURE 4-1   Percentage of Voting-Age Population and of the Politically Eligible and the Voting-Eligible Population, 1920–2008

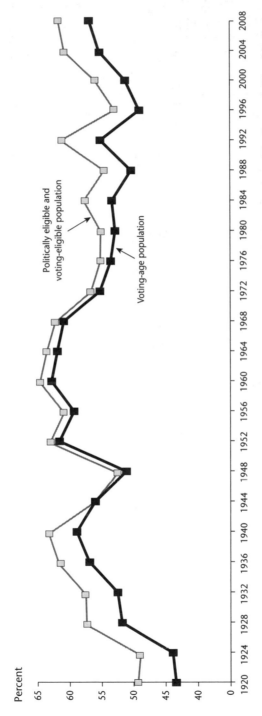

Sources: Voting-age population, see Table 4-3, this volume; politically eligible population, 1920–1944: Walter Dean Burnham, "The Turnout Problem," in *Elections American Style*, ed. A. James Reichley (Washington, D.C.: Brookings, 1987), 113–114; voting-eligible population, 1948–2000: Michael P. McDonald and Samuel L. Popkin, "The Myth of the Vanishing Voter," *American Political Science Review* 95 (December 2001): 966; 2004: Michael P. McDonald, "2004 General Election Turnout Rates," http://elections.gmu.edu/Turnout_2004G.html; 2008: Michael P. McDonald, "2008 General Election Turnout Rates," http://elections.gmu.edu/Turnout_2008G.html.

turnout is 61.7 percent. If we use McDonald's measure to calculate turnout in all sixteen postwar presidential elections, turnout would rise from 55.7 percent to 58.2 percent. However, U.S. turnout would still be lower than turnout in parliamentary elections in any country except Switzerland and lower than in presidential elections in any country except Ireland.

In 2004 George W. Bush won more votes than any previous presidential candidate, but in 2008 Obama won 7.4 million more votes than Bush. Obama's tally is far less impressive, however, when one compares his success with the vote shares of previous winners. As Table 4-3 shows, only 30.0 percent of voting-age Americans voted for Obama. In eight of the previous twenty-two elections, the winner exceeded Obama's share, and in three other elections the winner tied it. In 1960 Richard Nixon, the losing candidate, exceeded Obama's share. As in all of these elections except 1964, the percentage that did not vote clearly exceeded the share cast for the winning candidate.[16]

Turnout among the voting-age population generally rose between 1920 and 1960 (Figure 4-1). Two of the exceptions—1944 and 1948—resulted from the social dislocations during and after World War II. Specific conditions account for increases in turnout in certain elections. The jump in turnout in 1928 resulted from the candidacy of Alfred Smith, the first Catholic candidate to receive a major-party nomination, and the increase in 1936 resulted from Franklin Roosevelt's efforts to mobilize the lower social classes, especially the industrial working class. The extremely close contest between Nixon and the second Catholic candidate, John Kennedy, partly accounts for the high turnout in 1960, when it rose to 62.8 percent of the voting-age population and was slightly higher among the politically eligible population.[17] This figure was far below the percentage of eligible Americans that voted between 1840 and 1900, although it was the highest level of voting-age Americans that had ever voted in a presidential election. Nevertheless, the U.S. turnout in 1960 was still well below the average level of turnout in most advanced democracies (see Table 4-1).

Although short-term forces drove turnout upward in specific elections, long-term forces also contributed to the increase in turnout. For example, women who came of age before the Nineteenth Amendment often failed to exercise their right to vote, but women who came of age after 1920 had higher levels of turnout and gradually replaced older women in the electorate.[18] Because all states restricted voting to citizens, immigrants enlarged the voting-age population, but could not increase the number of voters until they became citizens. After 1921, however, as a result of restrictive immigration laws the percentage of the population that was foreign-born declined. Moreover, levels of education rose throughout the twentieth century, a change that boosted turnout. Americans who have attained higher levels of education are much more likely to vote than those with lower levels of education.

From 1960 to 1988, however, turnout declined, and the turnout among the voting age population was clearly higher in 1960 than it was in 2008. This change occurred even though there were institutional changes that should have increased turnout. Between 1960 and the century's end, the country underwent changes that tended to increase turnout. After passage of the Voting Rights Act of 1965, turnout rose dramatically among African Americans in the South, and their turnout spurred voting among southern whites. Less restrictive registration laws introduced over the last three decades also have made it easier to vote. The National Voter Registration Act, better known as the "motor voter" law, went into effect in January 1995, and it may have added nine million additional registrants to the rolls.[19] And, as we saw in Chapter 2, in 2008 many states allowed voters to vote early. According to McDonald's analysis of the 2008 Current Population Survey conducted by the U.S. Census Bureau, 29.7 percent of self-reported voters cast their ballots before election day.[20]

And yet despite these changes turnout declined. Except for a small increase in turnout in 1984, turnout among the voting-age population clearly declined between 1960 and 1988, falling most between 1968 and 1972.[21] Turnout then rose almost five points in 1992, perhaps as a result of Ross Perot's candidacy.[22] But in 1996 turnout fell some six percentage points, reaching only 48.9 percent. In 2000, in the expectation that the election would be close, both campaigns made major efforts to mobilize their supporters, but turnout rose only 2.3 percentage points. In 2004 the election was again expected to be close, and there were even greater get-out-the-vote efforts. This time, these efforts were more successful, and turnout rose 4.2 points. In 2008 few people expected the election to be close, but the Obama campaign had an effective ground game and launched a major GOTV campaign. Although some observers expected a large increase in turnout, it rose only 1.4 percentage points. Turnout among the voting-age population was 6.0 percentage points below the 1960 high-water mark. By contrast, turnout among the voting-eligible population was only 2.1 percent below the level in 1960.

VOTER TURNOUT AMONG SOCIAL GROUPS

Although turnout was relatively low in 2008, especially when compared with that of other advanced democracies, it was not equally low among all social groups. To compare groups, we rely on the 2008 ANES survey. Since 1992, the ANES measure of turnout has been based exclusively on a survey asking respondents whether they voted.[23] In 2008, 61.7 percent of the voting-eligible population voted, but 76.9 percent of the respondents interviewed in the ANES postelection survey said they voted.

The ANES surveys overestimate turnout for three reasons. First, even though the ANES respondents are asked a question that provides reasons for not voting, some voters falsely claim to have voted.[24] Validation efforts, in which the ANES checked voting and registration records, suggest that about 15 percent of the respondents who say that they voted did not do so, whereas only a handful of actual voters claim they did not vote.[25] Second, the ANES surveys do not perfectly represent the voting-age population. Lower socioeconomic groups, which have very low turnout, are underrepresented. Third, during presidential election years the same respondents are interviewed before and after the election. Being interviewed before the election provides a stimulus to vote and thus increases turnout among the ANES sample.[26]

Race, Gender, Region, and Age

In Table 4-4, we compare for the 2008 election reported turnout among social groups using the ANES surveys.[27] Our analysis begins by comparing African Americans with whites.[28] Whites and blacks are equally likely to report that they voted, and in a historical context that is a striking finding. In the first three elections we studied—1980, 1984, and 1988—we were able to compare turnout using actual checks of voting and registration records—the so-called vote validation studies. In those elections, whites were eighteen points more likely to vote than blacks. Unfortunately, in 1992 the ANES discontinued its checks of voting records, but we found blacks just as likely to report voting as whites in 2000, but less likely to report voting in 1992, 1996, and 2004. For these elections, whites were an average of 6.5 points more likely to report voting. Earlier ANES surveys based on reported voting show that blacks were less likely to vote than whites in all seven presidential elections between 1952 and 1976 and in all six midterm elections between 1958 and 1978.[29] The CPS also reveals that whites were more likely to report voting in every presidential election between 1964 and 2004 and in every midterm election between 1966 and 2006. But these differences have declined. In 1964, according to the CPS, whites were 12.2 percentage points more likely to vote than blacks;[30] in the 2004 election this difference was reduced to 5.4 percent.[31] According to the CPS, in 2008 turnout among non-Hispanic whites was 66.4 percent and 64.7 percent among black citizens. McDonald estimates that white turnout fell about one percentage point between 2004 and 2008, while black turnout rose five points. The exit polls conducted for a consortium of news organizations in 2004 and 2008 also suggest that black turnout increased. In 2004, 11 percent of voters were black; in 2008, 13 percent were.[32] All the same, if blacks continue to be more likely than whites to claim falsely that they voted, it is possible that blacks were still somewhat less likely to vote than whites.[33]

The relatively small number of blacks in the 2008 sample prevents us from making many comparisons among blacks.[34] As in earlier ANES surveys, blacks with higher levels of formal education were more likely to vote than those with lower levels of education, and young blacks were less likely to vote than their elders. Unlike earlier elections, however, black men were as likely to vote as black women and southern blacks were as likely to vote as blacks outside the South.[35]

TABLE 4-4   Percentage of Electorate Who Reported Voting for President, by Social Group, 2008

Social group	Did vote	Did not vote	Total	(N)[a]
Total electorate	77	23	100	(2,103)
Electorate, by race				
African American	78	22	100	(257)
White	78	22	100	(1,667)
Other	66	34	100	(174)
Latinos (of any race)	62	38	100	(191)
Whites, by gender				
Female	81	19	100	(920)
Male	75	25	100	(747)
Whites, by region				
New England and Mid-Atlantic	74	26	100	(232)
North Central	77	23	100	(373)
South	75	25	100	(476)
Border	90	10	100	(69)
Mountain and Pacific	84	16	100	(352)
Whites, by birth cohort				
Before 1940	87	13	100	(246)
1940–1954	84	16	100	(362)
1955–1962	78	22	100	(279)
1963–1970	79	21	100	(217)
1971–1978	73	27	100	(215)
1979–1986	68	32	100	(254)
1987–1990	62	38	100	(73)
Whites, by level of education				
Not high school graduate	45	55	100	(166)
High school graduate	70	30	100	(524)
Some college	83	17	100	(482)
College graduate	92	8	100	(342)
Advanced degree	95	5	100	(150)

(Continued)

TABLE 4-4   Percentage of Electorate Who Reported Voting for President, by Social Group, 2008 *(continued)*

Social group	Did vote	Did not vote	Total	(N)[a]
Whites, by annual family income				
Less than $15,000	56	44	100	(89)
$15,000–34,999	70	30	100	(230)
$35,000–49,999	73	27	100	(162)
$50,000–74,999	78	22	100	(274)
$75,000–89,999	85	15	100	(127)
$90,000–119,999	84	15	100	(171)
$120,000–149,999	91	9	100	(74)
$150,000 and over	89	11	100	(106)
Whites, by union membership[b]				
Member	82	18	100	(204)
Nonmember	77	23	100	(1,460)
Whites, by religion				
Jewish	96	4	100	(26)
Catholic	80	20	100	(330)
Protestant	80	20	100	(945)
None	71	32	100	(342)
White Protestants, by whether born again				
Not born again	77	23	100	(381)
Born again	81	19	100	(551)
White Protestants, by religious commitment				
Medium or low	77	33	100	(485)
High	82	18	100	(276)
Very high	84	16	100	(183)
White Protestants, by religious tradition				
Mainline	87	13	100	(234)
Evangelical	73	27	100	(395)

Source: Authors' analysis of the 2008 ANES survey.

[a] Numbers are weighted.

[b] Respondent or family member in union.

The mobilization of blacks in the 2008 election is a major story in its own right, but we cannot do justice here to this development.

The ANES study includes only citizens. As Table 4-4 reveals, the reported turnout among Latinos was low. But because relatively few Latinos were sampled, we cannot probe their behavior in any depth. The ANES survey divided Latinos into seven categories: Mexican, Puerto Rican, Cuban, Latin American, Central American, Spanish, and other. Forty-eight percent of Latinos were Mexican Americans. They were less likely to vote than Latinos who were not Mexican Americans. Among Mexican American citizens ($N = 121$), 60 percent reported voting; among other Latinos ($N = 133$), 74 percent did. According to the CPS, 49.8 percent of Hispanic citizens said they voted in 2008. McDonald estimates that there was a 2.7 percent increase in the Latino turnout in 2008 compared with 2004. The pool polls also suggest a slight increase in voting among Latinos. They made up 9 percent of voters in 2008, up 1 percent from four years earlier.

In 2008 white women were seven points more likely than white men to report voting, the largest female advantage in any of the eight presidential elections we have studied. Several of these studies, including 2004, reveal a slight female advantage. The 1980 election may be a turning point, because it is the last year in which the ANES surveys show white males to have a clear tendency to report voting more often than white females. ANES surveys from an earlier period show a clear decline in the turnout differential. In 1952, 1956, and 1960, the average male advantage was just over ten points, while in the 1964, 1968, 1972, and 1976 elections the gap narrowed to an average of just over five points. A similar trend is evident for the midterm elections during these years. According to the 2008 CPS, white women (66.3 percent) were more likely to report voting than white men (62.4 percent).[36]

Surveys are not needed to study turnout in the various regions of the country. Because we have estimates of both the voting-age population and the voting-eligible population for each state, we can measure turnout once we know the number of votes cast for president. According to McDonald's estimates, turnout among the voting-age population ranged from a low of 45.1 percent in Hawaii (50.7 percent of the voting-eligible population) to a high of 73.2 percent in Minnesota (78.2 percent of the voting-eligible population). But regional differences as a whole were small. According to our calculations, among the voting-age population in the South 55.0 percent voted; outside the South, 57.7 percent did. Among the voting-eligible population, 61.4 percent of southerners voted; outside the South, 61.9 percent did. There are small regional differences among whites. As the data in Table 4-4 show, 75 percent of southern whites said they voted; among whites outside the South, 80 percent did. The CPS also showed small regional differences among whites.[37] Among white citizens in the South, 62.3 percent said they voted; outside the South, 65.5 percent did. This relatively small difference reflects fundamental change in postwar voting patterns since the Voting Rights Act of 1965. The one-party South was destroyed, electoral competition increased, and, with blacks enfranchised for the first time since the turn of the twentieth century, turnout increased among whites as well. Outside the South, turnout has declined.

As described in Chapter 2, in 2008 there was a great effort, especially by the Obama campaign, to mobilize younger voters. But this effort had mixed success (Table 4-4). Turnout probably did increase somewhat among the young, but not very much. Among whites between the ages of eighteen and twenty-nine (the two youngest birth cohorts), 67 percent claimed to have voted; among whites fifty-five years and older, 85 percent did. Analyses of earlier NES surveys also show that young Americans are less likely to report voting, although they suggest that between 1952 and 1976 (or between 1958 and 1978) there was a decline in turnout among the cohort born before 1895.[38] The CPS data consistently show low levels of reported turnout among the young.[39] McDonald's analysis of the CPS data does suggest that between 2004 and 2008 there was a slight increase (2.1 percentage points) in turnout among Americans between the ages of eighteen and twenty-nine, whereas among all older cohorts there was a slight decline. But the CPS still found a strong relationship between age and turnout. In 2008 among white citizens eighteen to twenty-four years, 47.7 percent said that they voted; twenty-five to forty-four, 60.0 percent; forty-five to sixty-four, 70.2 percent; sixty-five to seventy-four, 73.8 percent; and seventy-five and over, 69.0 percent.[40] Moreover, the pool polls also suggest a slight increase in turnout among the young. In 2004, 17 percent of respondents were between the ages of eighteen and twenty-nine; in 2008, 18 percent were.

Young Americans are more likely to have higher levels of formal education than their elders, and one might therefore expect them to have higher levels of turnout. But they do not. As they age, young Americans tend to participate more, although the reasons for their increased participation are not well understood.[41]

Income and Union Membership

Respondents' family income was also related to electoral participation, which was especially low among whites with annual incomes of less than $15,000.[42] Reported turnout was very high among whites with incomes of $120,000 and over. We found strong relationships between income and turnout in 1980, 1984, and 1988 and between income and reported turnout in all the presidential elections between 1982 and 2004. Earlier analyses of the ANES data using five income percentiles showed a strong relationship between family income and turnout in all the presidential elections between 1952 and 1986 and all the midterm elections between 1958 and 1978.[43] The CPS also shows a strong tendency for Americans in households with higher incomes to be more likely to vote than those with lower incomes, and that relationship was present in 2008.[44]

However, educational attainment has a greater effect on turnout than does income.[45]

Surveys over the years have found a weak and inconsistent relationship between union membership and turnout. Being in a household with a union member may create organizational ties that encourage voting. In their *Sourcebook,* scholars at the University of Michigan report that members of union households were more likely to vote than nonmembers in most of the presidential elections between 1952 and 1976, as well as most of the midterm elections between 1958 and 1978.[46] We found no differences in turnout between members of union households and nonmembers in the 1980 presidential election, but in all the remaining elections, including 2008, members of union households were more likely to either vote (1984 and 1988) or to report voting (1992–2008) than nonmembers. However, these differences were relatively small in 2008 because reported turnout among union members fell slightly between 2004 and 2008. This finding is consistent with the finding of the pool polls that members of union households made up 24 percent of the electorate in 2004 and only 21 percent in 2008.

Religion

In the earlier postwar years, Catholics were more likely to vote than Protestants, but these differences have declined.[47] The low turnout of Protestants, clearly documented by ANES surveys conducted between 1952 and 1978, resulted largely from two factors.[48] First, Protestants were more likely to live in the South, which was once a low turnout region. And, second, Protestants were more likely to be black, a group that had much lower turnout than whites. We have always compared turnout or reported turnout by comparing white Catholics with white Protestants. Except for the 1980 election, when there were no differences between Catholics and Protestants, Catholics were more likely to vote when vote validation measures were used (1984 and 1988). And they were more likely to report voting in the five elections between 1992 and 2004. But as Table 4-4 shows, in 2008 Protestants and Catholics were equally likely to vote. According to the pool polls, the shares of the electorate made up of white Protestants and of white Catholics fell by one percentage point between 2004 and 2008.

The Michigan team found that Jews had higher reported turnout than either Protestants or Catholics in six of the seven presidential elections between 1952 and 1996 as well as in five of the six midterm elections between 1958 and 1978. And we found Jews to have higher levels of turnout or reported turnout in all seven elections between 1980 and 2004. In 2008 Jews once again had a higher level of turnout than Catholics or Protestants (see Table 4-4), although the small number of Jews sampled makes any conclusion based on the ANES survey alone problematic.

In recent elections, fundamentalist Protestants have launched get-out-the-vote efforts to mobilize their supporters. In examining turnout among white Protestants since the 1992 election, we have found that the success of these groups in mobilizing their supporters has varied from election to election. In 2008 social conservatives were not enthusiastic about John McCain, but they were enthusiastic about his running mate, Sarah Palin.

Table 4-4 reveals for 2008 our comparison of white Protestants who say they are born-again Christians with those who say they are not.[49] As in previous years when we examined this question (1992, 1996, and 2000), there was no difference between Protestants who were born again and those who did not have this religious experience.

Lyman A. Kellstedt argues that religious commitment is an important factor contributing to voting behavior.[50] To score "very high" on this measure respondents had to report praying several times a day and attending church at least once a week. In addition, they had to say that religion provided "a great deal" of guidance in their lives and to believe that the Bible is literally true or the "word of God." In 1992, 1996, 2000, and 2004, respondents who scored very high on this measure were the most likely to report voting. But in 2008 there was only a weak relationship between religious commitment and whether white Protestants said they voted (Table 4-4).[51]

Since 1990, the ANES has asked detailed questions that allow us to distinguish among Protestant denominations and thus to conduct analyses of religious differences that could not be conducted earlier. We can now divide Protestants into four main groups: evangelicals, mainline, ambiguous affiliation, and nontraditional. Most white Protestants can be classified into the first two categories, which, according to Kenneth D. Wald, make up more than two-fifths of the total U.S. adult population.[52] As R. Stephen Warner has pointed out, "The root of the [mainline] liberal position is the interpretation of Christ as a moral teacher who told his disciples that they could best honor him by helping those in need." By contrast, says Warner, "the evangelical interpretation sees Jesus (as they prefer to call him) as one who offers salvation to anyone who confesses in his name." Liberal or mainline Protestants stress the importance of sharing their abundance with the needy, whereas evangelicals see the Bible as a source of revelation about Jesus.[53]

In classifying Protestants as mainline or evangelical, we rely on their denomination. For example, Episcopalians, Congregationalists, and most Methodists are classified as mainline, whereas Baptists, Pentecostals, and many small denominations are classified as evangelicals.[54] In 1992, 1996, 2000, and 2008, white mainline Protestants were more likely than white evangelicals to report voting. These results are scarcely surprising because mainline Protestants have higher levels of formal education than evangelicals. Only in 2004, when fundamentalist churches launched a massive get-out-the-vote effort, were white evangelicals as likely to report voting as white mainline Protestants.

Education

In the 2008 election, there was a strong relationship between education and reported electoral participation (see Table 4-4). Among whites who have not graduated from high school, less than half claim to have voted, the lowest level of turnout we have ever found among this group. Among college graduates, nine in ten say they voted. And among whites with advanced degrees, nineteen in twenty say they voted. Earlier reports that divided the entire electorate into three educational categories (grade school, high school, and college) revealed a consistent relationship between levels of education and reported turnout in every presidential election between 1952 and 1976 and every midterm election between 1958 and 1978.[55] And we found a strong relationship between educational level and turnout among whites in 1980, 1984, and 1988, and between educational level and reported turnout between 1992 and 2004. Likewise, the CPS has found a strong relationship between education and reported voting in every presidential election between 1964 and 2004 and in every midterm election between 1966 and 2006.

Analyses of the 2008 CPS data once again show a strong relationship between education and reported voting. Among white citizens without a high school diploma, only 37.6 percent said they voted; among those with a diploma, 54.6 percent; among those with some college, 68.5 percent; among those with a bachelor's degree, 78.5 percent; and among those with an advanced degree, 84.9 percent.[56]

Even though surveys may somewhat exaggerate the relationship between formal education and electoral participation, the tendency of better-educated Americans to be more likely to vote is one of the most extensively documented facts of American political life.[57]

WHY DID VOTER TURNOUT DECLINE AFTER 1960?

Even though turnout rose four percentage points in 2004 and one and a half points in 2008, turnout among the voting-age population is still 6.0 points lower than it was in 1960, and 2.1 percentage points lower among the voting-eligible population.

The research by McDonald and Popkin helps explain why turnout among the voting-age population has declined. The percentage of Americans who were not citizens increased markedly between 1960 and 2008. Moreover, in 1960 fewer than half a million people were ineligible to vote because they were incarcerated or were convicted felons, whereas in 2008 about five million were.[58] Both of these changes would tend to reduce turnout among the voting-age population.

Still, because education is so strongly related to turnout and because educational levels have risen continuously since 1960, it is difficult to explain why turnout has declined. According to the U.S. Census Bureau, in 1960, 43.2 percent of whites and 20.1 percent of blacks twenty-five years and older were high school graduates. By 2007, 86.2 percent of whites and 82.3 percent of blacks were high school graduates. In 1960 only 8.1 percent of whites and 3.1 percent of blacks were college graduates. By 2007, 29.1 percent of whites and 18.5 percent of blacks had achieved this goal.[59] Clearly, turnout within educational groups must have been declining so quickly that the effect of higher levels of education was cancelled out. This finding suggests that changes in turnout resulted from some forces that stimulated turnout and others that depressed it.

Analysts have studied the decline in turnout extensively. Some have focused on social factors, such as the changing levels of education among the electorate, while others have investigated political attitudes, such as the decline in party loyalties, as a major source of turnout decline. Some scholars have examined institutional changes, such as the easing of registration requirements. Others have pointed to the behavior of political leaders, arguing that they are not trying as hard to mobilize the electorate. Certain changes, such as the rise in educational levels and the easing of registration requirements, should have increased turnout in national elections. Richard A. Brody views the decline in turnout as a major puzzle for students of political participation.[60]

We begin our own attempt to solve this puzzle by examining the relationship between education and voting among whites in all presidential elections from 1960 to 2008. (Because African Americans have substantially lower levels of formal education than whites, and southern blacks have been enfranchised only since 1965, including blacks in our analysis would obscure the relationships we are studying.) We divided whites into four educational levels: college graduates, those with some college, high school graduates, and those who did not graduate from high school.

Although the ANES surveys show no decline in turnout among college graduates, they do show declines in the remaining three categories, with the greatest declines among the two lowest educational categories. (Several studies of the CPS also suggest that turnout has declined most among Americans who are relatively disadvantaged.[61]) Ruy A. Teixeira's analysis of the CPS shows a ten-point drop among college graduates from 1964 to 1988, although the decline was greater among those who had not graduated from college.[62]

The rise in educational levels did not prevent the decline in turnout, but it played a major role in slowing down its decline. Between 1960 and 2008, there was a remarkable increase in educational levels among the white electorate. According to the ANES surveys, the percentage of whites who had not graduated from high school fell from 47 percent to 11 percent. During this same period, the percentage who graduated from college rose from 11 percent to 33 percent. Among whites who could be classified according to their educational levels, reported turnout fell four percentage points between 1960 and 2008. Our estimate based on an algebraic standardization procedure suggests that if educational levels had not increased, turnout would have declined nineteen percentage points.[63] Although this procedure provides only a preliminary estimate of the impact of education, it strongly suggests that turnout would have declined much more if educational levels had not increased.

Other social factors also tended to slow the rate of decline. In a comprehensive attempt to explain the decline in turnout between 1960 and 1988, Teixeira studied changes in turnout using the ANES surveys. He found that increases in income and the growth of white-collar employment tended to retard the decline in turnout. But the rise in educational levels, according to Teixeira's estimates, was far more important than these two changes; its influence was three times as great as the impact of occupation and income combined.[64]

Steven J. Rosenstone and John Mark Hansen, too, have used the ANES surveys to develop a comprehensive explanation for the decline in turnout during these years. Their analyses demonstrate that formal education was the most important factor preventing an even greater decline in voter participation. They also examined the effects of easing registration requirements. They found that reported turnout declined eleven percentage points from the 1960s to the 1980s, but that turnout would have declined sixteen points had it not been for the combined effect of rising educational levels and liberalized election laws.[65]

Although some forces slowed down the decline in turnout after 1960, other forces contributed to it. After 1960, the electorate became younger as baby boomers (that is, those born between 1946 and 1964) came of age. As we have seen, younger Americans have lower levels of turnout, although as baby boomers aged (by 2008 they were between the ages of forty-four and sixty-two), one might have expected turnout to rise. The proportion of Americans who were married declined, and because married people are more likely to vote than the unmarried, this change also reduced turnout. Church attendance declined, reducing the ties of Americans to their communities. Teixeira identifies these three changes as the major shifts contributing to the decline in turnout and argues that the decline in church attendance was the most important of them.[66] Rosenstone and Hansen also examined changes that contributed to the decline in turnout, and their analysis suggests that a younger electorate was the most important factor reducing electoral participation.[67]

Warren E. Miller argues that the decline in turnout after 1960 resulted mainly from the entry of a post–New Deal generation into the electorate.[68] That change, Miller contends, resulted not only from these Americans being young, but also from generational differences that contributed to lower levels of electoral participation. During the late 1960s and early 1970s, a series of events—the Vietnam War, the Watergate scandal, the failed presidencies of Gerald Ford and Jimmy Carter—created a generation that withdrew from political activity. Robert D. Putnam also argues that political disengagement was largely the result of the baby boom generation, and that generational succession reduced other forms of civic activity as well. Putnam writes: "The declines in church attendance, voting, political interest, campaign activities, associational membership, and social trust are attributable almost entirely to generational succession."[69]

Most analysts agree that attitudinal changes have contributed to the decline in electoral participation. Our own analysis has focused on the effect of attitudinal changes. We have studied the impact of changes in party identification, and we have examined what George I. Balch and others have called "feelings of external political efficacy"—that is, the belief that political authorities will respond to attempts to influence them.[70] These are the same two political attitudes that Teixeira studied in his first major analysis of turnout, and they are among the attitudes studied by Rosenstone and Hansen.[71] Like Teixeira, we found that these attitudinal changes contribute to the decline in turnout.[72] We have now analyzed the impact of these attitudes in every presidential election from 1980 to 2008.[73]

The measure of party identification we used is based on a series of questions designed to measure attachment to a partisan reference group.[74] Between 1952 and 1964, the percentage of strong partisans among the white electorate never fell below 35 percent. It then fell to 27 percent in 1966 and continued to fall, reaching its lowest level in 1978, when only 21 percent of voters identified strongly with either party. After that, party identification rose, and by 2004 it had reached the 1952–1964 levels. But it fell in 2008 mainly because of a move away from the Republicans. In 2008 only 29 percent of whites were strong party identifiers. Even though the percentage of strong partisans was off its all-time low, it was substantially lower than during the surveys between 1952 and 1964. Moreover, during the 1962–1964 period the percentage of white independents who leaned toward a party was about 15 percent; in 2008 it was 29 percent. And even the percentage of independents with no party leanings increased, from about 8 percent during the 1952–1964 period to 12 percent in 2008. Strong partisans are more likely to vote than any other group, and in most elections independents who lean toward a party are less likely to vote than weak partisans. Independents who do not feel closer to either party consistently have low turnout. Partisan loyalties should be expected to contribute to electoral participation for several reasons. Strong party ties contribute to a psychological involvement in politics. And from a rational choice perspective, strong party loyalties will reduce a citizen's information costs.[75] For a detailed discussion of party identification from 1952 to 2008, along with tables showing the distribution of party identification among whites and blacks during these years, see Chapter 8 in this volume, as well as the Appendix.

Feelings of political effectiveness also contribute to electoral participation. Citizens may expect to gain benefits if they believe the government is responsive to their demands. Conversely, those who believe that political leaders will not or cannot respond to their demands may see little reason for voting. In thirteen of the fourteen elections between 1952 and 2004, Americans with high feelings of political efficacy were the most likely to vote, and in all thirteen elections those with low feelings of political efficacy were the least likely to vote.[76] As we will see, feelings of political effectiveness were less related to reported voting than in any of the previous fourteen elections.

TABLE 4-5   Percentage of Whites Who Reported Voting for President, by Strength of Party Identification and Sense of External Political Efficacy, 2008

Score on external political efficacy index	Strength of party identification							
	Strong partisan		Weak partisan		Independent who leans toward a party		Independent with no partisan leaning	
	%	(N)	%	(N)	%	(N)	%	(N)
High	91	(76)	87	(60)	76	(68)	25	(24)
Medium	96	(51)	87	(52)	74	(69)	76	(25)
Low	92	(104)	82	(121)	58	(110)	50	(52)

Source: Authors' analysis of the 2008 ANES survey.

Note: Numbers in parentheses are the totals on which percentages are based. Numbers are weighted.

From 1960 to 1980, scores on the measure of political efficacy declined markedly. Between 1956 and 1960, 64 percent of whites scored high on feelings of political efficacy; only 15 percent scored low. After 1960, feelings of effectiveness began to fall, reaching an all-time low in 1996, when only 35 percent of whites scored high and 46 percent scored low. Although there was some rebound in 2000 and 2004, feelings of political efficacy fell to a new all-time low in 2008. Only 28 percent of whites scored high on our measure of sense of political efficacy, and 48 percent scored low.

In 2008 strength of party identification was strongly related to reported voting among the white electorate. Among strong party identifiers ($N = 486$), 91 percent said they voted; among weak partisans ($N = 492$), 83 percent voted; among independents who leaned toward a party ($N = 484$), 71 percent voted; and among independents who did not feel closer to either party ($N = 194$), only 52 percent voted. But feelings of political effectiveness were weakly related to reported voting, although whites with low feelings of external political efficacy were somewhat less likely to vote than the two other groups. Among whites with high feelings of political efficacy ($N = 229$), 78 percent said they voted; among those with medium feelings ($N = 198$), 83 percent voted; and among whites with low feelings ($N = 395$), 73 percent voted.

Table 4-5 shows the joint relationship between strength of party identification, feelings of political efficacy, and reported electoral participation. First, strength of party identification and feelings of political efficacy are relatively weakly related. Second, reading across each row reveals that strength of party identification is strongly related to reported electoral participation. Reading down each column, however, reveals a strong and consistent relationship between feelings of political efficacy and reported voting in only one partisan group, independents who lean toward a political party.

We estimated the impact of attitudinal changes on the decline in turnout by using an algebraic standardization procedure.[77] Among whites who could be measured for both strength of party identification and feelings of political efficacy, reported turnout fell 5.4 percent. According to our analyses, the decline in party loyalties contributed to 64 percent of this decline, and weakening feelings of political efficacy contributed to 30 percent. The combined shift in both of these attitudes contributed to 78 percent of the decline in turnout among the white electorate.

Our estimates demonstrate that attitudinal changes are important, but they do not represent a final estimate of the impact of such changes. We do not claim to have solved the puzzle of declining political participation. Comprehensive analyses such as those conducted by Teixeira and by Rosenstone and Hansen are needed to study the 1992, 1996, 2000, 2004, and 2008 survey results. As Teixeira demonstrates, a comprehensive explanation of the impact of attitudinal changes must calculate the contribution that attitudinal changes would have made to the decline in turnout if there had been no social changes slowing the decline. In Teixeira's analysis, for example, the decline in party loyalties and the erosion of political efficacy contributed to 62 percent of the decline in turnout between 1960 and 1980. But these attitudinal changes contributed to only 38 percent of the decline if changes in educational levels, income, and occupational patterns had not slowed it.

We analyzed the combined impact of rising levels of education, the erosion of feelings of political efficacy, and the decline in party identification between 1960 and 2008. Our estimates show that attitudinal changes would have had little effect on the decline that would have occurred if rising educational levels had not slowed it.[78] In this sense, our findings differ from those of our analyses of the 1988, 1992, 1996, 2000, and 2004 elections, for in all of these elections attitudinal changes contributed to the decline in turnout even when we controlled for the decline in educational levels.[79]

A comprehensive analysis of the impact of attitudinal factors would have taken into account other factors that might have eroded turnout. As has been well documented, there has been a substantial decline in trust during the past four decades, a decline that might be under way in a large number of democracies.[80] In 1964, when political trust among whites was highest, 77 percent of whites trusted the government to do what was right just about always or most of the time, and 74 percent of blacks endorsed this view.[81] Political trust reached a very low level in 1980, when only 25 percent of whites and 26 percent of blacks trusted the government. Trust rebounded during the Reagan years, but it fell after that, and by 1992 trust was almost as low as it was in 1980. After that, trust rose in most elections, and by 2004, 50 percent of whites and 34 percent of blacks trusted the government. But trust dropped markedly among whites during the next four years, and it dropped somewhat among blacks. In 2008, 30 percent of whites and 28 percent of blacks trusted the government.[82]

Back in 1964, 63 percent of whites and 69 percent of blacks said the government was run for the benefit of all.[83] By 1980 only 20 percent of whites and 19 percent of blacks trusted the government on this question. Once again, trust rose during the Reagan years, but it fell after that, and by 1992 trust had fallen back to its 1980 levels among whites, and blacks were even less trusting than they were four years earlier. But trust rose in 1996 and again in 2000. In 2004 trust rose among whites, while falling among blacks: 44 percent of whites, but only 27 percent of blacks, thought the government was run for the benefit of all. During the next four years, trust clearly fell among whites, while rising somewhat among blacks. In 2008 only 29 percent of whites and 33 percent of blacks believed the government was run for the benefit of all citizens.

Although many scholars have studied the decline in trust, this decline has had little impact on the decline in turnout. In most years, including 2008, Americans who distrusted the government were as likely to vote as those who were politically trusting. In 2008 this was true for whites for both of these standard political trust questions, although among blacks for both of these questions those who were politically cynical were more likely to vote than those who were politically trusting.

ELECTION-SPECIFIC FACTORS

In any election there will be political circumstances that affect turnout. Research by Rosenstone and Hansen points to the importance of political parties in mobilizing voters, and study of this activity may shed light on changes in turnout. This activity is similar to education—changes in educational levels prevented the decline in turnout from being even greater. Likewise, changes in mobilization of the electorate may have had the same effect. The percentage of Americans who say they have been contacted by a political party increased after the 1960 election. In 1960, 22 percent of the electorate said a political party had contacted them; in 1980, 32 percent said they had been contacted.[84] In 1992 only 20 percent said they had been contacted by a political party, but turnout was higher in 1992 than in 1980. The percentage that said they had been contacted by a political party grew in 1996 and in 2000, and it increased slightly between 2000 and 2004. It grew again somewhat in 2008, when 43 percent said they had been contacted, with whites somewhat more likely to claim they were contacted (45 percent) than blacks (38 percent). As in previous elections, Americans who were more likely to be contacted by a party were more likely to report voting than those who were not contacted. In 2008, among whites who said they had been contacted by a political party ($N = 747$), 88 percent said they voted; among those who had not been contacted ($N = 921$), only 69 percent did. Likewise, among blacks who said they were contacted ($N = 97$), 87 percent reported voting; among those who had not been contacted ($N = 160$), 72 percent did. But even though there was a consistent relationship between being contacted by a party and voting, and even though the percentage that was contacted increased, turnout declined among the white electorate during this period.[85]

In most elections, Americans who think the election will be close are more likely to vote than those who think the winner will win by quite a bit. Indeed, Orley Ashenfelter and Stanley Kelley Jr. report that the single most important factor accounting for the decline in turnout between 1960 and 1972 was "the dramatic shift in voter expectations about the closeness of the race in these two elections."[86] Although the differences are usually not large, the percentage who thinks the election will be close varies greatly from election to election. For example, in 1996 only 52 percent of whites thought the election between Bill Clinton and Bob Dole would be close, but in 2000, 88 percent thought the contest between Gore and Bush would be close. In 2004, 81 percent did. The percentage who thought the election would be close fell only slightly, to 79 percent, in 2008, but there were clear racial differences. Among whites, 82 percent thought the election would be close; among blacks, only 69 percent did. Among whites who thought the election would be close ($N = 1,342$), 80 percent said they voted; among those who thought the winner would win by "quite a bit" ($N = 430$), 70 percent did. Among blacks, however, the perceived closeness of the election was not related to turnout.

DOES LOW VOTER TURNOUT MATTER?

For nearly three decades, Democratic Party leaders have debated the importance of increasing turnout. The Democrats could win, some argued, if they could mobilize disadvantaged Americans. In 1984 the Democrats made major get-out-the-vote efforts, but turnout increased less than one percentage point, and turnout among the voting-age population reached a postwar low. Other Democrats argued that the main problem facing the party was defections by its traditional supporters. Of course, increasing turnout and winning back defectors are not mutually exclusive strategies, but they can lead to contradictory tactics. For example, mobilizing African Americans may not be cost-free if doing so leads to defections among white Democrats.

As James DeNardo has pointed out, from 1932 to 1976 there was only a weak relationship between turnout and the percentage of the vote won by Democratic presidential candidates.[87] In our analyses of the 1980, 1984, and 1988 presidential elections, we argued that, among most reasonable scenarios, increased turnout would not have led to Democratic victories.[88] In 1992 increased turnout went along with the Democratic victory, but not a higher share of the Democratic vote. Our analyses suggest that Bill Clinton benefited from increased turnout, but that he benefited more by converting voters who had supported George H. W. Bush four years earlier.[89] Despite the six percentage point decline in turnout between 1992 and 1996, Clinton was easily reelected. Even so, there is some evidence that the decline in turnout cost Clinton votes.[90]

In view of the closeness of the 2000 contest, it seems plausible that a successful get-out-the-vote effort by the Democrats could have swung the election to Al Gore. As Gerald M. Pomper argued in 2001, "If every citizen had actually voted, both the popular and electoral votes would have led to an overwhelming Gore victory."[91] A CBS poll released on November 5, two days before the election, showed that Americans who did not expect to vote favored Gore by a 42 percent to 28 percent margin over Bush. And a CBS poll released on November 13 showed that Americans who regretted not voting favored Gore by 53 percent to 33 percent over Bush. This latter evidence is questionable, however, because, although the outcome was not definitive, Gore was trailing Bush in Florida, and Bush seemed more likely to win the presidency than Gore.

In 2004 turnout rose by over four percentage points, regardless of how it is measured. But Bush won with a majority of the popular vote, even though his margin over Kerry was small. Our analyses suggest that the Republicans were more successful in mobilizing their supporters than the Democrats. Some argue that the GOP gained because in eleven states proposals to ban same-sex marriages were on the ballot. But, as we have shown, turnout was only one point higher in the states that had these propositions on the ballot than in the states that did not.[92] Bush won nine of the eleven states with such a proposition, but of those nine states only Ohio was closely contested, and turnout increased by nine percentage points there. We do not know the extent to which the presence of this ballot proposition brought voters to the polls in Ohio or whether the voters who came to the polls to vote on the proposition were crucial for Bush's 2.1 percent margin over Kerry in the Buckeye State.[93]

Table 4-6 examines whether respondents reported voting for president in 2008, controlling for their party identification, their position on the issues (the "balance of issues" measure), and their evaluations of the performance of George W. Bush, the government, and the Republican Party (the summary measure of "retrospective" evaluations). We have already employed party identification in Table 4-5, in which we looked at the "strength" of party identification. We discuss the balance of issues measure in Chapter 6 and our measure of retrospective evaluations in Chapter 7.

We begin our discussion of the significance of low turnout by examining party identification. In 1980, 1984, and 1988, strong Republicans were more likely to vote than strong Democrats.[94] In 1992 partisan differences were small because voter turnout increased more among Democrats than among Republicans. But in 1996, 2000, and 2004, strong Republicans were once again more likely to report voting than strong Democrats. Among other partisan categories, the Republican turnout advantage varies from year to year. In the 2004 election, we estimate that Kerry would have gained 3.4 percentage points in the vote if Democrats had been as likely to vote as Republicans. Depending on the states in which these votes were cast, Kerry could have won the election.

TABLE 4-6   Percentage of Electorate Who Reported Voting for President, by Party Identification, Issue Preferences, and Retrospective Evaluations, 2008

	Voted	Did not vote	Total	(N)
Electorate, by party identification				
Strong Democrat	89	11	100	(390)
Weak Democrat	76	24	100	(320)
Independent, leans Democratic	66	34	100	(345)
Independent, no partisan leaning	50	50	100	(236)
Independent, leans Republican	75	25	100	(246)
Weak Republican	86	14	100	(274)
Strong Republican	94	6	100	(270)
Electorate, by scores on balance of issues measure				
Strongly Democratic	77	23	100	(70)
Moderately Democratic	80	20	100	(108)
Slightly Democratic	75	25	100	(179)
Neutral	62	37	100	(85)
Slightly Republican	73	26	100	(228)
Moderately Republican	82	18	100	(222)
Strongly Republican	90	10	100	(140)
Electorate, by scores on summary measure of retrospective evaluations of incumbent party				
Strongly opposed	80	20	100	(855)
Moderately opposed	74	26	100	(363)
Slightly opposed	65	35	100	(263)
Neutral	55	45	100	(11)
Slightly supportive	76	24	100	(208)
Moderately supportive	85	15	100	(199)
Strongly supportive	87	13	100	(174)

Source: Authors' analysis of the 2008 ANES survey.

Note: Numbers are weighted. Chapter 6 describes how the balance of issues measure was constructed, and Chapter 7 describes how the summary measure of retrospective evaluations was constructed.

Despite the speculation before the election about Obama mobilizing new voters, the ANES data suggest that Republicans were more likely to vote than Democrats. Table 4-6 shows that strong Republicans were somewhat more likely to report voting than strong Democrats, weak Republicans were more likely to vote than weak Democrats, and independents who felt closer to the Republican Party were more likely to vote than those who felt closer to the Democrats. If we assume that each of the Democratic groups had turnout as high as each of the comparable Republican groups, and if we assume that the additional Democrats drawn to the polls voted the same way as the Democrats who did vote, Obama would have gained about 3.5 percentage points.

In Chapter 6 we examine the issue preferences of the electorate. For every presidential election between 1980 and 2008, we built a measure of overall issue preferences based on the seven-point scales used by the ANES surveys to measure the issue preferences of the electorate.[95] In 1980 there was no systematic relationship between policy preferences and turnout, but in 1984, 1988, 1992, and 1996 respondents with pro-Republican views were more likely to vote than those with pro-Democratic views. Obviously, the tendency of respondents with pro-Republican views could not have affected the outcome in the two elections the Democrats won, and in 1984 Ronald Reagan won by such a massive margin that it is difficult to imagine that the relationship of issue preferences to turnout cost Walter Mondale the election. Although we estimate that the turnout advantage of Americans with pro-Republican views cost Michael Dukakis two percentage points in 1988, it seems unlikely that turnout gains would have overcome George H. W. Bush's 7.7 percentage point margin. In 2000 the only Republican turnout advantage was that respondents who were slightly Republican were more likely to vote than those who were slightly Democratic. But this difference could have affected the outcome, because more than three in five voters who were slightly Democratic voted for Gore.[96] In 2004 there was no systematic relationship between issue preferences and the vote. In fact, respondents who were strongly Democratic were more likely to report voting than those who were strongly Republican. On balance, differential turnout on these measures had little effect on the percentage of Americans who voted for Kerry or Bush.

In 2008 our overall measure of issue preferences is based on scales measuring the respondent's position on seven issues: (1) reducing or increasing government services, (2) decreasing or increasing defense spending, (3) government health insurance, (4) government job guarantees, (5) government helping blacks, (6) protecting the environment, and (7) the role of women in society.[97] As Table 4-6 shows, there is only one clear difference. Respondents who are strongly Republican on the issues are more likely to report voting than those who are strongly Democratic. But Americans who are strongly Democratic made up only 7 percent of the electorate. On balance, turnout biases on issue preferences have a negligible effect on the overall share of the vote for Obama.

In Chapter 7 we discuss the retrospective evaluations of the electorate. Voters, some analysts argue, make their decisions based not just on their evaluation of policy promises, but also on their evaluation of how well the party in power is doing. Between 1980 and 2000, we used a summary measure based on presidential approval, an evaluation of the job the government was doing dealing with the most important problem facing the country, and an assessment of which party would do a better job dealing with this problem. In 1980 respondents who expressed negative views toward Jimmy Carter and the Democrats were more likely to vote than those with positive views, but these biases cannot account for Reagan's 9.7 percentage point margin over Carter. In 1984 and 1988, respondents with positive views of the Republicans were more likely to vote than those with negative views. Because Reagan won by a landslide in 1984, these biases did not cost Mondale the election. In 1988 they cost Dukakis about two percentage points. In 1992 these biases were eliminated. In 1996 respondents with pro-Republican views were more likely to vote, and this bias probably cost Clinton about one percentage point. But in 2000 there was no consistent relationship between retrospective evaluations and turnout.

In 2004 we could not use the measure we employed between 1980 and 2000, and so we developed an alternative measure.[98] We found no consistent relationship between retrospective evaluations and reported participation, and correcting for differences in turnout had virtually no effect on the vote.

In 2008 we had to employ yet another measure—one based on the respondent's approval of the incumbent president, the respondent's evaluation of how good a job the government had been doing over the last four years, and the respondent's assessment of which party would better be able to deal with the most important problem facing the country. Our most important finding is that in 2008 the electorate was overwhelmingly negative toward President Bush and the Republican Party. Yet the turnout advantage was clearly won by the Republicans. For every retrospective subgroup, respondents who were favorable toward the Republicans were more likely to report voting than those who were negative toward the GOP. Had these turnout differences been eliminated, Obama would have gained about one percentage point.

Clearly, then, in most elections higher turnout is unlikely to affect the outcome. There could be conditions in which turnout increases dramatically, but it is hard to imagine conditions under which turnout would surge among Democrats without also rising among Republicans. The 1928 contest provides an excellent example. In 1924 only 12.7 percent of the voting-age population voted for John W. Davis, the Democratic candidate, but in 1928, 21.1 percent voted for Democrat Alfred Smith. In 1924, 23.7 percent of the voting-age population voted for Republican Calvin Coolidge, but in 1928, 30.1 percent voted for the Republican candidate, Herbert Hoover (see Table 4-3).

Because in most presidential contests increased turnout would not have affected the outcome, some analysts might argue that low turnout does not matter. Moreover, some scholars have argued that in many elections the policy preferences of Americans who do not vote have been similar to those who do go to the polls. Thus, even if turnout has been low in postwar elections, in most of them voters have reflected the sentiments of the electorate as a whole.[99]

Despite this evidence, we do not accept the conclusion that low turnout is unimportant. We are especially concerned that turnout is low among the

disadvantaged. Some observers believe this is so because political leaders structure political alternatives in a way that provides disadvantaged Americans with
relatively little political choice. Frances Fox Piven and Richard A. Cloward, for
example, acknowledge that the policy preferences of voters and nonvoters are
similar, but they argue that this similarity exists because of the way that elites
have structured policy choices:

> Political attitudes would inevitably change over time if the allegiance of
> voters from the bottom became the object of partisan competition, for
> then politicians would be prodded to identify and articulate the griev-
> ances of and aspirations of the lower-income voters in order to win their
> support, thus helping to give form and voice to a distinctive political
> class.[100]

We cannot accept this argument either, mainly because it is highly speculative
and there is little evidence to support it. The difficulty in supporting this view
may in part stem from the nature of survey research itself because questions
about public policy are usually framed along lines of controversy as defined by
mainstream political leaders. Occasionally, however, surveys pose radical policy
alternatives, and they often ask open-ended questions that allow respondents to
state their own preferences. We find no concrete evidence that low turnout leads
American political leaders to ignore the policy preferences of the electorate.

Nevertheless, low turnout can scarcely be healthy for a democracy. Even if low
turnout seldom affects electoral outcomes, it may undermine the legitimacy of
elected political leaders. The existence of a large bloc of nonparticipants in the
electorate may be potentially dangerous because it means that many Americans
have weak ties to the established parties and political leaders. The prospects for
electoral instability and perhaps political instability thus increase.[101]

Does the low turnout of the American electorate provide clues about the
prospects for a partisan realignment? Low turnout in 1980 led scholars to question whether Reagan's victory presaged a pro-Republican realignment. As
Pomper pointed out at the time, "Elections that involve upheavals in party coalitions have certain hallmarks, such as popular enthusiasm."[102] In 2004 turnout
increased, and it increased again in 2008, but it was still well below the level
attained in other advanced industrialized democracies.

Past realignments have been characterized by increases in turnout. As Table
4-2 shows, turnout rose markedly between 1852 and 1860, a period during
which the Republican Party formed, replaced the Whigs, and gained the presidency. Turnout also rose in the Bryan-McKinley contest of 1896, generally
considered a realigning election (Table 4-2). And turnout rose markedly as
well after 1924, increasing in 1928 and again in 1936, a period that saw the
Democrats emerge as the majority party (see Table 4-3 and Figure 4-1).

The increase in turnout in 2004 gave Republicans hopes that the election heralded the beginning of GOP dominance. As Rhodes Cook wrote a few months after the 2004 election,

> Obviously it is much too soon to say whether the election of 2004 will be remembered as a watershed event, one that seals Republican dominance for a generation. But with its sky high turnout, it already suggests a different legacy. By galvanizing voters as no election in decades, it just might launch a whole new era in voter engagement in the political process.[103]

Turnout rose only modestly in 2008, but, according to the CPS data, it led to a modest increase in turnout among non-Hispanic blacks (up 4.9 percent), Hispanics (up 2.7 percent), and voters ages eighteen to twenty-nine (up 2.1 percent). And, as we will see, both the ANES data and the pool polls show that these groups all voted heavily for Obama. Nevertheless, turnout among Latinos and the young remained low, and it would be premature to say that the election mobilized new groups into the electorate.

Chapter 5

Social Forces and the Vote

More than 131 million Americans voted for president in 2008. Although voting is an individual act, group characteristics influence voting choices because individuals with similar social characteristics may share similar political interests. Group similarities in voting behavior may also reflect past political conditions. The partisan loyalties of African Americans, for example, were shaped by the Civil War; black loyalties to the Republican Party, the party of Lincoln, lasted through the 1932 election. The steady Democratic voting of southern whites, the product of those same historical conditions, lasted even longer, perhaps through 1960.

It is easy to see why group-based loyalties persist over time. Studies of pre-adult political learning suggest that partisan loyalties are often transmitted from generation to generation. And because religion, ethnicity, and, to a lesser extent, social class are often transmitted from generation to generation, social divisions have considerable staying power. Moreover, the interactions of social group members may reinforce similarities in political attitudes and behaviors.

Politicians often think in group terms. They recognize that to win an election they need to mobilize the social groups that often supported them in the past and that it may be helpful to cut into their opponents' bases of support. Democrats think in group terms more than Republicans because Democrats are a coalition of minorities. To win, Democrats usually need a high level of support from the social groups that have traditionally supported their broad-based coalition, which was formed by Franklin Roosevelt during the 1930s.

The 1992 election was unique, however. Bill Clinton earned high levels of support from only two of the groups that made up the New Deal coalition formed by Roosevelt—African Americans and Jews. Most of the other New Deal coalition groups gave fewer than half of their votes to Clinton. Fortunately for him, in a three-way contest (it included independent candidate Ross Perot) only 43 percent of the vote was needed to win. Despite a second candidacy by Perot, the 1996 election was much more of a two-candidate fight, and Clinton won 49 percent of the popular vote. He gained ground among the vast majority of groups analyzed in this chapter, making especially large gains among union members (a traditional component of the New Deal coalition) and Latinos. In many respects, the Democratic losses after 1964 can be attributed to the party's failure to hold the loyalties of the New Deal coalition groups. In winning in 1992 and 1996, Clinton only partly revitalized that coalition.

In 2000 Democrat Al Gore won only one percentage point less of the popular vote than Clinton had won in 1996, whereas Republican George W. Bush won seven points more than Bob Dole had won in 1996. Among most groups, Gore won about the same share of the vote as Clinton, but Bush won a larger share than Dole. As a result, group differences were smaller than in previous elections. In 2004 John Kerry made some gains among union members (and members of their families), and he may have made gains among Latinos, although the evidence here is mixed. Kerry's most striking failure was his inability to win majority support among white Catholics. He was only the third Catholic to be a major-party presidential nominee (the other two were Democrats Alfred Smith in 1928 and John Kennedy in 1960). But the ANES data show him winning only 49 percent of the vote among white Catholics.

HOW SOCIAL GROUPS VOTED IN 2008

Table 5-1 presents the results of our analysis of how social groups voted in the 2008 presidential election.[1] Among the 1,590 respondents who said they voted for president, 53.8 percent said they voted for Obama, 44.2 percent for McCain, and 2.0 percent for other candidates—results very close to the actual results (see Table 3-1). The American National Election Studies are the best source of data for analyzing change over time, but the total number of self-reported voters is small.[2] Therefore, we will often supplement our analysis with the pool polls conducted by Edison Research Media/Mitofsky International for a consortium of news organizations. For the 2008 polls, 17,836 voters were surveyed at three hundred polling places around the nation, and 2,378 telephone interviews were conducted with absentee and early voters. For the 2004 poll, 13,110 voters were interviewed as they left 250 polling places throughout the United States on election day, and five hundred telephone interviews were conducted with early voters.[3]

Race, Gender, Region, and Age

Political differences between African Americans and whites are far sharper than any other social cleavage.[4] According to the ANES survey, 99 percent of black voters supported Obama (Table 5-1), whereas the pool poll indicates that 95 percent did. Both surveys suggest that Obama did better among black voters than did Kerry, who won 88 percent of the black vote in 2004, according to both polls. Based on the ANES survey, we estimate that 23 percent of Obama's vote

TABLE 5-1　How Social Groups Voted for President, 2008 (percent)

Social group	Obama	McCain	Other	Total	(N)[a]
Total electorate	54	44	2	100	(1,590)
Electorate, by race					
African American	99	1	0	100	(196)
White	44	53	2	99	(1,277)
Other	79	18	4	101	(113)
Latino (of any race)	75	23	2	100	(118)
Whites, by gender					
Female	47	51	2	100	(732)
Male	41	56	3	100	(545)
Whites, by region					
New England and Mid-Atlantic	55	44	1	100	(169)
North Central	46	51	3	100	(279)
South	35	62	2	99	(470)
Border	13	87	0	100	(69)
Mountain and Pacific	59	39	1	99	(290)
Whites, by birth cohort					
Before 1940	35	65	c	100	(201)
1940–1954	43	54	2	99	(299)
1955–1962	39	56	5	100	(218)
1963–1970	46	54	0	100	(168)
1971–1978	48	49	3	100	(158)
1979–1986	57	40	3	100	(171)
1987–2000	58	42	0	100	(45)
Whites, by level of education					
Not high school graduate	57	43	0	100	(72)
High school graduate	46	54	1	101	(359)
Some college	42	55	3	100	(392)
College graduate	43	54	2	99	(312)
Advanced degree	43	53	4	100	(139)
Whites, by annual family income					
Less than $15,000	54	44	2	100	(50)
$15,000–34,999	59	39	1	99	(160)
$35,000–49,999	53	44	3	100	(118)
$50,000–74,999	44	54	2	100	(212)
$75,000–89,999	42	58	0	100	(108)
$90,000–119,999	38	60	2	100	(144)

(Continued)

TABLE 5-1   How Social Groups Voted for President, 2008 (percent) *(continued)*

Social group	Obama	McCain	Other	Total	(N)[a]
$120,000–149,999	30	70	0	100	(67)
$150,000 and over	20	78	1	99	(93)
Whites, by union membership[b]					
Member	52	46	2	100	(166)
Nonmember	43	54	2	99	(1,109)
Whites, by religion					
Jewish	84	16	0	100	(25)
Catholic	50	49	1	100	(261)
Protestant	35	63	2	100	(736)
None	62	35	3	100	(240)
White Protestants, by whether born again					
Not born again	49	47	4	101	(289)
Born again	25	74	1	100	(440)
White Protestants, by religious commitment					
Medium or low	49	48	3	100	(363)
High	28	70	3	101	(219)
Very high	10	88	2	100	(153)
White Protestants, by religious tradition					
Mainline	44	53	3	100	(200)
Evangelical	27	70	3	100	(283)

Source: Authors' analysis of the 2008 ANES survey.

[a] Numbers are weighted.

[b] Respondent or family member in union.

[c] Less than 1 percent.

came from blacks; our analysis of the pool poll suggests that 27 percent did. No Democratic presidential winner has ever received this large a share of his vote from the black electorate. Even in the three-candidate contest of 1992, when the white vote was split among three candidates, Clinton received only a fifth of his votes from blacks. This large black contribution to the Democrats in 2008 results from two factors: black turnout was the same as white turnout, and blacks voted overwhelmingly Democratic, equaling the black vote for two white Democrats, Lyndon Johnson in 1964 and Hubert Humphrey in 1968. Because only a handful of blacks voted for McCain, we cannot examine variation among black McCain voters.[5]

The ANES data suggest that Latinos (of any race) shifted toward the Democrats in 2008. In 2004 Kerry won 67 percent of the Latino vote, and in 2008 Obama won 75 percent—an eight percentage point difference. The pool polls show an even greater shift, with Kerry winning only 53 percent of the Latino vote and Obama winning 67 percent—a fourteen percentage point difference.[6] But then Latinos are not a homogeneous group.[7] For example, Cuban Americans in South Florida usually vote Republican. But there were too few Cuban Americans in the ANES survey to evaluate their behavior.[8]

Gender differences in voting behavior have been pronounced in some European societies, but they have been relatively weak in the United States.[9] Gender differences emerged in the 1980 election and have been found in every election since. According to the exit polls, the "gender gap" was eight percentage points in 1980, six points in 1984, seven points in 1988, four points in 1992, eleven points in 1996, twelve points in 2000, and seven points in 2004. According to the 2008 pool poll, 56 percent of women and 49 percent of men voted for Obama, a gap of seven points. Among white women, Obama received 46 percent of the vote; among white men he received 41 percent, for a gap of five points.

As the gender gap began to emerge, some feminists hoped that women would play a major role in defeating the Republicans. But as we pointed out more than two decades ago, a gender gap does not necessarily help the Democrats.[10] For example, in 1988 George H. W. Bush and Michael Dukakis each won half of the female vote, but Bush won a clear majority of the male vote. Thus Bush benefited from the gender gap in 1988. However, two decades later the role of gender was reversed, with Obama and McCain each winning half of the male vote, while Obama won a clear majority among women. By the same logic, then, Obama benefited from the gender gap. During the intervening elections, Clinton benefited from the gender gap in both 1992 and 1996, and George W. Bush benefited in 2000 and 2004.

As just noted, the 2008 ANES reveals a modest gender gap, because white women were five points more likely to vote for Obama than white men (Table 5-1). Among all voters in the ANES survey, 56 percent of women but only 51 percent of men voted for Obama, once again suggesting that Obama may have benefited from a gender gap.

In studying previous elections, we found that the gender gap was greatest among women with higher socioeconomic status, but this was not true in 2004. In 2008 the gap was actually greatest among the small number of white voters who had not graduated from high school, but it was also large among whites with advanced degrees. Among white women with advanced degrees ($N = 65$), 54 percent voted for Obama; among white men with advanced degrees ($N = 75$), only 33 percent did.

As for marital status, as in all of our analyses of ANES surveys between 1984 and 2004 we found clear differences between married women and single women.[11] Among all women voters who were married ($N = 462$), 47 percent voted for Obama; among those who were never married ($N = 194$), 74 percent did—a twenty-seven-point difference. In some years, the gap between married and single women has resulted largely from white women being about twice as likely as black women to be married. But the gap in 2008 had little to do with race. There was still a twenty-five-point gap between married white women and white women who had never been married. The marriage gap among men was substantially smaller. Among all men, married voters were nineteen points less likely to vote for Obama than men who had never been married, while among white men the difference was fifteen points.

Since the 2000 election, exit polls have shown that sexual orientation is related to the way people vote. In 2000, 70 percent of the respondents who said they were gay, lesbian, or bisexual voted for Gore; in 2004, 77 percent voted for Kerry; and in 2008, 70 percent voted for Obama. But in all three surveys, self-acknowledged homosexuals made up only 4 percent of the electorate.[12] In 2008 the ANES asked respondents their sexual orientation, and 5 percent said they were gay, lesbian, or bisexual.[13] Among homosexual or bisexual voters ($N = 79$), 79 percent voted for Obama.

As described in Chapter 3, in the 2008 election the political variation among states was greater than in any election since 1964. Regional differences were even greater among whites. If we overlook the very high level of Republican voting among the border states (in which the overall sample was small),[14] McCain did best in the South where he won 62 percent of the white vote; Obama won only 35 percent. In fact, Obama won a minority of the white vote in the three southern states he carried: 40 percent in Florida, 35 percent in North Carolina, and 39 percent in Virginia.[15]

Between Ronald Reagan's election in 1980 and Clinton's reelection in 1996, young voters were more likely to vote Republican than their elders, and the Democrats did best among Americans who came of age before World War II (born before 1924). This was not the case in the 2000 and 2004 elections. In both of these elections, the ANES surveys show Bush doing best among voters born between 1963 and 1970. These were the voters who entered the electorate in the 1980s, and who may have been influenced by the pro-Republican tide during the Reagan years. The one hopeful sign for the Democrats was that in both 2000 and 2004 they did best among the young, even though among young whites they gained just over half of the vote.

In 2008 Obama did especially well among young voters. According to the ANES surveys, Obama won 57 percent of the vote among whites born between 1979 and 2000 (that is, those between the ages of eighteen and twenty-nine). The pool poll shows a strong shift toward the Democrats among young voters. In 2004, 54 percent of voters between the ages of eighteen and twenty-nine voted for Kerry; in 2008, 66 percent voted for Obama. The 2008 pool poll reveals that McCain prevailed only among voters sixty-five and over, and even among these voters he won only 53 percent of the vote. According to Chuck Todd and Sheldon Gawiser, "The consistent growth in the margins among the youth vote over the last eight years is one of the best signs for the Democratic Party in terms of their push for realignment."[16]

Social Class, Education, Income, and Union Membership

Traditionally, the Democratic Party has fared well among the relatively disadvantaged. It has done better among the working class, voters with lower levels of formal education, and the poor. Moreover, since the 1930s most union leaders have supported the Democratic Party, and union members have been a mainstay of the Democratic presidential coalition. We are not able to measure social class differences using the 2008 ANES because the occupational codes we use to classify respondents as working class (manually employed) and middle class (nonmanually employed) were not available at the time of this writing. But we do have substantial evidence that class differences as defined by occupation have been declining—a trend found in other advanced democracies.[17]

In his victories in 1992 and 1996, Clinton clearly fared better among the poor than among the affluent. The relationship between income and voting preferences was weak and inconsistent in 2000. In the 2004 ANES survey, the relationship between family income and the vote was once again relatively weak, although whites with an annual family income of $50,000 and above were more likely to vote for Bush. The pool poll found a consistent tendency for the more affluent to vote Republican in 2004, although a national exit poll sponsored by the *Los Angeles Times* revealed a very weak relationship between income and voting preferences.[18]

In 2008, however, the ANES data reveal a sharp relationship between the respondent's family income and voting choice. As Table 5-1 shows, among whites with annual family incomes below $50,000 a majority voted for Obama. In all income groups above that level, a majority voted for McCain. Moreover, among whites with family incomes of $150,000 and above, over three in four voted Republican. The relationship between income and vote choice in the pool poll was much weaker. As in the ANES data, a majority of respondents (of all races) with annual family incomes below $50,000 voted for Obama, but McCain split the vote with Obama with higher-income groups. Even among voters with family incomes of $200,000 and above, McCain prevailed over Obama by only 52 percent to 46 percent. The pool poll results provide little support for scholars such as Jeffrey M. Stonecash and Larry M. Bartels who argue that voting differences according to income have been growing.[19]

In 1992 and 1996, Clinton fared best among whites who had not graduated from high school, whereas both George H. W. Bush and Bob Dole fared best among whites who were college graduates (but without advanced degrees). In 1992 Clinton won over half of the major-party vote among whites with advanced degrees, and in 1996 he won almost half the major-party vote among this group. In 2000 there was a weaker relationship between education and voting preferences. In 2004 Kerry did best among whites in the highest and lowest educational categories. The 2004 pool poll also revealed the same pattern, with Kerry winning half the vote among whites who were not high school graduates and 55 percent among those with some postgraduate education.

As Table 5-1 reveals, however, the 2008 ANES survey found only a weak relationship between level of education and the vote among whites. Moreover, the only educational group among which Obama won a majority of the vote was the small number who had not graduated from high school. The pool poll, however, shows a different relationship, albeit with no controls for race. Obama won 63 percent of the vote among those who had not graduated from high school. The only other group handing him a clear majority of the vote (58 percent) was voters with postgraduate education.

Some scholars of American politics such as Walter Dean Burnham and Everett Carll Ladd Jr. argue that the Democrats now tend to fare better among the upper and lower socioeconomic groups.[20] All of the major exit polls from 1988 to 2008 found that respondents who were not high school graduates and those with postgraduate education were the most likely to vote Democratic.[21] The Democrats may be appealing to disadvantaged Americans because of their party's economic policies and to better-educated Americans—especially better-educated women—because they may reject the interpretation of traditional values that the Republicans have emphasized in recent elections.

According to the ANES surveys, Clinton made major gains among white union households between 1992 and 1996. But the 2000 ANES survey shows that Gore slipped twelve percentage points from Clinton's 1996 total, while George W. Bush gained sixteen points over Dole's. The 2004 ANES survey shows that Bush made no gains among union households, but gained six points among nonunion households. Exit polls show similar results for 2000 and 2004. According to the pool poll, voters who were in union households gave 59 percent of their votes to Kerry, but of those who were not, only 44 percent did—results that are very similar to the 2000 Voter News Service (VNS) exit poll. And the 2004 *Los Angeles Times* poll yielded results very close to the pool poll.

The 2008 ANES survey shows a five-point loss for the Democrats among white union households, but a seven-point gain among nonunion households. According to the 2008 pool poll, Obama received the same share of the union vote as Kerry (59 percent), whereas Democratic support among nonunion households rose from 44 percent in 2004 to 51 percent in 2008.[22]

Religion

Religious differences, partly reflecting ethnic differences between Protestants and Catholics, have long played a major role in American politics.[23] Catholics have tended to support the Democrats, and white Protestants, especially outside the South, have tended to favor the Republicans. Throughout the postwar years, Jews have consistently voted more Democratic than any other major religious group. In 2008, according to the ANES, over four in five Jews voted for Obama, but the number of Jews sampled is too small to be meaningful (Table 5-1). However, the pool poll, based on a much larger sample, shows a similar result: nearly four in five Jews voted for Obama.

In the 2008 election, white Catholics split evenly between Obama and McCain, but more than three in five white Protestants voted for McCain (Table 5-1). These results are similar to the ANES results in 2004. The pool poll shows a similar result for white Protestants, because in both years about two in three voted Republican. By contrast, the pool poll suggests that white Catholics may have shifted slightly toward the Democrats. In 2004, 43 percent voted for Kerry; in 2008, 47 percent voted for Obama.

Although the Republican Party has been successful among white Protestants, it has been more successful among some than others. The Republican emphasis on traditional values may have special appeal to Protestants who share them. Bush's policies such as limiting funding for embryonic stem cell research, calling for an amendment to the U.S. Constitution to ban same-sex marriage, and appointing conservatives to the federal courts may have appealed to Christian conservatives. But McCain had not shown a commitment to these values throughout his career, and even though he had embraced an antiabortion position, he had not adopted all the policies favored by social conservatives. He favored embryonic stem cell research and opposed an amendment to the U.S. Constitution to ban same-sex marriage because he believed that marriage was an issue that should be determined by the states. Social conservatives were, however, enthusiastic about his running mate, Sarah Palin, who took positions on social issues more similar to Bush's.

We focus here on differences among white Protestants. For example, for the 1992, 1996, and 2000 ANES surveys we examined differences between white Protestants who said they were "born again" and those who had not had this religious experience.[24] In all three surveys, white born-again Protestants were more likely to vote Republican than those who were not. This relationship was also found in 2008. Nearly half the white Protestants who said they had not had this religious experience voted for Obama; among those who said they were born again, only one in four did.

As we noted in Chapter 4, Lyman A. Kellstedt argues that religious commitment has an important effect on voting behavior.[25] Table 5-1 reveals that among white Protestants with very high levels of religious commitment nearly nine in ten voted for McCain. Among those with medium or low levels of commitment, McCain won just about half the vote. The variation in the percentage voting for McCain is impressive when one considers that we are looking at a subset of the electorate that is already predisposed to vote Republican because it is both white and Protestant. As Table 5-1 shows, 63 percent of all white Protestants voted for McCain, and yet there is still a thirty-nine-point difference between Protestants with very high or high levels of religious commitment and those with medium or low levels.

Morris P. Fiorina and his colleagues have pointed out that ANES surveys suggest that the relationship between church attendance and the tendency to vote Republican was substantially higher in 1992 than in 1972, although the relationship leveled off or declined slightly between 1992 and 2004.[26] Both the pool poll and the *Los Angeles Times* poll indicate that in 2004 church attendance was strongly related to the vote. And the pool poll suggests that the relationship between church attendance and the vote may have increased somewhat in 2008. Among voters who said they never attended church, 67 percent voted for Obama, while among those who attended weekly and those who attended more than once a week, only 43 percent did.[27]

Our analyses of the 1992, 1996, 2000, and 2004 ANES surveys reveal that white evangelical Protestants were more likely to vote Republican than white mainline Protestants. And this was true once again in 2008. By contrast, the pool poll conflates being "born again" with being evangelical. Among white Protestants who were born again or evangelical, seven in ten voted for McCain, while among those who did not fall into one of these categories, just over half did. This was about the same relationship found in the 2004 pool poll.

HOW SOCIAL GROUPS VOTED DURING THE POSTWAR YEARS

How does the 2008 election compare with other presidential elections? Do the relationships between social variables and the vote found in 2008 result from long-term trends that have changed the importance of social factors? To answer these questions, we will examine the voting behavior of social groups that have been an important part of the Democratic coalition during the postwar years. Our analysis, which will begin with the 1944 election between Roosevelt and Thomas Dewey, uses a simple measure to assess the effect of social forces.

In his lucid discussion of the logic of party coalitions, Robert Axelrod analyzed six basic groups that made up the Democratic coalition: the poor, southerners, blacks (and other nonwhites), union members (and members of their families), Catholics and other non-Protestants such as Jews, and residents of the twelve largest metropolitan areas.[28] John R. Petrocik's more comprehensive study identified fifteen coalition groups and classified seven of them as predominantly Democratic: blacks, lower-status native southerners, middle- and upper-status southerners, Jews, Polish and Irish Catholics, union members, and lower-status border state whites.[29] A more recent analysis by Harold W. Stanley, William T. Bianco, and Richard G. Niemi analyzes seven pro-Democratic groups: blacks, Catholics, Jews, women, native white southerners, members of union households, and the working class.[30] Our own analysis focuses on race, region, union membership, social class, and religion.[31]

The contribution that a social group can make to a party's coalition depends on three factors: the relative size of the group in the total electorate, its level of turnout compared with that of the total electorate, and its relative loyalty to the political party.[32] The larger a social group, the greater its contribution can be. African Americans make up 12 percent of the electorate; the white working class makes up about 30 percent. Thus the potential contribution of blacks is smaller than that of the white working class. In most elections, the electoral power of blacks has been limited by their relatively low turnout. However, because blacks

FIGURE 5-1 Major-Party Voters Who Voted Democratic for President, by Race, 1944–2008 (percent)

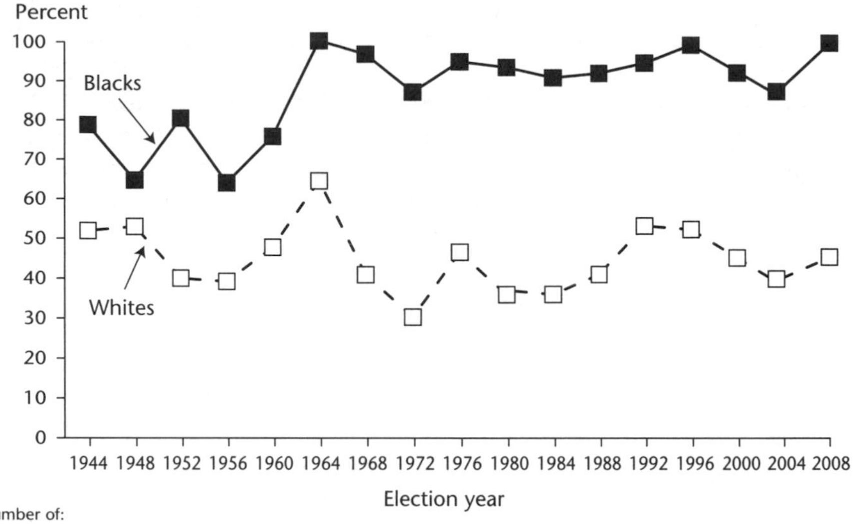

Number of:

	1944	1948	1952	1956	1960	1964	1968	1972	1976	1980	1984	1988	1992	1996	2000	2004	2008
Blacks	(52)	(17)	(51)	(50)	(75)	(94)	(87)	(138)	(133)[a]	(105)	(129)	(122)	(188)[a]	(102)[a]	(123)[a]	(111)[a]	(196)[a]
Whites	(1,564)	(364)	(1,257)	(1,253)	(1,340)[a]	(1,104)	(816)	(1,430)	(1,459)[a]	(765)	(1,220)	(1,041)	(1,134)[a]	(900)[a]	(851)[a]	(595)[a]	(1,250)[a]

Source: Authors' analysis of a 1944 NORC survey and ANES surveys.

[a] Number is weighted.

vote overwhelmingly Democratic, their contribution to the Democratic Party can be greater than their group size would indicate. And the relative size of their contribution grows as whites desert the Democratic Party.

Race

We begin by examining racial differences, which we can trace back to 1944 by using the National Opinion Research Center (NORC) study for that year.[33] Figure 5-1 shows the percentages of white and black major-party voters who voted Democratic for president from 1944 to 2008. (All six figures in this chapter are based on major-party voters.) Although most African Americans voted Democratic from 1944 to 1960, a substantial minority voted Republican. However, the political mobilization of blacks spurred by the civil rights movement and by the Republican candidacy of Barry Goldwater in 1964 ended that Republican voting, and the residual Republican loyalties of older blacks were discarded between 1962 and 1964.[34]

Although the Democrats made substantial gains among blacks, they lost ground among whites. From 1944 to 1964, the Democrats gained a majority of the white vote in three of six elections. Since then, they have never won a majority of the white vote. However, in a two-candidate contest a Democrat can win with just under half the white vote, as the 1960, 1976, and 2008 elections demonstrate. In the three-candidate contests of 1992 and 1996, Clinton was able to win with only about two-fifths of the white vote.[35]

The gap between the two trend lines in Figure 5-1 illustrates the overall difference in the Democratic vote between whites and blacks. Table 5-2 shows the overall level of "racial voting" in the six elections from 1944 to 1964, as well as four other measures of social cleavage.

From 1944 to 1964, racial differences in voting ranged from a low of twelve percentage points to a high of forty points. These differences then rose to fifty-six percentage points in 1968 (sixty-one points if Wallace voters are included with Nixon voters), and did not fall to the forty percentage point level until 1992.[36] Racial voting was higher in the 1996, 2000, and 2004 contests, but higher still in 2008, when there was a fifty-four percentage point gap between blacks and whites. This was the highest level of racial voting in any election that the Democratic candidate had won.

Not only did African American loyalty to the Democratic Party increase sharply after 1960, but black turnout rose markedly from 1960 to 1968 because southern blacks were reenfranchised. And while black turnout rose, white turn-out outside the South declined. Between 1960, when overall turnout was highest, and 1996, when postwar turnout was lowest, turnout fell by about fifteen per-centage points among the voting-age population. Even though black turnout fell in 1996, it was still well above its levels before the Voting Rights Act of 1965.[37] Since then, turnout has been rising, although, as we saw in Chapter 4, turnout among the voting-age population is still substantially lower than it was in 1960 and somewhat lower among the voting-eligible population. In the 2008 election, turnout clearly rose among blacks, whereas it changed very little among whites. Both the ANES and the Current Population Survey indicate that in 2008 the black turnout was only one percentage point lower than white turnout.

From 1948 to 1960, African Americans never accounted for more than one Democratic vote in twelve. In 1964, however, Johnson received about one in seven of his votes from blacks, and blacks contributed a fifth of the Democratic totals in both 1968 and 1972. In the 1976 election, which saw Democratic gains among whites, Jimmy Carter won only about one in seven of his votes from blacks, and in 1980 one in four. In the next three elections, about one in five Democratic votes were from blacks. In 1996 about one in six of Clinton's votes came from black voters, and in 2000 about one in five of Gore's votes did. In 2004 between a fifth and a fourth of Kerry's total vote was provided by black voters. Both Gore and Kerry came very close to winning, even with this heavy reliance on African American vot-ers. As we pointed out earlier in this chapter, black voters accounted for about one-fourth of Obama's total vote. And, as we noted, no Democratic presidential winner had ever drawn this large a share of his total vote from these voters.

Region

White southerners' desertion of the Democratic Party has been the most dramatic change in postwar American politics. As we saw in Chapter 3, regional differences

TABLE 5-2   Relationship of Social Characteristics to Presidential Voting, 1944–2008

								Election year (percentage point difference)									
	1944	1948	1952	1956	1960	1964	1968	1972	1976	1980	1984	1988	1992	1996	2000	2004	2008
Racial voting[a]	27	12	40	25	23	36	56	57	48	56	54	51	41	47	47	49	54
Regional voting[b]																	
Among whites	—	—	12	17	6	−11	−4	−13	1	1	−9	−5	−10	−8	−20	−10	−14
Among entire electorate (ANES surveys)	—	—	9	15	4	−5	6	−3	7	3	3	2	0	0	−10	1	−11
Among entire electorate (official election results)	23	14	8	8	3	−13	−3	−11	5	2	−5	−7	−6	−7	−8	−8	−10
Union voting[c]																	
Among whites	20	37	18	15	21	23	13	11	18	15	20	16	12	23	12	21	8
Among entire electorate	20	37	20	17	19	22	13	10	17	16	19	15	11	23	11	18	6
Class voting[d]																	
Among whites	19	44	20	8	12	19	10	2	17	9	8	5	4	6	−6	3	—
Among entire electorate	20	44	22	11	13	20	15	4	21	15	12	8	8	9	2	4	—

(Continued)

TABLE 5-2 Relationship of Social Characteristics to Presidential Voting, 1944–2008 (*continued*)

	Election year (percentage point difference)																
	1944	1948	1952	1956	1960	1964	1968	1972	1976	1980	1984	1988	1992	1996	2000	2004	2008
Religious voting[e]																	
Among whites	25	21	18	10	48	21	30	13	15	10	16	18	20	14	8	19	15
Among entire electorate	24	19	15	10	46	16	21	8	11	3	9	11	10	7	2	5	9

Sources: Authors' analysis of a 1944 NORC survey, official election results, and ANES surveys.

Notes: All calculations are based upon major-party voters. — indicates not available.

[a] Percentage of blacks who voted Democratic minus percentage of whites who voted Democratic.

[b] Percentage of southerners who voted Democratic minus percentage of voters outside the South who voted Democratic. Comparable data for region were not available for the surveys conducted in 1944 and 1948.

[c] Percentage of members of union households who voted Democratic minus percentage of members of households with no union members who voted Democratic.

[d] Percentage of working class that voted Democratic minus percentage of middle class that voted Democratic. The data for occupation needed to classify respondents according to their social class for 2008 were not available as of this writing.

[e] Percentage of Catholics who voted Democratic minus the percentage of Protestants who voted Democratic.

FIGURE 5-2   White Major-Party Voters Who Voted Democratic for President, by Region, 1952–2008 (percent)

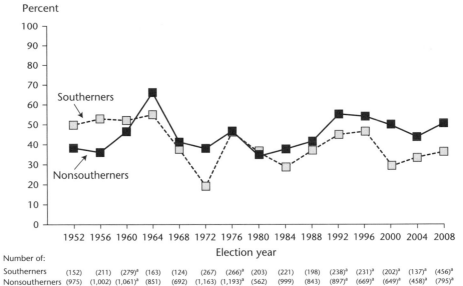

Source: Authors' analysis of ANES surveys.

[a] Number is weighted.

can be analyzed using official election statistics, but these statistics are of limited use in examining race-related differences in regional voting because election results are not tabulated by race. However, we are able to rely on survey data to document the dramatic shift in voting behavior among white southerners.

As the data in Figure 5-2 reveal, white southerners were somewhat more Democratic than whites outside the South in the 1952 and 1956 contests between Dwight Eisenhower and Adlai Stevenson and in the 1960 contest between John Kennedy and Richard Nixon.[38] But in the next three elections, regional differences were reversed, with white southerners voting more Republican than whites outside the South. In 1976 and 1980, when the Democrats fielded Jimmy Carter of Georgia as their standard-bearer, white southerners and whites outside the South were very much alike. In 1984 and 1988, white southerners were less likely to vote Democratic than whites from any other region. In 1992 and 1996, Bill Clinton and his running mate, Al Gore, were both from the South. Even so, George H. W. Bush in 1992 and Bob Dole in 1996 did better among white southerners than among whites from any other region.[39] In 2000 the Democrats ran Al Gore, a southern presidential candidate, with Joseph Lieberman of Connecticut as his running mate. The Republican candidate, George W. Bush, the governor of Texas, was also a southerner, and his running mate, Dick Cheney, who had become a resident of Texas, moved back to

Wyoming to reestablish his residence.[40] In 2004 the Democrats ran John Kerry, the junior senator from Massachusetts, although John Edwards, his running mate, was from North Carolina. But in both these contests, the Democratic vote in the South was low, and the Democrats did substantially better outside the South. In Obama's 2008 victory, in which neither party ran a southerner on its ticket, the Democrats made gains among both white southerners and among whites outside the South. But, as Figure 5-2 shows, the Democrats did substantially better outside the South.

Regional differences among whites from 1952 to 2008 are summarized in Table 5-2. The negative signs for 1964, 1968, 1972, and 1984–2008 reveal that the Democratic candidate fared better outside the South than he did in the South. As we saw in Chapter 3, in 1968 Wallace had a strong regional base in the South. If we include Wallace voters with Nixon voters, regional differences change markedly, moving from –4 to –12.

Table 5-2 also presents regional differences for the entire electorate. Here, however, we present two sets of estimates: (1) the ANES results from 1952 to 2008, and (2) the results we computed using official election statistics. Both sets of statistics indicate that regional differences have been reversed, but these results are often different, and in many cases would lead to substantially different conclusions. The 2004 election provides a clear example. According to the 2004 ANES survey, voters in the South were as likely to vote Democratic as voters outside the South. But we know that this result is wrong. After all, Bush won all the southern states, whereas Kerry won nineteen states outside the South, as well as the District of Columbia. In fact, the official statistics show that southerners were eight points more likely to vote Republican than voters outside the South. The ANES results are based on eight hundred voters, whereas the official results are based on 122 million voters. And it is obvious that the latter are correct. This should remind us of a basic caution in studying elections: always turn to the actual election results before turning to the survey data.

Surveys are useful in demonstrating the way in which the mobilization of southern blacks and the defection of southern whites from the Democratic Party dramatically transformed the Democratic coalition in the South.[41] According to our analysis of ANES surveys, between 1952 and 1960 Democratic presidential candidates never received more than one in fifteen of their votes in the South from blacks. In 1964 three in ten of Johnson's southern votes came from black voters, and in 1968 Hubert Humphrey received as many votes from southern blacks as from southern whites. In 1972, according to these data, George McGovern received more votes from southern blacks than from southern whites.

Blacks were crucial to Carter's success in the South in 1976; he received about a third of his support from African Americans. Even though he won ten of the eleven southern states, he won a majority of the white vote only in his home state of Georgia and possibly in Arkansas. In 1980 Carter again received about a third of his southern support from blacks. In 1984 Walter Mondale received about four in ten of his southern votes from blacks, and in 1988 one in three of the votes Michael Dukakis received came from black voters. In 1992 and 1996, Clinton won about a third of his southern support from African Americans. In 2000 four in ten of the southern votes Gore received came from blacks. A southern running mate helped Kerry very little among southern whites in 2004. According to the ANES survey, about half of Kerry's votes in the South came from blacks.

Our analysis of the 2008 ANES survey indicates that about a third of Obama's votes in the South came from black voters. And blacks were crucial to the three southern states he carried, because he won a minority of the white vote in those states. Our calculations based on exit polls in these states reveal that about a fifth of his votes in Florida, over two-fifths of his votes in North Carolina, and a third of his votes in Virginia were cast by black voters.[42]

Union Membership

In Figure 5-3 we show the percentage of white union members and nonmembers who voted Democratic for president from 1944 to 2008. In all six elections between 1944 and 1964, the majority of white union members (and members of their households) voted Democratic. In 1968, Humphrey won a slight majority of the union vote, although his total would be cut to 43 percent if Wallace voters were included. The Democrats won about three-fifths of the union vote in 1976, when Jimmy Carter defeated Gerald Ford. In 1988 Dukakis appears to have won a slight majority of the white union vote, although he fell well short of Carter's 1976 tally. In 1992 Clinton won three-fifths of the major-party union vote and won nearly half the total union vote. In 1996 the ANES data show him making major gains and winning 70 percent of the major-party vote among union members. In 2000 Gore won a majority of the union vote, but he was well below Clinton's 1996 tally. In 2004 Kerry did slightly better than Gore among white union voters, but Bush did somewhat better among nonmembers. Because there are more nonmembers than members, this shift worked to Bush's advantage. But as we have noted, the 2008 ANES survey shows Obama losing slightly among white union members while gaining among nonmembers, obviously a net benefit for the Democrats.

Differences in presidential voting between union members and nonmembers are presented in Table 5-2. Because in 1968 Wallace did better among union members than nonmembers, including Wallace voters with Nixon voters reduces union voting from thirteen percentage points to ten points. Union voting was highest in 1948, a year when Truman's opposition to the Taft-Hartley Act gained him strong union support.[43] Union voting was low in 1992 and 2000, when white union members were only slightly more likely to vote Democratic than nonmembers. Because Bush did better among nonmembers in 2004, the differences between members and nonmembers rose to twenty-one points. However, differences between members and nonmembers were sharply reduced in 2008, reaching the lowest level in any of these seventeen elections. Table 5-2 also shows the results for the entire electorate, but because

FIGURE 5-3   White Major-Party Voters Who Voted Democratic for President, by
Union Membership, 1944–2008 (percent)

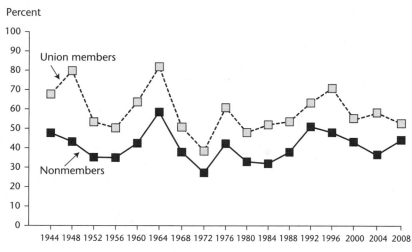

Number of:

Union members[a]	(332)	(94)	(305)	(334)	(342)[c]	(259)	(197)	(366)	(347)[c]	(193)	(278)	(209)	(207)[c]	(175)[c]	(141)[c]	(133)[c]	(163)[c]
Nonmembers[b]	(1,215)	(226)	(815)	(877)	(979)[c]	(775)	(617)	(1,049)	(1,099)[c]	(569)	(941)	(828)	(925)[c]	(723)[c]	(706)[c]	(461)[c]	(1,095)[c]

Source: Authors' analysis of a 1944 NORC survey and ANES surveys.

[a] Union member or in household with union member.
[b] Not a union member and not in household with union member.
[c] Number is weighted.

blacks are about as likely to live in union households as whites, including blacks has little effect.

The percentage of the total electorate composed of white union members and their families has declined during the postwar years. White union members and their families made up 25 percent of the electorate in 1952; in 2008, according to the ANES survey, they made up only 13 percent. Turnout among white union members has declined at about the same rate as turnout among nonunion whites. In addition, in many elections since 1964 the Democratic share of the union vote has been relatively low. All of these factors, as well as increased turnout by blacks, have reduced the contribution of white union members to the Democratic presidential coalition. Through 1960, a third of the total union vote came from white union members and their families; between 1964 and 1984 only about one Democratic vote in four; in 1988, 1992, and 1996 only about one Democratic vote in five; and in 2000 only about one Gore vote in six. In 2004, with a drop in Democratic support among whites who did not live in union households, the share of Kerry's vote from union households rose back to one vote in five. The 2008 ANES survey shows that only 10 percent of Obama's votes came from members of a white union household. Although this percentage may

FIGURE 5-4   White Major-Party Voters Who Voted Democratic for President, by Social Class, 1944–2004 (percent)

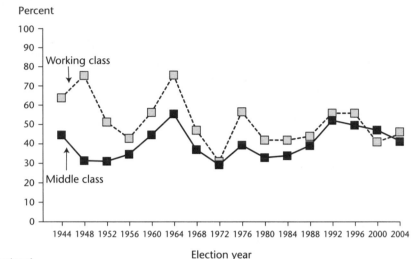

Number of:

Working class	(597)	(134)	(462)	(531)	(579)[a]	(425)	(295)	(587)	(560)[a]	(301)	(473)	(350)	(393)[a]	(279)[a]	(224)[a]	(149)[a]
Middle class	(697)	(137)	(437)	(475)	(561)[a]	(454)	(385)	(675)	(716)[a]	(376)	(634)	(589)	(569)[a]	(507)[a]	(540)[a]	(379)[a]

Source: Authors' analysis of a 1944 NORC survey and ANES surveys.

[a] Number is weighted.

well be too low, there is no doubt that the contribution of union members to the Democratic presidential coalition has declined.[44]

Social Class

The broad social cleavage between manually employed workers (and their dependents) and nonmanually employed workers (and their dependents) is especially valuable for studying comparative behavior.[45] For this reason, we present the results of our analysis in Figure 5-4, even though we are not yet able to analyze the ANES results for 2008. The figure shows the percentage of white major-party voters who voted Democratic among the working class and the middle class in all the presidential elections between 1944 and 2004.

In all fourteen presidential elections between 1944 and 1996, the white working class voted more Democratic than the white middle class. But as Figure 5-4 shows, the percentage of white working-class voters who voted Democratic has varied considerably from election to election. It reached its lowest level in 1972 during the Nixon-McGovern contest. Carter regained a majority of the white working-class vote class in 1976, but he lost it four years later. In 1992 Clinton won only two-fifths of the vote among working-class whites, although he did win a clear majority of the major-party vote. In 1996 he won half of the working-class vote and a clear majority of the major-party vote. In 2000 Gore won only two-fifths of the vote among working-class whites, and 2000 is the only election during these years in which the Democratic presidential candidate did better among middle-class whites than among working-class whites. According to the ANES data, Kerry did somewhat better in 2004, and Bush did somewhat worse. Even so, the data suggest that Kerry fell short of a majority.

Although levels of class voting have varied over the last six decades, they have clearly followed a downward trend, as Table 5-2 reveals.[46] Class voting was even lower in 1968 if Wallace voters are included with Nixon voters, because 15 percent of white working-class voters supported Wallace, while only 10 percent of white middle-class voters did. Class voting was very low in 1972, mainly because many white working-class voters deserted McGovern. Only in 2000 do we find class voting to be negative.[47]

Class voting trends are affected substantially if African Americans are included in the analysis. Blacks are disproportionately working class, and they vote overwhelmingly Democratic. In all the elections between 1976 and 1996, class voting is higher when blacks (and other nonwhites) are included in the analysis. In 2000 class voting is positive (although very low) when blacks are included in our calculations. In 2004 class voting is only one point higher. The overall trend toward declining class voting is somewhat dampened when blacks are included. However, black workers vote Democratic because they are black, not because they are working class. In 2004 middle-class blacks were more likely to vote for Kerry than working-class blacks. Obviously, there was no relationship between social class and voting choice among blacks in 2008 because 99 percent of blacks voted Democratic.[48]

During the postwar years, the proportion of the electorate made up of working-class whites has remained relatively constant, while that of the middle class has grown. The percentage of whites in the agricultural sector has declined dramatically. Turnout fell among both the middle and working classes after 1960, but it fell more among the working class. Declining turnout and defections from the Democratic Party by working-class whites, along with increased turnout by blacks, have reduced the total white working-class contribution to the Democratic presidential coalition.

In 1948 and 1952, about half the Democratic vote came from working-class whites, and from 1956 through 1964 this social group supplied more than four in ten Democratic votes. Its contribution fell to just over a third in 1968 and then to under a third in 1972. In 1976, with the rise in class voting, the white working class provided nearly two-fifths of Carter's total, but it provided just over a third four years later in Carter's reelection bid. In 1984 over a third of Mondale's total support came from this group, and in 1988 Dukakis received more than two in five of his votes from this group. In both 1992 and 1996, working-class whites provided three in ten votes of Clinton's total, but in 2000 this group accounted for only about a fifth of Gore's votes. In 2004, with a drop in middle-class support for the Democratic candidate, Kerry received just under a fourth of his vote from working-class whites.

The white middle-class contribution to the Democratic presidential coalition amounted to fewer than three in ten votes in 1948 and 1952, and just under one-third in 1956, stabilizing at just over one-third in the next five elections. In 1984 Mondale received just under two in five of his votes from middle-class whites, and in 1988 Dukakis received more than two in five. In 1992 more than two in five of Clinton's total votes came from this group, rising to a half in 1996. In 2000 Gore received two-fifths of his total vote from middle-class whites, and in 2004 Kerry received just over two-fifths. In all of the elections between 1984 and 2004, the Democrats received a larger share of their vote from middle-class whites than from working-class whites. The increasing middle-class contribution stems from two factors: (1) the middle class is growing, and (2) class differences are eroding. The decline in class differences is a widespread phenomenon in advanced industrialized societies.[49]

Of course, our argument that class-based voting is declining depends on the way in which we have defined social class. Different definitions may yield different results. For example, in a major study depending on a far more complex definition that divides the electorate into seven social categories, Jeff Manza and Clem Brooks, using ANES data from 1952 to 1996, conclude that class differences are still important.[50] But their findings actually support our conclusion that the New Deal coalition has eroded. For example, they found that professionals were the most Republican class in the 1950s, but that by the 1996 election they had become the most Democratic.

Religion

Voting differences among major religious groups have also declined during the postwar years. Even so, as Figure 5-5 reveals, in every election since 1944 Jews have been more likely to vote Democratic than Catholics, and Catholics have been more likely to vote Democratic than Protestants.[51]

As Figure 5-5 shows, a large majority of Jews voted Democratic in every election from 1944 to 1968, and although the percentage declined in Nixon's landslide over McGovern in 1972, even McGovern won a majority of the Jewish vote. In 1980 many Jews (like many Gentiles) were dissatisfied with Carter's performance as president, and some resented the pressure he had exerted on Israel to accept the Camp David Accords, which returned the Sinai Peninsula— captured by Israel in 1967—to Egypt. A substantial minority of Jews supported third-party candidate John Anderson that year, but Carter still outpolled Reagan. Both Mondale in 1984 and Dukakis (whose wife, Kitty, is Jewish) in 1988 won a clear majority of the Jewish vote. The Jewish Democratic vote surged in 1992, with Clinton winning nine in ten major-party voters. With Lieberman, an observant Jew, as his running mate, Gore, too, won overwhelming Jewish support in 2000. Bush was strongly pro-Israel in his foreign policy, but Kerry did win solid support among Jewish voters, although there may have been some Republican gains. In 2008 some Jews may have had reservations about Obama's

FIGURE 5-5   White Major-Party Voters Who Voted Democratic for President, by Religion, 1944–2008 (percent)

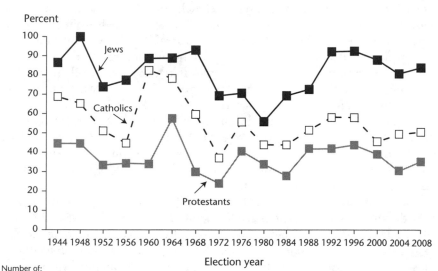

Source: Authors' analysis of a 1944 NORC survey and ANES surveys.

[a] Number is weighted.

commitment to Israel's security, but even so he may have made slight gains among Jewish voters.

A majority of white Catholics voted Democratic in six of the seven elections from 1944 to 1968. The percentage of Catholics voting Democratic surged in 1960, when the Democrats fielded a Catholic candidate, John Kennedy, but it was still very high in Johnson's landslide four years later.[52] In 1968 a majority of white Catholics voted Democratic, although Humphrey's total is reduced from 60 percent to 55 percent if Wallace voters are included. In 1976 Carter won a majority among white Catholics, but the Democrats did not win a majority of the major-party vote among white Catholics again until 1992. In his 1996 reelection, Clinton again won over half of the major-party vote among white Catholics. Four years later, George W. Bush outpolled Al Gore among white Catholics. Even in 2004, when the Democrats ran a Catholic presidential candidate, Bush outscored Kerry among white Catholic voters. Figure 5-5 and Table 5-1 show that Obama won half the vote among white Catholics, although, as we noted earlier, he won slightly less than half in the pool poll. But both polls show Obama doing better among white Catholics than among white Protestants.

Our measure of religious voting shows considerable change from election to election, although there was a downward trend from 1968 to 2000, when religious differences reached their lowest level. Religious differences were somewhat higher in both 2004 and 2008 (see Table 5-2). Even though white Protestants were more likely than white Catholics to vote for Wallace in 1968, including Wallace voters in our total has little effect on religious voting (it falls from thirty points to twenty-nine points). Religious differences were small in the 1980 Reagan-Carter contest, but since then they have varied. Because most Latinos are white Catholics, religious voting may rise in future elections.

Including African Americans in our calculations reduces religious voting. Blacks are much more likely to be Protestant than Catholic, and including blacks in our calculations adds a substantial number of Protestant Democrats. In 2008, for example, religious voting is reduced from fifteen points to nine points when blacks (and other nonwhites) are included.

The Jewish contribution to the Democratic Party has declined, in part because Jews did not vote overwhelmingly Democratic in 1972, 1980, 1984, 1988, and 2004, and in part because Jews make up a small and declining share of the electorate. During the 1950s, Jews were about a twentieth of the electorate. But the most recent estimates suggest that only about one American in fifty is Jewish.[53]

Although Jews make up only about 2 percent of the population, three-fourths of the nation's Jews live in seven large states—New York, California, Florida, New Jersey, Pennsylvania, Illinois, and Massachusetts—which together had 182 electoral votes in 2004 and 2008.[54] More important, two of these states are battleground states: Florida, where Jews make up 3.6 percent of the population, and Pennsylvania, where they make up 2.3 percent. Because exit polls suggest that Jews made up 4 percent of the Florida electorate, and because Obama won the state by only 2.2 percentage points, Jews may have provided enough votes to swing the Sunshine State toward Obama. Overall, however, the electoral significance of Jews is lessened because five of these large states are not battleground states. For example, Jews make up 8.4 percent of the population in New York, far more than any other state. Although Jews could influence New York's thirty-one electoral votes, a Democratic candidate who does not win by a comfortable margin in New York is very likely to lose the election.[55]

According to our estimates based on ANES surveys, in 1948 Truman received about a third of his total vote from white Catholics. In 1952 Stevenson won three-tenths of his vote from white Catholics, but only one-fourth in 1956. In 1960 Kennedy received 37 percent of his vote from Catholics, but the Catholic contribution grew to just under three in ten votes when Johnson defeated Goldwater in 1964. In 1968 three-tenths of Humphrey's total vote came from white Catholics, but only a fourth of McGovern's vote in 1972. White Catholics provided just over a fourth of Carter's vote in his 1976 victory, but in his 1980 loss to Reagan just over a fifth came from this source. Mondale received just under three in ten of his votes from white Catholics, and Dukakis received a fifth of his vote from this group. According to our analysis based on ANES surveys, just over a fifth of Clinton's vote came from white Catholics in 1992, and just over a fourth in 1996. The ANES surveys suggest that both Kerry and Bush received about a fifth of their votes from white Catholics. Similar results can be derived from the 2000 VNS exit polls and the 2004 pool poll. In 2008 both the ANES survey and the pool poll suggest that less than a fifth of Obama's vote came from white Catholics.

The contrast between the 1960 and 2004 elections is the most striking in these six-decade comparisons. In both elections, the Democrats fielded a Catholic presidential candidate. But Kennedy received over twice as large a share of the Catholic vote as Kerry. Religious differences were massive in 1960 and relatively modest in 2004. Well over a third of Kennedy's votes came from white Catholics, but only about one-fifth of Kerry's did, so that they made up barely more of Kerry's voter coalition than they made up of Obama's in 2008. Obviously, the social characteristics of the Catholic community changed over the span of forty-four years. And then there were social issues that may have led many Catholics to vote Republican in 2004 that were simply not on the political agenda four decades earlier.

As the data reveal, in all of the elections between 1944 and 1996 the effects of class and religion were cumulative (Figure 5-6). In every one of these fourteen elections, working class-Catholics were more likely to vote Democratic than any other group. And in all these elections, middle-class Protestants were the most likely to vote Republican. In 2000 middle-class Catholics were the most likely to vote Democratic, and middle-class Republicans the most likely to vote Republican. In 2004, as in the vast majority of past elections, working-class Catholics were the most Democratic group. Middle-class Protestants were somewhat more likely to vote Republican than middle-class Catholics. All the same, middle-class Protestants are the most consistent group, supporting the Republicans in all sixteen elections.

The relative importance of social class and religion can be assessed by comparing the voting behavior of middle-class Catholics with that of working-class Protestants. Religion was more important than social class in predicting the vote in all elections between 1944 and 2004, except those in which social class was more important than religion—1948 (by a considerable margin), 1976, and 1980—and the one, 1964, in which class and religion were equally important. However, all of these trend lines have been converging, suggesting that traditional sources of cleavage are declining in importance.

WHY THE NEW DEAL COALITION BROKE DOWN

The importance of race increased substantially after 1960, but all of the other factors we have examined have declined in importance. The effects of region on voting behavior have been reversed, with the Republicans now enjoying an advantage in the South, especially when we compare southern whites with

FIGURE 5-6   White Major-Party Voters Who Voted Democratic for President, by Social Class and Religion, 1944–2004 (percent)

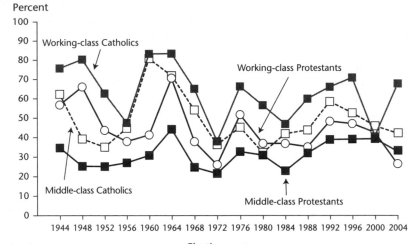

Number of:															
Catholics															
Working class	(152)	(61)	(158)	(168)	(179)[a]	(126)	(83)	(176)	(163)[a]	(76)	(156)	(100)	(100)[a]	(86)[a]	(79)[a]	(41)[a]
Middle class	(130)	(28)	(94)	(96)	(109)[a]	(121)	(96)	(176)	(179)[a]	(96)	(177)	(164)	(166)[a]	(167)[a]	(161)[a]	(108)[a]
Protestants															
Working class	(405)	(59)	(279)	(329)	(374)[a]	(280)	(198)	(383)	(367)[a]	(197)	(286)	(218)	(234)[a]	(159)[a]	(115)[a]	(79)[a]
Middle class	(479)	(91)	(302)	(336)	(405)[a]	(287)	(254)	(430)	(457)[a]	(226)	(359)	(349)	(303)[a]	(256)[a]	(292)[a]	(185)[a]

Source: Authors' analysis of a 1944 NORC survey and ANES surveys.

[a] Number is weighted.

whites outside the South. As the national Democratic Party strengthened its appeals to African Americans during the 1960s, party leaders endorsed policies that southern whites opposed, and many of them deserted the Democratic Party. The migration of northern whites to the South also may have reduced regional characteristics.

Although the Democratic Party's appeals to blacks may have weakened its hold on white groups that traditionally supported it, other factors were at work as well.[56] During the postwar years, these groups have changed. Although union members do not hold high-paying professional and managerial jobs, they have gained substantial economic advantages (however, these advantages may erode as the result of globalization). Differences in income between the working and the middle class have diminished. And Catholics, who often came from more recent European immigrant groups than Protestants, have become increasingly middle class as the proportion of second- and third-generation Americans among Catholics has grown. This trend is only partially offset by the growing number of Catholic Latinos.

Not only have these social groups changed, but the historical conditions that led union members, the working class, and Catholics to become Democrats have receded further into the past. Although the transmission of partisan loyalties from generation to generation gives historically based coalitions some staying power, the ability of the family to transmit partisan loyalties has decreased as the strength of party identification among the electorate has weakened.[57] Moreover, with the passage of time the proportion of the electorate that directly experienced the Roosevelt years has progressively declined. By 2004 only 3 percent of the voting-age population was old enough to have voted during the Roosevelt years. New policy issues, unrelated to the political conflicts of the New Deal era, have tended to erode party loyalties among traditionally Democratic groups. Edward G. Carmines and James A. Stimson provide strong evidence that race-related issues have been crucial in weakening the New Deal coalition.[58] And more recently, social issues such as abortion may have weakened Democratic Party loyalties among Catholic voters.[59]

Despite the weakening of the New Deal coalition, the Democrats managed to win the presidency in 1992 and 1996, came very close to holding it in 2000, and came close to regaining it in 2004. In 2008 they did regain the presidency, winning a majority of the popular vote for the first time since 1976. In his 1992 victory, Clinton boosted his share of the major-party vote among union members, the white working class, and even among white southerners. He focused on appeals to middle America, and in both 1992 and 1996 he paid as low a price as possible to gain the black vote. Clinton was the first Democrat to win in an election in which blacks made up more than 15 percent of the Democratic vote. In 1996 Clinton once again won with over 15 percent of his votes provided by blacks. But the 1992 election and to a lesser extent the one in 1996 were three-candidate contests. Our calculations suggest that it would be difficult for a Democrat to win a two-candidate contest in which blacks made up a fifth or more of his or her total coalition. Difficult, but not impossible. The 2008 contest is clearly an exception, for Obama gained about a fourth of his total tally from black voters. This was possible because black turnout equaled white turnout and because blacks voted overwhelmingly Democratic.

But Obama did not restore the New Deal coalition. Among the groups we examined, apart from blacks only Jews gave a clear majority of their vote to Obama. Obama had only a slight edge among white union members, and he split the white Catholic vote with McCain. Among white southerners, a mainstay of the New Deal coalition, he won only a third of the vote.

Perhaps as James W. Ceaser and Andrew E. Busch argued after the 1992 election, future coalitions will be formed on the basis of common issue positions rather than on the demographic groups that both politicians and political scientists now employ.[60] Turning to the issue preferences of the electorate provides an opportunity to see how the Democrats can move from their 2008 victory to form a winning coalition and may provide insights into how the Republicans might regain political power.

Chapter 6

Candidates, Issues, and the Vote

In Chapter 5 we discussed the relationship between social forces and the vote. The impact of these forces is indirect. Even though the New Deal coalition was constructed of members of different groups, the people who belonged to them did not vote Democratic simply because they were African Americans, white southerners, union members, Catholics, or Jews. Rather, they usually voted Democratic because that party offered symbolic and substantive policies and candidates that appealed to the concerns of members of these groups, and because the party's platforms and candidates were consistent, encouraging many voters to develop long-term partisan loyalties. Today, the long-term decline in class voting, for example, is evidence of the decreasing importance members of the working and middle classes place on the differences between the parties on concerns that divide blue-collar and white-collar workers. That race is the sharpest division in American politics today does not mean that blacks vote Democratic simply because they are black. As Supreme Court justice Clarence Thomas demonstrates, African Americans may also be conservative ideologically and may identify with and vote for Republicans.

In this chapter and the two that follow, we examine some of the concerns that underlie voters' choices for president. Even though scholars and politicians disagree about what factors voters employ and how they employ them, there is general consensus on several points. First, voters' attitudes or preferences determine their choices. There may be disagreement over exactly which attitudes shape behavior, but most scholars agree that voters deliberately choose to support the candidate they believe will make the best president. There is also general agreement that attitudes toward the candidates, the issues, and the parties are the most important attitudes in shaping the vote.[1] In these three chapters, we start with voters' considerations just before casting their ballots, and then turn to their earlier ones, ending with the most important long-term attitudinal force shaping the vote, party identification.

In this chapter, we look first at the relationship between several measures of candidate evaluation and the vote, beginning with the "feeling thermometers" used by the American National Election Studies to measure attitudes toward the candidates. After this brief analysis, we examine aspects of the major components of these evaluations: voters' perceptions of the candidates' personal qualities and voters' perceptions of the candidates' professional qualifications and competence to serve as president.[2] As we will see, there is a very powerful relationship between thermometer evaluations of candidates and the vote, and a somewhat less strong one between evaluations of candidate traits and the vote. It might seem obvious that voters support the candidate they like best, but in 1968, 1980, 1992, 1996, and 2000 the presence of a significant third candidate complicated decision making for many voters.[3]

We conceive of attitudes toward the candidates as the most direct influence on the vote itself, especially the summary evaluations encapsulated in the "feeling thermometers." But attitudes toward the issues and the parties help to shape attitudes toward the candidates and thus the vote. With that in mind, we turn to the first part of our investigation of the role of issues. After analyzing the problems that most concerned the voters in 2008, we discuss the two basic forms of issue voting: that based on prospective issues and that based on retrospective issues. In this chapter, we investigate the impact of prospective issues. In doing so, we consider one of the controversies surrounding issue voting: how much information the public has on the issues and candidates' positions on them. Our analyses provide an indication of the significance of prospective issues in 2008, and compare their impact as shown in earlier election surveys. Chapter 7 then examines retrospective issues and the vote, and Chapter 8 examines partisan identification and assesses the significance of both parties and issues for voting in 2008 and in earlier elections.

ATTITUDES TOWARD THE CANDIDATES

Although the United States has a two-party system, there are still ways in which other candidates can appear on the ballot or they can run a write-in candidacy. The 2008 presidential election was a two-person race for all intents and purposes, but many other candidates, such as Ralph Nader, were running as well. Nader was running in his third consecutive election, this time, as in 2004, as an independent, write-in candidate, whereas he had been the Green Party nominee in 2000. He received the most votes of any "third-party" candidate in 2008, over 700,000. In 2008 a former member of Congress, Georgia Democrat Cynthia McKinney, was the Green Party candidate, receiving over 150,000 votes. Another former member of Congress from Georgia, Bob Barr, was the candidate of the Libertarian Party, receiving over a half-million votes.

Here, though, we limit our attention to Senators Barack Obama and John McCain. We want to know why people preferred one candidate over the other,

TABLE 6-1   Relative Ranking of Presidential Candidates on Feeling
Thermometer: Response Distribution and Vote Choice, 2008

	Rated Obama higher than McCain on thermometer	Rated Obama equal to McCain on thermometer	Rated McCain higher than Obama on thermometer	Total	(*N*)
	A. Distribution of responses				
Percent	50	14	36	100	(2,288)
	B. Major-party voters who voted for Obama				
Percent	97	50	6	55	(1,549)
(*N*)	(764)	(145)	(639)		

Source: Authors' analysis of the 2008 ANES survey.

Note: The numbers in parentheses in part B of the table are the totals on which the percentages are based. Numbers are weighted. Only respondents who rated both candidates on the scale are included.

and therefore how they voted and, by extension, why Obama won the election. The obvious starting point in two-person races is to imagine that people voted for the candidate they preferred. This may sound obvious, but in races with three or more candidates—such as many recent contests—people do not necessarily vote for the candidate they most prefer.[4]

Happily for understanding the 2008 presidential election, in a strictly two-person race people almost always vote for the candidate they prefer. This close relationship can be demonstrated by analyzing the "feeling thermometer"—a scale that runs from 0 to 100 degrees, with 0 indicating "very cold" or negative feelings, 50 indicating neutral feelings, and 100 indicating a "very warm" or positive evaluation.[5] Respondents who rank a major-party candidate highest among three candidates vote overwhelmingly for the major-party candidate. By contrast, respondents who rank a third-party or independent candidate highest often desert that candidate to vote for one of the major-party candidates, which we believe may result from voters using strategic considerations to avoid "wasting" their votes on a candidate who has little chance of winning.[6] The data for 2008 are reported in Table 6-1.

As the data in part A of the table illustrate, exactly half of the respondents rated Obama higher than McCain on the thermometer (in the pre-election wave of the survey), while a bit more than a third rated McCain higher, with the rest scoring them equally. Part B depicts the powerful relationship between these assessments and the vote, in which well over nine in ten supported the candidate they rated higher. Those who rated the candidates at the same score divided their votes equally. This finding is commonplace, and so it is worth noting that much smaller percentages report voting for a third candidate, such as Nader. Nader was an extreme case in 2000, because he received votes from only three in ten of those who ranked him first on the postelection feeling thermometer, but no third candidate in this era has ever captured the votes of over 95 percent of his support, which major-party nominees invariably do.[7] Overall, then, an important factor in Obama's victory was the larger proportion of the electorate who rated him more highly on the feeling thermometer.

These summary evaluations are, therefore, quite close to the vote, especially in an election with only the nominees of the two major parties garnering any significant attention and support. The next obvious question is: why did more people rate Obama more warmly? The ANES asked a series of questions about how people view the candidates as people and as potential presidents (see Table 6-2A). The 2008 campaign was perhaps unusual in that the two major-party nominees were justly viewed as quite honorable and decent men. Thus in response to such questions as how well "moral" and "honest" described the candidates, the two were rated quite positively and nearly identically. Overall, most respondents believed both would provide strong leadership. However, McCain held a small advantage in this regard—it was, after all, a central aspect of his campaign, which was not surprising in view of his much longer experience in politics compared with Obama. Conversely, the Ivy League–trained law professor held a large advantage on the "intelligence" measure, and the nature of his "change you can believe in" campaign theme and his manner of presenting himself gave him an edge over McCain in assessments of the candidates' optimism. McCain's weakest trait (as seen by respondents, at least) was that he did not seem to "really care about people like [the respondent]," a disadvantage Republicans often face but one likely exacerbated by Obama's mixed race and his upbringing by a single mother and his grandparents.

In Table 6-2B, we report the percentage of major-party voters with differing assessments of the candidates who voted for Obama. It shows, for example, that among the 193 voters who said that "moral" described Obama extremely well, 88 percent voted for him. Among the 189 voters who said that "moral" described McCain extremely well, only 19 percent voted for Obama. As we see, these assessments are strongly related to the way people vote. This is especially true of those who thought a given trait did *not* describe the candidate well (let alone not at all well), because never more than one in four supported that candidate. Thus not only did the public's views of these candidate traits fit well with the candidates and their campaign themes, but the views were strongly related to the vote.[8]

PROSPECTIVE EVALUATIONS

Underlying these evaluations of the candidates are the public's attitudes toward the issues and toward the parties, as well as more specific evaluations of the

TABLE 6-2A   Distribution of Responses on Presidential Candidate Trait Evaluations, 2008 (percent)

	Extremely well	Quite well	Not too well	Not well at all	Total	(N)[a]
Obama						
Moral	24	47	21	8	100	(1,080)
Provides strong leadership	24	41	26	9	100	(1,111)
Really cares about people like you	24	40	23	12	99	(1,106)
Knowledgeable	28	50	18	5	101	(1,120)
Intelligent	48	44	6	2	100	(1,123)
Honest	18	43	26	13	100	(1,092)
Optimistic	37	48	12	4	101	(1,103)
McCain						
Moral	21	45	25	8	99	(1,090)
Provides strong leadership	23	42	27	9	101	(1,101)
Really cares about people like you	10	32	38	19	99	(1,103)
Knowledgeable	23	55	17	5	100	(1,118)
Intelligent	24	56	15	5	100	(1,118)
Honest	19	41	30	11	101	(1,088)
Optimistic	15	48	29	8	100	(1,095)

Source: Authors' analysis of the 2008 ANES survey.

Note: Questions were asked of a randomly selected half-sample.

[a] Numbers are weighted.

candidates. We begin by considering the role of issues in elections. Public policy concerns enter into the voting decision in two very different ways. In an election in which an incumbent is running, two questions become important: How has the incumbent president done on policy? And how likely is it that his opponent (or opponents) would do any better? Voting based on this form of policy appraisal is called retrospective voting and will be analyzed in Chapter 7.

The second form of policy-based voting involves examining the candidates' policy platforms and assessing which candidate's policy promises conform to what the voter believes the government should be doing. Policy voting, therefore, involves comparing sets of promises and voting for the set that is most like the voter's own preferences. Voting based on these kinds of decisions is called prospective voting, because it involves examining the promises of the candidates about future actions. In this chapter, we examine prospective evaluations of the two major-party candidates in 2008 and how these evaluations relate to voter choice.

TABLE 6-2B   Major-Party Vote for Obama and McCain by Presidential
Candidate Trait Evaluations, 2008 (percent)

	Extremely well	Quite well	Not too well	Not well at all
Obama				
Moral	88	66	14	9
(N)	(193)	(323)	(150)	(68)
Provides strong leadership	89	73	15	7
(N)	(188)	(289)	(198)	(75)
Really cares about people like you	91	66	25	8
(N)	(195)	(282)	(170)	(101)
Knowledgeable	84	55	19	14
(N)	(224)	(360)	(129)	(43)
Intelligent	75	40	8	2
(N)	(384)	(316)	(43)	(14)
Honest	94	73	20	9
(N)	(141)	(304)	(192)	(99)
Optimistic	75	48	16	22
(N)	(295)	(357)	(67)	(29)
McCain				
Moral	93	86	53	19
(N)	(189)	(333)	(161)	(59)
Provides strong leadership	95	92	47	17
(N)	(194)	(300)	(177)	(75)
Really cares about people like you	93	77	26	10
(N)	(81)	(262)	(265)	(139)
Knowledgeable	89	85	56	27
(N)	(193)	(401)	(117)	(40)
Intelligent	89	86	54	34
(N)	(198)	(412)	(107)	(37)
Honest	94	83	48	16
(N)	(157)	(320)	(190)	(69)
Optimistic	95	83	44	21
(N)	(131)	(350)	(203)	(55)

Source: Authors' analysis of the 2008 ANES survey.

Note: The numbers in parentheses are the totals on which the percentages are based. Numbers are weighted. The questions were asked of a randomly selected half-sample.

The last ten elections show some remarkable similarities in prospective evaluations and voting. Perhaps the most important similarity is the perception of where the Democratic and Republican candidates stood on issues. In these elections, the public saw clear differences between the major-party nominees. In all cases, the public saw the Republican candidates as conservative on most issues, and most citizens scored the GOP candidates as more conservative than the voters themselves. And in all elections, the public saw the Democratic candidates as liberal on most issues, and most citizens viewed the Democratic candidates as more liberal than the voters themselves. As a result, many voters perceived a clear choice based on their understanding of the candidates' policy positions. And the candidates presented the voters with, as the 1964 Goldwater campaign slogan put it, "a choice, not an echo." The *average* citizen, however, faced a difficult choice. For many, the Democratic nominees were considered to be as far to the left as the Republicans were to the right. On balance, the net effect of prospective issues was to give neither party a clear advantage.

One of the most important differences among the last ten elections was the mixture of issues that concerned the public. Each election presented its own mixture of policy concerns. Moreover, the general strategies of the candidates on issues differed in each election.[9] In 1980 Jimmy Carter's incumbency was marked by a general perception that he was unable to solve pressing problems. Ronald Reagan attacked that weakness both directly (for example, by the question he posed to the public during his debate with Carter, "Are you better off today than you were four years ago?") and indirectly. The indirect attack was more future-oriented. Reagan set forth a clear set of proposals designed to convince the public that he would be more likely to solve the nation's problems because he had his own proposals to end soaring inflation, to strengthen the United States militarily, and to regain respect and influence for the country abroad.

In 1984 the public perceived Reagan to be a far more successful president than Carter had been. Reagan chose to run his reelection campaign by focusing primarily on the theme that things were much better by 1984 (as illustrated by his advertising slogan "It's morning in America"). Walter Mondale attacked that claim by arguing that Reagan's policies were unfair and by pointing to the rapidly growing budget deficit. But Reagan countered that Mondale was another "tax and spend, tax and spend" Democrat, and the "Great Communicator," as some called him, captured a second term.

The 1988 campaign more resembled the 1984 campaign than the 1980 one. George H. W. Bush continued to run on the successes of the Reagan-Bush administration and promised no new taxes. ("Read my lips," he said. "No new taxes!") Michael Dukakis initially attempted to portray the election as one about "competence" rather than "ideology," arguing that he had demonstrated his competence as governor of Massachusetts and that Bush, by implication, was less competent. Bush countered that it really was an election about ideology, and that Dukakis was just another liberal Democrat from Massachusetts.

The 1992 election presented yet another type of campaign. Bush used the success of the 1991 Persian Gulf War to augment his claim that he was a successful world leader, but Bill Clinton attacked the Bush administration on domestic issues, barely discussing foreign affairs at all. He sought to keep the electorate focused on the current economic woes and argued for substantial reforms of the health care system, hoping to appeal to Democrats and to spur action should he be the first Democrat in the White House in twelve years. At the same time, he sought to portray himself not as another "tax and spend" liberal Democrat, but as a moderate "New Democrat."

In 1996 Clinton ran a campaign typical of a popular incumbent; he focused on what led people to approve of his handling of the presidency and avoided mentioning many specific new programs. His policy proposals were a lengthy series of relatively inexpensive, limited programs. Bob Dole, having difficulties deciding whether to emphasize Clinton's personal failings in the first term or to call for different programs for the future, decided to put a significant tax cut proposal at the center of his candidacy under either of those campaign strategies.

In 2000 the candidates debated a broad array of domestic issues—education, health care, Social Security, and taxes the most prominent among them—often couched in terms of a newfound "problem," federal government budget surpluses. Typically these issues (except for taxes) have favored Democratic contenders, and Republicans have often avoided detailed discussions of all except taxes on the grounds that doing so would make the issues more salient to voters and would highlight the Democratic advantages. George W. Bush, however, spoke out on education, in particular, as well as on health care and Social Security to a lesser extent, believing he could undercut the traditional Democratic advantage. For his part, Al Gore had the advantage of his belief (backed by public opinion polls) that the public was less in favor of tax cuts than usual and more in favor of allocating budget surpluses to buttress popular domestic programs.

In 2004, by contrast, Bush and Kerry had less choice about what issues to consider. With wars under way in Iraq, Afghanistan, and against terrorism, neither candidate could avoid foreign policy considerations. Bush preferred to emphasize that Iraq was part of the war on terrorism, while Kerry argued that it was not, and indeed that it was a costly distraction from it. Similarly, 2004 opened with the economy slumping. The Democrats, including Kerry, attacked the Bush administration policies, while Bush countered by saying that the economy was actually improving—in large part because of his successful policies. As the year wore on, the economy did in fact improve, although not so much as to remove all criticism.

The 2008 campaign began as one in which the Democrats tried to emphasize their opposition to the Bush policies in Iraq and its policies on the "detainees" being held in Iraq, Guantanamo Bay, and elsewhere, tempered by concerns about the war in Afghanistan and terrorism. On the domestic front, Obama emphasized health care reform, improved environmental policies, and other aspects of his agenda that called for "change." McCain, conversely, began with a spirited defense of the war in Iraq, and especially the "surge" in the war effort there. By fall, however, the economy had swept aside virtually every other issue but war from consideration, and replaced war as topic number one. Indeed, so worrisome were the economic events of the fall, as we saw in Chapter 2, that candidates could ill afford to do anything but relate any domestic issue to their plans for fighting the economic downturn.

THE CONCERNS OF THE ELECTORATE

The first question to ask about prospective voting is what kinds of concerns move the public. In its presidential election surveys from 1952 to 2000, the ANES asked respondents, "What do you think are the most important problems facing the country today?" A similar question was asked in 2004.[10] Data from the 2008 survey are not available as of this writing, but we can compare results from earlier ANES surveys to those reported by the pool poll for 2008. In Table 6-3, we have listed the percentage of responses to what respondents, choosing from broad categories of concerns, claimed was the most important problem at the time of the last nine elections (1972–2004).

In the four elections preceding the one in 2004, the great majority of responses revolved around domestic issues rather than foreign policy, perhaps because of the end of the Cold War (although concerns about foreign policy were also low in 1976, during the Cold War). In the eight elections prior to 2004, two major categories of domestic issues dominated. From 1976 to 1992, in good times and bad, by far the more commonly cited issue was the economy. In 1972, 1996, and 2000, the most frequently cited problems were in the social issues category, and an absolute majority cited some social welfare problem (such as welfare reform, the environment, or health care) or public order (such as crime, terrorism, or drugs). In 2004 social issues once again captured the most responses, but social welfare concerns (the largest specific category of concern in 2000) were virtually absent, declining from 45 percent to merely 4 percent of respondents. Instead, the various considerations under the rubric "public order" had taken social welfare's place at the center of concerns about social issues, with public order concerns selected by two in five respondents. Virtually all of these responses (42 percent) were recorded as in the category "terrorism, Islamic extremists, homeland security." In 1992, 1996, and 2000, about nine in ten respondents named either an economic or a social problem. In 2004 over one in four selected a foreign policy problem, and for most (18 percent) that was the war in Iraq in particular. From 1972 through 2004, very few cited problems in the "functioning of government" category, such as "gridlock," term limits, other reforms, or government corruption. Finally, in all of these elections, very few— only 3 percent in 2004, for example—cited no problem at all.

TABLE 6-3   Most Important Problem as Seen by the Electorate, 1972–2004 (percent)

Problem	1972	1976	1980	1984	1988	1992	1996	2000	2004[b]
Economic	*27*	*76*	*56*	*49*	*45*	*64*	*29*	*19*	*19*
Unemployment/recession	9	33	10	16	5	23	7	5	4
Inflation/prices	14	27	33	5	2	a	a	1	a
Deficit/government spending	1	9	3	19	32	16	13	4	2
Social issues	*34*	*14*	*7*	*13*	*38*	*28*	*56*	*67*	*49*
Social welfare	7	4	3	9	11	17	33	45	4
Public order	20	8	1	4	19	10	23	21	45
Foreign and defense	*31*	*4*	*32*	*34*	*10*	*3*	*5*	*10*	*29*
Foreign	4	3	9	17	6	2	3	6	27
Defense	1	1	8	17	3	1	2	4	3
Functioning of government (competence, corruption, trust, power, etc.)	*4*	*4*	*2*	*2*	*1*	*2*	*5*	*5*	*3*
All others	*4*	*3*	*3*	*3*	*6*	*2*	*4*	*0*	*0*
Total	100	101	100	101	100	100	100	101	100
(N)	(842)	(2,337)	(1,352)	(1,780)	(1,657)	(2,003)	(794)	(907)	(1,033)
(Number "missing")	(63)	(203)	(56)	(163)	(118)	(54)	(27)	(31)	(32)
Percentage missing	7	7	4	7	7	2	4	3	3

Source: Authors' analysis of ANES surveys.

Note: Foreign in 1972 includes 25 percent who cited Vietnam. Foreign in 1980 includes 15 percent who cited Iran. Questions were asked of a randomly selected half-sample in 1972, 1996, and 2000. Numbers for 1976, 1992, 1996, 2000, and 2004 are weighted. The main categories are in italics. Not all of the subcategories are included. The total percentages for the subcategories, therefore, will not equal the percentages for the main categories. In 1984 total *N* is 1,943, because forty-six respondents were not asked this question (they were given a shortened postelection questionnaire). In 1992 the total *N* is 2,057, because 431 respondents either had no postelection interview or were given a shortened form via telephone.

a Less than 1 percent of responses.

b For 2004, "foreign" includes the war in Iraq (18 percent) and "public order" includes terrorism, Islamist extremists, and homeland security (42 percent).

In 2008, by contrast, the pool poll offered respondents a list of problems from which they were to cite their most important concern. Because this is a procedure very different from the open-ended responses solicited by the ANES, comparisons are especially difficult to make. That being said, the pool poll indicated that 63 percent of respondents cited the economy as the most important issue, followed by the war in Iraq, although that concern had dropped to 10 percent, followed by terrorism at 9 percent.

Although the economy and social issues have been by far the dominant concerns of the public over the last three decades, the specific concerns of the public have varied from election to election. Within the economy, for example, inflation was a common concern throughout the 1970s, but by 1984 it had all but dropped from sight, becoming a literal "asterisk in the polls" by 1992, as in 2004 (and most likely in 2008 as well, although ANES data are not yet available). Unemployment as a concern has risen and fallen in rough accord with the actual level of unemployment in the nation. Likewise, concern about the federal budget deficit has tracked closely with the rate of growth (or, in 2000, decline) in the actual deficit. In the social issues category, the particular concerns also have varied from year to year, corresponding with the headlines in the news media and the issues the candidates emphasized in the campaigns. Thus in 1992 Clinton's emphasis on the "health care crisis" was apparent in the public's concerns on this topic. By 1996 those concerns had waned somewhat, replaced by crime, education, and welfare policy, and then education, health care, and the environment loomed large in 2000. By 2004 it was the ability of the government to address the domestic consequences of terrorism, among other considerations, and terrorism was also one of the more commonly chosen responses in 2008.

The concerns of the electorate are the backdrop of campaigns. Health care and energy policy were important components of the 2008 campaigns, especially Obama's. And the economic crisis dramatically shaped not only the public's concerns but also the candidates' strategies. The economy probably pushed Iraq and terrorism off the front burner. Earlier, opposition to the Iraq War had been a central part of Obama's push for the Democratic nomination. Then, the decline in violence in Iraq fueled McCain's support of Bush's "surge" strategy in the war, and criticism of Obama's opposition to the surge remained a key part of McCain's campaign because concern about the Iraq War remained high, even as economic concerns loomed larger. Still, being concerned about a problem does not directly indicate which candidate the voter intends to back. A vote, after all, is a choice among alternatives. To investigate these questions, we must look at the voters' issue preferences and their perceptions of where candidates stood on the issues.

ISSUE POSITIONS AND PERCEPTIONS

Since 1972, the ANES surveys have included issue scales designed to measure the preferences of the electorate and voters' perceptions of the positions the

FIGURE 6-1   Example of a Seven-Point Issue Scale: Jobs and Standard of Living
Guarantees

Questions the interviewers asked:

> Please look at page 9 of the [respondent] booklet
>
> Some people feel the government in Washington should see to it that every person has
> a job and a good standard of living. Suppose these people are at one end of a scale,
> at point 1. Others think the government should just let each person get ahead on their
> own. Suppose these people are at the other end, at point 7. And, of course, some other
> people have opinions somewhere in between at points 2, 3, 4, 5, or 6.
>
> Where would you place YOURSELF on this scale, or haven't you thought much about this?
>
> Where would you place BARACK OBAMA on this issue?
>
> Where would you place JOHN MCCAIN (on this issue)?

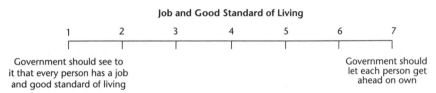

Source: 2008 ANES, Pre-Election Interview Schedule and Respondent Booklet.

Note: The order of the candidates was determined randomly.

candidates have taken on the issues.[11] The questions are therefore especially
appropriate for examining prospective issue evaluations. We hasten to add,
however, that voters' perceptions of where the incumbent party's nominee
stands may well be based in part on what the president has done in office, as well
as on the campaign promises he made as the party's nominee. The policy
promises of the opposition party candidate may also be judged in part by what
that candidate's party did when it last held the White House. Nevertheless, the
issue scales generally focus on prospective evaluations and are very different
from those used to make the retrospective judgments examined in Chapter 7.[12]

The issue scales will be used to examine several questions: What alternatives
did the voters believe the candidates were offering? To what extent did the voters
have issue preferences of their own and relatively clear perceptions of candidates'
positions? Finally, how strongly were voters' preferences and perceptions related
to their choice of candidates?

Figure 6-1 presents one of the seven-point issue scale questions, along with an
example of the illustration presented to respondents as they considered their
responses. Figure 6-2 shows the seven-point issue scales used in the 2008 ANES
survey. The figure presents the average (median) position of the respondents
(labeled "S" for self) and the average (median) perceptions of the positions of
McCain and Obama (labeled "M" and "O").[13] The issues raised in 2008 probe
the respondents' own preferences and perceptions of the major-party nominees
on whether government should spend more or less on social services, whether
defense spending should be increased or decreased, whether health insurance

FIGURE 6-2   Median Self-Placement of the Electorate and the Electorate's Placement of Candidates on Issue Scales, 2008

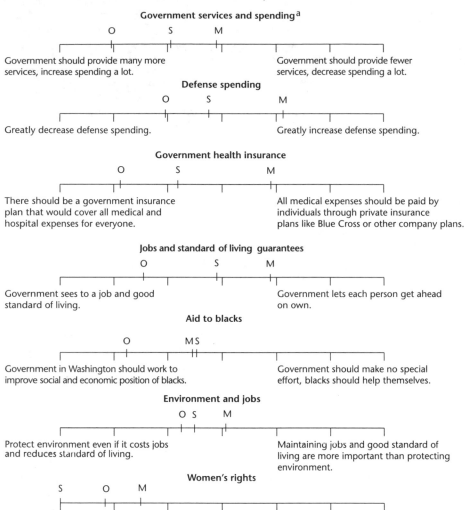

Source: Authors' analysis of the 2008 ANES survey.

Note: S = median self-placement of the respondents; O = median placement of Obama; M = median place-ment of McCain. Questions were asked of a randomly selected half-sample, except for the aid to blacks issue, which was asked in the same form to all respondents.

[a] Reversed from actual scoring to make a "liberal" response closer to point 1 and a "conservative" response closer to point 7.

should be provided by the government or by private insurance, whether the government should see to it that everyone has a job and a good standard of living or let citizens get ahead on their own, whether the government should provide aid to blacks or whether blacks should help themselves, whether the government should protect the environment at the cost of jobs and a good standard of living, and whether women should play a role equal to men in society or whether they should stay at home ("a woman's place is in the home").

These issues were selected because they are (or, in the case of the role of women, were) controversial and generally measure long-standing partisan divisions. As a result, the average citizen comes out looking reasonably moderate on these issues—that is, five in seven cases fall between the positions corresponding to the average placements of the two candidates. On many issues raised in 2008, the typical citizen is very near the center of the scale, especially on defense spending and jobs and standard of living, and is slightly to the left of the midpoint on aid to blacks and environmental scales and very far to the left on women's rights.[14] The average citizen is at about point 3 on the government services and spending and government health insurance issues.

Although many of these average citizen stances are quite similar from one election to the next, there are some important changes. For example, self-placement on the jobs scale was rather more conservative in Reagan's initial victory in 1980 than earlier and more conservative again in George W. Bush's victory in 2000 than in other preceding elections, but moved in a more liberal direction again in 2004. On the government spending and services scale, the average citizen has typically been just to the left of the middle, but was a bit more liberal in 2004, and in 2008 moved a full point to the left, perhaps reflecting one of the expectations about government action in light of the troubled economy. In those surveys that included the same women's rights scale used in 2008 (all but 1984), most citizens placed themselves about as close to the "equal role" end as possible, just as in 2000. As for the environment and jobs, the average citizen has been about one point to the pro-environmental side of the midpoint of that scale since it was introduced for the 1996 election survey, and thus the self-placement moved a bit in the conservative direction in 2008, perhaps also reflecting the economic situation and the expectation of higher unemployment.

Generally, on every issue scale used between 1980 and 2008 the public has viewed the Democratic candidate as more liberal and the Republican candidate as more conservative than the average member of the public except on women's rights. Indeed, these differences are often quite large. They exceed two points (or the maximum difference of six points) on the government services and spending, defense spending, government health insurance, and jobs scales. These issues have differentiated the two parties for decades, and the public perceived that the 2008 nominees were continuing that traditional division. Still, even in the face of large differences, McCain was able to break with past Republican nominees, including Bush. Although in the public's eyes the Republican always stood to the right of the scale on these issues in all preceding elections, McCain appeared to be in the middle (even very slightly to the left of center) on government spending and services. And the public believed that McCain was a full half-point to the left of center on aid to blacks—a substantial change from the traditional perception of Republicans. The public saw little difference overall between the two candidates on the environment and jobs scale and on women's rights, although Obama was seen as more liberal on both. Indeed, Obama was seen as quite liberal on several of these issues, especially government services, government health insurance, aid to blacks, and women's rights. Overall, the public saw quite large differences between the offerings of the two candidates. No matter how much or how little the public may have been polarized in 2008, it saw that alleged polarization dividing the two candidates.[15]

Although voters saw clear differences between the candidates, the average voter faced a difficult choice. Obama was seen to the left of the average respondent and McCain was seen to the right on most issues. Overall, the public saw Obama as somewhat farther to the left of where the average voter fell than it saw McCain to the right. On the scale measuring aid to blacks, McCain was seen as just to the left of where the average voter was placed. On the jobs and standard of living scales, the average voter was once again much closer to where McCain was placed. Even though, as we see later, McCain was advantaged by being closer to the average voter overall, not too much should be made of these differences. The average voter stood closer to Obama on defense spending and on government health insurance, for example. Of course, we cannot at this point go much further on these overall figures. The choice is made not by the average voter choosing over what the respondents as a whole thought the candidates offered; it is made by individual voters considering what they think about these issues. To consider a voter's choices, we must look beyond these averages.

ISSUE VOTING CRITERIA

The Problem

Because voting is an individual action, we must look at the preferences of individuals to see whether prospective issues influenced their votes.

The question of prospective voting is controversial. In their classic study of the American electorate, *The American Voter,* Angus Campbell and his colleagues point out that the public is often ill-informed about public policy and may not be able to vote on the basis of issues.[16] They asked themselves what information voters would need before an issue could influence the decision on how to vote, and they answered by posing three conditions. First, the voters must hold an opinion on the issue; second, they must learn what the government is doing on the issue; and third, they must perceive a difference between the policies of the two major parties. According to the authors' analysis, only about one-quarter to one-third of the electorate in 1956 could meet these three conditions.

Although it is impossible to replicate the analysis in *The American Voter,* we can adapt the authors' procedures to the 2008 electorate. In some ways, recent ANES data focus more directly on the actual choice citizens must make—the choice among the candidates. The first criterion is whether respondents claim to have an opinion on the issue.[17] This is measured by whether they could place themselves on the issue scale. Second, the respondents should have some perception of the positions taken by the candidates on an issue. This is measured by whether they could place both major-party candidates on that issue.[18] Although some voters might perceive the position of one candidate and vote on that basis, prospective voting involves a comparison between or among alternatives, so the expressed ability to perceive the stands of the contenders seems a minimal requirement of prospective issue voting. Third, the voter must see a difference between the positions of the candidates. Failing to see a difference means that the voter perceived no choice on the issue, perhaps because he or she failed to detect actual distinctions between the candidates. This failure might arise from lack of attention to the issue in the campaign, which may have been true about the environment in 2008. It also may arise from the fact that the candidates took very similar positions on the issue, and respondents were thus, on average, reflecting that similarity, as we believe was truer of the candidates in 1976 than in other recent campaigns.

A voter might be able to satisfy these criteria but misperceive the offerings of the candidates. This leads to a fourth condition, which we are able to measure more systematically than was possible in 1956: do the respondents accurately perceive the relative positions of the two major-party candidates—that is, do they see McCain as more "conservative" than Obama? This criterion does not demand that the voter have an accurate perception of what the candidate proposes, but it does expect the voter to recognize that Obama, for example, favored spending more on social services than did McCain.

The Data

In Table 6-4, we report the percentages of the sample that met the four criteria on the seven issue scales used in 2008.[19] We also show the average proportion that met these criteria for all scales and compare those averages with comparable averages for all issue scales used in the nine preceding elections.[20] Column I of Table 6-4 reveals that most people felt capable of placing themselves on the issue scales, and this capability was common to all election years.[21] If all criteria were met at such high levels, considerably less controversy would surround prospective issue voting.

For all seven issues, however, fewer people could place both the candidates and themselves on an issue scale than could place just themselves (see column II of Table 6-4). Nevertheless, over three in four respondents met these two criteria in 2008. Note that there was relatively little variation across issues: 70–82 percent met these criteria on each issue scale. The relatively consistent ability to satisfy these criteria is similar to that observed in 1984 and thereafter, but different from findings in earlier elections. In 1980, for example, there were three issue scales on which fewer than half of the respondents could place

TABLE 6-4   Four Criteria for Issue Voting, 2008, and Comparisons with
1972–2004 Presidential Elections

	Percentage of sample who …			
	I	II	III	IV
Issue scale	Placed self on scale	Placed both candidates on scale[a]	Saw differences between Obama and McCain	Saw Obama more "liberal" than McCain
Government spending/ services	84	78	67	57
Defense spending	86	80	69	62
Government health insurance	91	82	69	60
Jobs and standard of living	89	81	66	58
Aid to blacks	85	72	60	52
Environment and jobs	84	70	50	38
Women's rights	98	82	45	30
Average[b]				
2008 (7)	88	78	61	51
2004 (7)	89	76	62	52
2000 (7)	87	69	51	41
1996 (9)	89	80	65	55
1992 (3)	85	71	66	52
1988 (7)	86	66	52	43
1984 (7)	84	73	62	53
1980 (9)	82	61	51	43
1976 (9)	84	58	39	26
1972 (8)	90	65	49	41

Source: Authors' analysis of ANES surveys.

Note: Columns II, III, and IV compare the Democratic and Republican nominees. Third-party or independent candidates John Anderson (1980), Ross Perot (1992 and 1996), and Ralph Nader (2000 and 2004) were excluded. The 2008 questions were asked of a randomly selected half-sample, except for aid to blacks, which was asked of the full sample.

[a] Until 1996, respondents who could not place themselves on a scale were not asked to place the candidates on that issue scale. Although they were asked to do so in 1996, 2000, 2004, and 2008, we excluded them from further calculations to maintain comparability with prior surveys.

[b] Number in parentheses is the number of seven-point issue scales included in the average for each election year survey.

themselves and both candidates, and in 1976 fewer than six in ten could meet both criteria on average. The average of 78 percent who met these two conditions in 2008 is only slightly less than that for 1996, and thus near its highest level. Note that the percentage meeting these two criteria seems to be increasing over time, at least on average, perhaps reflecting the greater divergence between the two parties and their leaders.

Column III of Table 6-4 reveals that three in five respondents met the first two criteria and also were able to see a difference between the positions of the two candidates. The 2008 result is thus on a par with those for the other high-water mark elections—1984, 1992, 1996, and 2004—and is noticeably higher than those for 1972, 1980, 1988, and 2000, and substantially higher than that for 1976. What are we to conclude about these differences in the ability of the electorate to satisfy the criteria and thus be able to vote on the basis of issues? It seems highly unlikely that the ability of the public to comprehend the electoral process varies so greatly from election to election. There is very little difference among elections in self-placement on issue scales, for example. Rather, the differences stem from perceptions of the candidates' positions. What seems to make the election of 1976 unique is the lower ability of the electorate to place both candidates on the scales. Perhaps the reason is that Gerald Ford had not run for president before and had been the incumbent for only two years, and Jimmy Carter was a relatively unknown challenger. Perhaps other elections had higher scores because, except for 2008, the incumbent party's candidate had served four or more years in the presidency or the vice presidency. In 1984 the candidates adopted particularly distinctive positions on issues, and this relative clarity was perceived by the electorate. The same seems to be true in 1992, 1996, 2004, and 2008. In 1972, 1980, 1988, and 2000, the candidates were only slightly less distinctive in their positions, and the electorate saw the differences only slightly less clearly. In 1976, by contrast, Ford and Carter were generally described as moderates, albeit moderately conservative and moderately liberal, respectively. The electorate appears to have reacted to the relative lack of differences.

In summary, we agree with Morris P. Fiorina's argument that failure to satisfy the criteria for issue voting does not mean that the electorate has ill-formed preferences and perceptions.[22] Rather, the electorate's ability to perceive differences between the candidates varies because political conditions differ from election to election, and these differences result mainly from differences in the strategies candidates follow. Thus the "quality" of the responses to these issue questions is based in part on how clearly the candidates articulate their issue positions and on how distinctly the alternative policy platforms are presented to the public.

The data in column IV of Table 6-4 reflect the ability of the electorate to discern distinctions between the candidates' policy offerings. The average of the seven issues reveals that in 2008 over half of the respondents satisfied all four issue voting conditions, including the criterion that they saw Obama as more liberal than McCain. The 2008 data thus indicate that the potential for issue voting is quite high, similar to the findings for 1984, 1992, 1996, and 2004 in these terms, all of which are higher than those for 1972, 1980, and 1988. Once again, however, the 1976 election stands out in very sharp contrast, because barely more than one in four voters could assess the relative positions of the two candidates.

The data in Table 6-4 suggest that the potential for prospective issue voting was high in 2008. Therefore, we might expect these issues to be rather closely related to voter choice. We examine voter choice on these issues in two ways. First, how often did people vote for the closer candidate on each issue? Second, how strongly related to the vote is the set of all issues taken together?

APPARENT ISSUE VOTING IN 2008

Issue Criteria and Voting on Each Issue

The first question is to what extent did people who were closer to a candidate on a given issue actually vote for that candidate—that is, how strong is apparent issue voting?[23] In Table 6-5, we report the proportion of major-party voters who voted for Obama by where they placed themselves on the issue scales. We divided the seven points into the set of positions that were closer to where the average citizen placed McCain and Obama (see Figure 6-2).[24]

Table 6-5 shows the clear relationship between the voters' issue positions and the candidate they supported on six of the seven scales (the exception was the women's rights issue, which reflected little relationship to the vote). Those who adopted positions at the "liberal" end of each scale were very likely to vote for Obama. If we define *liberal* as adopting position 1 or 2, Obama received three in four votes or even more on six of those seven scales. Obama rarely received three in ten votes from those at the conservative end of the scales, and those with moderate views on each issue fell in between these two extremes of support. The pattern of support we would expect from voting on the basis of these issues is particularly clear on those issues that have long defined the traditional cleavages between the two parties (the top five scales on the table). Over these issues, then, there are substantial relationships between the public's opinions and their perceptions of candidates on prospective issues.

The information on issues can be summarized, as it is in Table 6-6, to illustrate what happens when voters met the various conditions for issue voting. In the first column of Table 6-6, we report the percentage of major-party voters who placed themselves closer to the average perception of McCain or Obama and who voted for the closer candidate. To be more specific, the denominator is the total number of major-party voters who placed themselves closer to the electorate's perception of McCain or Obama. The numerator is the total number of major-party voters who were both closer to Obama and voted for him plus the total number of major-party voters who were both closer to McCain and voted for him.

TABLE 6-5 Major-Party Voters Who Voted for Obama, by Seven-Point Issue Scales, 2008 (percent)

Issue scale	Closer to median perception of Obama				Closer to median perception of McCain			
	1	2	3	4	5	6	7	(N)
Government services/spending[a]	74	80	64	54	27	17	12	
(N)	(78)	(88)	(158)	(149)	(94)	(62)	(51)	(680)
Defense spending	87	84	65	49	45	34	31	
(N)	(54)	(54)	(80)	(198)	(145)	(94)	(69)	(694)
Government health insurance	80	80	58	62	36	14	24	
(N)	(132)	(91)	(91)	(134)	(102)	(79)	(89)	(720)
Jobs and standard of living	88	81	74	58	55	28	21	
(N)	(71)	(54)	(79)	(142)	(135)	(122)	(102)	(695)
Aid to blacks	95	85	80	63	49	40	27	
(N)	(94)	(78)	(129)	(297)	(185)	(230)	(332)	(1,345)
Environment and jobs	85	82	65	51	36	30	36	
(N)	(53)	(57)	(135)	(186)	(130)	(71)	(53)	(685)
Women's rights	58	45	50	52	22	61	35	
(N)	(508)	(120)	(43)	(54)	(22)	(12)	(11)	(770)

Source: Authors' analysis of the 2008 ANES survey.

Notes: Questions were asked of a randomly selected half-sample, except for aid to blacks, which was asked of the full sample. Numbers in parentheses are the totals on which the percentages are based. Numbers are weighted.

[a] Reversed from actual scoring to make a "liberal" response closer to 1 and a "conservative" response closer to 7.

TABLE 6-6   Apparent Issue Voting, 2008, and Comparisons with 1972–2004
Presidential Elections

	Percentage of voters who voted for closer candidate and …		
Issue scale	Placed self on issue scale	Met all four issue voting criteria	Placed self but failed to meet all three other criteria
Government services/ spending	62	65	52
Defense spending	62	63	36
Government health insurance	67	73	51
Jobs and standard of living	64	71	47
Aid to blacks	63	69	50
Environment and jobs	64	75	53
Women's rights	55	80	42
Averages[a]			
2008 (7)	62	71	47
2004 (7)	67	75	51
2000 (7)	60	68	40
1996 (9)	63	74	41
1992 (3)	62	70	48
1988 (7)	62	71	45
1984 (7)	65	73	46
1980 (9)	63	71	48
1976 (9)	57	70	50
1972 (8)	66	76	55

Source: Authors' analysis of ANES surveys.

Note: An "apparent issue vote" is a vote for the candidate closer to one's position on an issue scale. The closer candidate is determined by comparing self-placement to the median placements of the two candidates on the scale as a whole. Respondents who did not place themselves or who were equidistant from the two candidates are excluded from the calculations.

Analyses conducted on the randomly selected half-sample asked questions with the traditional wording, except aid to blacks, which was asked of the full sample with the same (traditional) wording.

[a] Number in parentheses is the number of seven-point issue scales included in the average for each election year survey.

If voting were unrelated to issue positions, we would expect 50 percent of voters to vote for the closer candidate on average, not unlike the problematic women's rights scale, for example. In 2008 on average 62 percent voted for the closer candidate, which was very similar to the percentage doing so in most elections—not as high as in 2004 but slightly higher than in 2000, for example. These figures do not tell the whole story, however, because those who placed themselves on an issue but failed to meet some other criterion were unlikely to have cast a vote based on that issue. In the second column of Table 6-6, we report the percentage of those who voted for the closer candidate on each issue among voters who met all four conditions on that issue. The third column reports the percentage that voted for the closer candidate among voters who placed themselves but failed to meet all three of the remaining conditions.

Those respondents who met all four conditions were much more likely to vote for the closer candidate on any issue. Indeed, there is relatively little difference, on average, across all ten elections. In each case, about seven in ten such voters supported the closer candidate. By contrast, for those respondents who failed to meet the last three of the conditions on issue voting, voting was essentially random with respect to the issues.

The strong similarity of all election averages in the second and third columns suggests that issue voting seems more prevalent in some elections than others because elections differ in the number of people who clearly perceive differences between the candidates. In all elections, at least seven in ten who satisfied all four conditions voted consistently with their issue preferences; in all elections those who did not satisfy all the conditions on perceptions of candidates voted essentially randomly with respect to individual issues. As we saw earlier, the degree to which such perceptions vary from election to election depends more on the strategies of the candidates than on the qualities of the voters. Therefore, the relatively low percentage of apparent issue voting in 1976, for example, results from the perception of small differences between the two rather moderate candidates. The larger magnitude of apparent issue voting in 2008, as in most other elections, especially other recent elections, stems from the greater clarity with which most voters saw the positions of the two nominees.

The Balance of Issues Measure

In prospective issue voting, voters compare the full set of policy proposals made by the candidates. Because nearly every issue is strongly related to the vote, we might expect the set of all issues to be even more strongly so. To examine this relationship, we constructed an overall assessment of the issue scales to arrive at what we call the balance of issues measure. We give individuals a score of +1 if their positions on an issue scale were closer to the average perception of McCain, a score of −1 if their positions were closer to the average perception of Obama, and a score of 0 if they had no preference on an issue.[25] The scores for all seven issue scales were added together, creating a measure that ranged from −7 to +7.

For example, respondents who were closer to the average perception of Obama's positions on all seven scales received a score of −7. A negative score indicated that the respondent was, on balance, closer to the public's perception of Obama, while a positive score indicated the respondent was, overall, closer to the public's perception of McCain.[26] We collapsed this fifteen-point measure into seven categories, running from strongly Democratic through neutral to strongly Republican.[27] The results are reported in Table 6-7.

As can be seen in part A of Table 6-7, 7 percent of respondents were strongly Democratic; almost twice as many were strongly Republican. One in four was moderately or slightly Democratic, and four in ten fell in the two comparable Republican categories. Thus the balance of issues measure tilted noticeably in the Republican direction, even though the respondents were often just slightly closer to McCain than Obama on specific issues.[28]

The balance of issues measure, however, was strongly related to the vote, as the findings for the individual issues would suggest (see part B of Table 6-7). Obama won the vast majority of the votes from those in the strongly and moderately Democratic categories, and three in four from those in the slightly Democratic category. He won a bit more than six in ten votes from those in the neutral category and then about the average level of support from those in the slightly Republican category. His support dropped off dramatically from that point. Indeed, the decline in Democratic voting across the net balance of issues categories is about as strong in 2008 as it was in 1984, 1996, 2000, and 2004.

The Abortion Issue

We give special attention to the public policy controversy over abortion for two reasons. First, it is an especially divisive issue. The Republican national platform has taken a strong pro-life stand since 1980, while the Democratic Party has became increasingly pro-choice. Indeed, abortion is one of the most contentious issues in government at all levels, between the two parties, and among the public. In addition, it is one of a complex of issues that define much of the social issues dimension, one of two major dimensions of domestic policy (economics being the second) into which most domestic policies—and most controversial issues—fall. Although same-sex marriage is a relatively new aspect of social issues (as conservatives would put it, a new addition to the set of family issues), abortion has been central to the rise of social conservatism in America, virtually back to its modern emergence in the wake of *Roe v. Wade* (1973), the Supreme Court decision that made abortion legal throughout the United States.

The second reason for examining this issue is that it is another policy question about which respondents were asked their own views as well as what they thought McCain's and Obama's positions were—a battery that has been asked for the last several elections. It differs from (and is therefore hard to compare directly with) the seven-point issue scales, however, because respondents were given only four alternatives, but each was a specified policy option:

TABLE 6-7 Distribution of Electorate on Net Balance of Issues Measure and Major-Party Vote, 2008

	Net balance of issues								
	Strongly Democratic	Moderately Democratic	Slightly Democratic	Neutral	Slightly Republican	Moderately Republican	Strongly Republican	Total	(N)
A. Distribution of responses									
Percent	7	10	17	10	22	21	13	100	(1,167)
B. Major-party voters who voted for Obama									
Percent	96	91	74	62	55	28	21	54	(788)
(N)	(52)	(85)	(130)	(49)	(164)	(175)	(126)		

Source: Authors' analysis of the 2008 ANES survey.

Notes: Numbers in parentheses in part B of the table are the totals on which the percentages are based. Numbers are weighted. Table is based on the random half-sample that received the traditional wording of the issue questions.

1. By law, abortion should never be permitted.
2. The law should permit abortion only in the case of rape, incest, or when the woman's life is in danger.
3. The law should permit abortion for reasons *other than* rape, incest, or danger to the woman's life, but only after the need for the abortion has been clearly established.
4. By law, a woman should always be able to obtain an abortion as a matter of personal choice.

The electorate's responses, reported in Table 6-8, were clearly toward the pro-choice end of the measure in 2008. Among the major-party voters who chose among these four alternatives, four in ten said that abortion should be a matter of personal choice. This is a substantial decrease from four years earlier, when half selected that option, but it was almost exactly the same as in 2000. In 2008, 19 percent (up from 15 percent in 2004 and 17 percent in 2000) were willing to allow abortions for reasons other than rape, incest, or danger to the woman's life, while 26 percent said abortion should be allowed only under those conditions (the same as in 2004). Only 14 percent said that abortion should never be permitted, which is up from the 8 percent in 2004 and 12 percent in 2000. Thus, although 2004 stood out for its increase in pro-choice sentiments, respondents in 2008 still tilted toward the pro-choice end of the scale, with six in ten favoring abortion for a variety of reasons and only one in seven supporting a complete ban.

A voter's opinion on this issue was strongly related to the way he or she voted. Table 6-8 presents the percentage of major-party voters who voted for Obama according to their view on the abortion issue. Because the survey asked respondents what they thought McCain's and Obama's positions were, we can look into whether the basic issue voting criteria apply. If they do, we can expect to find a very strong relationship between the respondents' positions and how they voted if they met three additional conditions, beyond having an opinion on this issue themselves. First, they had to have an opinion about where the candidates stood on the issue. Second, they had to see a difference between the positions of the two major-party nominees. Third, to cast a policy-related vote reflecting the actual positions of the candidates, they had to recognize that Obama held a more pro-choice position than McCain. In 2008 seven in ten major-party voters met all these conditions, similar to the figures obtained in many other recent election surveys (particularly 1992). Note that this level of satisfaction of all of the issue voting conditions is considerably higher than for the seven-point issue scales discussed earlier (see Table 6-6).

CONCLUSION

Our findings suggest that for major-party voters prospective issues were important in the 2008 election, perhaps not quite as important as at their high-water

TABLE 6-8 Percentage of Major-Party Voters Who Voted for Obama, by Opinion about Abortion and What They Believe McCain's and Obama's Positions Were, 2008

	Respondent's position on abortion							
	Abortion should never be permitted		Abortion should be permitted only in the case of rape, incest, or danger to health of the woman		Abortion should be permitted for other reasons, but only if a need is established		Abortion should be a matter of personal choice	
	%	(N)	%	(N)	%	(N)	%	(N)
All major-party voters	27	(99)	44	(203)	45	(149)	73	(321)
Major-party voters who placed both candidates, who saw a difference between them, and who saw Obama as more pro-choice than McCain	16	(64)	33	(120)	44	(105)	79	(232)
Major-party voters who did not meet all three of these conditions	45	(35)	60	(83)	48	(44)	55	(89)

Source: Authors' analysis of the 2008 ANES survey.

Note: Numbers in parentheses are the totals on which percentages are based. Numbers are weighted. Results are restricted to respondents who were in the random half-sample that was asked the traditional version of the seven-point issue scales.

mark in 1996 and 2004, but still important considerations of voters. Prospective issues are particularly important for understanding how citizens voted. They cannot account for Obama's victory in the popular vote. Those for whom prospective issues gave a clear choice voted consistently with those issues. But not only were somewhat more voters closer to McCain than Obama, but also most people were located between the candidates as the electorate saw them. Indeed, on most issues the majority of people were relatively moderate, and the candidates were perceived as more conservative and more liberal, respectively. Moreover, even though abortion and other prospective issues were strongly related to the vote in 2008, these results do not prove that policy preferences shape voting decisions. Some voters may have projected the position they favored onto the candidate they favored.[29] And it does appear that unless all the basic conditions for issue voting are present, issue voting does not occur. When the conditions are present, there can be a strong relationship between the position voters hold and their choice between the major-party candidates. For these reasons, we conclude that voters took prospective issues into account in 2008, but that they also considered other factors. In the next chapter, we will see that the second form of policy voting, that based on retrospective evaluations, was among those other factors, as it has been in previous presidential elections.

Chapter 7

Presidential Performance and Candidate Choice

Just as in 2004, in 2008 the presidential candidates focused mostly on war and the economy.[1] Although both candidates took very different stances on these concerns in 2008, as their counterparts did in 2004, the 2008 campaign differed from the 2004 one in several important ways. In both contests, the Democratic candidate argued about the failures of the Bush administration, particularly its handling of the war in Iraq and of the economy. On the Republican side, however, George W. Bush campaigned in 2004 on the record of his administration, claiming that his policies were working. His relatively close reelection owed much to the somewhat more positive than negative evaluations of those policies. In 2008 the Republican candidate, John McCain, was not a part of the Bush administration, and so he could at least attempt to say that the voters should not hold him responsible for Bush's policies. And McCain wanted to make that argument because by 2008 the Bush administration was very unpopular in general, and its war policies, especially in Iraq, and its handling of the economy were very unpopular in particular.

Voters might well have reasoned along similar lines in 2008 as they did in 2004 in determining whom they would support—that is, they would choose McCain if they thought Bush had done a good job dealing with problems or at least thought that McCain would handle them well, and they would choose Barack Obama if they thought he would handle the problems better. In many respects, the 2008 campaign was likely to be all but dominated by retrospective evaluations because of the apparent strength of opinion about such concerns. At the least, voters would choose on this basis to the extent that they held the McCain-Palin ticket responsible for the successes and failures they attributed to the Republican Party and its outgoing presidential administration.

In the aftermath of the very close election in 2000, many Democrats, as well as pundits, had criticized Al Gore for his failure to campaign on the successes of the

Clinton-Gore administration. They believed that, by doing so, he could have reminded voters of the positive performance of the American economy in the late 1990s.[2] These criticisms were easy to understand because there has often been a close correspondence between the performance of the economy and the electoral fortunes of the incumbent president's party, both directly and indirectly. A strong economy enhances the incumbent's approval ratings, thereby strengthening his party's support among the electorate. Indeed, in 1988 George W. Bush's father was aided in his bid to rise from vice president to president by the strong economy during the Reagan-Bush administration.[3] But by 1992 the voters had concluded that it was time to "throw the rascals out," and Bush the incumbent lost to Bill Clinton.[4] To the extent that voters were considering the successes and failures of the incumbent president and his party in these cases, perhaps in comparison to what they thought his opponent and the opponent's party would have done had they been in office, voters were casting a retrospective vote.

Retrospective evaluations are concerns about policy, but they differ significantly from the prospective evaluations considered in the last chapter. Retrospective evaluations are, as the name suggests, concerns about the past. These evaluations focus on outcomes, with what actually happened, rather than on the policy means for achieving outcomes, which are at the heart of prospective evaluations. For example, after his reelection in 2004 George W. Bush argued that there was a looming problem in Social Security and proposed private accounts as a solution. Even though other events soon intervened to draw attention away from this policy, some Democrats argued against the president on the grounds that creating private accounts would actually make the problem worse. These Democrats agreed with Bush that there was a problem, but they were focusing on concerns they had about the policy means that Bush proposed to solve that problem, a classic response in terms of prospective evaluations. Other Democrats argued that there really was no serious problem with Social Security in the first place. Such arguments focused on policy outcomes, which are the basis of retrospective judgments. This scenario illustrates the difference between prospective and retrospective judgments, but also illustrates that the two are often different sides of the same policy coin.

WHAT IS RETROSPECTIVE VOTING?

A voter who casts a ballot for the incumbent party's candidate because the incumbent was, in the voter's opinion, a successful president or votes for the opposition because, in the voter's opinion, the incumbent was unsuccessful is said to have cast a retrospective vote. In other words, retrospective voting decisions are based on evaluations of the course of politics over the last term in office and on evaluations of how much the incumbent should be held responsible for what good or bad occurred. V. O. Key Jr. popularized this argument by suggesting that the voter might be "a rational god of vengeance and of reward."[5]

The more closely a candidate can be tied to the actions of the incumbent, the more likely it is that voters will decide retrospectively. The incumbent president cannot escape such evaluations, and the incumbent vice president is usually identified with (and often chooses to identify himself with) the administration's performance. The electorate has frequently played the role of Key's "rational god," because an incumbent president or vice president has stood for election in twenty-three of the twenty-eight presidential elections since 1900 (all but 1908, 1920, 1928, 1952, and 2008). Thus 2008 is the first election in which we can examine whether the nominee of the incumbent's party was held responsible for the successes and failures of the incumbent administration, even though he was not a part of that administration.

Key's thesis has three aspects. First, retrospective voters are oriented toward outcomes rather than the policy means to achieve them. Second, these voters evaluate the performance of the incumbent only, all but ignoring the opposition. Finally, they evaluate what has been done, paying little attention to what the candidates promise to do in the future.

Anthony Downs presents a different picture of retrospective voting.[6] He argues that voters look to the past to understand what the incumbent party's candidate will do in the future. According to Downs, parties are basically consistent in their goals, methods, and ideologies over time. Therefore, the past performances of both parties' nominees may prove relevant for making predictions about their future conduct. Because it takes time and effort to evaluate campaign promises and because promises are just words, voters find it faster, easier, and safer to use past performance to project the administration's actions for the next four years. Downs also emphasizes that retrospective evaluations are used in making comparisons among the alternatives presented to the voter. Key sees a retrospective referendum on the incumbent's party alone. Downs believes that retrospective evaluations are used to compare the candidates as well as to provide a guide to the future. Even incumbents may use such Downsian retrospective claims. In 1996, for example, Clinton attempted to tie his opponent, Sen. Bob Dole, to the performance of congressional Republicans because they had assumed the majority in the 1994 election. Clinton pointedly referred to the 104th Congress as the "Dole-Gingrich" Congress.

Morris P. Fiorina elaborates on and extends Downs's thesis. For our purposes, Fiorina's major addition to the Downsian perspective is his argument that party identification plays a central role. He argues that "citizens monitor party promises and performances over time, encapsulate their observations in a summary judgment termed 'party identification,' and rely on this core of previous experience when they assign responsibility for current societal conditions and evaluate ambiguous platforms designed to deal with uncertain futures."[7] We return to Fiorina's views on partisanship in Chapter 8.

Retrospective voting and voting according to issue positions, as analyzed in Chapter 6, differ significantly. The difference lies in how concerned people are with societal outcomes and how concerned they are with the policy means to achieve desired outcomes. For example, everyone prefers economic prosperity. The disagreement among political decision makers lies in how best to achieve it. At the voters' level, however, the central question is whether people care only about achieving prosperity or whether they care about, or even are able to judge, how to achieve this desired goal. Perhaps they looked at high inflation and interest rates in 1980 and said, "We tried Carter's approach, and it failed. Let's try something else—anything else." They may have noted the long run of relative economic prosperity from 1983 to 1988 and said, "Whatever Reagan did, it worked. Let's keep it going by putting his vice president in office." In 1996 they may have agreed with Clinton that he had presided over a successful economy, and so they decided to remain with the incumbent. In 2004 just how these concerns would play was uncertain. Would the public judge the economy as improving sufficiently or was its recent improvement too little, too late? Would Iraq be viewed as a success or a failure?

Economic policy and foreign affairs issues are especially likely to be discussed in these terms because they share several characteristics. First, the outcomes are clear, and most voters can judge whether they approve of the results. Inflation and unemployment are high or low; the economy is growing or it is not. The country is at war or at peace; the world is stable or unstable. Indeed, one thing that made 2004 unusual was that economic conditions, though improving, were still a mixture of good and bad results, and that the outcome of the war in Iraq was uncertain. Even so, voters could and did make these assessments. Second, there is often near consensus on the desired outcomes; no one disagrees with peace or prosperity, with world stability, or with low unemployment. Third, the means to achieving these ends are often very complex, and information is hard to understand; experts as well as candidates and parties disagree over the specific ways to achieve the desired ends. How should the economy be improved, and how could terrorism possibly be contained or democracy established in a foreign land?

As issues, therefore, peace and prosperity differ sharply from policy areas such as abortion, in which there is vigorous disagreement over ends among experts, leaders, and the public. On still other issues, people value both ends *and* means. The classic cases often revolve around the question of whether it is appropriate for government to take action in a particular area at all. Ronald Reagan was fond of saying, "Government isn't the solution to our problems; government *is* the problem." For example, should the government provide national health insurance? Few disagree with the end of better health care, but they do disagree over the appropriate means to achieve it. The choice of means touches on some of the basic philosophical and ideological differences that have divided Republicans and Democrats for decades.[8] For example, in the 1984 presidential campaign Walter Mondale agreed with Reagan that the country was in a period of economic prosperity and that prosperity was a good thing, but he also argued that Reagan's policies were unfair to the disadvantaged. In the 1992 campaign, Bill Clinton and Ross Perot claimed that Reagan's and

George H. W. Bush's policies, by creating such large deficits, were creating the conditions for future woes. Clearly, then, disagreement was not over the ends, but over the means and the consequences that would follow from using different means to achieve them.

Two basic conditions must be met before retrospective evaluations can affect voting choices. First, individuals must connect their concerns (especially the problems they feel are among the most important) with the incumbent and the actions he took in office. This condition would not be present if, for example, a voter blamed earlier administrations with sowing the seeds that grew into the huge deficits of the 1980s, blamed a profligate Congress, or even believed that the problems were beyond anyone's control. Second, individuals, in the Downs-Fiorina view, must compare their evaluations of the incumbent's past performance with what they believe the nominee of the opposition party would do. For example, even if they thought George W. Bush's performance on the economy was weak, voters might have compared that performance with John Kerry's programs in 2004 and concluded that his efforts would not result in any better outcome and might even make things worse.

In this second condition, a certain asymmetry exists, one that benefits the incumbent. Even if the incumbent's performance has been weak in a certain area, the challenger still has to convince voters that he could do better. It is more difficult, however, for a challenger to convince voters who think the incumbent's performance has been strong that he, the challenger, would be even stronger. This asymmetry advantaged Republican candidates in the 1980s, but worked to Bob Dole's disadvantage in 1996 and to Bush's in 2000. Would this asymmetry apply to 2008? Or perhaps, would both sides have the more difficult problem of convincing the electorate they could handle important problems, not having been in a presidential administration?

We examine next some illustrative retrospective evaluations and study their impact on voter choice. In Chapter 6 we looked at issue scales designed to measure the public's evaluations of candidates' promises. For the incumbent party, the public can evaluate not only its promises but also its actions. We compare promises with performance in this chapter, but one must remember that the distinctions are not as sharp in practice as they are in principle.[9] The Downs-Fiorina view is that past actions and projections about the future are necessarily intertwined.

EVALUATIONS OF GOVERNMENT PERFORMANCE
ON IMPORTANT PROBLEMS

"Now thinking about the performance of the government in Washington in general, how good or bad a job do you think the government in Washington has done over the past four years?"[10] This question is designed to measure retrospective judgments, and the responses are presented in Table 7-1. In the appendix to this book, we report responses to the question the American National Election Studies had asked in prior surveys, comparing the respondents' evaluations of government performance on the problem that each respondent identified as the single most important one facing the country.[11] The most striking finding in part A of Table 7-1 is that in 2008 few thought the government was doing a very good job or even a good job. Barely more than one in four chose either of these top two categories. Two in five thought the government was doing a bad job, and another one in three said it was doing a very bad job—that is, seven in ten thought the government's performance was bad. In 2004 six in ten said Bush was doing a good or very good job, and only four in ten said he was not, which is obviously a much more positive result than in 2008. It is difficult to compare these results with those from earlier years because the question was worded differently then, but it is clear that evaluations were extremely negative in 2008 (see Table A7-1 in the appendix). To the extent that we can make comparisons with earlier elections, 2008 is most similar to 1980 and 1992, elections with negative opinions and in which the incumbent party was soundly defeated. By contrast, 2004 looked most like 2000 and

TABLE 7-1   Evaluation of Government Performance and Major-Party Vote, 2008 (percent)

Evaluation	2008
A. Evaluation of government performance during the last four years	
Very good job	2
Good job	24
Bad job	42
Very bad job	31
Total	100
(N)	(2,083)
B. Percentage of major-party vote for incumbent party's nominee	
Very good job	69
(N)	(24)
Good job	75
(N)	(359)
Bad job	47
(N)	(658)
Very bad job	21
(N)	(512)

Source: Authors' analysis of the 2008 ANES survey.

Note: The numbers in parentheses in part B are the totals on which the percentages are based. The numbers in parts A and B are weighted.

not that dissimilar from 1976, 1984, and 1996—two elections that did return the incumbent party to office (1984 and 1996) and two that narrowly did not (1976 and 2000).[12]

If the voter is a rational god of vengeance and reward, we can expect to find a strong relationship between the evaluation of government performance and the vote. Such is indeed the case for all elections (see Table A7-1 in the appendix), and 2008 was no exception (see part B of Table 7-1). Typically, seven to nine out of every ten major-party voters who thought the government was doing a good job on the most important problem voted for the incumbent party's nominee in each election. In 1996 those who thought the government was doing a good job with the most important problem supported Clinton even more strongly than they had supported incumbents in previous elections, and in 2004 Bush came very close to holding the same level of support. By 2008, however, and even though the question asks more generally about problems, Bush's unpopularity was bad news for McCain, because just over two in three who thought the government had done poorly voted against the nominee of the incumbent's party. Although McCain did hold on to nearly three in four who thought the Bush administration had done a good job, there were just too few such voters.

According to Downs and Fiorina, it is important for voters not only to evaluate how things have been going but also to assess how that evaluation compares with the alternative. In most recent elections, including 2008, respondents have been asked which party would do a better job of solving the problem they named as the most important. Part A of Table 7-2 shows the responses to these questions (also see the appendix for comparison to earlier elections). These questions are clearly oriented toward the future, but they may call for judgments about past performance, consistent with the Downs-Fiorina view. Respondents were not asked to evaluate policy alternatives, and thus responses were most likely based on a retrospective comparison of how the incumbent party handled things with a prediction about how the opposition would fare. We therefore consider these questions to be a measure of comparative retrospective evaluations.

Part A in Table 7-2 shows that the public had different views about which party was better at handling their important concerns. In prior elections, slightly more than one in four had thought the Republicans were better able to handle their most important concern. This is not much different from some earlier elections, including major Republican defeats (such as in 1996), solid victories (such as in 1988), and major landslide victories (such as in 1972).

The difference from these earlier elections is that in 2008 very few voters thought neither party was better. Rather, a majority thought the Democrats were better able to handle their most important concern. In no other contest was it true that a majority of the public thought a party was better in this regard. The closest was in 1980 when a near majority thought the Republicans would be better, and, as in 2008, the incumbent party was ousted. But even then, in 1980 more thought neither party was better able to handle the most

TABLE 7-2   Evaluation of Party Seen as Better on Most Important Political Problem and Major-Party Vote, 2008 (percent)

Better party	2008
A. Distribution of responses on party seen as better on most important political problem	
Republican	27
No difference[a]	18
Democratic	55
Total	100
(N)	(1,932)
B. Major-party voters who voted Democratic for president	
Republican	6
(N)	(429)
No difference[a]	39
(N)	(237)
Democratic	87
(N)	(800)

Source: Authors' analysis of the 2008 ANES survey.

Note: The numbers in parentheses are the totals on which the percentages are based. Numbers are weighted. Question wording: "Thinking of the most important political problem facing the United States, which party do you think is best in dealing with it?"

[a] In 2008 the middle response allowed was "other." Most respondents in the middle category volunteered no difference.

important problem. In 2008 very few selected the "neither party" option, and thus the Democratic Party held a huge advantage on this measure.

Why was 2008 so different from all preceding elections in this regard? We cannot be certain, but it is likely a mixture of two things. One is the genuine dissatisfaction with the Bush administration, combined with the fact that the Republicans had controlled both houses of Congress for six of Bush's eight years in office, with McCain supporting Bush's Iraq policy. Also, during the campaign McCain did not handle the unfolding national economic crisis well. The second is the public's very positive opinion of Obama, as we saw in Chapter 6. His positive image and his message of "change" may have convinced the public that he actually might well do better than the Republicans in handling the most important problems facing the country.

Part B of Table 7-2 reveals that the relationship between the party seen as better on the most important political problem and the vote is very strong. Obama won nearly nine in ten votes from those who thought the Democrats would be better. McCain was able to hold nearly all of those who thought the Republican Party better able to handle the most important problem and about three in ten of those who saw no difference between the two parties. McCain's problem, therefore, was not that this variable was related to the vote differently than in prior elections. His problem was that opinion was so strongly against his party.

The data presented in Tables 7-1 and 7-2 have an important limitation. The first question, analyzed in Table 7-1, refers to how the government is doing and not the incumbent president. The question examined in Table 7-2 refers to which political party would handle the problem better and does not directly refer to the incumbent—we believe it is the assessment of the incumbent that relates most directly to voters' evaluations of the candidates. Thus we look more closely at the incumbent and at people's comparisons of his and the opposition's performance where the data are available to permit such comparisons.

ECONOMIC EVALUATIONS AND THE VOTE FOR THE INCUMBENT

More than any other, economic issues have been highlighted as suitable retro-spective issues. The impact of economic conditions on congressional and presidential elections has been studied extensively.[13] Popular evaluations of presidential effectiveness, John E. Mueller has pointed out, are strongly influenced by the economy. Edward R. Tufte suggests that because the incumbent realizes his fate may hinge on the performance of the economy, he may attempt to manipulate it, leading to what is known as a "political business cycle."[14] A major reason for Jimmy Carter's defeat in 1980 was the perception that economic performance had been weak during his administration. Reagan's rhetorical question in the 1980 debate with Carter, "Are you better off than you were four years ago?" indicates that politicians realize the power such arguments have over the electorate. Reagan owed his sweeping reelection victory in 1984 largely to the perception that economic performance by the end of his first term had become, after a deep recession in the middle, much stronger.

If people are concerned about economic outcomes, they might start by looking for an answer to the sort of question Reagan asked. Part A of Table 7-3 presents ANES respondents' perceptions of whether they were financially better off than one year earlier. From 1972 to 1980, about a third of the sample felt they were better off. Over that period, however, more and more of the remainder felt they were worse off. By 1980, "worse now" was the most common response. But by 1984 many respondents were feeling the economic recovery, and more than two in five said they were better off than in the previous year; only a little more than one in four felt worse off. But because 1984 was only two years after a deep recession, many may have seen their economic fortunes improve considerably over the prior year or so. By 1988 that recovery had been sustained, and the distribution of responses to this question in 1988 was very similar to that of 1984. By 1992 there was a return to the feelings of the earlier period, and responses were nearly evenly divided between "better now," "same," and "worse now." In 1996 the responses were like those of the 1984 and 1988

TABLE 7-3 Public's Assessment of Personal Financial Situation and Major-Party Vote, 1972–2008 (percent)

"Would you say that you (and your family) are better off or worse off financially than you were a year ago?"

Response	1972[a]	1976	1980	1984	1988	1992	1996	2000[a]	2004	2008
A. Distribution of responses										
Better now	36	34	33	44	42	31	46	33	43	32
Same	42	35	25	28	33	34	31	53	25	18
Worse now	23	31	42	27	25	35	24	14	32	50
Total	101	100	100	99	100	100	101	100	100	100
(N)	(955)	(2,828)[b]	(1,393)	(1,956)	(2,025)	(2,474)[b]	(1,708)[b]	(907)[b]	(1,203)[b]	(2,307)[b]
B. Major-party voters who voted for the incumbent party nominee for president										
Better now	69	55	46	74	63	53	66	56	65	53
(N)	(247)	(574)[b]	(295)	(612)	(489)	(413)[b]	(462)[b]	(164)[b]	(354)[b]	(491)[b]
Same	70	52	46	55	50	45	52	51	50	52
(N)	(279)	(571)[b]	(226)	(407)	(405)	(500)[b]	(348)[b]	(291)[b]	(207)[b]	(280)[b]
Worse now	52	38	40	33	40	27	47	45	28	38
(N)	(153)	(475)[b]	(351)	(338)	(283)	(453)[b]	(225)[b]	(56)[b]	(219)[b]	(778)[b]

Source: Authors' analysis of ANES surveys.

Note: The numbers in parentheses are the totals on which the percentages are based.

[a] This question was asked of a randomly selected half-sample in 1972 and 2000.

[b] Number is weighted.

elections—and even slightly more favorable than in those years. In 2000 about a third felt better off, similar to responses through 1980. However, far fewer felt worse off in 2000 than in any of the seven preceding elections. Over half responded in 2000 that they were about the same as a year ago. In 2004 we see a return to the pattern more typical of the 1984, 1988, and 1996 elections, with over two in five feeling better off, the most popular response. Unlike the preceding comparisons, however, nearly a third felt worse off and a quarter felt about the same. The year 2008, however, was a different story, because half the respondents said they were worse off, with only a third saying they were better off (the same as in 1992), and very few feeling their finances were the same. As before, we can see that these figures presented the Republicans with bad news and the Democrats with good news.

In part B of Table 7-3, we see how the responses to this question are related to the two-party presidential vote. That relationship, however, is not particularly strong. McCain was able to win just over half the votes of those who felt better off, just as he did among those relatively few who felt neither better nor worse off. Obama won support from a clear majority of that half of the electorate who felt worse off, winning over three in five of their votes. That is clearly a weaker relationship than in 2004, which was one of the strongest of all the elections we have analyzed. The closest comparison with 2008 is 1976, another year in which the incumbent Republicans lost the White House. Perhaps the weaker relationship in 2008 stems from the dramatic changes in the economy during the campaign, changes that had not yet fully affected the individual. Layoffs, the housing crisis, and other economic setbacks were expected to worsen dramatically over the coming months, as they in fact did—as the public perhaps anticipated—so that their immediate circumstances were less relevant than what they expected to be coming soon.

People may "vote their pocketbooks," but they are even more likely to vote retrospectively based on their judgments of how the economy as a whole has been faring. And personal and national economic experiences can be quite different. In 1980, for example, about 40 percent of respondents thought their own financial situation was worse than the year before, but responses to the 1980 ANES survey revealed that twice as many (83 percent) thought the national economy was worse off than the year before. In 1992 the public gave the nation's economy a far more negative assessment than they gave their own financial situations. That was not the case in 1996 and 2000, when respondents gave broadly similar assessments of their personal fortunes and those of the nation. Thus those two elections most resemble the 1984 one. But then in 2004 the public had very negative views of the economy as a whole, with nearly half describing it as worse, three in ten as the same, and only one in four as better. And what about 2008? According to the data in Table 7-4, the public saw the economy in 2008 in the most negative terms ever observed in these surveys. Fully nine in ten respondents believed that the economy was worse off.

TABLE 7-4 Public's View of the State of the Economy and Major-Party Vote, 1980–2008 (percent)

Response	"Would you say that over the past year the nation's economy has gotten …?"							
	1980	1984	1988	1992	1996	2000[b]	2004[b]	2008[b]
A. Distribution of responses								
Better	4	44	19	4	40	39	24	2
Stayed same	13	33	50	22	44	44	31	7
Worse	83	23	31	73	16	17	45	90
Total	100	100	100	99	100	100	100	99
(N)	(1,580)	(1,904)	(1,956)	(2,465)[a]	(1,700)[a]	(1,787)[a]	(1,196)[a]	(2,313)[b]
B. Major-party voters who voted for the incumbent party nominee for president								
Better	58	80	77	86	75	69	87	69
(N)	(33)	(646)	(249)	(62)[a]	(458)[a]	(408)[a]	(211)[a]	(34)[a]
Stayed same	71	53	53	62	45	45	88	57
(N)	(102)	(413)	(568)	(318)[a]	(443)[a]	(487)[a]	(243)[a]	(109)[a]
Worse	39	21	34	32	33	31	20	44
(N)	(732)	(282)	(348)	(981)[a]	(130)[a]	(154)[a]	(319)[a]	(1,425)[a]

Source: Authors' analysis of ANES surveys.

Note: The numbers in parentheses are the totals on which percentages are based.

[a] Number is weighted.

[b] We combine the results using standard and experimental prompts that contained different word ordering in 2000, 2004, and 2008.

In part B of Table 7-4, we show the relationship between responses to these items and the major-party vote for president. The relationship between these measures and the vote is always strong. Moreover, a comparison of part B of Table 7-3 and part B of Table 7-4 reveals that, in general, the vote is more closely associated with perceptions of the nation's economy than it is with perceptions of one's personal economic well-being. In 2008, however, the perceptions of the economy were so one-sidedly negative that there is very little room for a strong relationship. To be sure, McCain won the votes of those who thought the economy was doing better, and, as in most elections, the incumbent party held a majority of those who thought the economy was just the same as in the year before. But very few people were in either category. Thus the percentage backing Obama among those who thought the economy was worse off differed only slightly from the electorate as a whole, because virtually the whole electorate thought the economy was worse off!

To this point, we have looked at personal and national economic conditions and the role of the government in shaping them. We have not yet looked at the extent to which such evaluations are attributed to the incumbent. In Table 7-5, we report responses to the question of whether people approved of the incumbent's handling of the economy in the elections of 1980–2008. Although a majority approved of Reagan's handling of the economy in both 1984 and 1988, fewer than one in five held positive views of the economic performance of the Carter administration in 1980. In 1992 evaluations of George H. W. Bush were also very negative. In 1996 evaluations of Clinton's handling of the economy were stronger than those of incumbents in the previous surveys. By 2000 evaluations of Clinton's handling of the economy were even stronger, with three of every four respondents approving. Evaluations of George W. Bush's handling of the economy in 2004 were more negative than positive, although not nearly as negative of those of Jimmy Carter or of George H. W. Bush. By 2008 evaluations of Bush's handling of the economy were very negative. Because different question wording was used in 1980 and 2008, it is hard to be certain, but evaluations were at least as negative of Bush as of Carter, and quite possibly even more so.

The bottom-line question is whether these views are related to voter choice. According to the data in part B of Table 7-5, the answer is yes. Those who held positive views of the incumbent's performance on the economy were very likely to vote for that party's candidate, while those who did not were just as likely to vote against him. As we have seen before, in 2008 those few who gave positive marks to the incumbent supported McCain's candidacy, in this case about as strongly as at any time. Obama won the support of two in three of the vast majority who evaluated Bush's handling of the economy negatively. Again, it is hard to be certain, but this relationship looks most similar to those in 1980 (albeit with its different question wording) and 1992, two bad years for the economy—and for the incumbent party.

TABLE 7-5 Evaluations of the Incumbent's Handling of the Economy and Major-Party Vote, 1980–2008 (percent)

Response	1980[a]	1984	1988	1992	1996	2000	2004	2008
	Approval of incumbent's handling of the economy							
	A. Distribution of responses							
Positive view	18	58	54	20	66	77	41	18
Balanced view	17	[b]	[b]	[b]	[b]	[b]	[b]	[b]
Negative view	65	42	46	80	34	23	59	82
Total	100	100	100	100	100	100	100	100
(N)	(1,097)	(1,858)	(1,897)	(2,425)[c]	(1,666)[c]	(1,686)[c]	(1,173)[c]	(2,227)[c]
	B. Major-party voters who voted for the incumbent party nominee							
Positive view	88	86	80	90	79	67	91	89
(N)	(130)	(801)	(645)	(310)[c]	(688)[c]	(768)[c]	(341)[c]	(313)[c]
Balanced view	60	[b]	[b]	[b]	[b]	[b]	[b]	[b]
(N)	(114)							
Negative view	23	16	17	26	13	11	17	33
(N)	(451)	(515)	(492)	(1,039)[c]	(322)[c]	(233)[c]	(431)[c]	(1,200)[c]

Source: Authors' analysis of ANES surveys.

[a] In 1980 the questions asked whether the respondent approved or disapproved of President Carter's handling of inflation (unemployment). A positive (negative) view was approve (disapprove) on both; balanced responses were approve on one, disapprove on the other.

[b] In 1984, 1988, 1992, 1996, 2000, 2004, and 2008, responses were whether the respondent had a positive or a negative view (balanced view was omitted) of the (president's) handling of the economy.

[c] Number is weighted.

FOREIGN POLICY EVALUATIONS AND THE VOTE
FOR THE INCUMBENT

Foreign and economic policies are, as we noted earlier, commonly evaluated by means of retrospective assessments. These policies share the characteristics of consensual goals (peace and prosperity, respectively, plus security in both cases), complex technology, and difficulty in ascertaining relationships between means and ends. Foreign policy differs from economic policy in one practical way, however. As Table 6-3 illustrates, economic problems are invariably a major concern, but foreign affairs are salient only sporadically. Indeed, foreign affairs are of sufficiently sporadic concern that most surveys, including the ANES, only occasionally have many measures to judge their role in elections.

Three questions included in the 2004 and 2008 ANES surveys examined evaluations of foreign affairs over the recent past. One question asked whether the standing of the United States in the world had become stronger or weaker or stayed the same, and thus called for a general assessment about how well things had gone for the nation in the world. The other two asked respondents to evaluate aspects of the war in Iraq, specifically whether that war was worth the cost and whether it had increased or decreased the threat of terrorism—a point of particular partisan contention. The responses to these questions are reported in Table 7-6.

Part A of Table 7-6 reveals that nearly two-thirds of the respondents thought the United States had become weaker in the world, up from the nearly half (46 percent) who thought so in 2004. Conversely, the 26 percent in 2004 who thought the United States had become stronger had dropped to only 8 percent in 2008. This was hardly good news for the incumbent party, and we can see that in part B of Table 7-6 that Obama won two in three votes of those who thought the United States had weakened, whereas McCain won just under three in four votes of those few who thought the United States had strengthened and two in five of those who saw little change. This relationship was slightly weaker than in 2004, but still quite strong.[15]

In 2004, 40 percent of respondents thought the war in Iraq was worth the cost; the rest thought it was not. In 2008 this measure, too, became more negative, with exactly one-quarter thinking the war was worth the cost, and three-quarters thinking it not. Part B of Table 7-6 shows that opinion about Iraq was quite closely related to the vote, with McCain winning support from eight in nine of those who thought the war was worth the cost but only three in ten from those who disagreed. This pattern is similar to that in 2004 in which 91 percent of those who thought the war was worth the cost backed Bush and 80 percent of those who did not voted for Kerry. The question about Iraq and terrorism was not asked in 2004. In 2008 there was a balanced relationship, with nearly half of respondents saying that the war in Iraq had neither increased nor

TABLE 7-6   Evaluations of Three Foreign Policy Issues and Major-Party Vote, 2008 (percent)

	U.S. standing in the world over the past year	Iraq War worth the cost		Iraq War increased or decreased the threat of terrorism	
A. Evaluation of issues					
Stronger	8	Worth it	25	Decreased	26
Stayed the same	27			Stayed the same	46
Weaker	65	Not worth it	75	Increased	29
Total	100		100		101
(N)	(2,295)		(2,251)		(2,298)
B. Major-party voters holding these views who voted Republican for president					
Stronger	72	Worth it	86	Decreased	78
(N)	(119)		(418)		(413)
Stayed the same	60			Stayed the same	42
(N)	(384)				(719)
Weaker	37	Not worth it	29	Increased	18
(N)	(1,045)		(1,102)		(418)

Source: Authors' analysis of the 2008 ANES survey.

Note: Numbers are weighted. The numbers in parentheses in part B are the totals on which the percentages are based.

decreased the threat of terrorism; the rest were nearly evenly divided between the war increasing and decreasing the threat. Part B shows as well that responses to this question were strongly related to the vote, with each candidate winning about eight in ten votes from those who supported the position claimed by that candidate's party, while Obama won only a modest majority of those who said the threat had stayed the same. Thus the relationship between opinion and the vote on all three of these measures belies the belief that "voting ends at water's edge"—that is, that voters choose on the basis of domestic considerations and pay little attention to and care little about foreign affairs.

Table 7-7 presents data on two measures of approval of Bush's performance: how well he handled the war in Iraq and foreign relations more generally. Part A of Table 7-7 demonstrates that three in ten respondents approved of Bush on both measures. Once again, these ratings are more negative than in 2004, when Bush gained the approval of 42 and 44 percent on these issues respectively. And, as is evident in part B of Table 7-7, these measures were strongly related to the vote, with McCain winning 88 and 83 percent support on these two measures, respectively—only slightly less than Bush had won in 2004 when he was supported by 92 and 93 percent, respectively.

TABLE 7-7   President's Handling of Two Foreign Policy Issues and Major-
Party Vote, 2008 (percent)

"Do you approve or disapprove of the way George W. Bush is handling ...?"		
	War in Iraq	Foreign relations
A. Distribution of responses		
Approve	30	31
Disapprove	70	69
Total	100	100
(*N*)	(2,254)	(2,215)
B. Major-party voters who voted for the incumbent party's nominee		
Approve	88	83
(*N*)	(526)	(536)
Disapprove	22	24
(*N*)	(999)	(967)

Source: Authors' analysis of the 2008 ANES survey.

Note: Numbers are weighted. The numbers in parentheses in part B of the table are the totals on which the percentages are based.

EVALUATIONS OF THE INCUMBENT

Fiorina distinguishes between "simple" and "mediated" retrospective evaluations. By simple, Fiorina means evaluations of the direct effects of social outcomes on the person, such as one's financial status, or direct perceptions of the nation's economic well-being. Mediated retrospective evaluations are evaluations seen through or mediated by the perceptions of political actors and institutions.[16] Approval of George W. Bush's handling of the economy and the assessment of which party would better handle the war in Iraq are examples.

As we have seen, the more politically mediated the question, the more closely the responses align with voting behavior. Perhaps the ultimate in mediated evaluations is the presidential approval question: "Do you approve or disapprove of the way [the incumbent] is handling his job as president?" From a retrospective voting standpoint, this evaluation is a summary of all aspects of the incumbent's service in office. Table 7-8 reports the distribution of overall evaluations and their relationship to major-party voting in the last ten elections.[17]

Part A of Table 7-8 reveals that incumbents Richard Nixon (1972), Gerald Ford (1976), Ronald Reagan (1984), and Bill Clinton (1996) enjoyed widespread approval, whereas only two respondents in five approved of Jimmy Carter's and of George H. W. Bush's handling of the job in 1980 and 1992, respectively. This situation presented Carter and Bush with a problem. Conversely, highly approved incumbents, such as Reagan in 1984 and Clinton in 1996—and their vice presidents as beneficiaries in 1988 and 2000, respectively—had a major

TABLE 7-8 President's Handling of Job and Major-Party Vote, 1972–2008 (percent)

	1972[a]	1976	1980	1984	1988	1992	1996	2000	2004	2008
"Do you approve or disapprove of the way [the incumbent] is handling his job as president?"										
A. Distribution of responses										
Approve	71	63	41	63	60	43	68	67	51	27
Disapprove	29	37	59	37	40	57	32	33	49	73
Total	100	100	100	100	100	100	100	100	100	100
(N)	(1,215)	(2,439)[b]	(1,475)	(2,091)	(1,935)	(2,419)[b]	(1,692)[b]	(1,742)[b]	(1,182)[b]	(2,245)[b]
B. Major-party voters who voted for the incumbent party's nominee										
Approve	83	74	81	87	79	81	84	74	91	88
(N)	(553)	(935)[b]	(315)	(863)	(722)	(587)[b]	(676)[b]	(662)[b]	(408)[b]	(441)[b]
Disapprove	14	9	18	7	12	11	4	13	6	26
(N)	(203)	(523)[b]	(491)	(449)	(442)	(759)[b]	(350)[b]	(366)[b]	(372)[b]	(1,075)[b]

Source: Authors' analysis of ANES surveys.

Note: The numbers in parentheses in part B are the totals on which percentages are based.

[a] Question was asked of a randomly selected half-sample in 1972.

[b] Number is weighted.

advantage. Clinton dramatically reversed any negative perceptions held of his incumbency in 1994, so that by 1996 he received the highest level of approval in the fall of an election year since Nixon's landslide reelection in 1972. Between 1996 and 2000, Clinton suffered through several scandals, one of which culminated in his impeachment in 1998. Such events might be expected to lead to substantial declines in his approval ratings, but instead his ratings remained high—higher even than Reagan's at the end of his presidency. The evaluations in 2004 present a more varied picture. For the first time in nine elections, the proportions approving and disapproving of George W. Bush were almost exactly the same. In view of what we have seen so far, it should come as no surprise that evaluations of Bush turned dramatically by 2008, so that he was by far the least approved incumbent during this period, with nearly three in four respondents disapproving of his handling of the office.

If it is true that the more mediated the evaluation, the more closely it seems to align with behavior, and if presidential approval is the most mediated evaluation of all, then we would expect a powerful relationship with the vote. As part B of Table 7-8 illustrates, that is true over the full set of elections for which we have the relevant data. In 2008 McCain won the support of just under nine in ten of the minority who approved of Bush's performance, and he won the support of a quarter of those who disapproved. Both of these percentages are higher than in most other elections, suggesting that McCain did at least slightly better than others in his circumstances. The problem for him, of course, lies in the fact that so many disapproved of Bush's performance.

THE IMPACT OF RETROSPECTIVE EVALUATIONS

Our evidence strongly suggests that retrospective voting has been widespread in all recent elections. Moreover, as far as data permit us to judge, the evidence is clearly on the side of the Downs-Fiorina view. Retrospective evaluations appear to be used to make comparative judgments. Presumably, voters find it easier, less time-consuming, and less risky to evaluate the incumbent party based on what its president did in the most recent term or terms in office than on the nominees' promises for the future. But few people base their votes on judgments of past performance alone. Most use past judgments as a starting point for comparing the major contenders with respect to their likely future performances. Furthermore, it appears that voters were nearly as willing to apply their judgments about what proved to be a generally unpopular incumbent administration to McCain, who shared a party with the incumbent but was not a part of his administration, as they were to apply their judgments of incumbent performance to predecessors who were either the incumbent president or vice president.

In analyzing previous elections, we constructed an overall assessment of retrospective voting and compared that overall assessment across elections. We then compared that net retrospective assessment with our balance of issues measure.

Our measure is constructed by combining the presidential approval measure with the evaluation of the job the government has done on important problems, and with the assessment of which party would better handle the problem the respondent thinks is the single most important. We were not able to build this measure for studying the 2004 election, however, because the survey did not include the question about which party would better handle the most important problem. And, although we can (and do) construct a measure for 2008 similar to that for the 1972–2000 election surveys, one of the questions is worded differently, and so comparisons must be considered tentative.[18] The combination of responses to these three questions creates a seven-point scale ranging from strongly opposed to the job the incumbent and his party have done to strongly supportive of that performance. For example, those who approved of Bush's job performance, thought the government was doing a good job, and thought the Republican Party would better handle the most important problem are scored as strongly supportive of Bush in their retrospective evaluations in 2008.

In Table 7-9, we present the results of this measure.[19] The figures indicate that there was a substantial diversity of responses, but that the measure was skewed decidedly against the incumbent—hardly a surprise by this point. By this measure, two in five were strongly opposed to the performance of the Bush administration, with another one in three moderately or slightly opposed. Hardly anyone was neutral, and fewer than one in three was supportive of the Bush administration. Part B of Table 7-9 presents a remarkably clear example of a very strong relationship between responses and votes, with over nine in ten in each of the "strong" categories voting for the appropriate candidate, and very strong majorities doing so in the two "moderate" categories as well. These data strongly suggest that dissatisfaction with the Bush administration lay at the heart of Obama's victory.

We cannot compare 2008 with any other election on this measure, but we can at least make broad generalizations.[20] In earlier years, it was reasonable to conclude that the 1980 election was a clear and strong rejection of Carter's incumbency. In 1984 Reagan won in large part because voters perceived that he had performed well and because Mondale was unable to convince the public that he would do better. In 1988 George H. W. Bush won in large part because Reagan appeared to have performed well—and people thought Bush would stay the course. In 1992 Bush lost because of the far more negative evaluations of his administration and of his party than had been recorded in any recent election except for 1980. In 1996 Clinton won reelection in large part for the same reasons that Reagan won in 1984: he was viewed as having performed well on the job, and he was able to convince the public that his opponent would not do any better. In 2000 Gore essentially tied George W. Bush, because the slightly pro-incumbent set of evaluations combined with a very slight asymmetry against the incumbent in translating those evaluations into voting choices. In 2004 there was a slight victory for the incumbent because, by our different measure, more thought he had performed well than poorly. And 2008 was most like 1980, with

TABLE 7-9 Summary Measure of Retrospective Evaluations of the George W. Bush Administration and Major-Party Vote, 2008

	Strongly opposed	Moderately opposed	Slightly opposed	Neutral	Slightly supportive	Moderately supportive	Strongly supportive	Total (N)
	A. Distribution of responses							
Percent	41	18	13	1	10	10	8	101 (2,075)
	B. Major-party voters who voted for Obama							
Percent	91	62	31	[1]	13	8	4	55
(N)	(666)	(248)	(165)	(6)	(154)	(161)	(150)	(1,559)

Source: Authors' analysis of the 2008 ANES survey.

Note: Numbers are weighted. The numbers in part B are the totals on which the percentages are based. In the one instance in which a response includes fewer than ten major-party voters, the total number who voted for Obama appears in brackets.

a highly skewed distribution working against the Republicans (likely the most skewed measure of all, subject to wording differences).

How do retrospective assessments compare with prospective judgments? As described in Chapter 6, prospective issues, especially our balance of issues measure, have become more strongly related to the vote over the last few elections, peaking in 2004, with 2008 only somewhat more weakly related to the vote. Table 7-10 reports the impact of both types of policy evaluation measures on the major-party vote in 2008. Both policy measures were collapsed into three categories: pro-Democratic, neutral, and pro-Republican. Reading down each column, we see that, controlling for retrospective evaluations, prospective issues are modestly related to the vote in a positive direction. Or, to be more precise, they are modestly related to the vote among those whose retrospective evaluations incline them in the Democratic direction and not at all related to the vote among those in the comparable Republican category. It is thus only among those whose retrospective evaluations did not even moderately incline them toward either party that prospective evaluations are strongly related to the vote.

Reading across each row, we see that retrospective evaluations are very strongly related to the vote. This is true no matter what prospective evaluations

TABLE 7-10   Percentage of Major-Party Voters Who Voted for Obama, by Balance of Issues and Summary Retrospective Measures, 2008

	Summary retrospective						
	Strongly or moderately Democratic		Slightly supportive or slightly opposed or neutral		Strongly or moderately Republican		Total
Net balance of issues	%	(*N*)	%	(*N*)	%	(*N*)	%	(*N*)
Democratic	93	(223)	51	(32)	4	(12)	84	(267)
Neutral	86	(30)	[3]	(9)	17	(11)	62	(49)
Republican	68	(204)	15	(133)	6	(125)	36	(465)
Total	81	(457)	24	(176)	7	(148)	54	(783)

Source: Authors' analysis of the 2008 ANES survey.

Note: The numbers in parentheses are the totals on which the percentages are based. Numbers are weighted. Results are based on the randomly selected half-sample of respondents who were asked the traditional wording of the issue questions. For the condensed measure of retrospective voting, we combine respondents who are strongly positive (or negative) toward George W. Bush and the Republican Party with respondents who are moderately positive (or negative). We combine respondents who are slightly positive (or negative) with those who are neutral (see Table 7-9). For the condensed balance of issues measure, any respondent who is closer to McCain is classified as pro-Republican. The neutral category is the same as the seven-point measure (see Table 6-7). For the one entry with fewer than ten major-party voters, the number who voted for Obama is in brackets.

respondents held. Thus we can conclude that in 2008 retrospective evaluations shaped voting choices to a great extent. Prospective evaluations were still important, but only for those without a moderate or strong partisan direction to their retrospective judgments.

Together, the two kinds of policy measures take us a long way toward understanding voting choices. More than nine out of ten of those with pro-Republican stances on the two measures, for example, voted for McCain, while those with pro-Democratic stances were equally likely to vote for Obama. This accounting of voting choices is stronger when considering both forms of policy evaluations than when looking at either one individually. Note that the two largest percentages are for those with pro-Obama views on both measures and those with pro-McCain views on prospective evaluations but who evaluated the Bush administration negatively. And because over two-thirds of those in the latter category voted for Obama, it is clear why McCain and his running mate, Sarah Palin, attempted to portray themselves as "mavericks" who were independent of the Republican Party and, even more, of the Bush administration.[21]

CONCLUSION

In this and the previous chapter, we have found that both retrospective and prospective evaluations were strongly related to the vote in 2008. Indeed, 2008 presents an unusually clear case of retrospective evaluations being a very powerful reason for Obama's victory. Although such evaluations are always strong, they genuinely stand out in 2008. In 1992, for example, dissatisfaction with George H. W. Bush's performance and with his and his party's handling of the most important problem—usually an economic concern in 1992 (see Table 6-3)—goes a long way toward explaining his defeat, while satisfaction with Clinton's performance and the absence of an advantage for the Republicans in being seen as able to deal with the most important concerns of voters go a long way toward explaining his 1996 victory. In 2000 prospective issues favored neither candidate, because essentially the same number of major-party voters were closer to Bush as were closer to Gore. The Democrat had a modest advantage on retrospective evaluations, but Bush won greater support among those with pro-Republican evaluations than did Gore among those with pro-Democratic evaluations. The result was another even balance and, as a result, a tied outcome. Although Kerry was favored on prospective evaluations in 2004, his advantage was counterbalanced by Bush's slight advantage based on retrospective evaluations, leading to a Bush reelection victory with only a slight gain in the popular vote. By 2008 the public had turned quite negative on Bush's performance, and that led to a major advantage for the Democrats. Even so, our explanation remains incomplete. Most important, we have not accounted for *why* people hold the views they expressed on these two measures. We cannot provide a complete account of the origins of people's views, of course, but there is one important source we can examine: party identification. This variable, which we have used in previous chapters, provides a powerful way in which the typical citizen can reach preliminary judgments. As we will see, partisanship is strongly related to these judgments, especially to retrospective evaluations.

Moreover, party identification plays a central role in debates about the future of American politics. Will the Democratic rebound in Congress in 2006 and the Democrats' capturing of the White House in 2008 lead to long-term changes? Many political scientists believe that change in the political system of this magnitude will emerge only if there are changes in party loyalties in the electorate as well as in its voting behavior. Therefore, to understand voter choice better and to assess future partisan prospects, we must examine the role of party loyalties.

Chapter 8

Party Loyalties, Policy Preferences, and the Vote

Chapter 5 described the influence of social forces such as race, ethnicity, and social class on voting behavior. For example, African Americans do not vote Democratic simply because of their race; race and other social forces provide the context for electoral politics and thus influence how voters reach their decisions. Chapters 6 and 7 described the effects of issues and evaluations of the candidates on the vote. In 2008 reactions to issues such as abortion might have spurred voters to support John McCain, especially after he chose a running-mate who had demonstrated her opposition to abortion by carrying her pregnancy to term even though she knew her baby would have Down syndrome. And yet negative evaluations of George W. Bush's handling of his incumbency might have caused a voter to support Barack Obama. The question here is why did some voters disapprove of Bush's performance, while others did not?

Partisanship is an important part of the answer, because it is the most important factor connecting voters' backgrounds, social settings, and their more immediate assessments of issues and the candidates. Thus a major part of the explanation of why African Americans vote overwhelmingly Democratic are the various events and actions that made the Democratic Party attractive (and the Republican Party unattractive) to them. The reason why some people approved of Bush's performance while others did not is largely because some are Republicans and some are Democrats. Party is therefore the third of the triumvirate of "candidates, issues, and parties"—that is, evaluations of the parties are one of three major forces that shape voting behavior.

Partisanship is not the only force that helps connect context and evaluation, but it has proven to be by far the most important for understanding elections. Its dual role in directly and indirectly affecting voting makes it unusually critical in understanding why U.S. citizens vote as they do. Most Americans identify with a political party—one reason why it is so central. Their identification then influences their political attitudes and, ultimately, their behavior. In the 1950s and 1960s, Angus Campbell and his coauthors of *The American Voter*, along with other scholars, began to emphasize the role of party loyalties.[1] Although today few people deny that partisanship is central to political attitudes and behavior, many scholars question the interpretation of the evidence gathered during that period. Here we ask two questions: What is party identification? And how does it actually structure other attitudes and behavior? We then examine the role that party identification played in the 2008 presidential election.

PARTY IDENTIFICATION: THE STANDARD VIEW

According to Angus Campbell and his colleagues, party identification is "the individual's affective orientation to an important group-object in his environment," in this case a political party.[2] In other words, an individual recognizes that two major political parties are playing significant roles in elections and develops an affinity for one of them. Partisanship, therefore, represents an evaluation of the two parties, but its implications extend to a wider variety of political phenomena. Campbell and his colleagues measured partisanship by asking individuals which party they identified with and how strong that identification was.[3] If an individual did not identify with one of the parties, he or she may have either "leaned" toward a party or been a "pure" independent. Individuals who could not answer the party identification questions were classified as "apolitical."[4] Most Americans develop a preference for either the Republican or the Democratic Party. Very few identify with any third party. The rest are mostly independents, who, according to this classic view, are not only unattached to a party but also relatively unattached to politics in general. They are less interested, less informed, and less active than those who identify with a party.

Partisan identification in this view becomes an attachment or loyalty similar to that between the individual and other groups or organizations in society such as a religious body, a social class, or even a favorite sports team. As with loyalties to many of these groups, partisan affiliation often begins early. One of the first political attitudes children develop is partisan identification, and it develops well before they acquire policy preferences and many other political orientations. Furthermore, as with other group loyalties, once an attachment to a party develops, it tends to endure.[5] Some people do switch parties, of course, but they usually do so only if their social situation changes dramatically, if there is an issue of overriding concern that sways their loyalties, or if the political parties themselves change substantially.

Party identification, then, stands as a base or core orientation of electoral politics. Once formed, this core orientation, predicated on a general evaluation of the two parties, affects many other specific orientations. Democratic loyalists tend to rate Democratic candidates and officeholders more highly than Republican candidates and officeholders, and vice versa. In effect, one is predisposed to evaluate the promises and performance of one's party leaders relatively more favorably. It follows, therefore, that Democrats are more likely to vote for Democratic candidates than are Republicans, and vice versa.

PARTY IDENTIFICATION: AN ALTERNATIVE VIEW

In *The Responsible Electorate*, published in 1966, V. O. Key Jr. argued that party loyalties contributed to electoral inertia and that many partisans voted as "stand-patters" from election to election.[6] In other words, in the absence of any information to the contrary, or if the attractions and disadvantages of the candidates are fairly evenly balanced, partisans are expected to vote for the candidate of their party. That is voters' "standing decision" until and unless they are given good reasons not to follow it. More recently, scholars have reexamined the bases of such behavior. In this new view, citizens who consider themselves Democrats have a standing decision to vote for the Democratic nominee because of the past positions of the Democrats and the Republicans and because of the parties' comparative past performances while in office. In short, this view of partisan identification presumes that it is a "running tally" of past experiences (mostly in terms of policy and performance)—a sort of summary expression of political memory, according to Morris P. Fiorina.[7]

Furthermore, when in doubt about how, for example, a Democratic candidate is likely to handle a civil rights issue in comparison with the Republican opponent, voters can reasonably assume that the Democrat will be more liberal than the Republican—unless the candidates indicate otherwise. Because the political parties tend to be consistent on the basic historical policy cleavages, summary judgments of parties and their typical candidates will not change radically or often.[8] As a result, a citizen's running tally serves as a good first approximation, changes rarely, and can be an excellent device for saving time and effort that would be spent gathering information in the absence of this "memory."

Many of the major findings used in support of the conventional interpretation of party identification are completely consistent with this more policy-oriented view. We do not have the evidence to assert that one view is superior to the other. Indeed, the two interpretations are not mutually exclusive. Moreover, they share the important conclusion that party identification plays a central role in shaping voters' decisions.

These two views are still widely studied today, with adherents of each view enriching and extending the core positions on each side. For example, Robert S. Erikson, Michael B. MacKuen, and James A. Stimson recently argued that an updated version of the Key-Downs-Fiorina view of partisanship is one of the central concepts for understanding what they call the "macro polity"—that is, an explanation of how political leaders, institutions, and policy respond to changes in aggregate public opinion.[9] They argue that partisanship in the electorate changes, as do macro-level conditions such as inflation and unemployment rates, akin to the Key-Downs-Fiorina view. In turn, political elites react to changes in this "macro-partisanship," among other aspects of public opinion and beliefs. On the other side, Donald Green, Bradley Palmquist, and Eric Schickler developed an elegant account of the affective base of partisan identification and its stability over time.[10] This view is therefore the modern version of the original account by Campbell et al. And, as recent exchanges have shown, the two sets of authors differ substantially in their interpretations of what partisanship means, but empirical differences are slighter.[11]

Both views agree that partisan identifications are long-term forces in politics. Both agree that, for most people, such identifications are formed early in life; children often develop a partisan loyalty, which they usually learn from their parents, although these loyalties are seldom explicitly taught. And both views recognize that partisan loyalties contribute to voter participation, as we demonstrated in Chapter 4. Partisan identifications also are often closely associated with social forces, as discussed in Chapter 5, especially when a social group is actively engaged in partisan politics. An important illustration of this point is the affiliation of many labor unions with the New Deal Democratic coalition, which often reinforced the tendency of those who were in labor unions to identify with the Democratic Party. This affiliation is similar to that of evangelical and other religious groups on the right with the Republican Party today, reinforcing the tendency of those who share such religious beliefs to identify with that party. Finally, both views agree that partisanship is closely associated with more immediate evaluations, including prospective and retrospective evaluations of the issues and candidates, as analyzed in Chapters 6 and 7.

The two views disagree over the nature of the linkage between partisanship and other attitudes, such as those toward the candidates and issues. The standard view argues that partisanship, as a long-term loyalty, affects the evaluations of issues and candidates by voters, but that it, in turn, is largely unaffected by such evaluations, except in such dramatic circumstances as realigning elections. In this sense, partisanship is a "filter" through which the concerns relevant to the particular election are viewed. In the alternative view, partisanship as a running tally may affect, but also is affected by, more immediate concerns. Indeed, Fiorina's definition of partisanship makes clear that the running tally includes current as well as past assessments. Distinguishing empirically between these two views is therefore quite difficult. Although the alternative view may believe that partisan identification is affected by retrospective and prospective assessments of the issues and candidates in the current election, such assessments rarely change an individual's identification because of that person's past experiences and the impact of initial socialization. We will analyze the role of partisan identification in 2008 and other recent elections in ways consistent with both major views of partisan identification.

PARTY IDENTIFICATION IN THE ELECTORATE

If partisan identification is a fundamental orientation for most citizens, then the distribution of partisan loyalties is crucial. The American National Election Studies has monitored the party loyalties of the American electorate since 1952. In Table 8-1, we show the basic distributions of partisan loyalties in presidential elections from 1980 to 2008.[12] As the table shows, most Americans identify with a political party. In 2008 three in five claimed to think of themselves as a Democrat or as a Republican, and about three in ten more, who initially said they were independent or had no partisan preference, nevertheless said they felt closer to one of the major parties than to the other.[13] One in nine was purely independent of party, and fewer than one in one hundred was classified as "apolitical." One of the biggest changes in partisanship in the electorate began in the mid-1960s, when more people claimed to be independents.[14] This growth stopped, however, in the late 1970s and early 1980s. There was very little change in partisan loyalties between the 1984 and 1992 surveys.

There were signs in 1996 of reversals in the trends in party identification toward greater independence. All partisan groups increased slightly in 1996 compared with 1992, and the percentage of "pure" independents (that is, those with no partisan leanings) was at its lowest level, 8 percent, since 1968. That decline in independence stopped, however, so that the percentages of independents in 2004 and 2008 were at about the same levels as during the 1980s.

Table 8-1 also shows that more people think of themselves as Democrats than as Republicans. Over the last forty years, the balance between the two parties has favored the Democrats by a range of about 55/45 to about 60/40. The results from the last six presidential election years still fall within that range, although more often at the lower part of the range. From 1984 to 2000, there was a clear shift toward the Republicans. In 1980, 35 percent of partisans were Republicans; in 2000 Republicans accounted for 42 percent. The inclusion of independents who leaned toward a party would increase the percentage of Republicans to 38 percent in 1980 and 43 percent in 2000. The high point was 47 percent in 1988. In 2004 the (strong and weak) Democrats led comparable Republicans in the ANES survey with 33 percent to 29 percent (or 54/46). The Democratic advantage increased in 2008; the percentage of Republicans declined, and there was a one-point increase on the Democratic side. These two small differences nevertheless brought the ratio of Democrats to Republicans to 57/43. The percentage of independents who leaned toward a party remained the same as in 2004, and, as a result, including them maintained the Democrats' edge over Republicans at 57/43, keeping the partisan balance within the historical range of a noticeable Democratic lead. The Democratic advantage is smaller in practice, however, because of the tendency of the Republicans to have higher turnout than the Democrats (see Chapter 4).

TABLE 8-1 Party Identification in Presidential Years, Pre-election Surveys, 1980–2008 (percent)

Party identification	1980	1984	1988	1992	1996	2000	2004	2008
Strong Democrat	18	17	18	17	18	19	17	19
Weak Democrat	24	20	18	18	20	15	16	15
Independent, leans Democratic	12	11	12	14	14	15	17	17
Independent, no partisan leanings	13	11	11	12	8	12	10	11
Independent, leans Republican	10	13	14	13	12	13	12	12
Weak Republican	14	15	14	15	16	12	12	13
Strong Republican	9	13	14	11	13	12	17	13
Total	100	100	101	100	101	98	101	100
(N)	(1,577)	(2,198)	(1,999)	(2,450)[a]	(1,696)[a]	(1,777)[a]	(1,193)[a]	(2,301)[a]
Apolitical	2	2	2	1	1	1	[b]	[b]
(N)	(35)	(38)	(33)	(23)	(14)	(21)	(3)	(2)

Source: Authors' analysis of ANES surveys.

[a] Number is weighted.

[b] Less than 1 percent.

Gary C. Jacobson has provided two excellent analyses of the shift in party loyalties away from the Republican Party from a high-water mark in 2003 to a low-water mark in 2009. His analyses strongly suggest that the decline has been driven largely by the decline in approval of Bush's performance as president.[15] Jacobson relies mainly on Gallup data, which probably capture more short-term variation than the standard Michigan Survey Research Center (SRC) question.[16]

A variety of other data sets can be analyzed, some of which are more attuned to long-term changes in partisanship. The most useful is the General Social Survey (GSS) conducted by the National Opinion Research Center (NORC) at the University of Chicago. These national samples are based on in-person interviews, use the standard ANES party identification questions, and usually have a sample size of 1,500. The GSS has measured party identification since 1972.[17] Like the ANES surveys, the GSS reveals some Republican gains. From 1972 to 1982, the percentage of party identifiers supporting the Republicans never rose above 37 percent, and, even if independents who leaned toward a party are included, the percentage of Republicans never rose above 38 percent. In 1984 the percentage of party identifiers who were Republicans rose to 40 percent, and Republican strength peaked in the 1990 GSS, which showed 48 percent of all party identifiers as Republicans. If independents who leaned toward a party are included, 49 percent were. But the Republicans made no further gains, even in the 1991 survey conducted during and after the Persian Gulf War. In the February–April 2000 GSS survey, 43 percent of all party identifiers were Republicans, and the total is unchanged if independent leaners are included. In 2004, 47 percent of all party identifiers were Republicans (a similar percentage with leaners included). And like the 2004 ANES, the 2004 GSS registered the highest percentage of strong Republicans ever recorded, 14 percent. The overall percentage of Republicans was virtually the same in the 2006 GSS, although the percentage of strong Republicans fell to 11 percent. But there was a clear drop in the percentage of Republicans in 2008. Among party identifiers, only 42 percent were Republicans, and the same when independent leaners were included. Thus there was a five-point drop in the percentage of Republicans in only four years. The percentage of strong Republicans remained at 11 percent.

The 2008 GSS survey shows partisan strength to be somewhat weaker than in the 2008 ANES survey. In the GSS survey, 30 percent of respondents were strong partisans, only negligibly less than the 32 percent in the ANES survey (see Table 8-1). But 16 percent of the respondents in the GSS survey were independents with no partisan leanings; in the ANES survey only 11 percent were (see Table 8-1).

Telephone surveys conducted by the *New York Times*/CBS News are also useful, because these surveys use the standard Michigan SRC party identification question. Between January 1992 and mid-July 2009, 144 polls measured party identification.[18] During this period, these telephone polls occasionally reported an even division between the Republicans and Democrats, and in one survey conducted in 2003 and another two conducted in 2004 the GOP had a marginal edge. But the Republicans began losing ground in February 2005. In the five surveys conducted during 2009, an average of 37 percent of party identifiers were Republicans.

Our analysis of earlier ANES surveys reveals that the shift toward the Republican Party was concentrated among white Americans.[19] As described in Chapter 5, the sharpest social division in U.S. electoral politics is race, and this division has been reflected in partisan loyalties for decades. Moreover, the racial gap has appeared to be widening, with a sharp increase in 2004. As we will show later in this chapter, although whites became somewhat more Democratic in their loyalties in 2008, blacks also increased their Democratic affiliation, thereby maintaining the large gap between the races in spite of Democratic gains among whites.

Although the distribution of partisanship in the electorate as a whole has changed slightly since 1984, this stability masks the growth in Republican identification among whites through 2004 and the compensating growth of already strong Democratic loyalties among African Americans. In Tables 8-2 and 8-3, we report the party identification of whites and blacks, respectively, between 1980 and 2008. In Tables A8-1 and A8-2 in the appendix, we report the party identification of whites and of blacks between 1952 and 1978. As these four tables show, black and white patterns in partisan loyalties were very different from 1952 to 2008. There was a sharp shift in black loyalties in the mid-1960s. Before then, about 50 percent of African Americans were strong or weak Democrats. Since that time, 60–70 percent—and even higher—of blacks have considered themselves Democrats.

The party loyalties of whites have changed more slowly. Still, the percentage of self-professed Democrats among whites declined over the Reagan years, while the percentage of Republicans increased. In the five elections that followed, partisanship among whites changed. If independents who lean Republican are included, there was close to an even balance among whites between the two parties in 1984. By 1988 the numbers of strong and weak Democrats and strong and weak Republicans were virtually the same, with more strong Republicans than strong Democrats for the first time. Adding in the two groups of independent leaners gave Republicans a clear advantage in identification among whites. In 1992, however, there were slightly more strong and weak Democrats than strong and weak Republicans. In 1996 all four of the partisan categories were larger, by one to three points, than in 1992. The result was that the balance of Republicans to Democrats changed very slightly, and the near parity of identifiers with the two parties among whites remained. By 2000 the parity was even more striking. But 2002 revealed a substantial increase in Republican identification among whites, one that was constant in terms of the three Republican groups in 2004. Democratic identification declined slightly, so that from 2000 to 2004 strong and weak Democrats fell by four points, partially balanced by a two-point gain among independent leaners. Pure independents declined sharply, to 8 percent, in both 2002 and 2004, a sign (along with the growth in strong Republicans) that

TABLE 8-2 Party Identification among Whites, 1980–2008 (percent)

Party identification[a]	1980	1982	1984	1986	1988	1990	1992	1994	1996	1998	2000	2002	2004	2008
Strong Democrat	14	16	15	14	14	17	14	12	15	15	15	12	13	14
Weak Democrat	23	24	18	21	16	19	17	19	19	18	14	16	12	14
Independent, leans Democratic	12	11	11	10	10	11	14	12	13	14	15	14	17	17
Independent, no partisan leanings	14	11	11	12	12	11	12	10	8	11	13	8	8	12
Independent, leans Republican	11	9	13	13	15	13	14	13	12	12	14	15	13	13
Weak Republican	16	16	17	17	15	16	16	16	17	18	14	17	15	15
Strong Republican	9	11	14	12	16	11	12	17	15	11	14	17	21	16
Apolitical	2	2	2	2	1	1	1	1	1	2	1	1	a	a
Total	101	100	101	101	99	99	100	100	100	101	100	100	99	101
(N)	(1,405)	(1,248)	(1,931)	(1,798)[b]	(1,693)	(1,663)	(2,702)[b]	(1,510)[b]	(1,451)[b]	(1,091)[b]	(1,404)[b]	(1,129)[b]	(859)[b]	(1,824)[b]

Source: Authors' analysis of ANES surveys.

[a] The percentage supporting another party has not been presented; it usually totals less than 1 percent and never totals more than 1 percent.

[b] Number is weighted.

TABLE 8-3 Party Identification among Blacks, 1980–2008 (percent)

Party identification[a]	1980	1982	1984	1986	1988	1990	1992	1994	1996	1998	2000	2002	2004	2008
Strong Democrat	45	53	32	42	39	40	40	38	43	48	47	53	30	47
Weak Democrat	27	26	31	30	24	23	24	23	22	23	21	16	30	23
Independent, leans Democratic	9	12	14	12	18	16	14	20	16	12	14	17	20	15
Independent, no partisan leanings	7	5	11	7	6	8	12	8	10	7	10	6	12	9
Independent, leans Republican	3	1	6	2	5	7	3	4	5	3	4	2	5	3
Weak Republican	2	2	1	2	5	3	3	2	3	3	3	4	2	1
Strong Republican	3	0	2	2	1	2	2	3	1	1	0	2	1	1
Apolitical	4	1	2	2	3	2	2	3	0	2	1	b	b	b
Total	100	100	99	99	101	101	100	101	100	99	100	100	100	99
(N)	(187)	(148)	(247)	(322)	(267)	(270)	(317)	(203)[c]	(200)[c]	(149)[c]	(225)[c]	(161)[c]	(193)[c]	(281)[c]

Source: Authors' analysis of ANES surveys.

[a] The percentage supporting another party has not been presented; it usually totals less than 1 percent and never totals more than 1 percent.

[b] Less than 1 percent.

[c] Number is weighted.

the white electorate was polarizing somewhat on partisanship. As a result, the three Republican groups constituted nearly half of the white electorate and led Democrats by a 49 percent to 42 percent margin. That situation changed in 2008.[20] Democratic identification (over the three Democratic categories) increased three percentage points, to 45 percent, while strong Republicans fell from 21 percent to 16 percent, dropping their three-category total to 44 percent. Thus in 2008 Democrats had at least regained parity with Republicans among white identifiers. And pure independents increased four points, to 12 percent, the highest level in over a decade.

Although the increased Republicanism of the white electorate was partly the result of long-term forces, such as generational replacement, the actual movement between 1964 and 1988 appears to be the result of two shorter-term increases in Republican identification. There were movements toward the GOP of five percentage points from 1964 to 1968 and ten points between 1982 and 1988. The latter movement waned modestly in the 1990s, as we saw. By 2000 the Republican categories, like the Democratic categories, had declined about equally, while the pure independent category had increased from 8 percent to 13 percent of the white electorate between 1996 and 2000. Obviously, the increase in Republican identification from 2000 to 2002 and 2004 constitutes a third short-term change, whereas the decline in 2008 may be the beginning of a strengthening of Democratic affiliation for the longer term among whites.

Party identification among blacks is very different. In 2008 there were very few black Republicans. Indeed, the percentage of black Republicans fell to near trace levels, with only 4 percent choosing any Republican option and a mere 2 percent being strong and weak Republicans. Because the Democrats were the first major party to choose an African American presidential candidate, we would expect this choice to exert a strong pull of blacks toward the party, perhaps limited only by blacks' already strong standing among Democrats. In 2008 nearly half of the blacks said they were strong Democrats, a very high proportion, although not as high as in 1964, 1968 (see Table A8-2), or 2002. Another 23 percent were weak Democrats, with 15 percent more leaning toward the Democratic Party. As a result, seven in every eight blacks chose one of the three Democratic options, with most of the rest claiming to be purely independent of either party.

These racial differences in partisanship are long-standing, and they have increased over time. Between 1952 and 1962, blacks were primarily Democratic, but about one in seven supported the Republicans. Black partisanship shifted massively and abruptly even further toward the Democratic Party in 1964. In that year, over half of all black voters considered themselves strong Democrats. Since then, well over half have identified with the Democratic Party. Black Republican identification fell to barely a trace in 1964 and edged up only slightly since then, only to fall back even further in recent years.

The abrupt change in black loyalties in 1964 reflects the two presidential nominees of that year: Democrat Lyndon Johnson and Republican Barry

Goldwater. President Lyndon Johnson's advocacy of civil rights legislation appealed directly to black voters, and his Great Society and War on Poverty programs made only slightly less direct appeals. Arizona senator Barry Goldwater voted against the 1964 Civil Rights Act, a vote criticized even by many of his Republican peers. In 1968 Republican nominee Richard Nixon began to pursue systematically what was called the "southern strategy"—that is, an attempt to win votes and long-term loyalties among white southerners. This strategy unfolded slowly but consistently over the years, as Republicans, particularly Ronald Reagan, continued to pursue the southern strategy. Party stances have not changed appreciably since then.[21]

In 1964 the proportion of blacks considered apolitical dropped from the teens to very small proportions, similar to those among whites. This shift resulted from the civil rights movement, the contest between Johnson and Goldwater, and the passage of the Civil Rights Act. The civil rights movement stimulated many blacks, especially in the South, to become politically active. The 1965 Voting Rights Act then enabled many of them to vote for the first time. Party and electoral politics were suddenly relevant, and blacks responded as all others by becoming engaged with the political—and party—system.

PARTY IDENTIFICATION AND THE VOTE

As we saw in Chapter 4, partisanship is related to turnout. Strong supporters of either party are more likely to vote than weak supporters, and independents who lean toward a party are more likely to vote than independents without partisan leanings. Republicans are somewhat more likely to vote than Democrats. Although partisanship influences whether people vote, it is more strongly related to how people vote.

Table 8-4 reports the percentage of white major-party voters who voted for the Democratic candidate across all categories of partisanship since 1952.[22] Clearly, there is a strong relationship between partisan identification and choice of candidate. In every election except 1972, the Democratic nominee has received more than 80 percent of the vote of strong Democrats and majority support from both weak Democratic partisans and independent Democratic leaners. In 1996 these figures were higher than in any other election in this period; nine in ten white Democratic identifiers voted for their party's nominee. Although the figures fell somewhat in 2000, especially in the independent-leaning Democrat category, that decline reversed in 2004, with John Kerry holding on to very large majorities of those who identified with the Democratic Party, including nearly nine in ten independents who were leaning toward the Democratic Party. In 2008 this very high level of Democratic voting continued, with slight declines among strong Democrats balanced by comparable increases among weak Democrats.

TABLE 8-4 White Major-Party Voters Who Voted Democratic for President, by Party Identification, 1952–2008 (percent)

Party identification	1952	1956	1960	1964	1968	1972	1976	1980	1984	1988	1992	1996	2000	2004	2008
Strong Democrat	82	85	91	94	89	66	88	87	88	93	96	98	96	97	92
Weak Democrat	61	63	70	81	66	44	72	59	63	68	80	88	81	78	83
Independent, leans Democratic	60	65	89	89	62	58	73	57	77	86	92	91	72	88	88
Independent, no partisan leanings	18	15	50	75	28	26	41	23	21	35	63	39	44	54	50
Independent, leans Republican	7	6	13	25	5	11	15	13	5	13	14	26	15	13	17
Weak Republican	4	7	11	40	10	9	22	5	6	16	18	21	16	10	10
Strong Republican	2	a	2	9	3	2	3	4	2	2	2	3	1	3	2

Source: Authors' analysis of ANES surveys.

Note: To approximate the numbers on which these percentages are based, see Table 8-2. Actual *N*s will be smaller than those that can be derived from these tables because respondents who did not vote (or voted for a nonmajor-party candidate) have been excluded from the calculations. Numbers also will be lower because the voting report is provided in the postelection interviews, which usually contain about 10 percent fewer respondents than the pre-election interviews in which party identification is measured.

a Less than 1 percent.

Since 1952 strong Republicans have given the Democratic candidate less than one vote in ten. In 1988 more of the weak Republicans and independents who leaned toward the Republican Party voted for Michael Dukakis than had voted for Walter Mondale in 1984, but, even so, only about one in seven voted Democratic. In 1992 Clinton won an even larger percentage of the two-party vote from these Republicans, and he increased his support among Republicans again in 1996. In 2000 George W. Bush held essentially the same level of support among the three white Republican categories as his father had in 1988 and 1992, and, if anything, increased his support among Republicans in 2004. In 2008 over 90 percent of the strong and weak Republicans voted for McCain, just as they did for Bush four years earlier. As for independent leaners, McCain was very slightly less successful than Bush; he lost 17 percent of votes among this group, whereas in 2004 Bush lost 13 percent.

The pure independent vote, which fluctuates substantially, has been more Republican than Democratic in ten of these fifteen elections (1952–2008), and was strongly Democratic only in 1964. Clinton did well among major-party voters in 1992. John Kennedy won 50 percent of that vote in 1960, but Bill Clinton won nearly two-thirds of the pure independents' vote among the two-party vote in 1992.[23] In 2004 Kerry was able to win 54 percent of the pure independent vote. Obama, like Kennedy, won exactly half of the vote among whites who are pure independents. However, that 50–50 percent vote in 1960 was the same as the overall vote, whereas Obama won a higher proportion from the full electorate than from white pure independents.

Thus, at least among major-party voters, partisanship is strongly related to the vote. In recent elections, the Democrats have been better able to hold support among their partisans, perhaps because the loss of southern white support has made the party more homogeneous in its outlook. Its partisan base has become essentially as strong as the Republicans', which has been consistently strong except in the very best years for the Democrats. Partisanship, then, has become more polarized in its relationship to the vote. Obama won because he broke even among independents and because he not only held his base well but also saw that base increase slightly.

Although nearly all blacks vote Democratic regardless of their partisan affiliations (most are, however, Democratic identifiers), among whites partisanship leads to loyalty in voting. Between 1964 and 1980, the relationship between party identification and the vote was declining, but in 1984 the relationship between party identification and the presidential vote was higher than in any of the five elections between 1964 and 1980. The relationship remained strong in 1988 and continued to be quite strong in the two Clinton elections and the Gore-Bush election, at least among major-party voters. The question of whether the parties are gathering new strength at the presidential level could not be answered definitively from the 2000 election data, but the 2004 and 2008 election data now make it clear that these growing signs have become a strong trend, to the point that party identification is as strongly related to the presidential vote as it has

been since the ANES surveys began. The relationship between party identification and voting in general will be reconsidered in Chapter 10, when we assess its
relationship to the congressional vote.[24]

Partisanship is related to the way people vote. The question, therefore, is why
do partisans support their party's candidates? As we shall see, party identification affects behavior because it helps structure (and, according to Fiorina, is
structured by) the way voters view both policies and performance.

POLICY PREFERENCES AND PERFORMANCE EVALUATIONS

In their study of voting in the 1948 election, Bernard R. Berelson, Paul F. Lazarsfeld, and William N. McPhee discovered that Democratic voters attributed to
their nominee, incumbent Harry Truman, positions on key issues that were
consistent with their beliefs—whether those beliefs were liberal, moderate, or
conservative.[25] Similarly, Republicans tended to see their nominee, Gov. Thomas
E. Dewey of New York, as taking whatever positions they preferred. Research
since then has emphasized the role of party identification not only in projecting
onto the preferred candidate positions similar to the voter's own views, but also
in shaping the policy preferences in the public.[26] In this section, we use four
examples to illustrate the strong relationship between partisan affiliation and
perceptions, preferences, and evaluations of candidates.

Partisanship and Approval of the President's Job Performance

Most partisans evaluate the job performance of a president from their party
more highly than do independents and, especially, more highly than do those
who identify with the other party. Figure 8-1A shows the percentage of each of
the seven partisan groups that approves of the way the incumbent has handled
his job as president (as a proportion of those approving or disapproving) in the
last three presidential elections in which there was a Democratic president
(1980, 1996, and 2000). Figure 8-1B presents similar results for the seven elections in which there was a Republican incumbent (1972, 1976, 1984, 1988, 1992,
2004, and 2008).[27] Strong partisans of the incumbent's party typically give overwhelming approval to that incumbent (Table A8-3 in the appendix presents
the exact values for each year). It is not guaranteed, however. In 1980 only
73 percent of strong Democrats approved of Jimmy Carter, which is just about
the same percentage of strong Republicans who approved of Bush's job performance in 2008.

We can draw two conclusions about 2008 from the data in Figures 8-1A and
8-1B. First, just as in every election, there was a strong partisan cast to evaluations
of the president in 2008. Democrats are very likely to approve of any Democratic
incumbent and very unlikely to approve of any Republican incumbent. In 2008
the highest Bush scored among the Democratic groups was the remarkably low

FIGURE 8-1A   Approval of Democratic Incumbents' Handling of Job, by Party
Identification, 1980, 1996, and 2000 (percent)

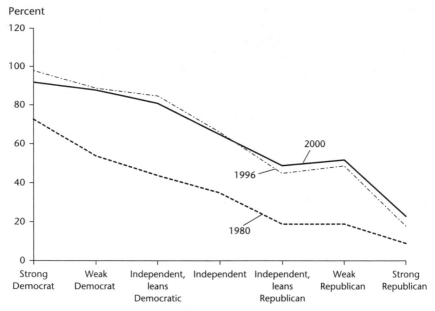

Source: Authors' analysis of ANES surveys.

11 percent approval rating of weak Democrats. Republicans are just the opposite, unlikely to approve of any Democratic incumbent and much more likely to approve of any Republican incumbent. And pure independents are just about halfway between the two partisan groups. In Figure 8-1B, the consistency with which the approval line rises steeply from left to right is clear. The second conclusion is that Bush had very low approval ratings, the lowest of any since the ANES started including presidential approval ratings in their surveys. For example, Figure 8-1B shows that support for Bush was lower than support for any other Republican since 1972 at each of the seven points along the partisanship scale. Moreover, often the gap between 2008 and the next worst year for a Republican incumbent's evaluation (usually 1976) is quite large. Approval ratings of Democratic incumbents were higher at each comparable point—that is, strong Democrats compared with strong Republicans, and so forth. What stands out about Bush's rating, then, is how low it is across the electorate.

Partisanship and Approval of the President's Handling of the Economy

Our second illustration extends the connection we have drawn between partisanship and approval of the incumbent's job performance. In this case, we examine the relationship between partisanship and approval of the incumbent's

FIGURE 8-1B   Approval of Republican Incumbents' Handling of Job, by Party
Identification, 1972, 1976, 1984, 1988, 1992, 2004, and 2008
(percent)

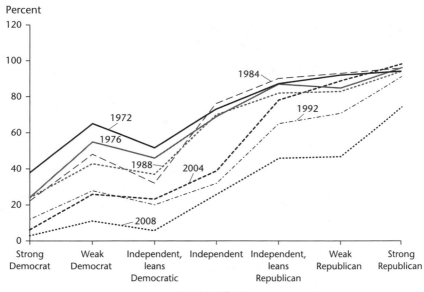

Source: Authors' analysis of ANES surveys.

handling of the economy. Table 8-5 shows the relationship among all seven partisan categories and approval of incumbent presidents' handling of the economy from 1984 to 2008.[28]

In 1984 and 1988, more than three-quarters of each of the three Republican groups approved of Reagan's handling of the economy, while more than half—and often more than two-thirds—of the three Democratic groups disapproved. Independents generally approved of Reagan's economic efforts, albeit more strongly in 1984 than in 1988. The 1992 election was dramatically different, with overwhelming disapproval of George H. W. Bush's handling of the economy among the three Democratic groups and the pure independents. Even two-thirds of the weak and Republican-leaning independents disapproved. Only strong Republicans typically approved, and even then one in three did not. The relationship in 1996 is most like that of 1984. In 2000 the vast majority of Democrats and even three in four of the pure independents approved of Clinton's economic performance—by far the highest economic approval mark independents have given. But then most Republicans also approved. In 2004 the weak but improving economy meant that George W. Bush was approved by "only" nine in ten strong Republicans and about seven in ten weak and independent-leaning Republicans. Democratic disapproval reached very high levels, and once again pure independents did not favor Bush, only one in three approving

TABLE 8-5　Approval of Incumbent's Handling of the Economy among Partisan Groups, 1984–2008 (percent)

	Attitudes toward handling of the economy	Party identification							
Year		Strong Democrat	Weak Democrat	Independent, leans Democrat	Independent	Independent, leans Republican	Weak Republican	Strong Republican	Total
1984	Approve	17	41	32	68	84	86	95	58
	Disapprove	83	59	68	32	16	14	5	42
	Total	100	100	100	100	100	100	100	100
	(N)	(309)	(367)	(207)	(179)	(245)	(277)	(249)	(1,833)
1988	Approve	19	35	32	57	76	79	92	54
	Disapprove	81	65	68	43	24	21	8	46
	Total	100	100	100	100	100	100	100	100
	(N)	(337)	(332)	(229)	(185)	(262)	(262)	(269)	(1,876)
1992[a]	Approve	3	9	6	9	31	34	66	20
	Disapprove	97	91	94	91	69	66	34	80
	Total	100	100	100	100	100	100	100	100
	(N)	(425)	(445)	(340)	(267)	(310)	(347)	(266)	(2,401)
1996[a]	Approve	96	82	76	58	46	49	30	66
	Disapprove	4	18	24	42	54	50	70	34
	Total	100	100	100	100	100	100	100	100
	(N)	(310)	(325)	(228)	(131)	(188)	(263)	(209)	(1,655)

(Continued)

2000[a]	Approve	95	90	84	73	60	70	47	77
	Disapprove	5	10	16	27	40	30	53	23
	Total	100	100	100	100	100	100	100	100
	(N)	(342)	(265)	(264)	(198)	(206)	(184)	(200)	(1,659)
2004[a]	Approve	5	18	10	34	68	72	89	40
	Disapprove	95	82	90	66	32	28	11	60
	Total	100	100	100	100	100	100	100	100
	(N)	(197)	(176)	(204)	(107)	(139)	(141)	(194)	(1,158)
2008[a]	Approve	4	7	5	16	27	25	58	18
	Disapprove	96	93	95	84	73	75	42	82
	Total	100	100	100	100	100	100	100	100
	(N)	(428)	(338)	(381)	(240)	(255)	(274)	(291)	(2,208)

Source: Authors' analysis of ANES surveys.

[a] Numbers are weighted.

of his handling of the economy. In 2008 the Wall Street meltdown occurred in the midst of the electoral campaign, and its effects were devastating to President Bush's approval ratings. Only 18 percent of respondents approved of Bush's handling of the economy. Even though these ratings were lower than the overall approval ratings, they displayed a clear partisan effect. Strong Republicans still approved more than they disapproved, and one in four in the other two Republican categories approved. These are very low percentages to be sure, but they are higher than among pure independents (note, however, that more pure independents approved in 2008 than in 1992) and much higher than the mere trace levels of any type of Democrat, with about one in twenty approving.

The 2008 figures are thus the worst we have measured, but the 1992 survey results are actually reasonably comparable. The difference was that in 1992 George H. W. Bush was running and therefore able to defend his handling of the economy, but he faced two strong challengers, both of whom focused their campaign on the economic failures of the Bush administration. In 2008 only Obama was campaigning against the Republicans, but George W. Bush was not on the trail to defend his policies, and McCain and Palin were distancing themselves from his administration. Thus even though some differences are apparent from election to election (typically related to changes in the economy), the relationship between partisanship and approval of the incumbent's economic performance is clear and strong.

Prospective Issues

The third example of the impact of partisanship on attitudes and beliefs is its relationship to positions on policy issues. In Table 8-6, we report this relationship among the seven partisan categories and our balance of issues measure developed in Chapter 6, collapsed into three groupings: pro-Republican, neutral, pro-Democratic in Chapter 7.[29] As we saw in Chapter 6, these issues favored the Republicans in 1972, 1976, and 1980, worked slightly to the Democratic advantage in 1984, 1988, and 1992, and then once again favored the Republicans in the elections from 1996 to 2008. In all cases, the balance of issues measure had only moderately favored one party over the other, but in 2008 clearly favored the Republicans.

As Table 8-6 shows for 1976–2008, there has been a steady, clear, moderately strong relationship between partisanship and the balance of issues measure, and it is one that, by 2000, had strengthened considerably and continued to strengthen into 2008. Until 1984 the relationship had been stronger among Republicans than among Democrats. In 1984 and 1988 (and also in 1992, but that measure depends on only three issues and is therefore less useful), the relationship was, if anything, stronger among Democrats than Republicans. That change very likely stemmed from the political context. In 1980, for example, more people, Democrats as well as Republicans, were closer to Reagan's median position than to Carter's on important issues such as defense spending

TABLE 8-6 Balance of Issues Positions among Partisan Groups, 1976–2008 (percent)

				Party identification				
Issue positions closer to …[a]	Strong Democrat	Weak Democrat	Independent, leans Democrat	Independent	Independent, leans Republican	Weak Republican	Strong Republican	Total
1976								
Democratic candidate	28	27	22	15	12	9	3	18
Neutral	32	26	37	29	27	23	27	29
Republican candidate	39	47	40	55	61	67	69	53
Total	99	100	99	99	100	99	99	100
(N)	(422)	(655)	(336)	(416)	(277)	(408)	(254)	(2,778)
1980								
Democratic candidate	26	23	27	20	12	10	9	19
Neutral	34	37	33	43	40	43	31	37
Republican candidate	40	40	40	37	48	48	60	43
Total	100	100	100	100	100	101	100	99
(N)	(245)	(317)	(161)	(176)	(150)	(202)	(127)	(1,378)
1984								
Democratic candidate	57	49	59	35	23	29	14	39
Neutral	32	37	28	48	46	40	39	38
Republican candidate	11	14	13	17	32	32	47	23
Total	100	100	100	100	101	101	100	100
(N)	(331)	(390)	(215)	(213)	(248)	(295)	(256)	(1,948)

(Continued)

TABLE 8-6 Balance of Issues Positions among Partisan Groups, 1976–2008 (percent) (continued)

	Party identification							
Issue positions closer to ...[a]	Strong Democrat	Weak Democrat	Independent, leans Democrat	Independent	Independent, leans Republican	Weak Republican	Strong Republican	Total
1988								
Democratic candidate	49	36	50	33	21	21	11	32
Neutral	34	40	38	48	46	43	35	40
Republican candidate	17	24	12	19	33	36	53	29
Total	100	100	100	100	100	100	99	101
(N)	(355)	(359)	(240)	(215)	(270)	(281)	(279)	(1,999)
1992[b]								
Democratic candidate	40	36	30	26	13	13	9	25
Neutral	55	57	65	70	74	77	74	67
Republican candidate	5	7	4	5	13	11	17	9
Total	100	100	99	101	100	101	100	101
(N)	(380)	(389)	(313)	(235)	(283)	(335)	(238)	(2,192)
1996[b]								
Democratic candidate	44	27	35	17	13	9	1	22
Neutral	27	36	34	43	27	23	14	29
Republican candidate	30	37	31	40	60	68	85	49
Total	101	100	100	100	100	100	100	100
(N)	(313)	(333)	(229)	(140)	(195)	(268)	(217)	(1,696)

(Continued)

2000[b]

Democratic candidate	30	26	25	20	8	10	2	19
Neutral	47	48	46	49	40	33	25	43
Republican candidate	23	25	29	31	51	57	73	38
Total	100	101	100	100	99	100	100	100
(N)	(188)	(161)	(157)	(113)	(134)	(101)	(99)	(953)

2004[b]

Democratic candidate	72	55	57	40	19	21	9	40
Neutral	8	11	9	10	9	6	5	8
Republican candidate	21	33	34	50	73	73	86	52
Total	100	99	101	100	100	99	100	100
(N)	(168)	(157)	(180)	(100)	(124)	(136)	(179)	(1,046)

2008[b, c]

Democratic candidate	60	46	47	28	16	14	8	34
Neutral	6	9	14	10	17	9	[2]	9
Republican candidate	34	45	40	63	67	77	90	56
Total	100	100	101	101	100	100	99	99
(N)	(219)	(163)	(203)	(135)	(143)	(148)	(142)	(1,153)

Source: Authors' analysis of ANES surveys.

Note: In the one instance in which the category included fewer than ten observations, we show the total number of people in that category in brackets.

[a] The Democratic category on the condensed balance of issues measure includes any respondent who is at least slightly Democratic; the Republican category includes any respondent who is at least slightly Republican. The neutral category is the same as the neutral category on the seven-point issue scale (see Table 6-5).

[b] Numbers are weighted.

[c] In 2008 the issue questions used to form the balance of issues scale were asked of a randomly selected half-sample.

and income tax cuts. However, after Reagan pushed increases in defense spending and cuts in income taxes through Congress in his first term, the electorate no longer favored as great an increase in defense spending and was more amenable to higher spending on some domestic programs.

Thus in the next three elections issues tended to divide the electorate along party lines, with Democrats closer to their party's nominee. The result was a sharper and more balanced relationship between partisanship and the balance of issues measure. In 1996, although the balance of issues measure favored the Republicans, its relationship to party identification was stronger. It was almost as strong in 2000 and was moderately strong on both sides of the competition.

Prospective issues appeared to be increasingly polarized by party, strikingly so by 2000. The data for the 2000, 2004, and 2008 elections are quite similar—that is, there is a strong relationship between party identification and the balance of issues measure. In 2008 three in five strong Democrats were closer to where the electorate placed Obama, while nine in ten strong Republicans were closer to where the electorate placed McCain. Thus the degree of polarization on this measure continues to increase.

Partisan polarization characterizes not only prospective issues but also most other factors we have examined. In our balance of issues measure, "polarization" really means "consistency"—that is, partisans find their party's candidate closer to them than the opposing party's nominee on more and more issues. On these measures, then, what we observe as growing polarization stems from the increased differentiation and consistency of positions of the candidates and not as much from changes in the issue positions among the public.

Finally, we find a strong relationship between party identification and our measure of retrospective evaluations in 2008. We cannot directly compare this measure in the 2008 election with those for earlier elections, because the questions that make up the summary retrospective measure in the last seven presidential elections differ from those available in 2004, and both differ from those available in earlier elections.[30] Still, it is worth noting that this measure was very strongly related to partisanship in those earlier elections. Table 8-7 shows the relationship in 2008, collapsing the summary retrospective measure into the three categories of pro-Democratic, neutral, and pro-Republican. The relationship is overwhelming. Almost all strong Democrats had negative retrospective evaluations, for example, while nearly three in five strong Republicans were moderately or strongly positive. In 2008 pure independents gave Obama a strong boost. We conclude that retrospective evaluations are invariably strongly related to partisanship, and if comparable measures were available, in 2008 partisanship would be even more strongly related to the vote than in most preceding elections.[31]

Not only are party identification and retrospective evaluations consistently and strongly related to the vote, but these two measures also are strongly related to each other in every election. Do they both still contribute independently to the vote? As we learned earlier about the 1976–2004 elections and we learn in Table 8-8 about the 2008 election, the answer is yes.[32] In Table 8-8, we examine

TABLE 8-7 Retrospective Evaluations among Partisan Groups, 2008 (percent)

Summary measure of retrospective evaluations[a]	Party identification							
	Strong Democrat	Weak Democrat	Independent, leans Democrat	Independent	Independent, leans Republican	Weak Republican	Strong Republican	Total
Pro-Democratic	93	82	84	57	29	27	11	59
Slightly supportive, opposed, or neutral	7	15	14	30	41	40	30	23
Pro-Republican	[b]	3	2	13	30	34	59	18
Total	100	100	100	100	100	101	100	100
(N)	(388)	(314)	(344)	(227)	(245)	(270)	(269)	(2,057)

Source: Authors' analysis of the 2008 ANES survey.

Note: Numbers are weighted.

[a] The Democratic category on the condensed measure of retrospective evaluations includes any respondent who is at least moderately opposed to the incumbent's party; the Republican category includes any respondent who at least moderately supports the incumbent's party. The middle retrospective category is the same as the middle retrospective category in Table 7-10.

[b] Less than 1 percent.

TABLE 8-8 Percentage of Major-Party Voters Who Voted for Obama, by Party Identification and Summary of Retrospective Evaluations, 2008

	Summary of retrospective evaluations[a]						
	Pro-Democratic		Neutral		Pro-Republican		Total	
Party identification	%	(N)	%	(N)	%	(N)	%	(N)
Democratic	94	(519)	75	(48)	[2]	(6)	92	(573)
Slightly supportive, opposed, or neutral	81	(306)	24	(117)	16	(72)	58	(495)
Republican	29	(88)	4	(159)	2	(233)	7	(480)
Total	83	(914)	22	(325)	6	(312)	55	(1,551)

Source: Authors' analysis of the 2008 ANES survey.

Note: The numbers in the parentheses are the totals on which the percentages are based. Numbers are weighted.

[a] The Democratic category on the condensed measure of retrospective evaluations includes any respondent who is at least moderately opposed to the incumbent's party; the Republican category includes any respondent who at least moderately supports the incumbent's party. The middle retrospective category is the same as the middle retrospective category in Table 7-10.

the combined impact of party identification and retrospective evaluations on voting choices. To simplify the presentation, we use the three groupings of the summary retrospective evaluations, and we collapse party identification into the three groups: strong and weak Republicans, all three independent categories, and strong and weak Democrats.

Table 8-8 shows the percentage of major-party voters who voted Democratic by both party identification and retrospective evaluations in 2008. Reading down the columns reveals that party identification is strongly related to the vote, regardless of the voter's retrospective evaluations, a pattern found in the eight elections before 2008. Not enough Democrats assessed the Republicans positively on retrospective evaluations to say much about that column, but the other two columns illustrate a very strong relationship. Reading across each row reveals that in all elections retrospective evaluations are related to the vote, regardless of the voter's party identification, and once again a pattern was discovered in all eight earlier elections. Moreover, as in all eight elections between 1976 and 2004 party identification and retrospective evaluations had a combined impact on how people voted in 2008. For example, in 2008 among Republicans with pro-Republican evaluations, 98 percent voted for McCain (100 percent minus 2 percent); among Democrats with pro-Democratic evaluations, 94 percent voted for Obama.

Finally, partisanship and retrospective assessments appear to have roughly equal effects on the vote, and certainly both are strongly related to the vote, even when both variables are examined together. For example, the effect of retrospective evaluations on the vote is not the result of partisans having positive retrospective assessments of their party's presidents and negative ones when the opposition holds the White House. Republicans who held pro-Democratic retrospective judgments were more supportive of Obama than other Republicans. Overall, then, we can conclude that partisanship is a key component of understanding evaluations of the public and its votes, but the large changes in outcomes over time must be traced to retrospective and prospective evaluations, simply because partisanship does not change substantially over time.

In summary, partisanship appears to affect the way voters evaluate incumbents and their performances. Positions on issues have been a bit different. Although partisans in the 1970s and early 1980s were likely to be closer to their party's nominee on policy, the connection was less clear than between partisanship and retrospective evaluations. It is only recently that prospective evaluations have emerged as being nearly as important a set of influences on candidate choice as retrospective evaluations. It may well be that the strengthening of this relationship is a reflection of the increasingly sharp cleavages between the parties.[33] Still, policy-related evaluations are influenced in part by history and political memory and in part by the candidates' campaign strategies. Partisan attachments, then, limit the ability of a candidate to control his or her fate in the electorate, but such attachments are not entirely rigid. Candidates have some flexibility in the support they receive from partisans, especially depending on the candidates' or their predecessors' performance in office and on the policy promises they make in the campaign.

Party loyalties affect how people vote, how they evaluate issues, and how they judge the performance of the incumbent president and the president's party. In recent years, research has suggested that not only do party loyalties affect issue preferences, perceptions, and evaluations, but also preferences, perceptions, and evaluations may affect partisanship. There is good reason to believe that the relationship between partisanship and these factors is more complex than any model that assumes a one-way relationship would suggest. Doubtless, evaluations of the incumbent's performance may also affect party loyalties.[34]

As we saw in this chapter, there was a substantial shift toward Republican loyalties over the 1980s; among whites, the clear advantage Democrats had enjoyed over the last four decades appeared to be gone. The 2008 election suggests that there is at least a chance that the Democrats will enjoy a resurgence, because they have moved toward having a somewhat stronger advantage. To some extent, the earlier shift in party loyalties must have reflected Reagan's appeal and his successful performance in office, as judged by the electorate. It also appears that he was able to shift some of that appeal in George H. W. Bush's direction in 1988 both directly, by the connection between performance judgments and the vote, and indirectly, through shifts in party loyalties among white Americans. Bush lost much of the appeal he inherited, primarily because of negative assessments of his handling of the economy, and he was not able to hold on to the high approval ratings he had attained in 1991 after the success in the Persian Gulf War. In 1996 Clinton demonstrated that a president could rebound from a weak early performance as judged by the electorate and benefit from a growing economy.

The 1996 election stood as one comparable to the reelection campaigns of other recent, successful incumbents, although Clinton received marks as high as or higher than Nixon's in 1972 and Reagan's in 1984 for his overall performance and for his handling of the economy. With strong retrospective judgments, the electorate basically decided that one good term deserved another.

The political landscape was dramatically different after the 1996 election compared with the time just before the 1992 election. Although the proportion of Democrats to Republicans in the electorate had been quite close for over a decade, the general impression was that Republicans had a "lock" on the White House, while the Democrats' forty-year majority in the U.S. House was thought to be unbreakable. The 1992 election demonstrated that a party has a lock on the presidency only when the public believes that party's candidate will handle the office better than the opposition. The 1994 election so reversed conventional thinking that some then considered Congress a stronghold for the Republican

Party. Conventional wisdom, a lengthy history of such outcomes, and the apparent strength of the Republican delegation seemed to ensure that the GOP would gain seats in the 1998 congressional elections, but they actually lost five House seats. A Democratic resurgence seemed to be in the making. The Republicans' handling of the impeachment and Senate trial of President Clinton seemed to further set the stage for Democratic gains. Perhaps the single most surprising fact leading into the 2000 presidential race was the high approval ratings an impeached, but not convicted, Clinton held.

The question for the 2000 campaign was why Vice President Al Gore was unable to do better than essentially tie George W. Bush in the election (whether counting by popular or electoral votes). We must remember, however, how closely balanced all other key indicators were. Partisanship among whites was essentially evenly split between the two parties, with a Republican advantage in turnout at least partially offsetting the Democratic partisanship of blacks. Prospective issues, as in most election years, only modestly favored one side or the other. Retrospective evaluations, however, provided Gore with a solid edge, as did approval ratings of Clinton on the economy. The failure, then, was in Gore's inability to translate that edge in retrospective assessments into a more substantial lead in the voting booth. Retrospective evaluations were almost as strongly related to the vote in 2000 as in other recent elections, but Gore failed to push beyond that slight popular vote plurality and turn a virtual tie into an outright win.

George W. Bush, it appears, learned some lessons from 2000 for his 2004 reelection. In 2004, he faced an electorate that, like its immediate predecessors, was almost evenly balanced in its partisanship, with a slight Democratic edge in numbers of identifiers balanced by their lower propensity to turn out than Republican identifiers. Meanwhile, because of the continuing decline in the proportion of pure independents, there were fewer opportunities to win over those not already predisposed to support one party or the other. Furthermore, although Bush held an edge in prospective evaluations, Kerry held an advantage on retrospective assessments, but in both cases the edges were small. Thus with fewer independents to woo and such an even balance, the contest became a race for both the remaining independents and the weakly attached and an effort to strengthen the base by motivating supporters to, in turn, motivate the base to actually turn out. Perhaps for this reason, we observed a strengthening of the affective component of partisan attachments—that is, a growth in strong partisans at the expense of the more weakly attached, at least during the campaign itself.

All of this was lost in 2008. Partisanship shifted toward the Democrats. The Bush administration was the least popular we have yet been able to measure. The public rejected his incumbency in general and his handling of the economy in particular. As a result, John McCain faced an unusually steep uphill battle. It is no wonder that he and Sarah Palin emphasized their "maverick" status as independent of the Bush administration. They did not, however, cut themselves loose from their partisan base. McCain might have been able to do so, but his selection of Palin as running mate indicated that his administration would be distinct from Bush's administration but nevertheless just as Republican. In view of the edge he held on prospective issues, that was a plausible choice. But the financial meltdown in the fall of 2008 probably sealed his fate. The election came down to being a partisan one, in which the Democrats turned out to hold an increased advantage, and a retrospective one, in which the Democrats held an overwhelming advantage. These two factors translated into a comfortable victory for Obama—and many other Democrats.

Despite the shifts in partisan identification during the last half-century, we should not exaggerate the change. The same two parties hold the loyalties of three-fifths of the electorate, and because at least some self-professed independents may actually be partisans, the share is probably higher. Moreover, the Democrats still hold an edge, although it may be offset by their somewhat lower turnout. The share of strong party identifiers, who form the most reliable core of supporters for each party, has grown from a low point of only about one in five in 1978 to about one in three in 2008. And the relationship between party identification and the vote was very strong in 2000, 2004, and 2008. Although none of these changes demonstrates that either party has won the "hearts and minds" of the electorate, they do call into question the thesis that a partisan dealignment has occurred.

No assessment of whether a realignment has occurred can be complete by looking at presidential voting alone. After all, between January 1953 and January 1993, during which the Republicans controlled the White House for twenty-eight of forty years, few scholars considered the GOP to be the dominant party because it controlled the U.S. House of Representatives for only two of these years. In fact, between 1954 and 1992 the Democrats won a majority of the House in twenty straight elections. That winning streak ended in 1994, but a new one may have started in 2006. We must now turn to a study of congressional elections to evaluate the prospects for partisan change.

PART III

The 2008 Congressional Elections

Presidential selection is the main event of the 2008 election. But the president shares responsibility with Congress, which must enact a legislative program and approve major appointments. Now that we have concluded our discussion of Barack Obama's election to the presidency, we turn to the Congress that governs with him. In Part III, we consider the selection of the 111th Congress.

In 2008 thirty-five U.S. Senate contests were held, and all 435 U.S. House seats were filled. In addition, eleven gubernatorial contests were waged, and forty-four states held legislative elections.[1] These state-level elections can have national importance, because in most states the redistricting that follows the constitutionally required decennial census (Article I, section 2) is a political process in which the partisanship of the state legislatures and governorships can be crucial. For the most part, however, the 2010 gubernatorial and state legislative elections will have the greatest impact on the redistricting struggle that will begin after the 2010 census.

Many other statewide contests, including 153 statewide ballot proposals, were also held in 2008.[2] The most controversial propositions were bans on same-sex marriage, which passed in Arizona, California, and Florida. The contest in California was the most bitterly fought because it reversed a California Supreme Court decision that legalized such marriages.

In Chapters 9 and 10, we focus on the U.S. House and Senate elections, which are by far the most consequential for national public policy. These results lack the drama of electing the nation's first African American president. And from a partisan standpoint they are less interesting because the Democrats had already won control of the House and Senate in the 2006 midterm elections, in which they scored net gains of thirty seats in the House and six seats in the Senate. But in 2008 the Democrats added to these gains, winning an additional twenty-one seats in the House and eight in the Senate. Moreover, with Pennsylvania senator Arlen Specter's defection to the Democratic Party in 2009, the Democrats held sixty seats, and the Democrats briefly held the number of seats needed to invoke cloture and end filibusters designed to prevent a Senate vote on a substantive issue. With the death of Sen. Edward Kennedy on August 25, 2009, they temporarily lost this supermajority, and many observers argued that the Democrats' best hopes for passing health care reform in the Senate lay in gaining the support of Republican moderate Olympia Snowe of Maine.[3]

The Democrats' gains in 2006 and 2008 marked the first time since 1930 and 1932 that a party had won twenty or more seats in two consecutive elections. The earlier shifts, however, were more dramatic because they came at the beginning of the Great Depression. At the beginning of the Seventy-first Congress, elected in 1928 when Republican Herbert Hoover won a landslide victory over his Democratic opponent, Alfred Smith, the Democrats held only 167 seats in the House, and the Republicans held 267. In the 1930 midterm, the Democrats gained fifty-three seats and held a narrow 220- to 214-seat edge. And with Franklin Roosevelt's election in 1932, the Democrats gained ninety-seven seats, giving them a 313- to 117-seat advantage.

Although the Democratic gains in 2006 and 2008 were not nearly as dramatic as those of the early 1930s, they were remarkable when we restate our original point. In the thirty-five pairs of consecutive elections between 1934 and 2004, no party won twenty or more seats in two consecutive elections. But this finding does not mean the Democrats will gain seats in 2010, especially in view of the tendency for the party holding the presidency to lose seats in the midterm elections. After all, the party holding the White House lost strength in the House in thirty-eight of the thirty-nine midterm elections held between 1842 and 1994.[4] And yet the party holding the presidency actually gained seats in the next two midterms (there were small Democratic gains in 1998 and small Republican gains in 2002), only to have the pattern of midterm losses return with a vengeance in 2006. But these Democratic gains in 2006 and 2008 make it more likely that Barack Obama will be able to implement his policies. If those policies succeed in solving the nation's economic problems, the prospects for future Democratic dominance will be greatly enhanced.

Our analysis of the 2008 congressional elections relies on two distinct approaches. In Chapter 9, we use the election results themselves, supplemented by information about candidates' spending and their elective experiences. We then turn to the American National Election Studies surveys, which we analyze in Chapter 10. Studies of elections should begin by examining election results, because at times survey results simply do not reflect reality. For example, in Table 10-1 we find that 85 percent of the whites in the border states voted Republican, a result based on the fifty-five white respondents who said they voted. Although the Republicans did do better in the border states than in the rest of the nation, winning sixteen of the thirty-one U.S. House seats, they would have won far more seats had they actually won 85 percent of the white vote in Kentucky, Maryland, Missouri, Oklahoma, and West Virginia. Faced with such incontrovertible evidence, one would have to conclude that the survey results were wrong.

Chapter 9 focuses mainly on congressional competition between the 1994 and 2008 elections. From 1954 to 1992, the Democrats won control of the U.S. House of Representatives in twenty consecutive elections, by far the longest winning streak in U.S. electoral history.[5] Recent histories of congressional elections often begin with 1994, when the Republicans broke the Democratic winning streak and then controlled the House over the course of the next five elections and the Senate for most of these years. Although some scholars predicted that the Democrats might regain control of the House in 2006, few thought they would regain control of the Senate.

Regardless of the partisan pattern, in most contests an incumbent will be running for reelection, and for the most part he or she will win. We review the pattern in incumbent success in House and Senate races between 1954, the first Democratic victory of their forty-year winning streak, and 2008. As we will see, House incumbents who choose to run succeed a vast majority of the time. Senate success is more erratic for reasons we explain, but since 1982 the vast majority of senators who have run for reelection have succeeded.

We also examine the overall pattern of partisan control of Congress over the last fifty-six years, from Dwight Eisenhower's first victory (Eighty-third Congress) to Obama's election in 2008 (111th Congress). In our look at the pattern of partisan success in 2008, controlling for both partisanship and incumbency, the most striking finding is the Democratic success in Senate races. In 2008 twelve Democratic senators sought reelection, and all were successful. Five Republican senators retired, and the Democrats gained three of these seats. Even more impressive, the Democrats won five seats when facing sixteen Republican incumbents.

As we argued in the introduction to Part I, realignments in the United States have always involved regional shifts in the basis of partisan support. We examine changes in the partisan composition of regional delegations in the House and Senate, examining the composition of the Eighty-third Congress, elected during Eisenhower's first victory; the Ninety-seventh Congress, elected during Ronald Reagan's first victory; and the 111th Congress, elected along with Obama. As we show, there has been regional change, which, while substantial, is not as dramatic as the regional change in presidential elections. These shifts have made a substantial change in the dynamics of regional power within Congress.

Despite the admonition of former Democratic House Speaker Thomas P. "Tip" O'Neill Jr. that "all politics is local," we find that national forces have a great impact on congressional races.[6] We show in Chapter 9 that the political climate continued to deteriorate for the Republicans throughout the spring and summer of 2008. The main Republican burden was that George W. Bush was suffering from low approval ratings. As a result, the Republican "brand" became increasingly harder to market as the election approached.

This situation made it difficult for Republican leaders to persuade their incumbents to run in 2008 and eased the way for Democrats, giving them an advantage in raising money for their candidates. Now that they again controlled the majority in Congress, the Democrats found it easier to raise funds from political action committees. Their majority control of the House even allowed the Democratic leadership to provide benefits to aid members from competitive districts.

We examine the success of candidates, controlling for their last political office, party, and whether they were an incumbent. Most House incumbents were successful regardless of the elective experience of their opponent. In the Senate, only a single incumbent, Republican Norm Coleman of Minnesota, was defeated by a challenger without previous elective experience, professional comedian Al Franken. We attempt to determine why incumbency is such a major advantage. Incumbents have huge advantages at raising money and can usually outspend their opponents. Because contributors do not like to support candidates who have little chance of winning, challengers find it even more difficult to overcome the obstacles encountered in defeating an incumbent who is better known, has more campaign experience, and is also likely to share the partisanship of a plurality of his or her constituents.

We also discuss in Chapter 9 the impact of Democratic gains on the 111th Congress. On the one hand, it will not be as important as the Democratic gains were for the 110th Congress, because the Democrats already controlled both chambers. But now they have an enhanced majority and a Democratic president. Although some pundits had emphasized that, with Arlen Specter's switch to the Democrats, the party found itself with a filibuster-proof majority, we did not think that having this supermajority was especially consequential.[7] To gain sixty votes to invoke cloture, the Democrats would need all sixty Democrats present and voting, unless they can win a few Republican votes. And if the Democrats can gain a handful of Republican votes, they can win even if they cannot muster all Democratic senators.

We then discuss the problems Obama may have in dealing with the 111th Congress. We turn briefly to a discussion of the 2010 midterm elections and of several academic models that political scientists have used to predict election outcomes. Although we do not use such models ourselves, we believe they can be useful in explaining why election results occur. We also briefly discuss the redistricting that will follow the 2010 census. Any state that loses or gains one or more House seats (unless it is reduced to one seat) must redraw its congressional districts. But even if a multidistrict state retains the same number of seats, it still must draw new district boundaries because court decisions have decreed that each state must have congressional districts of equal population after each census.

We end Chapter 9 by discussing demographic changes, especially the growing Latino population, that may transform congressional elections during the coming decades (also see Chapter 11).

After looking at congressional elections at the district and state levels to see how they formed a national result, we discuss in Chapter 10, using the ANES, congressional elections from the viewpoint of the individual voter.

We begin by examining the ways in which social forces relate to the congressional vote and find that, with a few exceptions, they relate in much the same way they do in accounting for presidential voting. One difference, scarcely surprising because of Obama's candidacy, is that blacks were less likely to vote Democratic for Congress than they were for president. When we examine issues, we find that voters' perceptions of where House candidates stood on a liberal–conservative continuum affected their vote. And we examine studies from past elections that evaluate the role of issues, and we briefly evaluate the impact of the respondents' positions on the same issues we studied in Chapter 6.

We then examine the relationship between party identification and congressional voting among whites in twenty-eight of the twenty-nine elections between 1952 and 2008.[8] That relationship was strongest between 1952 and 1964, the period that Philip E. Converse calls the "steady-state" period in American party identification.[9] The relationship declined after that, and defections from party identification were highest between 1972 and 1992. Since then, the relationship has rebounded. We discuss the reasons for these changes, which probably result from partisans defecting to vote for incumbents of the opposite party. A good part of our analysis examines the conditions under which party identifiers remain loyal or defect to support incumbents.

Congressional voting can be seen as a referendum on the performance of the president and on members of Congress, and we consider both possibilities. Most voters approve of the job their own representative is doing. But as we know from Chapter 7, in 2008 most voters disapproved of the job George W. Bush was doing as president. Within every category of partisanship and congressional incumbency, voters who disapproved of Bush's performance were more likely to vote Democratic for Congress, although there were so few Democrats in Democratic congressional districts who approved of Bush it is difficult to make meaningful comparisons. Of the 196 Democrats who lived in districts with a Democratic incumbent, only four voters approved of Bush, and all four voted Democratic for Congress.

We also discuss presidential coattails, attempting to determine whether a successful presidential candidate can carry fellow partisans into Congress on his or her coattails. We found some evidence of coattail effects, but these effects were far less important than those of party identification and congressional incumbency.

For decades, the Democratic majority in Congress was based on three pillars: (1) more Democrats than Republicans were in the electorate; (2) most incumbents (regardless of party) enjoyed high levels of approval from their constituents; and (3) incumbents had greater resources to contact their constituents than did challengers. Because the Democrats controlled the House for forty consecutive years, there were over those years more Democratic incumbents than Republican incumbents. When the Republicans gained a House majority in 1994, they enjoyed these last two advantages. But the Republican majority lasted only twelve years. The Democrats once again gained both of these last two advantages, and, as we saw in Chapter 8, they have also made recent gains in the party loyalties of the electorate.

Chapter 9

Candidates and Outcomes in 2008

In 1994 the Republicans unexpectedly won control of both chambers of Congress. It was the first time the GOP had won the U.S. House of Representatives since 1952. The electoral earthquake of 1994 shaped all subsequent congressional contests. Until 2008, as each election season began, there was significant doubt about who would control Congress after the voters chose. In 1996 the Republicans held the House for a second consecutive election (something they had not done since 1928), and defended their majority again in 1998 and in 2000. However, the Democrats gained ground in the House in all three of those elections. In the Senate, the Republicans added to their majority in 1996, broke even in 1998, and then lost ground in 2000. Then in 2002, the GOP made small gains in both the House and Senate, thereby getting a little breathing room, and in 2004 they gained a bit more in both chambers. Going into the election of 2006, the GOP still controlled Congress, but that year its luck ran out. The GOP suffered a crushing defeat, losing thirty seats in the House and six in the Senate, which shifted control of both bodies to the Democrats. In 2008 the Democrats achieved a second substantial gain in a row, adding twenty-one seats in the House and eight seats in the Senate.[1] In the House, the Democrats won 257 seats to the Republicans' 178. In the Senate, the result was a 57–41 division in favor of the Democrats, with two independents.[2]

In this chapter, we examine the pattern of congressional outcomes for 2008 and see how it compares with those for previous years. We explain why the 2008 results took the shape they did—what factors affected the success of incumbents seeking to return and what permitted some challengers to run better than others. We also discuss the likely impact of the election results on the politics of the 111th Congress. Finally, we consider the implications of the 2008 results for the 2010 midterm elections and for other elections to come.

ELECTION OUTCOMES IN 2008

Patterns of Incumbency and Party Success

One of the most dependable generalizations about American politics is that most congressional races include incumbents and most incumbents are reelected. Although this statement has been true for every set of congressional elections since World War II, the degree to which it has held has varied from one election to another. Table 9-1 presents election outcomes for House and Senate races that included incumbents between 1954 and 2008.[3] During this period, an average of 93 percent of House incumbents and 84 percent of Senate incumbents who sought reelection were successful.

Despite the strong showing nationally by the Democrats in 2008, the proportion of representatives reelected (94 percent) was slightly above the average for all twenty-eight elections (and virtually identical to 2006), while the success rate for senators was just one point below the average for that chamber. The results for the House contrasted markedly with those for some elections in the previous decade. For example, incumbent success was depressed in 1992 by the higher than usual defeat rates in both the primaries and general elections. The large number of losses occurred in part because it was the election after a census (when redistricting changed many district lines and forced a number of representatives to face one another in the same district), and in part because of a major scandal involving many House incumbents.[4] By contrast, 2004 saw very few primary defeats (two Democrats, both from Texas), and the proportion that lost in the general election was only a little higher (1.7 percent). The 2008 House results fell in between these extremes, with four primary defeats and nineteen general election losses. In the 2008 Senate races, not a single incumbent lost in a primary, but five were defeated in the general election.

During the period covered by Table 9-1, House and Senate outcomes were sometimes similar, and in other instances they exhibited different patterns. For example, in most years between 1968 and 1988, House incumbents were substantially more successful than their Senate counterparts. In the three elections between 1976 and 1980, the success rates of House incumbents averaged over 93 percent, whereas senators' success rates averaged only 62 percent. By contrast, the success rates in the last five elections before 2000 were fairly similar. More recently, in all but one of the five elections beginning in 2000 we have again seen some divergence, with House incumbents being more successful.

These differences between the two bodies stem from at least two factors. The first is primarily statistical: House elections routinely involve about four hundred incumbents, while Senate contests usually have fewer than thirty. A smaller number of cases is more likely to produce volatile results over time. Thus the proportion of successful Senate incumbents tends to vary more than that for the House. In addition, Senate races are more likely to be vigorously contested than House races, making incumbents more vulnerable. In many years, a substantial

TABLE 9-1 House and Senate Incumbents and Election Outcomes, 1954–2008

Year	Incumbents running (N)	Primary defeats %	Primary defeats (N)	General election defeats %	General election defeats (N)	Reelected %	Reelected (N)
House
1954	(407)	1.5	(6)	5.4	(22)	93.1	(379)
1956	(410)	1.5	(6)	3.7	(15)	94.9	(389)
1958	(394)	0.8	(3)	9.4	(37)	89.8	(354)
1960	(405)	1.2	(5)	6.2	(25)	92.6	(375)
1962	(402)	3.0	(12)	5.5	(22)	91.5	(368)
1964	(397)	2.0	(8)	11.3	(45)	86.6	(344)
1966	(411)	1.9	(8)	10.0	(41)	88.1	(362)
1968	(409)	1.0	(4)	2.2	(9)	96.8	(396)
1970	(401)	2.5	(10)	3.0	(12)	94.5	(379)
1972	(392)	3.3	(13)	3.3	(13)	93.4	(366)
1974	(391)	2.0	(8)	10.2	(40)	87.7	(343)
1976	(383)	0.8	(3)	3.1	(12)	96.1	(368)
1978	(382)	1.3	(5)	5.0	(19)	93.7	(358)
1980	(398)	1.5	(6)	7.8	(31)	90.7	(361)
1982	(393)	2.5	(10)	7.4	(29)	90.1	(354)
1984	(411)	0.7	(3)	3.9	(16)	95.4	(392)
1986	(393)	0.5	(2)	1.5	(6)	98.0	(385)
1988	(409)	0.2	(1)	1.5	(6)	98.3	(402)
1990	(407)	0.2	(1)	3.7	(15)	96.1	(391)
1992	(368)	5.4	(20)	6.3	(23)	88.3	(325)
1994	(387)	1.0	(4)	8.8	(34)	90.2	(349)
1996	(384)	0.5	(2)	5.5	(21)	94.0	(361)
1998	(401)	0.2	(1)	1.5	(6)	98.3	(394)
2000	(403)	0.7	(3)	1.5	(6)	97.8	(394)
2002	(398)	2.0	(8)	1.8	(7)	96.2	(383)
2004	(404)	0.5	(2)	1.7	(7)	97.8	(395)
2006	(404)	0.5	(2)	5.4	(22)	94.1	(380)
2008	(403)[a]	0.9	(4)	4.7	(19)	94.2	(380)
Senate
1954	(27)	—	(0)	15	(4)	85	(23)
1956	(30)	—	(0)	13	(4)	87	(26)
1958	(26)	—	(0)	35	(9)	65	(17)
1960	(28)	—	(0)	4	(1)	96	(27)
1962	(30)	—	(0)	10	(3)	90	(27)
1964	(30)	—	(0)	7	(2)	93	(28)

(Continued)

TABLE 9-1   House and Senate Incumbents and Election Outcomes,
1954–2008 *(continued)*

Year	Incumbents running (N)	Primary defeats %	Primary defeats (N)	General election defeats %	General election defeats (N)	Reelected %	Reelected (N)
Senate *(continued)*							
1966	(29)	7	(2)	3	(1)	90	(26)
1968	(28)	14	(4)	14	(4)	71	(20)
1970	(28)	4	(1)	11	(3)	86	(24)
1972	(26)	4	(1)	19	(5)	77	(20)
1974	(26)	4	(1)	8	(2)	88	(23)
1976	(25)	—	(0)	36	(9)	64	(16)
1978	(22)	—	(1)	27	(6)	68	(15)
1980	(29)	—	(4)	31	(9)	55	(16)
1982	(30)	—	(0)	7	(2)	93	(28)
1984	(29)	—	(0)	10	(3)	90	(26)
1986	(27)	—	(0)	22	(6)	78	(21)
1988	(26)	—	(0)	12	(3)	88	(23)
1990	(30)	—	(0)	3	(1)	97	(29)
1992	(27)	4	(1)	11	(3)	85	(23)
1994	(26)	—	(0)	8	(2)	92	(24)
1996	(20)	—	(0)	5	(1)	95	(19)
1998	(29)	—	(0)	10	(3)	90	(26)
2000	(27)	—	(0)	22	(6)	78	(21)
2002	(26)	4	(1)	8	(2)	88	(23)
2004	(25)	—	(0)	5	(1)	96	(24)
2006	(28)	—	(0)	21	(6)	79	(22)
2008	(29)	—	(0)	17	(5)	93	(24)

Source: Compiled by the authors.

[a] Incumbent representative Albert Wynn, a Democrat from Maryland, sought reelection in the Fourth District and was defeated in the primary and subsequently resigned. He was defeated by Donna Edwards, who won the interim special election and then won the general election. For the purposes of this table, Wynn is considered an incumbent and Edwards is not.

number of representatives have had no opponent at all, or have had one who was inexperienced, underfunded, or both. Senators, by contrast, often have had strong, well-financed opponents. Thus representatives have been electorally advantaged relative to senators. In the early 1990s, the competitiveness of House elections increased, reducing the relative advantage for representatives, although the election cycles since then have continued to see competition in House contests confined to a more narrow range of constituencies than Senate races. We will consider this issue in more detail later in the chapter.

FIGURE 9-1   Democratic Share of Seats in House and Senate, 1953–2009

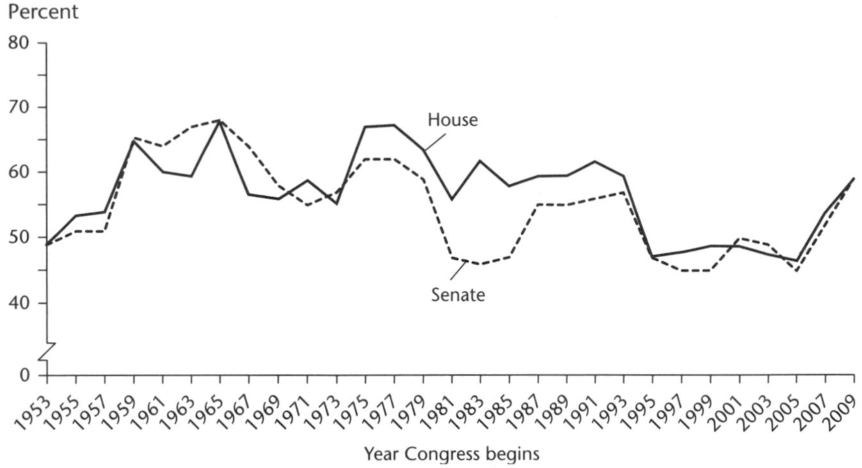

Percent

Year Congress begins

Sources: 1953–2007: Norman J. Ornstein, Thomas E. Mann, and Michael J. Malbin, *Vital Statistics on Congress 2008* (Washington, D.C.: Brookings Institution Press, 2008), 46–47; 2009: compiled by the authors.

Note: All percentages are based on party divisions on the first day of the Congress (except that for 2009 where Al Franken of Minnesota is included in the Senate share). Independents are included with the party with which they caucused.

Having considered the fortunes of incumbents, we now turn to success from the perspective of parties. Figure 9-1 shows the percentage of seats in the House and Senate held by the Democrats after each election since 1952. It graphically demonstrates how large a departure the elections of 1994–2004 were from those in the past. In House elections before 1994, the high percentage of incumbents running and the high rate of incumbent success led to fairly stable partisan control. Most important, the Democrats won a majority in the House in every election after 1954 and won twenty consecutive national elections. This winning streak, which was by far the longest period of dominance of the House by the same party in American history,[5] was ended by the upheaval of 1994, in which the GOP made a net gain of fifty-two representatives, winning 53 percent of the total seats. They held their majority in each subsequent election through 2004, although there were small shifts back to the Democrats in 1996, 1998, and 2000. Then in 2006, the Democrats took back the House and expanded their margin in 2008.

In the Senate, previous Republican control was much more recent. The Republicans took the Senate in the Reagan victory of 1980 and retained it in 1982 and 1984. When the class of 1980 faced the voters again in 1986, however, the Democrats made significant gains and won back the majority. They held it until the GOP regained control in 1994, and then the Republicans expanded their margin in 1996. In fact, the 55 percent of the seats they achieved that year (and repeated in 1998) was the highest Republican percentage in either chamber during this fifty-six-year period (1952–2008). Then in 2000 fortune turned against them, resulting in the fifty-fifty division of the chamber. This

TABLE 9-2   House and Senate General Election Outcomes, by Party and
Incumbency, 2008 (percent)

	Democratic incumbent	No incumbent		Republican incumbent	Total
		Democratic seat	Republican seat		
House					
Democrats	98	100	41	8	59
Republicans	2	0	59	92	41
Total	100	100	100	100	100
(*N*)	(229)	(7)	(29)	(170)	(435)
Senate					
Democrats	100	—	43	31	57
Republicans	0	—	57	69	43
Total	100	—	100	100	100
(*N*)	(12)	(0)	(7)	(16)	(35)[a]

Source: Compiled by the authors.

[a] Includes the two special election races held on the same general election calendar.

was followed a few months later by the decision of Sen. James Jeffords of
Vermont to become an independent and to vote with the Democrats on organizing the chamber, shifting majority control to them until after the 2002
elections. In 2004 the GOP gained four seats and again reached its high-water
mark of 55 percent. Finally, the combined Democratic gain of fourteen seats
in 2006 and 2008 restored solid control for that party.

The combined effect of party and incumbency in the general election of 2008
is shown in Table 9-2. Overall, the Democrats won 59 percent of the House races
and 57 percent of the Senate contests. Despite the sharp partisanship of both the
presidential and congressional races, incumbents of both parties did well in
House races. Ninety-eight percent of House Democratic incumbents won
reelection, and even though it was a bad year for the GOP, 92 percent of House
Republicans were successful. In Senate races, every Democratic incumbent won,
but only 69 percent of GOP incumbents were successful. One reason for the
Democrats' substantial success in 2008 was their performance in open-seat contests. Their record was similar in both chambers: they held every one of their
own open seats, and they won over 40 percent of the Republican ones.

Regional Bases of Power

The geographic pattern of 2008 outcomes in the House and Senate are evident
in the partisan breakdowns by region in Table 9-3.[6] For comparison, we also

TABLE 9-3   Party Shares of Regional Delegations in the House and Senate, 1953, 1981, and 2009 (percent)

	1953			1981			2009		
Region	Demo- crats (%)	Repub- licans (%)	(*N*)	Demo- crats (%)	Repub- licans (%)	(*N*)	Demo- crats (%)	Repub- licans (%)	(*N*)
House									
East	35	65	(116)	56	44	(105)	81	19	(84)
Midwest	23	76	(118)	47	53	(111)	56	44	(91)
West	33	67	(57)	51	49	(76)	64	36	(98)
South	94	6	(106)	64	36	(108)	45	55	(131)
Border	68	32	(38)	69	31	(35)	48	52	(31)
Total	49	51	(435)	56	44	(435)	59	41	(435)
Senate									
East	25	75	(20)	50	50	(20)	76	24	(20)
Midwest	14	86	(22)	41	59	(22)	65	35	(22)
West	45	55	(22)	35	65	(26)	48	52	(26)
South	100	0	(22)	55	45	(22)	27	73	(22)
Border	70	30	(10)	70	30	(10)	50	50	(10)
Total	49	51	(96)	47	53	(100)	59	41	(100)

Source: Compiled by the authors.

present corresponding data for 1981 (after the Republicans took control of the Senate in Reagan's first election) and for 1953 (the last Congress before 1995 in which the Republicans controlled both chambers). This series of elections reveals the enormous shifts in the regional political balance over the last half-century. In the House, comparing 2009 with 1981, we see that the GOP share declined in the East, Midwest, and West, while it increased in the South and border states. The most pronounced shifts were in the East and the South, with the Republican share decreasing by twenty-five percentage points in the East while increasing by nineteen points in the South. Overall, the Democrats won a majority of House seats in all regions but the South in 2008. The pattern is roughly similar in the Senate. Between 1981 and 2009, GOP gains were limited to two regions (the South and border), while it lost ground in the West, Midwest, and East.

The 2009 results are more interesting when viewed from the longer historical perspective. In 1953 there were sharp regional differences in party representation in both houses. Since then, these differences have diminished significantly. The most obvious changes have occurred in the East and the South. In 1953 the Republicans held nearly two-thirds of the House seats in the East, but by 2009 their share had fallen to less than one-fifth. Indeed, in New England, long a bastion of Republican strength, the GOP did not win even one of the twenty-two seats in 2008. The Republican decline in Senate seats in the East over the period was even greater, down from 75 percent to only 24 percent.

In the South, the percentage of House seats held by Democrats declined from 94 percent in 1953 to 45 percent in 2009. In 1953 the Democrats held all twenty-two southern Senate seats, but in 2009 they controlled only seven. This change in the partisan share of the South's seats in Congress has had an important impact on that region's influence within the two parties. The South used to be the backbone of Democratic congressional representation. This, and the tendency of southern members to build seniority, gave southerners disproportionate power within the Democratic Party in Congress. Because of the declining Democratic electoral success in the region, the numerical strength of southern Democrats in Congress has waned. In 1953, with the Republicans in control of both chambers, southerners accounted for about 45 percent of Democratic seats in the House and Senate. By the 1970s, southern strength had declined, to stabilize at between 25 and 30 percent of Democratic seats. In 2009 southerners accounted for 23 percent of Democratic House seats and only 12 percent of Democratic senators.

The South's share of Republican congressional representation presents the reverse picture. Minuscule at the end of World War II, it grew steadily, reaching about 20 percent in the House after the 1980 elections and 40 percent after 2008. As a consequence of these changes, southern influence has declined in the Democratic Party and grown in the GOP, to the point that southerners have recently held a disproportionate share of the Republican leadership positions in both houses of Congress. Because southerners of both parties tend to be more conservative than their colleagues from other regions, these shifts in regional strength have tended to make the Democratic Party in Congress more liberal and the Republican Party more conservative.[7]

Other regional changes since 1953, though not as striking as those in the South and East, are also significant. In the 1953 House, the Republicans controlled the West by a two-to-one margin and the Midwest by three to one; in 2009 they were a minority in both regions. The Senate also exhibited shifts away from substantial Republican strength in the West and Midwest. And yet with the increased Republican control of the South and Democratic dominance in the East, regional differences in party shares are somewhat more prominent in 2009 than they were in the 1990s. Still, partisan representation is more regionally homogeneous in the Congress of 2009 than it was in the Congress of 1953.

National Forces in Congressional Elections

The patterns of outcomes just discussed were shaped by a variety of influences. As with most congressional elections, the most important among these were the resources available to individual candidates and how those resources were distributed between the parties in specific races. We will discuss those matters shortly, but first we consider potential and actual national forces at work in the 2008 House and Senate elections.

The first national force to assess is whether there was a pattern in public opinion that advantaged one party over the other. Such "national tides" occur in presidential years and in midterms, and they can have a profound impact on the outcomes of congressional elections. Often these tides flow from reaction to presidents or presidential candidates. For example, in 1964 the presidential landslide victory of Lyndon Johnson over Barry Goldwater carried over to major Democratic gains in both congressional chambers, and Ronald Reagan's ten-point margin over Jimmy Carter in 1980 helped Republicans achieve an unexpected majority in the Senate and major gains in the House. Similarly, negative public reactions to events in the first two years of Bill Clinton's presidency played a major part in the Republicans' congressional victories in 1994.

Clearly, the 2008 election had a significant national tide working in favor of the Democrats in both the presidential and congressional arenas. From an historical point of view this is surprising, because 2006 had also exhibited a tide and in the same direction. And it is unusual for two consecutive elections to substantially advantage the same party. For example, before 2008 the last election in which a party gained at least thirty House seats followed by one in which the same party gained at least twenty seats was in 1932, when the Democrats gained ninety-seven seats after having gained fifty-three in 1930. It is clear, however, that the consecutive results in 2006 and 2008 grew largely from the same roots: negative public reactions to the Bush administration and its congressional co-partisans.

We examine the direct link between presidential approval and the congressional vote in the next chapter, but we note here that reactions to Bush were a negative weight for the GOP throughout the election campaign. As we discussed in Chapters 2 and 7, Bush's approval ratings were extremely low, as they had been in 2006. More generally, during the 2008 campaign Republicans were concerned about the reputation of their party among the public—the "Republican brand," as it is often called.[8]

Signs of the party's difficulties in 2008 emerged well before the November voting via the results in three special House elections needed to fill Republican vacancies. In March 2008, Illinois held an election to fill the longtime Republican seat of former House Speaker Dennis Hastert, who had resigned. The Democrats won. Then in May, two special elections took place in even friendlier Republican territory: Louisiana and Mississippi. The Democrats won both of these seats, too, despite GOP efforts to create unpalatable connections for the opposition candidates. In Mississippi, the Republicans sponsored an ad that said the Democrat was "endorsed by Barack Obama.... He took Obama's endorsement over our conservative values." And in Louisiana, an ad run by the Republican National Committee charged that a vote for the Democrat was "a vote for Barack Obama and Nancy Pelosi [the Democratic Speaker of the House].... He'll do what they tell him to do."[9] The expectation was that conservative southerners would find these connections unattractive, and so they would reject the Democratic candidates, but clearly that strategy did not work.

Until the third special election loss, GOP strategists and leaders had sought to paint the events as idiosyncratic—the result of special circumstances in the individual districts. But such a portrayal became more difficult after the Mississippi defeat, and some were willing to state publicly that there was a more general problem. For example, Rep. Tom Cole of Oklahoma, head of the National Republican Campaign Committee (NRCC, the official campaign committee for House Republicans), said, "When you lose three in a row, you have to get beyond campaign tactics and take a long hard look: Is there something wrong with your product?"[10] In another interview, Cole admitted that "voters remain pessimistic about the direction of the country in general and the Republican party in particular."[11] Probably the pithiest statement of the problem came from Rep. Tom Davis of Virginia, a former NRCC chair, who had announced he was retiring from the House in 2008. In a memo to GOP leaders he said, "The Republican brand is in the trash can.... If we were a dog food, they would take us off the shelf."[12]

It was, however, much easier to recognize the need to improve the Republican brand than to develop a strategy that would succeed in doing so. Well before the GOP saw the negative results in November, there were disagreements within the party about what to do and about who was to blame. Newt Gingrich, the former Republican House Speaker, called in early May for a complete overhaul of the NRCC and for a new GOP message by Memorial Day.[13] The Republican Study Committee (a group of the more conservative Republican members of the House) argued for pushing an agenda that would appeal to conservative voters, including "the end of pork-barrel spending" and reductions in federal spending, although they had great difficulty getting most members of the party to vote for these positions.[14] Other Republicans contended that their candidates would just have to fend for themselves. Rep. Peter King of New York said, "You are going to have to run on who you are, and establish some independence, and that is going to be rougher for some than others."[15]

To the party's misfortune, however, the rebranding efforts were plagued with difficulties. For example, in the midst of the May special election defeats the House Republican leadership proposed the first phase of a new agenda focused on family issues and a new slogan for the party: "Change You Deserve."[16] Within a couple of days, however, it came to light that the slogan was trademarked advertising copy, and worse, it was for an antidepressant (Effexor).

Another potential national force is public reaction to the performance of Congress. In the 1996 presidential race, Clinton and the Democrats tried to focus public attention on what they claimed was the extremism and excesses of the new GOP congressional majority, albeit with only very limited success.[17] In 2008 public opinion toward Congress turned very negative. For example, in an ABC News/*Washington Post* poll in mid-July, only 23 percent of respondents approved of the job Congress was doing, and 71 percent disapproved. Because the Democrats now controlled Congress, one might think this would be good news for the GOP. It was not. When the same people were asked their views of the job performance of Democratic leaders in Congress, 35 percent approved and 57 percent disapproved. For Republican leaders, the results were 25 and 69 percent, respectively.[18]

Efforts of National Parties and Their Allies

One important national-level force is the efforts of congressional party leaders and their allies to influence the races. Before the 1980s, the activities of national parties in congressional elections were very limited. Individual candidates were mostly self-starters who were largely on their own in raising money and planning strategy. More recently, this situation has changed substantially, and party leaders and organizations now are heavily involved in recruiting and funding their candidates.[19] The quality of candidates and their level of funding are two of the central determinants of election outcomes. Thus both the short-term and long-term fates of the parties in Congress provided incentives for the parties to be active in efforts to improve their circumstances in these respects.

Recruiting Candidates. National party organizations now play an ongoing role in candidate recruiting and fund-raising. As soon as the voting in one election ends, the organizations begin to gear up for the next one. The Republicans' main concern after their bad showing in 2006 was that many of their senior members would become frustrated by their minority status (and the expectation that it would continue) and retire. In 2007 and 2008, national campaign leaders and their staffs tried to stave off possible retirements and to promote candidacies for higher office. They monitored the plans of individual candidates, and the Republicans discussed possible strategies for eventually taking back the majority. The perceived prospects of success were key elements of the strategic calculations of potential recruits. It is much easier for a party to persuade a prospect to run if that party's national prospects look bright.

In the end, the Democrats were much more successful than the Republicans in persuading their incumbents to make another run, not surprising in view of the balance of public attitudes. In the House, only seven Democrats chose to leave, either to seek another office or to retire, whereas twenty-nine Republicans gave up their seats. In the Senate, not a single Democrat decided to quit, but five Republicans did. Because incumbents are favorites to hold on to their seats, this disproportion of open seats for the GOP just made their strategic position worse.

The Democrats also did better in persuading strong candidates to seek places in Congress. In Senate races, three former Democratic governors (of New Hampshire, Mississippi, and Virginia) and three sitting members of the U.S. House (representing Colorado, Maine, and New Mexico) opted to run, along with prominent state legislators in North Carolina and Oregon. The Republicans were generally perceived to have only one significant opportunity to take a Democratic seat (against Mary Landrieu in Louisiana), and they succeeded in convincing the Democratic state treasurer to switch parties to run. He lost. For Republican open seats, they were able to recruit two former governors (Nebraska and Virginia) and a lieutenant governor (Idaho), two of whom were winners.

House recruitment also revealed the GOP's difficult political circumstances. Potential Democratic candidates perceived an advantageous environment, and so high-quality candidates emerged in many open districts and against some incumbents who exhibited political weaknesses. The Republican Party was also able to convince potentially strong contenders to run in some districts, but far fewer than would have been expected in view of the fact that sixty-four Democrats held seats in districts that George W. Bush had won in 2004. Moreover, even in some districts where initial GOP recruitment efforts had been successful the party suffered reversals. For example, a state legislator in Indiana and a mayor in Illinois dropped out of congressional candidacies after winning primaries.

Money and Other Aid. In addition to recruitment, party leaders have grown increasingly active in fund-raising, pursuing many alternative strategies. For example, top party leaders solicit donations to the congressional campaign committees, such as the NRCC and the Democratic Congressional Campaign Committee (DCCC), and they appear at fund-raisers for individual candidates in their districts. Both parties develop lists of priority races (especially those involving endangered incumbents) on which to focus their efforts.

Raising campaign funds for the party has become a prominent obligation for members who hold or want to hold leadership posts and committee chairmanships, and the amounts they raise are a significant portion of money spent in campaigns. For example, during the two years leading up to the 2008 elections Rep. Charles Rangel of New York, Democratic chairman of the tax-writing Ways and Means committee, raised an incredible $5 million. He transferred over $1.1 million of this amount to other Democratic candidates, including $435,000 to the DCCC. In October, when some committee chairs were lagging behind the level of donations to the party that had been set for them, Speaker Nancy Pelosi pressured them to meet their obligations, resulting in hundreds of thousands of dollars in additional contributions.[20] In the Senate, the party campaign committees also sought and secured significant donations from members, which included a $1 million contribution from John Kerry of Massachusetts to the Democratic Senatorial Campaign Committee (DSCC).

The advantages that flowed from regaining majority status in 2006, as well as those that resulted from the tilt in the political environment, permitted the Democrats to dominate party campaign spending in 2008. The House Democrats received more donations from political action committees than the Republicans for the first election cycle since 1994 (the last time they were in the majority).[21] As Table 9-4 shows, Democratic spending was more than three times GOP spending in House races and about double GOP spending in

TABLE 9-4   Party Spending in House and Senate Contests, 2008

Spending	Democratic contests	Republican contests
House contests		
$2 million and over	10	0
$1.50–1.99 million	11	1
$1.0–1.49 million	17	3
$500,000–999,000	14	21
Less than $500,000	12	11
Total contests	64	36
Total spending (millions)	$75.25	$22.78
Senate contests		
$10 million and over	2	0
$7–9.99 million	3	0
$3–6.99 million	3	7
Less than $3 million	3	1
Total contests	11	8
Total spending (millions)	$70.08	$36.15

Source: "A First Look at Money in the House and Senate Elections," Campaign Finance Institute, November 8, 2008.

Senate contests. Moreover, the Democratic Party committees contributed to almost twice as many House races. The aggregate advantage for the Democrats resulted in advantages in individual contests. The party committees spent over $1.5 million in each of twenty-five House races, while the GOP reached that level in only one. Similarly, Democrats spent over $7 million in five Senate campaigns, a figure the Republicans could not match anywhere. The financial disadvantage for the GOP was particularly constraining as election day approached and they were unable to spend in many close races. In late October, the national Republicans decided to withhold support from all but two of the party's candidates in New York, including two in GOP districts in which the Republican incumbent was retiring.[22]

Party leaders are able to do more to help candidates' reelection efforts than just raise or spend campaign money, at least for the House majority. Because the majority has greater influence over the floor agenda and the content of bills, it can add or remove provisions in bills that will enhance their members' reelection chances, or permit vulnerable colleagues to bring popular bills to the floor. For example, in November 2007 fifty-four earmarks (spending on specific projects designated by congressional action) sponsored by Democratic freshmen or more endangered senior members were added to conference reports on three appropriations bills.[23] Republicans were unable to produce similar benefits for their members.

FIGURE 9-2   Competitive House Districts, 2007–2008

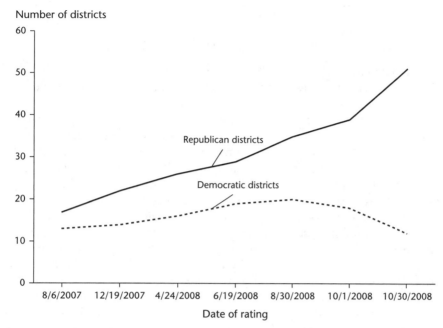

Source: Compiled by the authors from editions of *The Cook Political Report* on listed dates

In 2008 the Democrats' advantages in candidate recruitment and money, coupled with the shift in public opinion, helped to reinforce their competitive edge as the election season went on. Figure 9-2 presents the number of Democratic and Republican House seats that political analyst Charlie Cook estimated to be highly competitive at various points in the 2007–2008 election cycle.[24] In August 2007, more than a year before the elections, the two parties had nearly the same number of competitive seats: seventeen for the Republicans and thirteen for the Democrats. Over the next twelve months, the numbers increased for both parties. Then in October, the trends for both moved sharply in opposite directions, with the number of GOP competitive seats increasing. At the end of October, just before the election, the Republicans had more than four times as many competitive races as the Democrats—fifty-one and twelve, respectively. As we have seen, the final results reflected these expectations.

CANDIDATES' RESOURCES AND ELECTION OUTCOMES

Seats in the House and Senate are highly valued posts for which candidates compete vigorously. In contests for these offices, candidates draw on every resource they have. In this section, we discuss the most significant resources available to candidates and the impacts of those resources on the outcomes of congressional elections.

Candidate Quality

Election outcomes usually depend heavily on candidate quality. A strong, capable candidate is a significant asset for a party; a weak, inept one is a liability that is difficult to overcome. In his study of the activities of House members in their districts, Richard F. Fenno Jr. described how members try to build support within their constituencies, establishing bonds of trust between constituents and their representative.[25] Members attempt to convey to their constituents a sense that they are qualified for their job, that they identify with their constituents, and that they empathize with constituents and constituents' problems. Challengers of incumbents and candidates for open seats must engage in similar activities to win support. The winner of a contested congressional election will usually be the candidate who is better able to establish these bonds of support among constituents and to convince them that he or she is the person for the job (or that the opponent is not).

One indicator of candidate quality is previous success at winning elected office. The more important the office a candidate has held, the more likely it is that he or she has overcome significant competition to obtain the office. Moreover, the visibility and reputation for performance that usually accompany public office can be a significant electoral asset. For example, state legislators running for House seats can claim that they have experience that has prepared them for congressional service. State legislators may also have built successful organizations that are useful in conducting congressional campaigns. Finally, previous success in an electoral arena suggests that experienced candidates are more likely to be able to run strong campaigns than candidates without previous success or experience. Less adept candidates are likely to have been screened out at lower levels of office competition. For these and other reasons, an experienced candidate tends to have an electoral advantage over a candidate who has held no previous elected office.[26] The higher the office previously held, the stronger the candidate will tend to be in the congressional contest.

In Table 9-5, we present data showing which candidates were successful in 2008, controlling for elected office background, party, and incumbency. In House contests, the vast majority of candidates who challenged incumbents lost regardless of their elected office background or party, although those with elected office experience did better than those who had none. The impact of candidate quality is stronger in races without incumbents. Here candidates who had been state legislators were overwhelmingly successful, and those with other elective experience won at a much higher rate than those without any elected office experience. In Senate races, the patterns were similar. Only one incumbent was defeated by an inexperienced candidate (Al Franken of Minnesota, who beat incumbent Norm Coleman), and in Senate open-seat races, all of the winners had elected office experience.[27]

TABLE 9-5   Success in House and Senate Elections, Controlling for Office
Background, Party, and Incumbency, 2008 (percent)

Candidate's last office	Candidate is opponent of ...				No incumbent in district			
	Democratic incumbent		Republican incumbent		Democratic candidate		Republican candidate	
	%	(N)	%	(N)	%	(N)	%	(N)
House								
State legislature or U.S. House	7	(13)	13	(8)	67	(9)	62	(13)
Other elected office	5	(19)	10	(20)	75	(12)	57	(7)
No elected office	2	(155)	2	(128)	27	(15)	31	(16)
Senate								
U.S. House	—	(0)	0	(2)	67	(3)	50	(2)
Statewide elected office	0	(1)	50	(2)	50	(2)	67	(3)
Other elected office	0	(4)	29	(7)	—	(0)	50	(2)
No elected office	0	(6)	20	(5)	0	(2)	0	(0)

Source: Data on office backgrounds were taken from issues of *The Cook Political Report,* supplemented by other sources.

Over time, there has been substantial variation in the proportion of experienced challengers. During the 1980s, the proportion of House incumbents facing challengers who had previously won elected office declined. In 1980, 17.6 percent of incumbents faced such challenges; in 1984, 14.7 percent did; and in 1988 only 10.5 percent. In 1992, largely because of the perceptions of incumbent vulnerability stemming from redistricting and scandal, the proportion rose to 23.5 percent, but in 1996 it was back down to 16.5 percent, and it remained at that level in 2000.[28] In 2004, however, there was a substantial resurgence in the number of experienced candidates in both parties, with 22.4 percent of the total challengers having previously held elected office, followed by a decline again in 2008 to 14.8 percent.[29]

Whether experienced politicians actually run for the House or Senate is not an accident. Politicians must make big strategic decisions, and they have much to lose if they make the wrong choice. The choices are governed by the perceived chance of success, the potential value of the new office compared with what will be lost if the candidate fails, and the costs of running.[30] The chances of success of the two major parties vary from election to election, both locally and nationally. Therefore, each election offers a different mix of experienced and inexperienced candidates from the two parties for the House and Senate.

The most influential factor in whether a potential candidate will run is whether there is an incumbent in the race. High reelection rates tend to discourage potentially strong challengers from running, which, in turn, makes it even more likely that the incumbents will win. In addition to the general difficulty of challenging incumbents, factors related to specific election years (both nationally and in a particular district) will affect decisions to run. For example, the Republican Party had special difficulty recruiting strong candidates in 1986 because of fears about a potential backlash from the Iran-contra scandals. And the 2008 decline in experienced candidates likely stemmed from the inability of the minority Republicans to recruit strong candidates in many districts. And yet recent research indicates that potential House candidates are most strongly influenced in their decision by their perceived chances of winning their party's nomination.[31] Moreover, the actions of the incumbents may influence the choices of potential challengers. For example, an incumbent's success at building up a large reserve of campaign funds between elections may dissuade some possible opponents, although analyses of Senate contests (which usually involve experienced challengers) indicate that this factor does not have a systematic impact in those races.[32]

As we have seen, most congressional races do not include challengers who have held elected office. Given their slight chance of winning, why do challengers without experience run at all? As Jeffrey S. Banks and D. Roderick Kiewiet have pointed out, although the chances of success against incumbents may be small for such candidates, such a race may still be their best chance of ever winning a seat in Congress.[33] If inexperienced challengers were to put off their candidacies until a time when there is no incumbent, their opposition would likely include multiple experienced candidates from both parties. Moreover, as David Canon demonstrated, previous elected office experience is an imperfect indicator of candidate quality, because some candidates without such experience can still have significant political assets and be formidable challengers.[34] For example, four former television journalists who had never held office won House seats in 1992, and three of them defeated incumbents. They were able to build on their substantial name recognition among voters to win nomination and election.[35] For more recent examples, consider two 2000 contests, one from each chamber. The Republican candidate for the House in Nebraska's third district was Tom Osborne, the extremely popular former head coach of the University of Nebraska's football team. Osborne was elected to an open seat with a phenomenal 82 percent of the vote. In the New York Senate race, the very visible (and ultimately successful) Democratic candidate was the first lady at the time, Hillary Clinton.

Incumbency

One reason most incumbents win is that incumbency itself is a significant resource. Actually, incumbency is not a single resource, but rather a status that usually gives a candidate a variety of benefits. In some respects, incumbency works to a candidate's advantage automatically. For one thing, incumbents tend to be more visible to voters than their challengers.[36] Less automatic, but very important, incumbents tend to be viewed more favorably than challengers. Moreover, at least a plurality of the electorate in most districts will identify with the incumbent's political party. Incumbents can also use their status to gain advantages. Incumbents usually raise and spend more money than challengers, and they usually have a better developed and more experienced campaign organization. They also have assets, provided at public expense, such as a staff and franking privileges (free postage for mail to their constituents), that both help them perform their jobs and provide electoral benefits.

Increasing Electoral Margins. From the mid-1960s through the late 1980s, the margins by which incumbents were reelected increased (the pattern was less clear and more erratic in Senate elections than in House elections).[37] These changing patterns interested analysts primarily because they believed that the disappearance of marginal incumbents means less congressional turnover and a House that is less responsive to the electorate.

Edward R. Tufte offered an early explanation for the increased incumbency margins by arguing that redistricting had protected incumbents of both parties.[38] This argument seemed plausible because the increase in margins occurred about the same time as the massive redistrictings required by Supreme Court decisions of the mid-1960s. But other analysts showed that House incumbents had won by larger margins both in states that had redistricted and in those that had not, as well as in Senate contests.[39] Thus redistricting could not be the major reason for the change.

Another explanation offered for the increase in incumbents' margins was the growth in the perquisites of members and the greater complexity of government. Morris P. Fiorina notes that in the post–New Deal period the level of federal services and the bureaucracy that administered them grew tremendously.[40] More complex government means that many people encounter problems in receiving services, and people who have problems frequently contact their representatives to complain and seek help. Fiorina contends that in the mid-1960s new members of Congress emphasized such constituency problem solving more than their predecessors. This expanded constituency service developed into a reservoir of electoral support. Although analyses of the impact of constituency services have produced mixed conclusions, it is likely that the growth of these services offers a partial explanation for changing incumbent vote margins and for the incumbency advantage generally.[41]

The declining impact of party loyalties provided a third explanation for the growth in incumbent vote margins, either alone or in interaction with other factors. Until the mid-1960s, there was a very strong linkage between party identification and congressional voting behavior. Most Americans identified with a political party, many identified strongly, and most voters supported the candidate of their chosen party. Later, however, the impact of party identification declined, as we will see in Chapter 10. John A. Ferejohn, drawing on data from the American National Election Studies, showed that the strength of party ties weakened and that within any given category of party identification the tendency to support the candidate of one's party declined.[42] According to an analysis by Albert D. Cover, between 1958 and 1974 voters who did not identify with the party of a congressional incumbent were increasingly more likely to defect from their party and support the incumbent, whereas there had been no increase in defections from party identification by voters of the same party as the incumbents.[43] Thus weakened party ties produced a substantial net benefit for incumbents,[44] although, as we saw in Chapter 8, party loyalties among the electorate have grown stronger in recent years.

The Trend Reversed. Whatever the relative importance of these factors, and the others we will discuss, in explaining the increase in incumbents' victory margins, the increase continued through the 1980s, as the data in Table 9-6 show, peaking at 68.2 percent in 1986 and 1988.

Then in 1990, something changed. The average share of the vote for incumbents declined by nearly five percentage points. The decline was not the result of voters shifting toward one party, as it was with the decline from 1980 to 1982; rather, both parties' incumbents suffered. The shift in incumbents' electoral fortunes was apparently the result of what was called the "anti-incumbent mood" among the voters. Early in 1990, pollsters and commentators began to perceive stronger anti-Congress sentiments within the electorate.[45] For the first time, analysts began to question whether incumbency remained the asset it used to be. There was, of course, nothing new about Congress being unpopular; Congress had long suffered ups and downs in approval, just as the president had. What changed in 1990 was that Congress's unpopularity appeared to be undermining the approval of individual members by their own constituents. Yet as Table 9-1 showed, even though there was a drop in the average percentage of the vote received by incumbents in 1990, the rate of reelection still reached 96 percent. The decline in vote margins was not great enough to produce a rash of defeats. Many observers wondered, however, whether 1990 was the beginning of a new trend: would incumbents' electoral drawing power continue to decline?

In 1992 scandals damaged many representatives of both parties, and among the public the evaluation of Congress was very low. Opponents of incumbents emphasized that they were "outsiders" and not "professional politicians" (even when they had substantial political experience). The result was that incumbents' share of the vote dropped a bit more in 1992. Republicans rebounded a little from their bad 1990 showing, but Democrats fell more than two percentage points. Yet again, however, the casualty rate among incumbents who ran in the general election was lower than many expected: 93 percent were reelected. (It is important to note, though, that a substantial number of incumbents had already been defeated in the primaries, and many weak incumbents had retired.) Then

TABLE 9-6   Average Vote Percentages of House Incumbents, Selected Years, 1974–2008

Year	Democrats	Republicans	All incumbents
1974	68.5	55.2	61.7
1980	64.0	67.9	65.5
1982	67.9	59.9	64.1
1984	64.2	68.2	65.9
1986	70.2	65.6	68.2
1988	68.8	67.5	68.2
1990	65.8	59.8	63.5
1992	63.3	62.9	63.1
1994	60.0	67.6	62.8
1996	66.6	60.7	63.3
1998	65.0	61.6	63.3
2000	67.2	62.9	65.1
2002	66.4	66.1	66.3
2004	67.8	63.9	65.4
2006	71.5	60.0	65.0
2008	69.0	61.0	65.0

Sources: 1974–1990: "House Incumbents' Average Vote Percentage," *Congressional Quarterly Weekly Report,* November 10, 1990, 3800; 1994: *New York Times,* November 10, 1994; 1992 and 1996: *USA Today,* November 8, 1996, 4A; 1998–2008: computed by the authors.

Note: These figures include only races in which both major parties ran candidates. Thus they exclude contests in which an incumbent ran unopposed. Because such races were increasing in number over this period, the data actually understate the growth in incumbents' margins.

in 1994, although there was only a slight additional drop in incumbents' share of the vote overall, the drop was greater (and concentrated) for Democrats, and their casualty rate was high. The result was the loss of their majority. In 1996 there was a slight rebound in incumbents' vote share, with Democrats increasing sharply while the GOP fell. That vote shift translated into the defeat of eighteen Republican incumbents, but only three Democrats. The results from 2000–2008—with the continuing Democratic effort to whittle away at the GOP majority—fall in between the highs of the mid-1980s and the lows of 1994 and 1996.[46]

This discussion illustrates that incumbents' vote margins and incumbents' reelection success are related but distinct phenomena.[47] When—as was true in the 1980s—the average share of the vote received by incumbents is very high, they can lose a lot of ground in the vote advantage before they begin to fall to defeat. In 1990 many incumbents were probably subjected to vigorous contests for the first time in many years. Such challenges were then repeated or extended to additional incumbents in 1992, 1994, and 1996. Potential candidates apparently looked at the political situation and concluded that incumbents who had looked unbeatable could now be defeated, and thus there was a substantial increase in the number of candidates for Congress. These vigorous contests by challengers who were stronger than usual resulted in a decrease in the share of the vote received by many incumbents. In most cases in 1990, the decrease was not large enough to bring the challenger victory. In later years, however, the increased competition caught up with a greater number of incumbents. Now, in the twenty-first century, the aggregate level of competition varies from election to election, largely because of the political context and the deliberate crafting of safe districts for both parties' incumbents.

Campaign Spending

A third resource that strongly affects congressional elections is campaign spending. Campaign spending has received a great deal of attention in the last three decades because researchers have gained access to more dependable data than have been available.[48] The data on spending have consistently shown that incumbents usually outspend their challengers, often by large margins, and that through the early 1990s the disparity increased.[49] (As we shall see shortly, more recent data show significant changes.)

Disparities in campaign spending are linked to the increase in incumbents' election margins. Beginning in the 1960s, congressional campaigns relied more heavily on campaign techniques that cost money—for example, media time, campaign consulting, and direct mail—and these have become increasingly expensive. At the same time, candidates were progressively less likely to have available pools of campaign workers from established party organizations or from interest groups. This lack has made the use of expensive media and direct mail strategies relatively more important. Most challengers are unable to raise significant campaign funds. No one interested in the outcomes of congressional elections likes to throw money away; before making contributions they usually need to be convinced that the candidate has a chance. Yet in most election years few incumbents have been beaten. Thus it is often difficult to convince potential contributors that their money will produce results, and contributions are often not forthcoming, leaving most challengers at a strategic disadvantage, unable to raise sufficient funds to wage a competitive campaign.[50]

It is the ability to compete, rather than the simple question of relative amounts of spending, that is at the core of the issue. We have noted that incumbents have many inherent advantages that the challenger must overcome to win. But often the money is not there to overcome them. In 2008, for example, over 37 percent of challengers in House contests spent $25,000 or less, and 54 percent spent $75,000 or less. With so little money available, challengers are unable to make themselves visible to the electorate or to convey a convincing message.[51] Under such circumstances, most voters—being unaware of the positions, or perhaps even the existence, of the challenger—vote for the incumbent.

TABLE 9-7 Incumbents' Share of the Vote in the 2008 House Elections, by Challenger Campaign Spending (percent)

Challenger spending	Incumbents' share of two-party vote					
	70% or more	60%–69%	55%–59%	Less than 55%	Total	(N)
$0–25,000	60.9	36.7	2.3	0.0	99.9	(128)
$26,000–75,000	37.5	57.1	3.6	1.8	100.0	(56)
$76,000–199,000	10.8	67.6	16.2	5.4	100.0	(37)
$200,000–399,000	0.0	65.2	30.4	4.4	100.0	(23)
$400,000–799,000	7.1	53.6	21.4	17.9	100.0	(28)
$800,000 or more	0.0	14.1	39.4	46.5	100.0	(71)
All	30.6	42.0	15.2	12.2	100.0	(343)

Source: Federal Election Commission, www.fec.gov.

Note: Races without a major-party opponent are excluded and challenger campaign spending that was unavailable was coded in the $0–25,000 row. Totals do not always equal 100 because of rounding.

Data from 2008 on campaign spending and election outcomes seem consistent with this argument, and they show patterns similar to those exhibited in other recent elections. Linking spending to outcomes, Table 9-7 shows the relationship between the incumbent's share of the vote in the 2008 House elections and the amount of money spent by the challenger. Clearly, there is a strong negative relationship between how much challengers spend and how well incumbents do. In races in which challengers spent less than $26,000, 98 percent of the incumbents received 60 percent or more of the vote. At the other end of the spectrum, in races in which challengers spent $800,000 or more, 86 percent of the incumbents received less than 60 percent of the vote, and almost half received less than 55 percent. These results are consistent with those in earlier House elections for which comparable data are available.[52]

These findings are reinforced by other research that shows that challenger spending has a greater influence on election outcomes than does incumbent spending.[53] This generalization has been questioned on methodological grounds,[54] but further research by Gary C. Jacobson reinforced his earlier findings. Using both aggregate and survey data, he found that "the amount spent by the challenger is far more important in accounting for voters' decisions than is the amount of spending by the incumbent."[55] Analysis of Senate elections has also resulted in conflicting conclusions.[56]

Of course, challengers who appear to have good prospects will find it easier to raise money than those whose chances seem slim. Thus one might wonder whether these data simply reflect the fulfillment of expectations, in which money flows to challengers who would have done well regardless of spending.

Other research, however, indicates that that is probably not the case. In an analysis of the 1972 and 1974 congressional elections, Jacobson concluded, "Our evidence is that campaign spending helps candidates, particularly non-incumbents, by bringing them to the attention of the voters; it is not the case that well-known candidates simply attract more money; rather money buys attention."[57] From this perspective, adequate funding is a necessary but not a sufficient condition for a closely fought election contest, a perspective consistent with the data in Table 9-7. Heavily outspending one's opponent is not a guarantee of victory; the evidence does not support the conclusion that elections can be bought. If an incumbent outspends the challenger, the incumbent can still lose if the challenger is adequately funded and runs a campaign that persuades the voters. In eleven of the nineteen races in which incumbents lost in the 2008 election, the loser outspent the winner.[58] Indeed, in three of these contests the losing incumbent spent more than twice as much as the challenger. Perhaps most important, however, with one exception no victorious challenger spent less than $1 million.[59]

And yet a spending advantage is not a guarantee to a challenger. In an extreme example from 2000, in Texas Republican challenger Phil Sudan spent $3.247 million against the Democratic incumbent, Ken Bentsen, who spent $1.354 million. Despite being outspent over two to one, Bentsen won more than 60 percent of the vote. A somewhat less extreme case occurred in New York in 2008, when Republican Sandy Treadwell spent over $7 million to incumbent Democrat Kristen Gillibrand's $4.49 million. The Democrat was reelected with over 61 percent of the vote. Based on this analysis, our view can be summarized as follows: if a challenger is to attain visibility and get his or her message across to the voters, thereby neutralizing the incumbent's advantages in name recognition and perquisites of office, the challenger must be adequately funded. If both sides in a race are adequately funded, the outcome will tend to turn on factors other than just money, and the relative spending of the two candidates is unlikely to control the outcome.

This argument carries us full circle back to our earlier discussion and leads us to bring together the three kinds of resources that we have considered—candidate experience, incumbency, and campaign spending. Table 9-8 shows the impact of these three factors in the 2008 House elections. We categorize challenger experience as strong or weak, depending on previous elected office experience; challenger spending was classified as low or high, depending on whether it was above or below $200,000.[60] The data show that each element exerts some independent effect, but the impact of spending seems to be more consequential this year. When challengers had weak experience and low spending (198 of the 343 races), all incumbents won, and 94 percent won with more than 60 percent of the vote. In the opposite situation, in which the challenger had both strong experience and substantial spending (only thirty-seven of the 343 races), 73 percent of the races were relatively competitive. The combined results for the two intermediate categories fall between the extremes. Incumbent defeats occur with greater frequency

TABLE 9-8 Incumbents' Share of the Vote in the 2008 House Elections, by Challenger Experience and Spending (percent)

Challenger experience/ spending	Share of vote						Incumbents defeated (%)
	70% or more	60–69%	55–59%	Less than 55%	Total	(N)	
Weak/low	50.0	44.4	4.0	1.5	99.9	(198)	0.0
Strong/low	17.4	69.6	13.0	0.0	100.0	(23)	0.0
Weak/high	2.4	35.3	34.1	28.2	100.0	(85)	12.9
Strong/high	0.0	27.0	32.4	40.5	99.9	(37)	21.6

Source: See sources for Tables 9-5 and 9-7.

Note: Percentages read across. Strong challengers have held a significant elected office (challengers were categorized as having strong experience if they had been elected U.S. representative, to statewide office, to the state legislature, or to countywide or citywide office—for example, mayor, prosecutor, and so on). High-spending challengers spent more than $200,000. Races without a major-party opponent as well as those in which an incumbent lost in the primary have been excluded.

in situations in which the challenger is experienced and has strong spending. Yet note how few such races there were in 2008. Table 9-8 also reveals that over 60 percent of the challengers with strong experience were able to raise substantial funds (thirty-seven in sixty), whereas only 30 percent of challengers with little experience (eighty-five in 283) were able to do so.

This combination of factors also helps to explain the greater volatility of outcomes in the Senate races. Previous analysis has shown that the effects of campaign spending in Senate contests are consistent with what we have found true for House races: if challenger spending is above some threshold, the election is likely to be quite close; if it is below that level, the incumbent is likely to win by a large margin.[61] In Senate races, however, the mix of well-funded and poorly funded challengers is different. Senate challengers are more likely to be able to raise significant amounts of money than their House counterparts. Indeed, in recent elections a number of challengers (and open-seat candidates) have been wealthy individuals who could provide a large share of their funding from their own resources. The most extreme example comes from 2000, when Jon Corzine, the Democratic candidate for the open New Jersey Senate seat, spent more than $60 million of his own money to defeat his opponent by 50 percent to 47 percent. Corzine spent a total of $63 million; the Republican spent $6.4 million.[62]

Senate challengers are also more likely to possess significant elected office experience. Thus in Senate contests incumbents often face well-funded and experienced challengers, and the stage is then set for their defeat if other circumstances work against them. Consider the comment by David Johnson, director of the Democratic Senatorial Campaign Committee, to Rep. Richard C. Shelby of Alabama, who was challenging Republican senator Jeremiah Denton in 1986. Shelby, who eventually won, was concerned that he did not have enough campaign funds because Denton was outspending him two to one. Johnson responded: "You don't have as much money, but you're going to have enough— and enough is all it takes to win."[63]

THE 2008 ELECTIONS: THE IMPACT ON CONGRESS

The election of 1994 produced huge consequences for politics and governing, and each subsequent election over the next decade was seen in relation to that event: would GOP control be maintained or lost, strengthened or weakened? The GOP retained control in five elections, but then its luck ran out in 2006. A significant electoral tide gave the Democrats control of both chambers, and that result became the benchmark for speculation about the future. As we noted earlier, by historical standards the substantial shift to the Democrats in these elections was impressive. In the 2008 congressional elections, the immediate consequences were not as great as those of 2006, with their restoration of Democratic majority control in both chambers, but the numerical gains had important implications. (Perhaps most consequential was the reestablishment, with Obama's victory, of unified Democratic control of government.) The House "class of 2008" had fifty-five new members, 12.6 percent of the body. When the new members were added to the fifty-eight surviving representatives who had begun their service during the 110th Congress, the result was a chamber in which over one-fourth of its members had fewer than four years of seniority. In the Senate, ten members were new (10 percent). And twelve senators in the 111th Congress had begun their service in the 110th, so that 22 percent of that chamber had under four years of service.

The significant Democratic gains turned a narrow majority into a more comfortable one, particularly in the Senate. This development strengthened the hand of the majority party leaderships in the Senate and the House, but, as we discuss shortly, moderate members were still important because of the long-term decline of such members in Congress and the increase in the number of conservative Republicans and liberal Democrats. Twenty-five or thirty years ago, the ideological "overlap" between the parties was considerable. The Democrats had a substantial conservative contingent, mostly from the South, that was as conservative as the right wing of the Republican Party. Similarly, the GOP had a contingent (primarily northeasterners) who were as liberal as northern Democrats. In addition, each party had moderate members. During the intervening years, however, because of changes in the electorate and in Congress, this overlap between the parties began to disappear.[64] By the mid-1980s, each party in both houses of Congress had become more politically homogeneous, and that homogeneity continued to increase in subsequent elections. In each chamber, there was little departure from a complete ideological separation of the two parties.[65] Thus in the 111th Congress that emerged from the 2008 elections, substantial majorities of each party had policy preferences that were sharply different from those of the other party, with a small but influential group of members in the middle.

The House: Reinforcing Majority Party Control

In 1995 the new Republican majorities instituted major institutional changes, especially in the House.[66] By comparison, the changes in House organization for the 111th Congress were modest, although still consequential. Most were adjustments to rules the Democrats had adopted when they took over the House two years earlier. One change tweaked the "pay-as-you-go" budget rule. This rule requires increases in mandatory spending or tax cuts to be offset with spending cuts or tax increases elsewhere. The change permitted the House to designate legislation as "emergency" and thereby exempt it from the budget restrictions. Possible reasons for the designation included national security matters or a response to "a period of sustained low economic growth." In view of the economic crisis, this clause would offer the Democrats much more flexibility. Another change restricted the Republicans' ability to employ a legislative device called the "motion to recommit." This motion could be offered by the minority at the end of its consideration on the floor to try to alter or kill a bill. The change constrained the option to kill the bill, but retained the GOP's ability to use it to seek changes.

One interesting rules change was the abolition of the six-year term limits for Democratic committee chairs. The Republicans had adopted this rule when they took control in 1995. Before then, there was no limit on how long one could be a chair. To the surprise of many, the Democratic leadership retained the rule when the majority shifted back to the Democrats in 2007. Some observers thought that this choice was an effort to induce the Democratic chairs to be responsive to their leaders, and Speaker Pelosi did promise that the decision would be reconsidered at a later date. During the 110th Congress, Pelosi exerted a lot of influence over committees' actions and chairs' decisions, and it appears that she was satisfied that she could retain that influence without the term limits device.

The early evidence on the impact of this change does not indicate any significant change from the preceding Congress. Chairs in the 111th Congress appear to be usually, but not always, responsive to the Speaker's lead. One possible reason for both the term limits change and its apparent modest impact is that the Democrats had had a means of controlling chairs when they were last in the majority, and they reinstated it when they retook control. Rather than automatically remove all chairs at an arbitrary point, their rules permitted the removal by the membership of any chair at the beginning of any Congress. The operation of that rule was dramatically apparent in action at the outset of the 111th Congress. During the previous two years, the chair of the Energy and Commerce Committee had been John Dingell of Michigan. The longest-serving member of the House (he was first elected in 1955), Dingell had clashed over energy legislation and other bills with Pelosi.[67] After the 2008 election, Henry Waxman, the second-ranking member on Energy and Commerce, announced he was challenging Dingell for the chairmanship of the committee. He claimed that his record showed he had the experience and expertise to build consensus and produce legislation, but a subtext of the effort was the recognition that major aspects of Obama's agenda would go through the Energy and Commerce Committee and Waxman was more representative than Dingell of the views of the caucus (and Obama).[68]

Under the Democrats' rules, the choice in such a challenge first rested with the party's Steering and Policy Committee, a mix of party leaders, their appointees, and members elected to represent rank-and-file Democrats. If Waxman received at least fourteen of the committee's forty-seven votes, the final resolution would go to the full party caucus.[69] As it turned out, Waxman received twenty-five votes to Dingell's twenty-two, and the caucus confirmed his victory, 137–122. Waxman had long been an ally of Pelosi, and most observers believed she had favored him. In any event, after Waxman took the helm of Energy and Commerce, Pelosi was comfortable in delegating to him (and Ed Markey of Massachusetts, the third-ranking Democrat on the committee and another party loyalist) the task of writing the details of the climate change bill.[70] The relatively large amount of shared preferences within the majority party has made it easier and safer for the leadership to entrust the task of creating the details of legislation to the committee and subcommittee chairs.

The majority leadership's efforts to strengthen their party's hold on the levers of power and the restoration of unified Democratic control of the government have reinforced the partisan divisions in the chamber. The Democrats want to press their agenda, and House GOP members have largely decided that their best strategy is to resist. This is particularly true now that the increased Democratic majority has enough votes that it is usually not compelled to take Republican wishes into account.

And yet the majority's electoral gains have led to a somewhat more diverse caucus, and the extensive legislative ambitions of the Democrats make holding that majority together more challenging for Pelosi and the rest of the leadership. The Speaker has gone to great lengths to communicate with the various segments of the caucus. For example, Pelosi has regular weekly breakfasts with freshmen members, and she has sought to consult with and accommodate the fiscally conservative "Blue Dog" Democrats while not alienating liberal members.[71] This balancing act has produced tensions at times, but Pelosi avoided any major legislative defeats in the first six months of the 111th Congress.

Part of the reason Pelosi has pursued this strategy is her recognition that to maintain the Democratic majority her individual members must survive electorally. The majority was expanded in 2008 by means of the election of more Democrats from Republican-leaning areas. Forty-nine House Democrats won in districts that were carried by John McCain in the presidential race. Many of these members feel competing pressures from their party and their electorate.[72] And yet Democrats overall have exhibited high degrees of party voting on the floor, and their increased margin of control gives the leadership the luxury of permitting some cross-pressured members to stray from the party line on some votes without endangering the party's ability to win roll calls.

The Senate: How Effective Is Majority Control?

In the wake of the Senate elections, observers wondered whether the shift in margin would bring major changes in the operation of the body and its legislative product. In the weeks leading up to the November voting, there was much discussion about the possibility of the Democrats holding sixty seats— the number of votes the Senate's rules require to cut off extended floor debate that is intended to block a bill from final passage. This blocking strategy, called a filibuster, was used frequently in the 110th Congress and in earlier ones to frustrate the legislative program of the majority party.[73] As it happened, the Democrats fell short of the sixty-vote threshold in the elections, but the relevance of that margin and its implications was a recurring theme in the early months of the 111th Congress.

Like the House, the Senate faced some organizational issues related to committee leadership. One involved the Appropriations Committee. Sen. Robert Byrd of West Virginia had been chair in the previous Congress. But because he was ninety and experiencing health problems, some of his party colleagues sought to encourage him to step down in order to ensure that the heavy burdens of the committee would be handled effectively. Byrd balked initially, but then agreed to give up the chairmanship. The committee's leadership passed to Daniel Inouye of Hawaii, who was eighty-four but in better health than Byrd. The other committee issue involved Joseph Lieberman of Connecticut. Lieberman had been reelected to the Senate in 2006 as an independent after losing the Democratic primary that year to an opponent of the Iraq War. Despite his independent status, Lieberman wanted to remain in the Democratic caucus and retain his seniority. After some debate, the Democrats permitted him to retain his seniority on the Homeland Security and Governmental Affairs committee and to become its chair in 2007. However, because Lieberman had endorsed McCain in the presidential race and campaigned widely for him, many liberals wanted to deprive him of his chairmanship. In the end, a majority of Democratic senators (with the encouragement of President Obama) decided that such action could become a distraction from the party's legislative agenda, so they permitted Lieberman to remain as chair but took away one of this other committee assignments as a penalty for his actions in 2008. Sen. Ben Nelson of Nebraska said the decision was "less about retribution and more about reconciliation and atonement."[74]

Because of its rules, which vest more power in minorities and individuals, the Senate is less partisan and less party-dominated than the House.[75] However, over the last few decades polarization and party conflict have increased in the Senate as well. The election campaign ended with tense relations between the two top leaders, Majority Leader Harry Reid of Nevada and Minority Leader Mitch McConnell of Kentucky, in part because the Democrats, with Reid's support, had waged a vigorous campaign to try to defeat McConnell's reelection effort.[76] Reid made it clear at the outset that while he looked forward to working with the new president, he believed that under the Republicans Congress had ceded too much power to the White House. He said, "I don't work for Barack Obama. I work with him."[77]

In a move to counter Republicans' complaints that he had used his powers in the previous Congress to limit their ability to offer amendments on the Senate floor, Reid agreed early in the 111th Congress to open up the floor to greater participation.[78] However, the Democrats' numerical margin prevented Republicans from having much success when they did propose changes in the majority's proposals. As a result, the Democrats had substantial success in moving their agenda. After the first one hundred days of the new Congress, Reid said, "I've been here 25 years, and there's no question these first three months are the most productive by far I've ever been involved in."[79]

The spring of 2009 brought more bad news to Senate Republicans. On April 28, Republican senator Arlen Specter of Pennsylvania announced he was switching to the Democratic Party. Specter had long been one of the moderates in his party, and as the GOP became more conservative over the years, he came under greater pressure to conform. In 2004, when he sought his fifth term, Specter was nearly unseated in the Republican primary by a much more conservative House member, surviving by a 51 percent to 49 percent margin. In 2009 that conservative challenger, Pat Toomey, announced he would again run against Specter in the primary. However, Specter's political situation was now worse because many former moderate Republicans had become dissatisfied and changed their party registration.[80] Thus they would be unable to participate in the primary to support Specter. State polls showed the senator trailing Toomey by a substantial margin.

In announcing his switch, Specter listed a number of issues on which he had disagreed with the GOP, including embryonic stem cell research, Pell education grants, and funding for the National Institutes of Health. He particularly noted that he was one of only three Republicans to vote for the economic stimulus plan adopted in February. However, he also candidly admitted that personal political considerations dominated his decision, characterizing the poll data on his Pennsylvania race as "bleak."[81] He went on to say, "I am not prepared to have my 29-year record in the United States Senate decided by the Pennsylvania Republican primary electorate."[82]

Two potential effects of Specter's decision were its impact on the Senate's operation and its implications for the Republican Party. His switch, followed by the confirmation of Al Franken's Minnesota victory by the Minnesota Supreme Court, gave the Democrats sixty seats. The death of Massachusetts senator Edward Kennedy on August 25 again reduced the Democrats to fifty-nine votes, and because at the time Massachusetts's law did not permit the governor to fill the empty seat, the Democratic "filibuster-proof" majority disappeared, at least temporarily. But even before Kennedy's death, the media's trumpeting of the party's achievement of a "filibuster-proof" majority was misguided. The Democrats' ability to use their sixty votes to block a filibuster is contingent: it will work only if all Democrats vote together, and it is relevant only if no Republicans side with the Democrats. Certainly, Democratic solidarity will be important in legislative maneuvering, but it is not likely that there will be many situations in which these two conditions are met simultaneously. For example, on the stimulus vote that Specter cited, all fifty-five voting Democrats voted for it, as did three Republicans.[83] Both parties will often experience a few defectors, and it is unlikely that Specter's individual decisions will be affected much. Indeed, the day after announcing his decision Specter, in his last Senate vote as a Republican, voted against the Democratic budget resolution (along with all Republicans and three Democrats).

Probably more important in the long run is the fact that Specter *needed* to switch parties to survive. This is a reflection of the greater intraparty homogeneity and interparty polarization we have discussed. Increasingly, primary electorates, particularly in the GOP, have turned against moderate senators and representatives. For example, in 2008 House contests two Maryland members—one from each party—were defeated on the same day in primaries by challengers who were more ideologically typical of their parties.[84] Many Republicans, not all of them moderates, have publicly worried about their party's ability to compete effectively with the Democrats if moderate candidates are not tolerated. Rep. Fred Upton of Maryland pointed out that "to regain the majority you have to reach out to a lot of different groups."[85] And Sen. Olympia Snowe of Maine contended that "political diversity makes a party stronger, and ultimately we are heading to having the smallest tent in history."[86]

The Obama Administration and Unified Democratic Government

Obama's election restored unified Democratic government for the first time since 1994. Political scientists have debated whether unified party control results in more or different significant legislation compared with divided government.[87] Regardless of past patterns, however, Obama had campaigned on a theme of change from the governance of the Bush presidency, and he and congressional Democrats had argued for many new policies and programs. Obama also had promised to move away from the patterns of partisan conflict that had predominated in Washington in recent years. In his administration's early days, the new president appeared to pursue this course. For example, during the postelection transition he sought advice from prominent congressional Republicans on policy and appointments.[88] During the week after his inauguration, Obama also sought GOP support for and consultation on the economic stimulus package. This effort included a bipartisan meeting at the White House and an unusual presidential visit to Capitol Hill to meet with Republican members of Congress.[89]

A problem with such an effort at bipartisanship, however, is that Democrats and Republicans have both conflicting electoral interests and real policy differences. The latter is especially true because the vast majority of the GOP members who survived the 2008 elections were from the more conservative wing of the party. Thus what Republicans want from bipartisanship is for the Democrats to make concessions on policy, and usually their demands are more than the Democrats are willing to concede.

The Republicans' disagreements with the administration surfaced even before Obama was sworn in, when on January 15 the Senate had to vote on the release of the second half of the $700 billion that had been appropriated by the 110th Congress to bail out financially troubled banks. Obama supported the release, but Republican senators, led by Mitch McConnell, opposed it 32–6. After the president took office, there was conflict along partisan lines on every major administration initiative. For example, during Obama's first month in office three major bills were cleared by Congress for his signature: the economic stimulus bill, a proposal to expand the time period during which workers could bring lawsuits for employment discrimination, and a bill to more than double the amount of money allocated to the State Children's Health Insurance Program (SCHIP). In the Senate votes on initial passage of these three bills, the *total* vote by Republicans was 105 nays and 17 yeas, whereas Democrats were unanimously in favor. In the House, the corresponding totals were 50–474 for Republicans and 739–16 for Democrats. Republicans were unwilling to support the policies the Democrats favored, and members of the majority saw no reason to settle for less. These patterns of conflict then continued. The most significant partisan divisions have been over health care reform, an area in which Obama may receive no Republican support for his proposed changes.

The high levels of support exhibited by Democrats in the early votes just noted do not imply that Obama was able to get his way on all legislative details, nor that he did not experience intraparty conflict. Some liberal Democrats were unhappy with concessions that the administration had to make to secure adoption of initiatives in the Senate, such as the reductions in the stimulus bill. They also were sometimes disappointed that the changes from Bush policies were not greater. For example, fifty-one House Democrats voted against a bill to provide $96 billion in funding for the wars in Iraq and Afghanistan. Liberal Democrat Maxine Waters of California complained on the floor that "this bill simply amplifies and extends failed policies."[90]

More often, however, because of the administration's ambitious agenda, Obama's problems were with the more moderate Democrats. Many of them resisted going as far as Obama wanted to, some out of political concerns and others because of real policy disagreements. For example, when Obama sent his budget proposals to Congress, there was some resistance to specifics and much concern about the overall totals. In his plan for his chamber's budget resolution, Senate Budget Committee chair Kent Conrad, a Democrat from North Dakota, proposed only half as large an increase in discretionary spending as the administration wanted.[91] During the drafting and consideration of the two chambers' budget resolutions, Democratic Party leaders had to exert great efforts to rally their troops, and the president came to the Capitol personally to rally support among House Democrats.[92] In the end, Democrats were able to come together, producing a budget that was between the president's original high figure and the Senate's low proposal. (Even the initial proposals were only $54 billion apart on discretionary spending out of a total administration proposal of $1.133 trillion.[93])

In some cases, the conflicts between Congress and the president were less about party or ideology and more about Congress being unwilling to give the executive a free hand. This situation arose when the president requested funds to close the detention facility at Guantanamo Bay, Cuba. Because the proposal was not accompanied by a detailed plan specifying how it would be implemented and where detainees would be sent, when the relevant appropriations bill was adopted, no funds were allocated for the closure, and the bill contained a prohibition on the release of detainees in the United States.[94] And then like all presidents, sometimes in order to achieve things he wanted, Obama had to accept things he did not want. In one example, when Congress passed a bill imposing new regulations on the credit card industry in May 2009 (an administration priority), it included a provision permitting people to carry licensed loaded firearms in national parks. Obama did not want the provision, but decided not to fight it to avoid holding up the bill.[95]

Despite all of the conflicts and legislative interplay, the Obama administration and the Democratic Congress have compiled a substantial set of achievements from their point of view. *CQ Weekly*, a prominent objective chronicle of the legislative process and the executive branch, keeps a running tally of major legislation under the heading "Bills to Watch." By the end of June 2009, the Congress had completed action on twelve of these bills.[96] In addition to the budget, SCHIP, stimulus, employment discrimination, and omnibus and supplemental appropriations bills just mentioned, the list included credit card regulation, tobacco regulation, and vehicle trade-in incentives. In addition, the House adopted a major climate change bill and an authorization for State Department programs. All of these pieces of legislation, except the war supplemental, were opposed by a majority of Republicans. The Obama administration advocated a substantial legislative agenda, and congressional Democrats held together sufficiently to pass a major portion of it. In this polarized partisan era, then, it appeared that unified government was capable of achieving more than divided government. However, as Obama turned his focus to health care reform he found increasing resistance from the Republicans, with reservations among moderate "Blue Dog" Democrats. Throughout the summer of 2009, opposition to reform was voiced at "tea parties" and town hall meetings. The level of partisan acrimony was perhaps best illustrated by events surrounding Obama's major address to a joint session of Congress in early September. When Obama told members of Congress that people in the United States illegally would not benefit from the proposed reform, Republican backbencher Joe Wilson of South Carolina shouted, "You lie." The next week, in a largely party-line vote, the House formally rebuked Wilson.[97]

THE 2010 ELECTIONS AND BEYOND

Expectations about midterm elections are usually shaped by a strong historical pattern: the party of the president has lost strength in the House in twenty-three of the twenty-seven midterm elections since the beginning of the twentieth century. The first column in Table 9-9 shows the magnitude of these losses in midterms since World War II; they average 23.6 seats for the president's party. There has, however, been considerable variation in the outcomes, from the fifty-five-seat loss by the Democrats in 1946 to the six-seat Republican gain in 2002. Another consideration related to the president, however, clarifies the

TABLE 9-9   House Seat Losses by the President's Party in Midterm Elections, 1946–2006

All elections			First term of administration			Later term of administration		
1946	55	Democrats	1954	18	Republicans	1946	55	Democrats
1950	29	Democrats	1962	4	Democrats	1950	29	Democrats
1954	18	Republicans	1970	12	Republicans	1958	47	Republicans
1958	47	Republicans	1978	11	Democrats	1966	47	Democrats
1962	4	Democrats	1982	26	Republicans	1974	43	Republicans
1966	47	Democrats	1990	9	Republicans	1986	5	Republicans
1970	12	Republicans	1994	52	Democrats	1998	(+5)	Democrats
1974	43	Republicans	2002	(+6)	Republicans	2006	30	Republicans
1978	11	Democrats						
1982	26	Republicans		Average: 15.8			Average: 31.4	
1986	5	Republicans						
1990	9	Republicans						
1994	52	Democrats						
1998	(+5)	Democrats						
2002	(+6)	Republicans						
2006	30	Republicans						
	Average: 23.6							

Source: Compiled by the authors.

context for analysis. During the first midterm election of an administration, the president may be able to make a plausible appeal that the administration has not had enough time to bring about substantial change or to solidify many achievements. Moreover, even if things are not going very well, voters may not be inclined to blame a president who has served for such a short time. But four years later (if the president is fortunate enough to face a second midterm), appeals of too little time are unlikely to be persuasive. After six years, if the economy or foreign policy is not going well, voters may seek a policy change by reducing the number of the president's partisans in Congress.

The second and third columns of Table 9-9 indicate that this is what has usually happened in the past. Losses by the president's party in the first midterm election of a presidency have tended to be much smaller than losses in subsequent midterms.[98] Indeed, with the exception of the results in 1986, 1994, 1998, and 2002, the two categories yield two sets of outcomes that differ sharply. In the midterm elections during the first term except those in 1994 and 2002, the president's party lost between four and twenty-six seats, with an average loss of thirteen. In the elections after the first term (excluding 1986 and 1998), the range of losses was between twenty-nine and fifty-five seats, with an average loss of forty-two. (We discuss the atypical years later.)

Models of House Elections

In the 1970s and 1980s, several scholars constructed and tested models of congressional election outcomes, focusing especially on midterms. They were seeking to isolate the factors that most strongly influenced the results. The earliest models, constructed by Tufte and by Jacobson and Samuel Kernell, focused on two variables: presidential approval and a measure of the state of the economy.[99] Tufte hypothesized a direct influence by these forces on voter choice and election outcomes. The theory was that an unpopular president or a poor economy would cause the president's party to lose votes and therefore seats in the House. In essence, the midterm elections were viewed as a referendum on the performance of the president and his party. Jacobson and Kernell, by contrast, saw more indirect effects of presidential approval and the economy. They argued that these forces affected election results by influencing the decisions of potential congressional candidates. If the president is unpopular and the economy is in bad shape, potential candidates will expect the president's party to perform poorly. As a consequence, strong potential candidates of the president's party will be more inclined to forgo running until a better year, and strong candidates from the opposition party will be more inclined to run because they foresee good prospects for success. According to Jacobson and Kernell, this mix of weak candidates from the president's party and strong opposition candidates lead to a poor election performance by the party occupying the White House. To measure this predicted relationship, their model related the partisan division of the vote to presidential approval and the economic situation early in the election year. It is at this point, they argued, that decisions to run for office are being made, not at the time of the election, and so it is not appropriate to focus on approval and the economy at election time. This view is now called the "strategic politicians hypothesis."[100]

Subsequent research built on this base. One model, developed by Alan I. Abramowitz, Albert D. Cover, and Helmut Norpoth, considered a new variable: short-term party evaluations.[101] They argued that voters' attitudes about the economic competence of the political parties affect the impact of presidential approval and economic conditions on voting decisions. If the electorate judges that the party holding the presidency is better able to deal with the problems voters regard as most serious, the negative impact of an unpopular president or a weak economy will be reduced. The authors concluded from their analysis of both aggregate votes and responses to surveys in midterm elections that there is evidence for their "party competence" hypothesis.

All of these models used the division of the popular vote as the variable to be predicted, and they focused only on midterm elections. Later work merged midterm results with those of presidential years, contending that there should be no conceptual distinction between them. These efforts sought to predict changes in seats without reference to the division of the vote. For example, a study by Bruce I. Oppenheimer, James A. Stimson, and Richard W. Waterman argued that the missing piece in the congressional election puzzle is the degree of "exposure," or "the excess or deficit number of seats a party holds measured against its long-term norm."[102] If a party wins more House seats than normal, those extra seats will be vulnerable in the next election, and the party is likely to suffer losses. Thus the party that wins a presidential election does not automatically benefit in House elections. But if the president's party does well in the House races, it will be more vulnerable in the subsequent midterm elections. Indeed, the May 1986 article by Oppenheimer and his colleagues predicted only small Republican losses for 1986 because Reagan's large 1984 victory was not accompanied by substantial congressional gains for his party. The actual result in 1986 was consistent with this prediction, for the GOP lost only five seats.

Another model of House elections was constructed by Robin F. Marra and Charles W. Ostrom Jr.[103] They developed a "comprehensive referendum voting model" of both presidential year and midterm elections, and included factors such as foreign policy crises, scandals, unresolved policy disputes, party identification, and changes in the level of presidential approval. The model also incorporated measures reflecting hypothesized relationships in the models we discussed earlier: level of presidential approval, state of the economy, the strategic politicians hypothesis, exposure, and party competence. The model was tested on data from all congressional elections from 1950 to 1986.

The Marra-Ostrom analysis revealed significant support for most of the predicted relationships. The results indicated that the most powerful influences affecting congressional seat changes were presidential approval (directly and through various events) and exposure. The model was striking in its statistical accuracy: the average error in the predicted change was only four seats. The average error varied little whether presidential or midterm years were predicted, and the analysis demonstrated that the usually greater losses for the president's party in second midterm years resulted from negative shifts in presidential approval, exposure, and scandals. However, when the empirical analysis was extended by Ostrom and Brian Newman to include the election years 1988–1998, the accuracy of the model declined.[104] They produced a revised model that included some additional variables. In particular, they found that the relative number of open seats held by the two parties was important in determining losses. Moreover, once that variable was taken into account, the importance of the exposure variable decreased—that is, the most important form of exposure was open seats; incumbents were less vulnerable.

Drawing on the insights of these various models, we can now look at how these factors may influence outcomes in the 2010 House elections. How well the economy is doing and what proportion of the voters approves of Obama's performance early in the year may encourage or discourage high-quality potential challengers. And the same variables close to election time may lead voters to support or oppose Republican candidates based on their judgments of the job the Obama administration is doing. The usual midterm losses happen for reasons; they are not part of the laws of nature. Therefore, if the usual reasons for such losses, such as a recession or an unpopular president, are not present in 2010, we should not expect the losses to occur.[105] But if those reasons are present, the context will be quite different.

In the summer of 2009, Obama's approval was strong. The average of nine polls in June of that year yielded a mean approval rating of 61.4 percent, with the lowest of the nine results at 56 percent.[106] Moreover, there were signs that the dismal economic situation of 2008 was at least stabilizing, if not improving. Although Obama's approval ratings then began to slip somewhat, seven polls conducted through mid-September showed his mean approval rating at 54.4.[107] If Obama's popularity is relatively high in the fall of 2010 and the economy improves, Democrats could be somewhat insulated from suffering losses. In addition, the models indicate that other considerations are also important. Democratic exposure is high because of the large gains of 2006 and 2008. However, at this point it appears that few Democratic members of the House are planning to retire, which should limit the number of vulnerable Democratic seats.

As for recruiting, Republicans are unlikely to fear a third straight national tide against them. With so many Democrats holding seats that previously belonged to Republicans, and especially in view of the forty-nine Democratic districts in which McCain won the most votes, the GOP should find it now easier to recruit strong and experienced candidates than in the two previous cycles. Moreover, the analysis of short-term party evaluations reminds us that highly salient issues may offset the negative effects of poor economic conditions. Finally, the impact of events such as crises and scandals in the Marra-Ostrom model reminds us that unforeseeable events could influence the 2010 congressional election results.

Preparing for Redistricting

Many noncongressional contests in 2010 will have important implications for future House elections, because in most states the people chosen in the gubernatorial and state legislative races will control the redistricting process after the 2010 census. After the 2008 voting, the Democrats controlled twenty-nine governorships, but two of the fifty were up for grabs in November 2009, and thirty-six more will be contested in 2010. Similarly, at this time the Democrats control both chambers in twenty-seven state legislatures, and the Republicans control fourteen state legislatures. Eight states have split control, and the legislature in one (Nebraska) is both unicameral and officially nonpartisan.[108]

Early indications are that contests for governor in about half of the thirty-eight states with races in 2009 or 2010 will be competitive.[109] Of special importance are large states with many House seats, because in those situations it is easier to draw district lines to partisan advantage compared with states with few districts. Currently, thirteen states have ten or more House seats (although this list is likely to change based on the new census). In eleven of them, the governor and the legislature control redistricting, and in all but a few either the governorship or control of the legislature appears to be in doubt in the next set of elections.[110] Thus we expect that both parties will exert great effort and spend a lot of money to influence the results in these states.

Some Additional Considerations about House Races

A few further points related to the previous discussion must be made to complete our analysis of the prospects for the 2010 House races. The vulnerability of individual members varies between parties and across other attributes, and we do not expect those distributions to be similar from election to election. For example, in one year a party may have a relatively high percentage of freshmen or of members who won by narrow margins in the preceding election, whereas in another year the party's proportion of such potentially vulnerable members may be low. As Table 9-10 shows, both parties have a surprisingly similar (and relatively small) number of House members who won with less than 55 percent of the vote. Twenty-six Republicans and twenty-four Democrats fall into this category, which is fewer close races than in the 2000 election, and substantially fewer than the ninety-five in the 1996 election. It is in this type of district in which strong challengers are most likely to come forward and in which the challengers who do run are most able to raise adequate campaign funds. Thus based solely on these election margin figures, the political landscape does not present a very attractive prospect for challengers of either party. However, the Democrats' margins are from a year that was very

TABLE 9-10   Percentage of Vote Received by Winning House Candidates, by Party and Type of Race, 2008

Percentage of vote	Republican			Democratic		
	Reelected incumbent	Successful challenger	Open seat	Reelected incumbent	Successful challenger	Open seat
55 or less	16	4	6	7	11	6
55.1–60.0	32	0	6	20	3	7
60.1–70.0	76	1	4	68	0	5
70.1–100	32	0	1	129	0	1
Total	156	5	17	224	14	19

Source: Compiled by the authors.

Note: Table shows number of districts meeting the criteria for each cell. Open seats include races in which an incumbent lost in a primary.

good for them, and so they are at least somewhat inflated. There may, then, be more good GOP opportunities than the numbers would suggest. Similarly, the close Republican districts are from a very poor year. Probably fewer of them are vulnerable than would be true if 2008 were a more neutral year.

As our earlier analysis indicates, the parties' respective success in recruiting strong candidates for open seats and for opposing the other party's incumbents can be expected to play a significant role in shaping the outcomes for 2010. Both the Democratic and Republican campaign organizations were actively pursuing recruits during 2009, with some significant successes for both parties. However, the personal and financial costs of candidacies and the difficulty in defeating an incumbent often make recruitment difficult. Moreover, even successful recruitment efforts bring no guarantee of success. For example, in a New York special House election in April 2009 to replace Democrat Kirsten Gillibrand, who had been appointed to succeed Hillary Clinton in the Senate, the GOP candidate was a member of the state legislature from the area, and the district had a historically Republican tilt. The Democrat was a young businessman with no experience in public office. And yet the Democrat won.[111]

Worth noting here is the continuing impact of term limits in the states. Although the term limits movement failed to impose restrictions on members of Congress, it did succeed in imposing them on state legislators in fifteen states, and those limits have been taking effect. One potential outlet for a state legislator who cannot run for reelection is to seek a seat in Congress. This situation may lead to a greater number of strong challengers in House races than would otherwise be the case. For example, Ohio limits members to eight years in each chamber of the state legislature, and so some legislators will have to leave their current positions next year. Some of them are contemplating races for a U.S. House seat.[112]

As we have discussed, the potential number of open seats is also relevant to questions of candidate recruitment and district vulnerability. Our analysis shows that open seats are more likely to switch parties than those with incumbents, and that both parties are more likely to field strong candidates. As of the fall of 2009, few members of the House had confirmed their retirement. However, there were concerns that some representatives would leave the House to seek Senate seats or governorships, and by May 2009 thirteen members (four Democrats and nine Republicans) had committed to races.[113]

Finally, it should be remembered that the rules that shape elections are subject to change, and that such changes can have a substantial impact on the pattern of election outcomes. One source of such change is the courts. In 2009 the U.S. Supreme Court passed down two significant decisions related to the Voting Rights Act. In the first case, *Bartlett v. Strickland,* the Court decided by a 5–4 vote that the act did not require governments to create districts favorable to minority candidates in areas in which those minorities did not make up a majority of the population.[114] This ruling will surely have major consequences for the next round of congressional redistricting.

In the other case, *Northwest Utilities v. Holder,* the Court refused to strike down a provision of the Voting Rights Act that requires many state and local governments, mainly in the South, to seek permission from the U.S. Justice Department or a federal court before they can make changes to certain voting procedures. The provision, which had been reauthorized by Congress in 2006, had been challenged on the grounds that such restrictions on the rights of states were no longer required. However, the Court disposed of the case on a narrow technical issue.[115] Important cases are also still pending. For example, in the fall of 2009 the Court heard arguments on a challenge to the federal law that prohibits corporations from spending to favor or oppose political candidates.[116]

Senate Races in 2010

Because Senate terms are six years and staggered, the number of seats defended by each party varies from election to election. Even though the Democrats held sixty seats in the Senate in late September 2009, the same number of Republican and Democratic seats will be at risk in November 2010—eighteen for each party. The number of potentially vulnerable seats appears to be slightly greater for the GOP. The July 2009 ratings of *The Cook Political Report* show four Democratic seats as highly competitive, with two leaning toward the current party and two toss-ups. For the Republicans, six seats are equally competitive, with two leaning toward the GOP and four toss-ups. Thus the probability of a significant pro-Republican shift in the Senate appears to be low.

Still, the numerical balance in the Senate will have implications for the fate of the parties' legislative agendas, and so many seats will be hotly contested and each party is investing great efforts in recruiting candidates. As we write, seven seats will definitely be open because of the retirement of Republicans Christopher Bond of Missouri, Judd Gregg of New Hampshire, George Voinovich of Ohio, Mel Martinez of Florida, and Sam Brownback of Kansas, as well as Democrats Ted Kaufman of Delaware and Roland Burris of Illinois. Kaufman was appointed as a temporary replacement for Vice President Joe Biden, and Burris was appointed to succeed Obama. Obama's term would have expired in 2010. In addition, two Democratic seats are occupied by unelected incumbents who were appointed to fill vacancies: Gillibrand of New York and Michael Bennett of Colorado. It seems likely that the substantial number of Republican retirements stems in large part from these senators' recognition that their party will continue in minority status for some time.

Each party has had some significant recruitment success. The Democrats were able to recruit Missouri secretary of state Robin Carnahan to compete for the state's open Senate seat. One of the top candidates for the Republicans is Gov. Charlie Crist of Florida. However, the Crist candidacy demonstrates again the ideological divisions within the GOP and the policy motivations of party activists. Crist is very popular in his state and a moderate. He infuriated the party's conservative wing by publicly endorsing Obama's stimulus package. This and other issue positions led former Florida House Speaker Marco Rubio, an outspoken conservative, to oppose Crist in the Senate primary.[117] The Democrats have similar problems. Appointed senator Gillibrand of New York also had a moderate record, including opposition to certain gun control measures. Some prominent liberal Democrats considered running against Gillibrand in the primary, but they were dissuaded from doing so by Obama and the state's senior Democratic senator, Charles Schumer.[118] Democratic leaders were less successful in Pennsylvania, where Democratic representative Joe Sestak announced that he would contest Arlen Specter's attempt to secure the party's Senate nomination.

To summarize, then, House results are likely to depend heavily on the political context in late 2009 (when many candidate decisions will be made) and in November 2010. The context will probably determine whether the historical pattern of losses by the president's party occurs again or is broken as it was in the 1998 and 2002 midterms. As for Senate seats, the results probably depend more on the circumstances in individual races, largely fought independently of one another.

Beyond 2010: Solidifying the Democratic Majority or Renewed Uncertainty?

Just as every election has implications for those that follow, the elections of 2010 will have an impact on subsequent contests. Because we do not know the results, we cannot yet describe the effects, but a few general factors are likely to have an impact on future congressional contests.

The national demographic changes we touched on in Chapter 2 and that we discuss in Chapter 11 (see Table 11-2) will continue to be important. Although these shifts have slowed somewhat because of reduced immigration during the economic slump, the proportion of the population made up of Latinos and other minorities will continue to grow. The Democrats are currently advantaged among these groups, and they will pursue strategies that seek to retain that advantage and improve the activation of those constituencies. Meanwhile, the Republicans will look for ways to improve their standing among minorities, particularly Latinos. Indeed, they will have to succeed to a degree if they are to remain competitive as the distribution of the population changes. (We return to this subject in Chapter 11.)

As our earlier discussion indicated, one of the most important post-2010 issues will be reapportionment and then redistricting. The former term refers to the redistribution of House seats (and therefore electoral votes) among the states to reflect population changes. Nothing can be said with certainty about the seat changes associated with reapportionment until the census is completed, but projections indicate a continuation of the trend in recent decades of decreasing representation in the East and Midwest and an increasing number of seats in the West and South. The biggest gain will likely go to Texas, with four additional seats, and Arizona, with plus two. Six other states are slated to gain one each. The probable losses are more widely dispersed, with only Ohio (at minus two) projected to lose more than one seat.

Some observers argue that because the states that will be gaining seats are mostly "red" states, this trend will automatically benefit the Republicans. We disagree. The situation is potentially more complex than that. After all, California experienced its most explosive population growth when it was a dependable GOP bastion in presidential voting.[119] Moreover, a large share of the population increase in Texas is concentrated in areas with large numbers of Mexican Americans. That certainly does not guarantee GOP gains.

Finally, as was indicated earlier, some states have decided to delegate the task of redistricting to independent commissions rather than their state legislatures. The big change in 2008 was the addition of California to this group because of the adoption of a state constitutional amendment in a referendum. We will not know the exact consequences of this new system until we see it in action, but it is likely that the resulting district lines will be different from those that the legislators would have chosen in striving for personal protection. In any event, the next cycle of redistricting could affect significantly the fortunes of the two parties in House elections and their respective chances of majority control.

Chapter 10

The Congressional Electorate in 2008

In the preceding chapter, we viewed congressional elections at the district and state levels and saw how they formed a national result. In this chapter, we consider congressional elections from the point of view of the individual voter, using the same American National Election Studies surveys we employed to study presidential voting. We discuss how social forces, issues, partisan loyalties, incumbency, and evaluations of congressional and presidential performance influence the decisions of voters in congressional elections. We also try to determine the existence and extent of presidential coattails.

SOCIAL FORCES AND THE CONGRESSIONAL VOTE

In general, social forces relate to the congressional vote in the same way they relate to the presidential vote (Table 10-1).[1] These relationships were evident in our previous analyses of national elections, but they are somewhat tighter in 2008 than in the 1980s and 1990s. The vote for Democratic House candidates and the vote for Barack Obama are similar, both in the aggregate and in the categories we used in the presidential vote analysis (see Table 5-1).[2] This may reflect the closer relationship between party identification and the vote in recent elections for both the president and Congress as demonstrated in analyses by Larry M. Bartels.[3]

Not surprisingly, Obama did better among black voters (see Table 5-1) than did Democratic congressional candidates. All of our remaining comparisons are among white voters. Consider, for example, the relationship between voting and gender. Comparing white women and white men, we find that Obama failed to carry a majority of either sex, whereas House Democrats won a majority among women. In 1988 there was a small gender gap in the presidential vote (about three percentage points), with women more likely to vote Democratic than men, but there was no gap in the House vote. By 2000, however, the gender gap was

TABLE 10-1　How Social Groups Voted for Congress, 2008 (percent)

Social group	Democratic	Republican	Total	(N)[a]
Total electorate	54	46	100	(1,257)
Electorate, by race				
African American	86	14	100	(138)
White	48	52	100	(1,069)
Other	57	43	100	(148)
Latino (of any race)	85	15	100	(79)
Whites, by gender				
Female	52	48	100	(609)
Male	41	59	100	(459)
Whites, by region				
New England and Mid-Atlantic	46	54	100	(127)
North Central	56	44	100	(248)
South	39	61	100	(364)
Border	15	85	100	(55)
Mountain and Pacific	60	40	100	(241)
Whites, by birth cohort				
Before 1940	46	54	100	(175)
1940–1954	45	55	100	(253)
1955–1962	49	51	100	(185)
1963–1970	45	55	100	(146)
1971–1978	46	54	100	(120)
1979–1986	59	41	100	(124)
1987–2000	52	48	100	(21)
Whites, by level of education				
Not high school graduate	48	52	100	(62)
High school graduate	43	57	100	(289)
Some college	45	55	100	(317)
College graduate	52	48	100	(274)
Advanced degree	51	49	100	(127)
Whites, by annual family income				
Less than $15,000	75	25	100	(36)
$15,000–34,999	51	48	100	(126)

(Continued)

TABLE 10-1   How Social Groups Voted for Congress, 2008 (percent)
              (continued)

Social group	Democratic	Republican	Total	(N)[a]
Whites, by annual family income *(cont.)*				
$35,000–49,999	57	43	100	(94)
$50,000–74,999	47	53	100	(170)
$75,000–89,999	53	47	100	(92)
$90,000–119,999	39	61	100	(130)
$120,000–149,999	26	74	100	(61)
$150,000 and over	31	69	100	(75)
Whites, by union membership[b]				
Member	57	43	100	(138)
Nonmember	46	54	100	(894)
Whites, by religion				
Jewish	86	14	100	(22)
Catholic	57	43	100	(201)
Protestant	38	62	100	(637)
None	62	38	100	(200)
White Protestants, by whether born again				
Not born again	50	50	100	(252)
Born again	29	71	100	(375)
Whites Protestants, by religious commitment				
Medium or low	47	53	100	(317)
High	34	66	100	(182)
Very high	21	79	100	(136)
White Protestants, by religious tradition				
Mainline	39	61	100	(176)
Evangelical	36	64	100	(236)

Source: Authors' analysis of the 2008 ANES survey.

[a] Numbers are weighted. These results exclude sixteen respondents who did not know how they voted, seven who voted for independent or third-party candidates, and three for whom the results were not ascertained.

[b] Respondent or family member in union.

more pronounced in the vote both for the president and for representatives; the major-party share of the vote was nine percentage points more Democratic for women in the presidential vote and ten points more Democratic in the House vote. In 2004 gender differences were substantially reduced in both types of races, with the Democratic advantage among women down to seven percentage points for president and three points in House contests. Then in 2008, the gap declined a bit more for president, down to six points for Obama, but it increased to eleven points for House Democrats.

The presidential and congressional voting patterns are similar within many other social categories, including religion, income, and education. Catholics were nineteen points more likely to vote Democratic for representatives than were Protestants. Religious commitment was also related to congressional voting preferences, but the relationship was not as strong as that between religious commitment and presidential voting choices. Forty-seven percent of the white Protestants who had medium or low levels of religious commitment voted Democratic, while only 21 percent of white Protestants who scored very high in religious commitment voted Democratic. In addition, in congressional voting there was only a small difference between white mainline Protestants and white evangelicals.

There are some differences in the ways the presidential and congressional votes relate to income categories. It may be that these differences reflect the smaller number of cases in those categories, but overall patterns are similar and consistent: the propensity to vote Democratic generally is greater in the lower-income categories than in the higher ones.

As for education, the Democrats' support among those with advanced degrees was somewhat better for House members than for president. This is a reversal from 2004.

Among union voters in 2008, the Democrats were favored relative to non-union voters by similar amounts for the two offices: eleven percentage points better for the House and nine points better for the presidency. The relationship in 2004 was reversed and the differences were larger, with the Democrats faring only seven points better among union voters in House contests and nineteen points better in the presidential race. It should be noted, however, that all of these differences involve categories with relatively small numbers of respondents, and so the results may simply stem from sampling variation. The bottom line is that, overall, presidential voting and congressional voting among social groups were strikingly similar in 2008.

ISSUES AND THE CONGRESSIONAL VOTE

In Chapter 6 we analyzed the impact of issues on the presidential vote in 2008. Any attempt to conduct a parallel analysis for congressional elections is hampered by limited data. One interesting perspective on issues in the congressional vote is gained by asking whether voters are affected by their perceptions of where candidates stand on the issues. Previous analysis had demonstrated a relationship between a voter's perception of House candidates' positions on a liberal–conservative issue scale and the voter's choice,[4] and we found similar relationships in 2008. For example, among self-identified liberals in the ANES survey who viewed the Democratic House candidate as more liberal than the Republican candidate ($N = 121$), 92 percent voted Democratic; among self-identified conservatives who saw the Republican House candidate as more conservative than the Democrat ($N = 191$), 89 percent voted Republican.[5]

Research by Alan I. Abramowitz sheds additional light on this question. In two articles, he used the ANES surveys to demonstrate a relationship between candidate ideology and voter choice in both House and Senate elections.[6] For the 1978 Senate election, Abramowitz classified the contests according to the clarity of the ideological choice the two major-party candidates offered to voters. He found that the higher the ideological clarity of the race, the more likely voters were to perceive some difference between the candidates on a liberalism–conservatism scale, and the stronger the relationship was between voters' positions on that scale and the vote. Indeed, in races with a very clear choice ideology had about the same impact on the vote as party identification. In an analysis of House races in 1980 and 1982, Abramowitz found that the more liberal the voter was, the more likely the voter was to vote Democratic, but the relationship was statistically significant only in 1982.

Another perspective was offered in a series of analyses by Robert S. Erikson and Gerald C. Wright. They examined the positions of 1982 House candidates on a variety of issues (expressed in response to a *New York Times*/CBS News poll) and found that, on most issues, most of the districts offered a choice between a liberal Democrat and a conservative Republican.[7] They also found that moderate candidates did better in attracting votes than more extreme candidates. In a more recent study of the 1990 House elections, Erikson and Wright showed that both the issue stands of incumbents (measured by positions on roll call votes) and the district's ideology (measured by the district's propensity to vote for Michael Dukakis in the previous presidential election) were strongly related to the congressional vote.[8] A parallel analysis of the 2006 congressional voting demonstrates the same relationships, which are stronger for Democrats than for Republicans.[9] Finally, the same authors, in a study of the 1998 elections, employed a measure of candidate ideology that was derived from candidates' responses to questions about issues rather than from roll calls. That analysis confirmed that incumbent ideology has a substantial effect on vote share, with moderates gaining more votes relative to more extreme members. Challenger ideology did not have a consistent effect, reflecting the lesser visibility of their positions to the electorate.[10]

We examined the relationships between issues and congressional voting choices in 2008, analyzing the issues we studied in Chapter 6. For the most part, the relationship between issue preferences and congressional vote choices was fairly robust and consistent, especially among independents. However, partisan loyalties clearly affect congressional voting, even when we take issue preferences into account. Therefore, before considering the effects of other factors we will provide more information about the effects of party identification on House voting.

PARTY IDENTIFICATION AND THE CONGRESSIONAL VOTE

As our previous discussion demonstrates, party identification has a significant effect on voters' decisions. Table 10-2 (corresponding to Table 8-4 on the presidential vote) reports the percentage of whites voting Democratic for the House across all categories of partisanship from 1952 to 2008.[11] The data reveal that the proportion of voters who cast ballots in accordance with their party identification declined substantially over time through the 1980s. During the 1990s and 2000s, however, there was a resurgence of party voting for the House, especially among Republican identifiers.

Consider first the strong identifier categories. In every election from 1952 to 1964, at least nine in ten strong party identifiers supported the candidate of their party. After that, the percentage dropped, falling to four in five in 1980, and then fluctuating through 1992. From 1994 to 2008, strong identifiers showed levels of loyalty similar to those in the late 1960s. The relationship between party and voting among weak party identifiers shows a more erratic pattern, although defection rates tend to be higher in most years between 1970 and 1992 than earlier. (Because we present the percentage of major-party voters who voted Democratic, the defection rate for Democrats is the reported percentage subtracted from 100 percent.) Note that during this period the tendency to defect was stronger among Republicans, which reflected the Democrats' greater number of incumbents, as discussed in Chapter 9. Probably reflecting the effects of the Republicans' majority status and the corresponding increase in the number of Republican incumbents, from 1996 to 2000 the tendency of Democrats to defect rose, whereas among Republicans it fell. In the last three elections for which we have data (2002, 2004, and 2008), however, the Democratic defection rate was lower in all three Democratic categories (and the GOP defection rate was lower among strong Republicans) compared with the previous two elections. We consider these matters further in the next section.

Despite the general increase in defections from party identification since the mid-1960s, strong party identifiers continue to be notably more likely to vote in accord with their party than weak identifiers. In most years, weak Republicans were more likely to vote Republican than independents who leaned toward the Republican Party, although in 2008 these groups were about equally likely to vote Republican. Weak Democrats were more likely to vote Democratic than independents who leaned Democratic in most of the elections from 1952 to

TABLE 10-2　Percentage of White Major-Party Voters Who Voted Democratic for the House, by Party Identification, 1952–2008

Party identification	1952	1954	1956	1958	1960	1962	1964	1966	1968	1970	1972	1974
Strong Democrat	90	97	94	96	92	96	92	92	88	91	91	89
Weak Democrat	76	77	86	88	85	83	84	81	72	76	79	81
Independent, leans Democrat	63	70	82	75	86	74	78	54	60	74	78	87
Independent, no partisan leanings	25	41	35	46	52	61	70	49	48	48	54	54
Independent, leans Republican	18	6	17	26	26	28	28	31	18	35	27	38
Weak Republican	10	6	11	22	14	14	34	22	21	17	24	31
Strong Republican	5	5	5	6	8	6	8	12	8	4	15	14

Source: Authors' analysis of ANES surveys.

Note: To approximate the numbers on which these percentages are based, see Tables 8-2 and A8-1 (appendix). Actual Ns will be smaller than those that can be derived from these tables because respondents who did not vote (or who voted for a minor party) have been excluded from these calculations. Numbers also will be lower for the presidential election years because the voting report is provided in the postelection

1978, but in some elections since then this pattern has been reversed, and in 2008 almost identical proportions of the two groups voted Democratic. In general, then, the relationship between party identification and the vote was strongest in the 1950s and early 1960s, was less strong thereafter, but showing a substantial rebound in recent years.

If party identifiers were defecting more frequently in House elections over recent decades, to whom have they been defecting? As one might expect from the last chapter, the answer is: incumbents.

INCUMBENCY AND THE CONGRESSIONAL VOTE

In Chapter 9 we mentioned Albert D. Cover's analysis of congressional voting behavior from 1958 to 1974.[12] Cover compared the rates of defection from party identification among voters who were of the same party as the incumbent and those who were of the same party as the challenger. The analysis showed no systematic increase over time in defection among voters who shared identification with incumbents, and the proportions defecting varied between 5 percent and 14 percent. Among voters who identified with the challenger's party, however, the rate of defection—that is, the proportion voting for the incumbent instead of the candidate of their own party—increased steadily from 16 percent in 1958 to 56 percent in 1972, and then dropped to 49 percent in 1974. Thus the declining relationship between party identification and House voting results

1976	1978	1980	1982	1984	1986	1988	1990	1992	1994	1996	1998	2000	2002	2004	2008
86	83	82	90	87	91	86	91	87	87	87	88	88	93	92	92
76	79	66	73	66	71	80	80	81	73	70	60	69	73	74	82
76	60	69	84	76	71	86	79	73	65	70	62	71	75	74	81
55	56	57	31	59	59	66	60	53	55	42	45	50	42	46	43
32	36	32	36	39	37	37	33	36	26	19	23	27	28	30	21
28	34	26	20	33	34	29	39	35	21	19	25	15	26	19	22
15	19	22	12	15	20	23	17	16	6	2	8	11	6	8	7

interviews that usually contain about 10 percent fewer respondents than the pre-election interviews in which party identification was measured. The 1954 survey measured voting intention shortly before the election. Except for 1954, the off-year election surveys are based on a postelection interview. Note that no ANES survey was conducted in 2006.

largely from increased support for incumbents. Because there were more Democratic incumbents, this tendency was consistent with the higher defection rates among Republican identifiers, as seen in Table 10-2.

Controlling for party identification and incumbency, we present in Table 10-3 data on the percentage of respondents who voted Democratic for the House and Senate in 2008 that confirm this view. In both House and Senate voting, we find the same relationship discovered by Cover. Because we present the percentage of major-party voters who voted Democratic, the defection rate for Democrats is the reported percentage subtracted from 100 percent. Among Republicans, the percentage reported in the table is the defection rate. (By definition, independents cannot defect.) For the House, the proportion of voters defecting from their party identification is low when that identification is shared by the incumbent: 5 percent among Democrats and 3 percent among Republicans.[13] However, when the incumbent belongs to the other party, the rates are much higher: 16 percent among Democrats and 39 percent among Republicans. It is worth noting that the pro-incumbent defection rate for Democrats in 2008 is smaller than it was in 2000 and 2004, and for Republicans it is larger than in both years. This difference probably reflects the GOP's difficult political situation, as described in Chapter 9. Also note that the support of independents is skewed in favor of the incumbent, although the magnitude of this tilt is not as great as in the last few elections. When an incumbent Democrat was running, 66 percent of the independents voted Democratic; when an incumbent Republican was running, 59 percent of the independents voted Republican.

TABLE 10-3   Percentage Who Voted Democratic for the House and Senate, by
Party Identification and Incumbency, 2008

| | Party identification | | | | | |
| | Democrat | | Independent | | Republican | |
Incumbency	%	(N)	%	(N)	%	(N)
House						
Democrat	95	(197)	66	(137)	39	(92)
None	87	(55)	58	(53)	20	(69)
Republican	84	(202)	41	(198)	3	(245)
Senate						
Democrat	93	(79)	63	(46)	19	(38)
None	97	(40)	69	(35)	33	(23)
Republican	82	(167)	44	(142)	3	(182)

Source: Authors' analysis of the 2008 ANES survey.

Note: The numbers in parentheses are the totals on which the percentages are based. Numbers are weighted. In this table and in subsequent tables in this chapter, strong and weak Democrats and strong and weak Republicans are combined. Independents include those who lean toward either party and "pure" independents.

The pattern is similar in the data on the Senate except among Republicans. Given the opportunity to support a Republican House incumbent, 16 percent of the Democratic identifiers defected. Given the opportunity to support an incumbent Republican senator, 18 percent defected. However, 39 percent of Republicans supported a Democratic House incumbent, but only 19 percent backed an incumbent Democratic senator. Because the proportion of the electorate that has the chance to vote for Democratic and Republican senatorial candidates varies greatly from election to election, it is difficult to generalize from these data about the overall effects of incumbency on Senate contests. In the remainder of this chapter, we continue to explore this relationship among party identification, incumbency, and congressional voting.

THE CONGRESSIONAL VOTE AS REFERENDUM

In Chapter 7 we analyzed the effect of perceptions of presidential job performance on the vote for president in 2008, more or less viewing the election as a referendum on George W. Bush's job performance. A similar approach can be applied here, employing different perspectives. On the one hand, a congressional election can be considered as a referendum on the performance of a particular

TABLE 10-4   Percentage of Voters Who Supported Incumbents in House
Voting, by Party Identification and Evaluation of Incumbent's
Performance, 2008

| | Voters' evaluation of incumbent's job performance | | | |
| | Approve | | Disapprove | |
	%	(*N*)	%	(*N*)
Incumbent is of same party as voter	94	(329)	70	(37)
Incumbent is of opposite party	71	(322)	5	(186)

Source: Authors' analysis of the 2008 ANES survey.

Note: The numbers in parentheses are the totals on which the percentages are based. Numbers are
weighted. The total number of cases is somewhat lower than for previous tables because we have excluded
respondents who did not evaluate the performance of the incumbent and those who live in a district that
had no incumbent running.

member of Congress; on the other hand, it can be viewed as a referendum on
the president's performance. We will consider both possibilities here.

As we noted in Chapter 9, for some time public opinion surveys have shown
that constituents' approval ratings of congressional incumbents are very high,
even when judgments on the performance of Congress as an institution are not.
While traveling with House incumbents in their districts, Richard F. Fenno Jr.
noted that the people he met overwhelmingly approved of the performance of
their own representative, although at the time the public generally disapproved
of the job the institution was doing.[14] Data in the 2008 ANES survey again indicate widespread approval of House incumbents: among respondents who had
an opinion, 72 percent endorsed their member's job performance. This figure
was, however, about 10 percentage points lower than those for recent elections.
Approval was widespread, regardless of the party identification of the voter or
the party of the incumbent. Indeed, according to Table 10-4, approval is well
above 50 percent, even among identifiers of the party opposite that of the
incumbent (322 approve and 186 disapprove).

Further evidence indicates that the level of approval has electoral consequences. Table 10-4 presents the level of pro-incumbent voting among voters
who share the incumbent's party and among those who are of the opposite
party, controlling for whether they approve or disapprove of the incumbent's
job performance. If voters approve of the member's performance and share his
or her party identification, nineteen in twenty vote for the incumbent. At
the opposite pole, among voters from the opposite party who disapprove, only
one in twenty vote for the incumbent. In the mixed categories, incumbents
receive intermediate levels of support. Because approval rates are very high,

TABLE 10-5   Percentage Who Voted Democratic for the House, by Evaluation of Bush's Job Performance, Party Identification, and Incumbency, 2008

	Evaluation of Bush's job performance							
	Incumbent is Republican				Incumbent is Democrat			
	Approve		Disapprove		Approve		Disapprove	
Party identification	%	(N)	%	(N)	%	(N)	%	(N)
Democrat	[4]	(9)	87	(191)	[4]	(4)	95	(192)
Independent	14	(52)	52	(135)	30	(25)	74	(106)
Republican	1	(157)	8	(79)	36	(63)	46	(22)

Source: Authors' analysis of the 2008 ANES survey.

Note: The numbers in parentheses are the totals on which the percentages are based. Numbers are weighted. The number in brackets is the total number voting for the incumbent when there are fewer than ten total voters.

most incumbents are reelected by large margins, even in a difficult year for a party, such as for the Democrats in 1994.

In Chapter 9 we pointed out that midterm congressional elections, in particular, have been influenced by public evaluations of the president's job performance. Voters who think the president is doing a good job are more likely to support the congressional candidate of the president's party. We also saw that less scholarly attention has been given to this phenomenon in presidential election years, but the 2008 ANES survey provides us with the data needed to explore the question.

On the surface at least, there appears to be a strong relationship. Among voters who approved of Bush's job performance, only 16 percent voted Democratic for the House; among those who disapproved of the president's performance, 69 percent supported Democrats. In 1980 there was a similar relationship between the two variables, but when controls were introduced for party identification and incumbency the relationship all but disappeared.[15] Approval of Jimmy Carter increased the Democratic House vote by a small amount among Democrats, but had virtually no effect among independents and Republicans. In 2008, however, the results were somewhat different. Table 10-5 presents the relevant data on House voting, controlling for party identification, incumbency, and evaluation of Bush's job performance. It shows that even with these controls, evaluations of the president's job performance had an impact on House voting by all groups of identifiers. To be sure, Republicans were still more likely both to approve of Bush and to vote Republican than were independents and Democrats. Yet even after controlling for the pull of incumbency, within the

Republican and independent identification categories those who disapproved of Bush's job performance were more likely to vote Democratic for the House than were those who approved. (So few Democrats approved of Bush that there is little room for evidence of an effect in that category.)

PRESIDENTIAL COATTAILS AND THE CONGRESSIONAL VOTE

Another perspective on the congressional vote, somewhat related to the presidential referendum concept we just considered, is the impact of the voter's presidential vote decision, or the length of a presidential candidate's "coattails." In other words, does a voter's decision to support a presidential candidate make him or her more likely to support a congressional candidate of the same party, so that the congressional candidate, as the saying goes, rides into office on the president's coattails?

Expectations about presidential coattails have been shaped in substantial measure by the period of the New Deal realignment. Franklin Roosevelt won by landslide margins in 1932 and 1936 and swept enormous congressional majorities into office with him. Research has indicated, however, that such strong pulling power by presidential candidates may have been a historical aberration, and, in any event, candidates' pulling power has declined in the post–World War II period.[16] In an analysis of the coattail effect since 1868, John A. Ferejohn and Randall L. Calvert pointed out that the effect is a combination of two factors: how many voters a presidential candidate can pull to congressional candidates of his party and how many congressional seats can be shifted between the parties by the addition of that number of voters.[17] (The second aspect is called the seats/votes relationship, or the swing ratio.)

Ferejohn and Calvert discovered that the relationship between presidential and congressional voting from 1932 to 1948 was virtually the same as it was from 1896 to 1928 and that the impact of coattails was strengthened by an increase in the swing ratio. In other words, the same proportion of votes pulled in by a presidential candidate produced more congressional seats in the New Deal era than in the past. After 1948, they argued, the coattail effect declined because the relationship between presidential and congressional voting decreased. Analyzing data from presidential elections from 1956 to 1980, Calvert and Ferejohn reached similar conclusions about the potency of presidential coattails.[18] They found that although every election during the period exhibited significant coattail voting, over time the extent of such voting probably declined. More recently, James E. Campbell and Joe A. Sumners concluded from an analysis of Senate elections that presidential coattails exert a modest but significant influence on the Senate vote.[19]

Data on the percentage of respondents who voted Democratic for the House and Senate in 2008, controlling for their presidential vote and their party identification, are presented in Table 10-6. For both houses, the expected relationship is apparent. Within each party identification category, the proportion of McCain

TABLE 10-6   Percentage Who Voted Democratic for the House and Senate, by Party Identification and Presidential Vote, 2008

	Party identification					
	Democrat		Independent		Republican	
Presidential vote	%	(N)	%	(N)	%	(N)
House						
McCain	77	(38)	17	(159)	12	(379)
Obama	90	(428)	79	(220)	37	(30)
Senate						
McCain	48	(32)	20	(108)	6	(223)
Obama	92	(252)	83	(110)	50	(15)

Source: Authors' analysis of the 2008 ANES survey.

Note: The numbers in parentheses are the totals on which the percentages are based. Numbers are weighted.

voters who supported Democratic congressional candidates is lower than the proportion of Obama voters who supported Democratic candidates.

Because we know that this apparent relationship could be just a consequence of the distribution of different types of voters among Democratic and Republican districts, in Table 10-7 we present the same data on House voting in 2008, but this time controlling for the party of the House incumbent. When we made this comparison in 1996, we found that, despite this additional control, the relationship held up very well. Within every category for which comparisons were possible, Bob Dole voters supported Democratic candidates at substantially lower rates than did Clinton voters. In 2008 (as well as in 2000 and 2004), however, there are so few defectors within the two major parties that dependable comparisons are largely limited to independents, where the effect remains substantial. These limited data are consistent with the interpretation that the presidential vote exerted some small influence on the congressional vote, although not nearly as strong an influence as partisanship and congressional incumbency.

CONCLUSION

In this chapter we have considered a variety of possible influences on voters' decisions in congressional elections. We found that social forces have some impact on that choice. The work of other researchers has produced evidence that issues also have an effect.

TABLE 10-7   Percentage Who Voted Democratic for the House, by Presidential Vote, Party Identification, and Incumbency, 2008

Party identification	Voted for McCain %	Voted for McCain (N)	Voted for Obama %	Voted for Obama (N)
		Incumbent is Democrat		
Democrat	71	(14)	97	(182)
Independent	22	(46)	92	(82)
Republican	33	(84)	[5]	(5)
		Incumbent is Republican		
Democrat	87	(15)	84	(176)
Independent	7	(84)	68	(103)
Republican	4	(221)	18	(20)

Source: Authors' analysis of the 2008 ANES survey.

Note: The numbers in parentheses are the totals on which the percentages are based. Numbers are weighted. The number in brackets is the total number voting for either McCain or Obama when there are fewer than ten total voters.

Incumbency has a major and consistent impact on voters' choices as well. It solidifies the support of the incumbent's partisans, attracts independents, and leads to defections by voters who identify with the challenger's party. Incumbent support is linked to a positive evaluation of the representative's job by the voters. The tendency to favor incumbents currently appears to benefit the Democratic Party in House races. Within the context of this incumbency effect, voters' choices also seem to be affected by their evaluations of the job the president is doing and by their vote for president.

Partisanship has some direct impact on the vote, even after controlling for incumbency. The total effect of partisanship is, however, larger, because most incumbents represent districts that have more partisans of their party than of the opposition. Thus the long-term advantage of Democrats in congressional elections from the 1930s to the early 1990s was built on a three-part base: more Democrats than Republicans were in the electorate; most incumbents of both parties achieved high levels of approval in their constituencies; and the incumbents had resources that made it possible for them to create direct contacts with voters. After the 1994 Republican landslide, the GOP had the benefit of the last two factors, while mitigating their disadvantage in party identification. With the Democrats again in the majority in Congress and with recent Democratic gains in party identification (see Chapter 8), their members again are benefiting from all three parts of their previous support base.

PART IV

The 2008 Elections in Perspective

A careful analysis of voting patterns provides the information needed to speculate about future elections. Political leaders have always wanted advice about the future, and there were usually people willing to provide it. Few have fared as well as Themistocles, the Greek commander who correctly interpreted the cryptic advice of the Delphic oracle that the Greeks would be saved by a "wooden wall" and who defeated the Persians at the naval battle of Salamis (460 B.C.). Few have fared as badly as King Saul, who, even after the woman at En-dor raised the prophet Samuel from the grave, was told by Samuel that he faced certain defeat by the Philistines (1 Samuel 28: 7–20).

We do not have the powers attributed to the Delphic oracle, nor are we prophets like Samuel.[1] And we recognize that there is a great deal of uncertainty in politics, making any projections risky. As Niccolò Machiavelli wrote almost five centuries ago, "Fortune is arbiter of half of our actions, but ... she leaves the other half, or close to it, for us to govern."[2]

Both the 2000 and 2004 elections were shaped by events that were impossible to predict. Without the Monica Lewinsky scandal, Al Gore might have run a campaign emphasizing the accomplishments of Bill Clinton's administration and benefited more from positive evaluations of Clinton's presidency. Without a "butterfly ballot" in Palm Beach County, Florida—a ballot designed by a Democratic official—the conservative Pat Buchanan would not have won 3,400 votes, which was more than he won in any other county in the state. Because George W. Bush carried Florida by only 537 votes, there is compelling evidence that his victory resulted from voters misreading the butterfly ballot.[3] And because Bush needed Florida's twenty-five electoral votes to prevail nationwide, this minor flaw in ballot design may have cost Gore the election.

It is impossible to understand the 2004 election without taking into account the terrorist attacks on the United States on September 11, 2001, which were carried out by Osama bin Laden's al-Qaeda (The Base) terrorist organization and killed nearly three thousand people. In response to the 9/11 terrorist attacks, a U.S.-led coalition launched a series of attacks on the Taliban, an Islamist religious and political movement that had governed Afghanistan since 1996. Operation Enduring Freedom began on October 7, 2001. The military operation was based on the widely accepted assumption that Afghanistan was protecting al-Qaeda training bases. On March 20, 2003, the United States, with a much more limited coalition, launched Operation Iraqi Freedom against Saddam Hussein's regime in Iraq. In the justification for this operation, the links to al-Qaeda were much more tenuous, and subsequent findings revealed little direct relationship. Bush argued that Saddam was developing weapons of mass destruction (WMDs). Earlier, Saddam had used poison gas both against the Iranians in the Iran-Iraq War (1980–1988) and against the Kurdish minority in his own country. But after Saddam was ousted, no WMDs were found, nor was there any evidence that Iraq had a program that could have produced nuclear weapons.

It was within this unusual setting, rife with serious arguments about terrorism and foreign policy, that the 2004 election was held. Of course, Americans want to be protected from terrorists. But two questions remained: Who would do a better job of protecting them? What, if any, civil liberties should they be willing to sacrifice to be more secure?[4] Most Americans wanted to fight terrorists overseas, and most agreed that the Taliban regime in Afghanistan harbored terrorists. But the connection between Iraq and terrorism was much less clear. Once again, two questions were raised: How should the war against terrorism be fought? Who would do a better job of fighting it? And in addition to the importance of terrorism and war, voters also had economic concerns. Their votes, therefore, would be affected by the answers to two additional questions: What was the condition of the national economy? Who would do a better job taking care of it?

Voters in 2004 were also influenced by their positions on specific issues, as well as by their partisan loyalties and the ways in which those loyalties shaped their retrospective evaluations and their policy preferences. In our study of the 2004 election, we found that there was a virtual tie in the partisan loyalties of the electorate. Bush won, we concluded, because he held a slight advantage in the retrospective evaluations of the electorate. Additional analyses of the 2004 American National Election Studies that we conducted with Jill Rickershauser provide a multivariate assessment of the impact of these evaluations. We concluded that both the war in Iraq and perceptions of the economy hurt Bush, but that he was helped by positive evaluations of his handling of the war on terrorism.[5]

On balance, negative events affecting the United States may have aided Bush in gaining reelection. But more negative events were to come. One was an act of nature: Hurricane Katrina made landfall in Louisiana and Mississippi on August 25, 2005, killing almost two thousand people. Many people questioned the government's preparedness, and still more questioned its response. Sharp racial divisions characterized the public's assessments. In a survey conducted by the *New York Times*/CBS News between September 9 and September 13, 2005, 49 percent of whites approved of "the way George W. Bush is handling the response to Hurricane Katrina," whereas only 18 percent of blacks approved.[6] Many African Americans believed that the government would have been more forceful if most of the victims had been middle-class whites. The government's response to the hurricane was not an issue in the 2006 elections, and Bush's approval rating was already low when Katrina struck. All the same, Katrina may have undermined his ability to regain the confidence of the American people.

The most damaging events, however, emerged from the ongoing war in Iraq. When the war began, the public strongly backed the conflict, and in surveys conducted by a *USA Today*/Gallup poll a few days after it began, 71 percent approved of "the way George W. Bush is handling the situation in Iraq" and only 26 percent disapproved. His approval peaked in mid-April 2003, after the fall of Baghdad, when 76 percent approved and only 21 percent disapproved. But the U.S. military and its allies found it far more difficult to pacify Iraq than to topple Saddam. By the time of the 2004 presidential election, the United States had incurred more than 1,100 battle deaths and approval for the war had dropped dramatically. According to a *USA Today*/Gallup poll conducted at the time of the election, 47 percent approved of Bush's "handling of the situation in Iraq," whereas 51 percent disapproved. By the 2006 midterm election, the United States had suffered an additional 1,700 deaths, for a total of 2,800.[7] According to a *USA Today*/Gallup poll conducted between October 6 and October 8, 2006, only 30 percent approved of Bush's performance and 66 percent disapproved.[8]

In the 2006 midterm election, the Democrats made a net gain of thirty seats in the House, giving them 233 seats to the GOP's 202. The GOP had held the lower house for only twelve years. In the Senate, the Democrats scored a net gain of six seats, giving them a tenuous fifty-one to forty-nine–seat margin. It was clear that the war in Iraq had ended the Republican congressional majority.[9]

Although Bush acknowledged that the GOP had taken a "thumpin'" in the 2006 midterm election, he did not disengage from Iraq. Instead, as part of a "new way forward," on January 10, 2007, he ordered the deployment of an additional twenty thousand soldiers to Iraq and extended the tour of four thousand marines. Despite the Democrats' pledge to end the war, they were unable to prevent Bush from implementing this expansion. And despite considerable skepticism from Bush's critics, U.S. casualties in Iraq fell after the surge, and communal violence among Iraqis diminished.

But by the 2008 election neither the war nor terrorism was a major issue. As we saw in Chapters 2 and 7, the electorate's main concern was the U.S. economy. This concern was driven by the deterioration of economic conditions. The initial cause of the economic problems was a downturn in the housing market, which became apparent in 2006–2007 when housing prices began to decline. During the housing bubble, which peaked in 2005–2006, lenders were increasingly willing to issue credit to customers with relatively poor (or no) credit rating. The newly popular "subprime" mortgages usually had adjustable rates, and when home prices fell these rates began to rise. Many homeowners ended up with negative equity, owing more on their mortgages than their homes were worth. These factors contributed to foreclosures, especially among subprime borrowers. In the year before the election, some one million residences fell into foreclosure.[10] These problems at least in part resulted from both poor regulation by the government as well as deregulation. Some of these policies had begun during Bill Clinton's administration, and others during that of George W. Bush. But by 2008 few voters were likely to blame Clinton, and many blamed Bush.

The decline in the housing market, along with growing foreclosure rates, contributed to a decline in U.S. equities. Between January and mid-October 2008, U.S. stocks lost about 40 percent of their value. This decline eroded the retirement accounts of tens of millions of Americans, forcing some to delay their plans to retire and even forcing some older Americans back into the job market. Meanwhile, the unemployment rate rose from 4.3 percent in November 2006 to 6.5 percent in November 2008. Among the many economic indicators, only the inflation rate had improved. In November 2006, the consumer price index was increasing at an annual rate of 1.97 percent; in November 2008 the annual rate was 1.07 percent.

But these economic developments did not necessarily doom the GOP. As we saw in Chapter 3, among nine academic models developed by political scientists, six predicted an Obama victory, two a very close result, and one a McCain victory. We tracked daily contract prices posted at the Iowa Electronic Market (IEM) between June 2, 2006, when the market on the presidential election opened, to November 3, 2008, the day before the election.[11] Specifically, we studied the "Winner Take All" market in which one could buy or sell contracts on which party would receive the most popular votes for president.[12] There was not a single day during this twenty-six–month period in which the Republicans were favored, but there were several days in 2007 in which, for all intents and purposes, the parties had even chances.[13] On September 12, 2008, eight days after the Republican convention ended, the subjective probability of a Democratic win fell to a low of 0.525, and the probability of a Republican win rose to a high of 0.490.[14] But the odds were never this close again. On September 15, the day Lehman Brothers filed for Chapter 11 bankruptcy protection, the odds of a Democratic win rose to 0.563, and by September 17, the odds were 0.600. The Lehman Brothers bankruptcy precipitated a financial meltdown that led to a government bailout of over $700 billion. The odds for the Democrats remained at 0.600 or higher through the time the 2008 IEM closed. By October 8, the subjective probability of a Democratic win had risen to 0.807, and the probabilities consistently remained at or above this level. At the end of November 3, 2008, the day before the election, the probability of a Democratic victory was 0.903.

These probabilities, as well as the polling data we discussed in Chapter 2, suggest that until mid-September 2008, the Republicans had relatively good prospects, especially for the party of a president whose job performance was approved by fewer than three in ten Americans. As James W. Ceaser, Andrew E. Busch, and John J. Pitney Jr. argue, the entire campaign shifted in focus after Lehman Brothers announced that it would file for bankruptcy.[15] By October, the economy was the overwhelmingly dominant issue. The wars in Iraq and Afghanistan, cultural issues, and the threat of terrorism were pushed to the background.

As we pointed out in Chapter 6, the pool poll revealed that 63 percent of voters named the economy as the most important issue. Table 6-3, which is based on the open-ended results of the American National Election Studies surveys from 1972 to 2004, revealed that the incumbent party has lost all three elections (1976, 1980, and 1992) in which a majority thought the major problem facing the nation was the economy. The incumbent party has lost only one election (2000) in which the major concern was not the economy, and in that election it won a plurality of the popular vote. Using the pool poll to measure the concerns of the electorate, we found that this pattern held in 2008 as well. Obama won a comfortable victory, and the Democrats made gains of twenty-one seats in the House and eight seats in the Senate.[16] Obama's victory, we argue, resulted mainly from negative evaluations of George W. Bush and the Republican Party, particularly over the economy.

As this discussion then demonstrates, unexpected events can undermine any predictions, unless one issues cryptic predictions like the oracle at Delphi or malicious predictions like the witches who misled Macbeth. And, of course, as Samuel's example shows, divine guidance can be helpful as well.

Any short-term predictions rest heavily on the future of the economy. But as John Kenneth Galbraith observed, "The only function of economic forecasting is to make astrology look respectable." It is difficult to say how much progress Obama will need to make in dealing with the nation's problems to help the Democratic Party. After all, the U.S. economy had only modestly improved between March 1933, when Franklin Roosevelt became president, and November 1936, when he won his massive reelection victory. And, of course, there are even more drastic possibilities than a failed economy. North Korea already has some nuclear weapons capability, Iran may be close to achieving this capacity, and both have potentially unstable political systems.

Despite our inability to make specific predictions, the very nature of the U.S. political system creates some regularities absent in parliamentary elections. We know there will be no national legislative election until November 2, 2010, and that all 435 House seats will be open.[17] We know that there will be at least thirty-six Senate contests.[18] Indeed, we have already speculated about this upcoming midterm election (see Chapter 9).

We also know that there will be no presidential election until November 6, 2012.[19] We further know that, unlike the postwar elections of 1960, 1988, 2000, and 2008, when the incumbent president could not run for reelection as a result of the Twenty-second Amendment, Obama will be eligible to seek reelection in

2012. If he does, it seems unlikely that he will face any serious opposition for his party's nomination. However, if the Democrats should falter, the Republicans' prospects for victory will depend heavily on the quality of their standard-bearer. Most important of all, we know that the United States will hold a presidential election in 2012. The United States held a presidential election not only in 1944 during World War II, but even in 1864 during the Civil War.[20]

If Obama succeeds in solving the nation's economic crisis, he may cruise to reelection in 2012. If not, there may be a tight contest, although the Republicans will need to coordinate their strategies to make a credible challenge. In the chapter that follows, we examine four broad possibilities. First, we consider the prospects that the Democrats will retain the presidency, hold Congress, and once again become the nation's majority party. Second, we examine the prospects for a Republican comeback, noting that the party faces structural difficulties because of its shrinking demographic base and the internal divisions that often divide parties that have suffered political setbacks. Third, we discuss the prospects for a new political party, focusing on the demise of the Reform Party and showing why new parties find it difficult to break the Republican and Democratic duopoly. Finally, we examine the prospects for electoral volatility, the pattern that has prevailed in postwar American politics.

Chapter 11

The 2008 Elections and the Future
of American Politics

In his classic study of political parties, Maurice Duverger argued that in some democracies there is a clearly dominant party—that is, despite competitive elections a single party is consistently at the center of political power. A party, Duverger wrote, "is dominant when it holds the majority over a long period of political development." Although a dominant political party may occasionally lose an election, it remains dominant because "it is identified with an epoch" and because "its doctrines, ideas, methods, its style, so to speak, coincide with those of the epoch." One reason a party dominates is that it is believed to be dominant. "Even the enemies of the dominant party, even citizens who refuse to give it their vote," Duverger noted, "acknowledge its superior status and its influence; they deplore it, but admit it."[1]

Duverger's concept of the dominant party provides insights into the decline of the Democratic Party after 1964. Scholars of comparative politics have cited at least four clear examples of dominant parties in democratic political systems: Mapai in Israel (eventually succeeded by the Labor Party), the Christian Democratic Party (DC) in Italy, the Social Democratic Party in Sweden, and the Liberal Democratic Party (LDP) in Japan.[2] Duverger argued that if a country had free elections, a dominant party was always in peril. "The dominant party wears itself out in office, it loses its vigour, its arteries harden." And, he concluded, "every domination bears within itself the seeds of its own destruction."[3]

Duverger appears to have been prophetic.[4] Mapai was the dominant party even before Israel attained statehood in 1948. Asher Arian writes:

In the years immediately following independence, Mapai was presented with an opportunity shared by few parties in democratic polities—that of presiding over the creation of a constitutional and political order. As a consequence, it was closely identified with the new state, and it was the party of those segments of Israeli society most involved with those heroic years. It was able to translate this identification into an organizational network that complemented and amplified the advantages conveyed by its image. Furthermore, most of this network consisted of channels maintained largely at the expense of the state, with the result that the party and the government tended to merge in the popular mind.[5]

Mapai remained dominant until 1977, when an electoral upheaval drove the Alignment (the coalition Mapai joined) from office. Thereafter, the Likud (Union) ruled for fifteen years, although the Alignment joined the Likud in a national unity government between 1984 and 1990. The Labor Party, with Yitzhak Rabin as its head, regained power in 1992. Although the Alignment (Labor) was the largest party in the Knesset (Israel's legislature) after the 1996 elections, the Israeli electorate also voted for prime minister, and Benjamin Netanyahu, the leader of the right-of-center Likud, was elected. Labor thus again lost power. Labor came back to power briefly in 1999, but lost power only two years later when Ariel Sharon, the new leader of Likud, won a landslide election for prime minister.[6] In 2003 Labor won only nineteen of the 120 Knesset seats. In 2005 the Israeli system was again transformed when Sharon formed a new party, Kadima (Forward), and many Likud Knesset members and some Labor members joined the new party. Again in 2006, Labor won only nineteen seats and held a junior position in the newly formed government led by Ehud Olmert, who had become the new leader of Kadima after Sharon suffered a massive stroke in January 2006. But because of financial scandals, Olmert promised to give up his leadership. New elections were held in February 2009. Although Kadima won the most seats (twenty-eight), Likud came in only one seat behind, and Netanyahu, who had returned as Likud's leader, formed a government. Labor won only thirteen seats, its worst showing in Israel's eighteen Knesset elections.[7] Although Labor was a junior party in Netanyahu's government, it had gone from a position of overwhelming dominance to become a peripheral player on the Israeli political stage.

In Italy, the Christian Democratic Party, with U.S. support, won nearly half the votes cast in the lower-house election of 1948. It lost power more gradually than Mapai, but suffered a major loss in 1983, which brought Italy's first socialist prime minister to power.[8] In 1992 the "clean hands" investigation led to DC losses, and the party won only 34 percent of the vote. In 1993 the DC suffered major losses and a series of factional splits began. Some of these factions joined Casa delle Libertà (House of Freedoms), the coalition led by media magnate Silvio Berlusconi, and others joined the Ulivo (Olive Tree coalition), led by Romano Prodi. In the most recent election, held in April 2008, Berlusconi's coalition had become the People of Freedom, and the Olive Tree coalition, now led by Walter Veltroni, had become the Democratic Party. Berlusconi became prime minister for the third time since 1994. As for the DC, its successor parties split across the political center, to the center left, center, and center right.[9]

As Joseph A. LaPalombara points out, because the DC broke up into several factions aligned with larger competing coalitions, it is extremely difficult to assess the strength of its successor parties.[10] But, as Martin J. Bull notes, these successor parties are or have been "minnows by comparison with the old DC, and DC dominance is a thing of the past."[11]

The Swedish Social Democrats came to power in 1932. Although they were forced into the opposition in 1976 and 1979, they returned to power in 1982. But in 1991 the nonsocialists won a majority of the vote. The Social Democrats regained power in 1994, narrowly held power in 1988, and gained strength in 2002, winning 40 percent of the vote. But in September 2006 the four center-right parties, led by Fredrik Reinfeldt of the Moderate Party and campaigning under the same banner, won 48.1 percent of the vote, whereas the Social Democrats and their allies won 46.2 percent. The center-right had a seven-seat advantage in the parliament and formed Sweden's first majority government in twenty-five years. Even though the Swedish economy was doing well, and even though the Social Democrats also had "a privileged position as natural rulers of the country," they had been defeated. And yet, as *The Economist* wrote, "it was the presumption to rule that may have been their undoing."[12] Although the Social Democrats remain an important political force, their dominance has been seriously eroded.[13]

Since its formation in 1955, the Liberal Democratic Party had consistently been Japan's largest party in the House of Representatives, but in 1993, in the face of mounting scandals, the LDP split and the prime minister dissolved the House and called for new elections. Although it remained the largest party, the LDP was excluded from the governing coalition formed after the election. The LDP won nearly half the seats in the 1996 lower-house election and formed a government supported by several parties. It suffered major losses in the upper-house elections in 1998, forcing the resignation of the prime minister. In the 2000 House elections, the LDP did not win enough seats to reestablish its dominance, but it continued to rule in a coalition with other parties. A dynamic new leader, Junichirō Koizumi, provided the LDP with a majority of the seats in the upper-house elections of 2001. In fall of 2003, the LDP won the elections for the House of Representatives, but with a reduced majority. Most observers thought that the real winner was the Democratic Party (DPJ), which had strong appeal among the young and in urban areas. Commentators began to argue that Japan might be close to developing a two-party system. However, in the summer of 2005 Koizumi suddenly called an election for the House. Throwing the opposition onto the defensive, the LDP and its allies made major gains in the September 2005 elections, whereas the DPJ and its allies lost over a third of their seats.

A year after the election, Koizumi, having served three terms as prime minister, resigned. He was followed by Shinzō Abe. In July 2007, there was an election to choose half the members of the upper house, and the DPJ outpolled the LDP. A few months later, Abe resigned, to be replaced by Yazuo Fukuda and shortly thereafter by Taro Aso. After defeats in the municipal elections in Tokyo, Aso called for elections for the lower house, held on August 30, 2009. They were a disaster for the LDP. The DPJ, led by Yukio Hatoyama, won 308 seats of the 480 seats, and the LDP was reduced to only 119. *The Economist,* which had strongly argued that the LDP needed to be ousted, maintained that the election "marked the overdue destruction of Japan's post-war political system."[14] As the leader of the DPJ, Hatoyama became prime minister. But Japan continues to face serious economic difficulties resulting from stagnant economic growth, rising health care costs, and unfunded pensions in a rapidly aging society. If the DPJ fails to solve these problems, the LDP could return to political power.

Writing in 1958, Duverger argued that the Democrats were the majority party in the United States, even though Dwight Eisenhower, running as a Republican, had been elected president in 1952 and 1956. Duverger viewed Eisenhower's election as a personal triumph that did not change the balance of partisan power.[15] Scholars writing in 1964 might have perceived the Democrats to be even more dominant. The Democrats won the White House under Franklin Roosevelt in 1932 and then went on to win six of the next eight elections. In 1964, led by Lyndon Johnson, the Democrats won by a landslide over Barry Goldwater and gained thirty-eight seats in the House. The only Republican presidential victories were achieved by a former general, Eisenhower, who had been courted by both the Democratic and Republican Parties. The Republicans, much like the Whigs, who ran William Henry Harrison in 1840 and Zachary Taylor in 1848, defeated the Democrats by choosing a war hero as their standard-bearer. Between the Seventy-third Congress, elected in 1932, and the Eighty-ninth, elected in 1964, the Republicans held Congress only four years (the Eightieth Congress elected in 1946 and the Eighty-third Congress elected in 1952).

In retrospect, it is easy to see that the Democratic dominance had within it "the seeds of its own destruction," and that those seeds were in the composition of the coalition that supported it. The Democratic Party drew support from both northern blacks and southern whites. That coalition was sustainable only as long as discrimination against African Americans in the South was not a major issue. After the civil rights movement began in the mid-1950s, ignoring racial injustice in the South became untenable. By backing the Civil Rights Act of 1964 and the Voting Rights Act of 1965, Johnson chose a position that was morally correct, and he may have had strategic goals in mind as well, although he understood that signing these acts put Democratic support in the South at risk. In hindsight, the seeds of future Democratic defeats are apparent in Johnson's victory over Goldwater, who, in addition to winning his home state of Arizona, carried Alabama, Georgia, Louisiana, Mississippi, and South Carolina. By the end of the 1960s, African Americans in these states could vote, and, as Johnson expected, they voted overwhelmingly Democratic. Even so, in most subsequent elections these and the remaining southern states have voted Republican. Virginia voted Republican in all ten presidential elections between

1968 and 2004. And Alabama, Mississippi, South Carolina, and Texas voted Republican in eight elections between 1980 and 2008.

From 1968 to 1988, the Republicans won five of the six presidential elections. The exception was in 1976, when Democrat Jimmy Carter narrowly defeated Gerald Ford, the president who had pardoned Richard Nixon after he was forced from office by the Watergate scandal. Several political scientists, writing in 1988, argued that the Republicans had become the dominant party in presidential elections.[16] Yet after the 1988 election it appeared that the coalition that had supported Ronald Reagan and George H. W. Bush might also have had within it the seeds of its own destruction. Reagan had created a coalition of social conservatives, for whom the battle against abortion and for the right to pray in public schools were important issues, and economic conservatives, who believed that reducing the size and power of government was the key to economic growth. Although Reagan and Bush largely paid lip service to conservative social values, they provided tangible benefits through a series of court appointments, especially to the Supreme Court, that put *Roe v. Wade*, the 1973 case that legalized abortion, in jeopardy. In 1992, when Republican economic policies no longer appeared to provide economic growth, many economic conservatives and some social conservatives deserted the Republicans, although many turned to Ross Perot instead of to Bill Clinton. In the 1994 midterm election, two-thirds of the Perot voters who went to the polls in 1992 voted Republican, contributing to the party's legislative landslide. Although the Republicans had controlled the U.S. Senate for six years of Reagan's presidency, they had not controlled the U.S. House of Representatives since January 1955, a forty-year period during which the Democrats won twenty consecutive national elections for the House.

Despite Clinton's reelection in 1996, the Democrats did not return to electoral dominance because they failed to regain control of Congress. Between 1828 and 1996, the Democrats had won the presidency twenty times in forty-three elections, but 1996 was the first time they had won the White House without winning control of the U.S. House of Representatives. Although the Democrats unexpectedly gained House seats in 1998, the Republicans retained control of both chambers. In 2000 the Democrats gained another two seats in the House, but they were still short of control. Moreover, despite their plurality vote victory, they lost the presidency as well.

When George W. Bush became president in January 2001, the Republicans controlled the presidency, the House, and the Senate for the first time since the Eighty-third Congress ended in January 1955. But the Republicans had won a minority of the popular vote and had won just 271 electoral votes, only one more than the 270-vote majority required. They held only a 221 to 212-seat edge in the House and controlled the Senate only because Vice President Dick Cheney could cast the tie-breaking vote in a chamber equally divided between fifty Republicans and fifty Democrats. After Republican senator James Jeffords of

Vermont left the Republican Party to become an independent in May 2001, the Democrats regained control of the Senate.

The Republicans gained six House seats in the 2002 midterm elections, and they gained two seats in the Senate. Even though the net distribution of seats between the parties changed very little, the Republicans once again controlled the Senate as well as the House. The Republicans did better in 2004 than in 2000, but we should not exaggerate their success. George W. Bush did win a majority of the popular vote, but he held only a 2.4 percent margin over John Kerry, the narrowest popular vote margin for all seventeen incumbent victories since 1832.[17] His margin of thirty-five electoral votes was the second lowest of all twenty-one elections in which an incumbent was reelected.[18]

In 2004 the Republicans gained three seats in the House, extending their margin to 232 to 202, with one independent, Bernard Sanders of Vermont, who voted with the Democrats. But, according to Gary C. Jacobson, had it not been for the between-census redistricting in Texas in 2003, the GOP would have lost several House seats.[19] But the Republicans did very well in Senate contests. Winning all five open Democratic seats in the South, they made a net gain of four Senate seats, resulting in a total of fifty-five Republican seats to forty-four Democratic Senate seats and one independent. It was largely the Republican gains in these Senate contests that created a feeling of euphoria among many Republicans.

But in 2006 the Democrats regained both chambers, with net gains of thirty seats in the House and six seats in the Senate. Their House gains were a bit better than political scientists and pundits predicted before the election, but their Senate gains were much better than expected. Granted, the Democrats held a narrow majority in the House, holding 233 seats to the Republicans' 202, and their narrow majority in the Senate rested with two independents, Sanders and Joseph Lieberman of Connecticut, who was elected as an independent after losing in the Democratic primary to an antiwar Democrat, Ned Lamont.

In 2008 the Democrats recaptured the presidency by a comfortable margin. They also continued their congressional gains, winning a net of twenty-one seats in the House and eight seats in the Senate.[20] The Democrats held a 257 to 178-seat margin in the House. In July 2009, the Democrats briefly held a sixty to forty-seat margin in the Senate, enough seats to invoke cloture and to end Republican filibusters. With Sen. Edward Kennedy's death on August 25, 2009, their total fell to fifty-nine, until Kennedy was replaced by Paul G. Kirk Jr., who in September was appointed by the governor of Massachusetts to serve until a special election in January 2010.

Thus over the course of four years the overall prospects for the parties switched from a fairly rosy scenario for the GOP to a relatively even balance between the parties, and then to a political situation that left many Democrats feeling euphoric about their long-term prospects. But are those prospects as bright as optimistic Democrats believe?

PROSPECTS FOR THE DEMOCRATS

When Bill Clinton assumed the presidency in January 1993, the Democratic Party controlled the House and the Senate, ending twelve years of divided government. Although Clinton won only 43 percent of the popular vote, he had, in principle, the opportunity to provide a policy agenda that would make the Democrats the majority party for decades to come. Despite some early policy successes, the second year of his administration was marked by failures. The ambitious health care reforms proposed by Clinton received little legislative support, and he finally abandoned his own reforms to back a proposal by Senate leader George G. Mitchell. Ultimately, neither the House nor the Senate passed a health care reform bill. Clinton also failed to achieve another important policy goal, welfare reform.

Whatever prospects the Democrats had to seize the policy agenda disappeared with the Republican midterm victory of 1994. After the Democrats' defeat, Clinton moved to the political center. In 1996 he signed legislation significantly changing the welfare system, ending "welfare as we know it." But he did not entirely abandon liberal Democratic goals. Indeed, in the 1996 election the electorate saw substantial differences between Clinton and his opponent, Bob Dole, on policy issues. The main reason for Clinton's reelection was the favorable economy and the positive retrospective evaluations of the electorate.

In 2000 Al Gore, in attempting to minimize Democratic defections to the Green Party candidate, Ralph Nader, made some populist appeals. Even so, although the electorate saw sharp policy differences between Al Gore and George W. Bush, they had seen even sharper differences four years earlier. However, the electorate was favorably disposed toward Clinton, which should have worked to Gore's advantage. Perhaps Gore lost the election because he did not emphasize the successes of the Clinton presidency.

After the 2000 election, the Democrats could at least take solace in having won the plurality of the popular vote and having broken even with the Republicans in the Senate. The 2004 election was not as close, but the Democrats still had reasons for optimism. Our analyses suggest that the issue preferences of the electorate were somewhat closer to where Bush was perceived to be, but they were not as clearly pro-Republican as they had been four years earlier. Both the 2004 American National Election Studies survey and the 2004 General Social Survey still showed the Democrats with a small lead in the partisan loyalties of the electorate, although, because Republicans are somewhat more likely than Democrats to vote, there was, for all intents and purposes, an equal distribution of party support. The Democrats could still hope that Bush's success in 2004 was due to positive retrospective evaluations on issues such as terrorism and domestic security, which might not provide a long-term advantage for the GOP.

The Democrats did better in the 2006 midterm elections than could have been predicted even in late 2005, winning back control of the House and the Senate. The Republicans probably reached their high-water mark in party loyalties in

2003 and began declining thereafter. *New York Times*/CBS polls suggested that Republican Party loyalties declined in early 2005. But in the absence of a 2006 ANES survey, the most reliable measure was provided by the 2006 General Social Survey, which showed that the share of the Republican Party changed little between 2004 and 2006.

Along with their sweep of the presidency, the House, and the Senate, the Democrats made major gains in party loyalties in 2008, and these gains continued through mid-2009. Indeed, all the major data sources we have reviewed show Democratic gains. Most important, the two most reliable data sources, the ANES and the GSS, both show a five-point shift in the percentage of party identifiers who view themselves as Democrats.

To their credit, two scholars advanced an optimistic scenario for the Democrats only two years after Bush's 2000 election. In their widely discussed book *The Emerging Democratic Majority,* John B. Judis and Ruy Teixeira argue that many factors favor the Democrats.[21] For one thing, they claim that the demographic groups that tend to vote Democratic are growing as a percentage of the electorate, especially African Americans, Latinos, and Asian Americans. Moreover, the professionals who used to support the Republican Party are increasingly supporting the Democrats. Democratic strength, Judis and Teixeira argue, will be based in the high-tech and knowledge-producing urban areas, which they call "ideopolies." But they do not claim a Democratic majority is a certainty. "This survey is not intended to show that a Democratic majority is inevitable," they write. "What it shows is that over the next decade, the Democrats will enter elections at an advantage over the Republicans in securing a majority. Whether they actually succeed will depend, in any given race, on the quality of the candidates they nominate and on the ability of candidates and their strategists to weld what is merely a potential majority into a real one."[22]

Will Barack Obama succeed in restoring the Democrats to dominant-party status? Most overseers recognize that will depend on Obama's ability to solve the nation's economic problems. Perhaps it is more accurate to say it will largely depend on whether these problems are solved, for if they are, Obama and the Democrats will get the credit. If they are not, Obama and the Democrats will likely have to shoulder the blame. It also depends on other developments largely beyond Obama's control. Although Bush benefited from the events of 9/11, some Republicans will blame Obama if a major terrorist attack on the United States is carried out on his watch. And there are foreign policy developments that he cannot control and that could lead to devastating consequences, especially if a rogue state develops the capacity for delivering nuclear weapons, or, worse yet, actually delivers one. The ongoing wars in Iraq and Afghanistan pose problems. The United States may be able to withdraw its combat forces from Iraq, but no one can know the consequences of such a withdrawal. And if Obama's policies of winning support among the Afghan people fail, the war will eventually become Obama's war. Indeed, as U.S. battle deaths have increased in Afghanistan, support for the war has eroded.[23]

Problems for Obama are evident in the data we have presented. He was not elected because of his proposed policies—on many issues the electorate was actually closer to where it viewed John McCain. It is true that the Democrats benefited from gains in party identification, but, as Jacobson shows, those gains were largely the result of negative evaluations of Bush.[24] Indeed, as we have demonstrated, Obama's victory was based on negative evaluations of Bush and the Republican Party. The Democrats were able to win five consecutive elections between 1932 and 1948 by running against Herbert Hoover, and even tried to invoke memories of the Great Depression in Adlai Stevenson's campaign against Dwight Eisenhower in 1952. But the economic problems of 2008, as bad as they were, were not on the same order of magnitude as the Great Depression.

There is already evidence that many Americans who approve of Obama do not approve of his policies. For example, an NBC/*Wall Street Journal* telephone survey of 1,008 adults was conducted June 12–25, 2009. Fifty-six percent of respondents approved of the job Obama was doing as president, essentially the same approval rating he enjoyed in mid-September. Forty-eight percent liked Obama personally and approved of most of his policies, 27 percent liked him but disapproved of many of his policies, and 16 percent disliked him and disapproved of many of his policies. Few Americans blamed Obama for the nation's economic condition, but many did not approve of his policies for improving them. For example, 56 percent opposed his policies for aiding General Motors. By a smaller margin, most Americans (52 percent to 39 percent) opposed his plans to close the Guantanamo Bay detention center for terror suspects. And by a margin of 58 percent to 35 percent, Americans were more concerned about the budget deficit than about boosting the economy.[25] According to Democratic pollster Peter D. Hart who conducted the survey along with Republican Bill McInturff, "The public is really moving from evaluating him as a charismatic and charming leader to his specific handling of the challenges facing the country." Going forward, Hart added, Mr. Obama and his allies "are going to have to navigate in pretty choppy waters."[26] On the contentious issue of health care reform, an ABC News/*Washington Post* telephone survey of 1,007 adults conducted September 10–12, 2009, found that 48 percent of Americans approved of "the way Obama is handling health care," while 48 percent disapproved. But when asked, "Who do you trust to do a better job handling health care reform?" 48 percent chose Obama, and 36 percent chose the Republicans in Congress.

Obama has one clear advantage. It seems highly unlikely he will face any serious challenge, if any at all, for his party's presidential nomination. Intrade.com has already posted contract prices for the 2012 presidential elections and has generated contracts for the prices for the winners of both major-party nominations. The prospects for the Democratic nomination as of September 20, 2009, are presented in Table 11-1. Obviously, the betting public expects Obama to win the Democratic nomination. That the contract price is not even higher reflects the possibility that he may be unable to run or that he will choose not to. Even

TABLE 11-1   Possible Candidates for the 2012 Democratic Presidential
Nomination, as of September 20, 2009

Candidate	Current state	Year of birth	Year of election to highest office	Subjective probability of winning nomination
President				
Barack Obama	Illinois	1961	2008	0.811
Vice president				
Joe Biden	Delaware	1942	2008	0.020
Former U.S. senator				
Hillary Clinton	New York	1947	2000	0.050

Source: Biographical data on potential candidates taken from Jackie Koszczuk and Martha Angle, eds., *CQ's Politics in America, 2008: The 110th Congress* (Washington, D.C.: CQ Press, 2007).

Note: The subjective probabilities of these potential candidates winning the Democratic presidential nomination are based on the bid prices listed at www.intrade.com. These are the only potential candidates listed.

so, four-to-one odds are remarkably good for a result that will not be decided for over two and a half years.

PROSPECTS FOR THE REPUBLICANS

In some respects, the prospects for the Republicans to return to power are the flip side of the Democratic prospects. They depend in large part on America's economic future, as well as the success of Obama's foreign policies. But to a large extent, the present malaise of the Republican Party is the result of its own policies as well as its internal divisions. Just as George W. Bush was an albatross that John McCain could not escape, Bush's legacy may harm the Republican Party for years to come. But Bush was not Hoover, and the Democrats would be ill-advised to try to run against Bush.

One problem with the GOP is that it seems to have few new ideas, focusing instead on opposition to Obama's policies. But its problems were apparent well before Obama's election. The party is divided. One group is composed of economic conservatives who implemented tax cuts for wealthy Americans during the Bush administration. Although it is always difficult to determine causes and effects, after these tax cuts the federal budget deficits grew. In 1993, when Clinton became president, the federal debt was $4.35 trillion, and by 2001 it had grown to $5.77 trillion, a 33 percent increase. Over the eight years of Bush's presidency, the deficit increased to $9.65 trillion, a 67 percent increase. During the last year of the Clinton presidency, the federal government budget was running a surplus; in 2008 it was running an annual deficit of about $400 billion.

Social conservatives make up the second group within the Republican Party, and in some respects they have pushed it in directions that now make it more difficult to regain mainstream support. Social conservatives do hold the majority position in opposing same-sex marriages, but even Americans who oppose same-sex marriage may favor civil unions. On issues such as embryonic stem cell research, most Americans approve of federal funding. Most Americans do not favor the right to late-term abortions, but most are willing to allow women to end early-term pregnancies.

Pulling these disparate Republican views together will be a difficult task, and the GOP risks becoming a party of naysayers if it restricts itself to voting against all of Obama's proposals. In a widely quoted statement made in the summer of 2008, Tom Davis, a seven-term Republican from Virginia who was not seeking reelection, lamented that his party had run out of ideas. "If we were a dog food, they'd take us off the shelf and put us in a landfill."[27] And Republican strategist Ross Douthat concluded, "We're headed for a period of Democratic dominance, maybe four years, maybe eight years or more."[28]

In addition, demographic change appears to be working against the GOP. According to our analysis of the 2008 pool poll, 90 percent of McCain's voters were white, whereas the 2008 ANES suggests that 97 percent were. As we saw in Chapter 2, both parties attempted to win the Latino vote in 2008, but the Democrats were much more successful. What does this bode for the future? Although demographic projections are problematic, especially when they take immigration rates into account, the U.S. Census Bureau projects that the overall white population of the United States will decline dramatically during the next forty years (see Table 11-2).[29] According to these projections in Table 11-2, the white non-Hispanic population will make up just under two-thirds of the population in 2010, only three in five in 2020, less than three in five in 2030 and 2040, and only half by 2050.

The Hispanic population (which may be of any race) will rise from one in seven Americans in 2010 to one in four by 2050. Of course, it is difficult to predict the extent to which Hispanics will remain as politically distinctive as they were in 2008. Forty years is a long time, and it seems reasonable to speculate that many Hispanics will become economically successful, will accept mainstream American values, and, like many non-Hispanics, will become a less distinctive group within American society.[30] Even so, it seems obvious that the Republicans will not be able to win national elections in which nine in ten of their votes come from whites.

Finally, unlike the Democrats, who will not need to choose a presidential candidate in 2012 unless Obama is unable to run or if he chooses not to run, the Republicans are likely to produce many contenders for the GOP nomination. Even if Obama appears strong in 2012, many Republicans will want to challenge him, if only to establish their credentials for 2016.

TABLE 11-2   Projected Population of the United States, by Race and Hispanic Origin, 2010–2050 (percent)

	2010	2020	2030	2040	2050
Whites alone	79.3	77.6	75.8	73.9	72.1
Blacks alone	13.1	13.5	13.9	14.3	14.6
Asians alone	4.6	5.4	6.2	7.1	8.0
All other races[a]	3.0	3.5	4.1	4.7	5.3
Hispanics of any race	15.5	17.8	20.1	22.3	24.4
Whites alone, not Hispanic	65.1	61.3	57.5	53.7	50.1
Total population (thousands)	308,936	335,805	363,584	391,946	419,854

Source: U.S. Census Bureau, "U.S. Interim Projections by Age, Sex, Race, and Hispanic Origin," 2004, www.census.gov/ipc/www/usinteimproj.

[a] Includes the categories American Indian and Native Alaskan alone, Native Hawaiian and other Pacific Islander alone, and two or more races.

As we saw in Table 11-1, the list of likely Democratic candidates includes three names. For the Republican list, we include only prospects with a subjective probability of 0.005 or above (see Table 11-3).[31] As of September 20, 2009, twenty-three candidates met this criterion, and other candidates may emerge. Mitt Romney, the former governor of Massachusetts, appears to have a 0.280 chance of winning the Republican presidential nomination, which translates into odds of about one chance in three. The other candidates seen as having at least a one in ten chance of winning the nomination are Sen. John Thune of South Dakota, governors Bobby Jindal of Louisiana and Tim Pawlenty of Minnesota, former governors Mike Huckabee of Arkansas and Sarah Palin of Alaska, and former Speaker of the U.S. House Newt Gingrich. Some may argue that this long list of contenders reflects a weak field. Most pundits agree that Sarah Palin's decision to resign as governor of Alaska damaged her chances of winning the GOP nomination. And the Republicans may have lost a talented prospect when Utah governor Jon Huntsman accepted Obama's offer to serve as ambassador to China. All in all, the long list of Republicans in Table 11-3 may reflect a weak field or a surfeit of talent. Commenting on the GOP field as of July 2009, Republican strategist John Weaver argued, "You can call it the weakest field or the most wide open since Wendell Willkie won our nomination [in 1940]."[32] Of course, one reason the field seems weak is that very few of these potential candidates are well known to the public, and some might appear much stronger if and when the public comes to know them.

Even though most of these potential candidates will not run, there is likely to be a large field in a heavily front-loaded contest. In such a contest, the "invisible primary"—that is, the fund-raising the year before the delegate selection

TABLE 11-3   Possible Candidates for the 2012 Republican Presidential
Nomination, as of September 20, 2009

Candidate	Current state	Year of birth	Year of election to highest office	Subjective probability of winning nomination
Current or former senator				
Bob Corker	Tennessee	1952	2006	0.040
Rick Santorum	Pennsylvania	1958	1994 (defeated for reelection in 2006)	0.021
Fred Thompson	Tennessee	1942	1994 (did not run for reelection in 2002)	0.010
John Thune	South Dakota	1961	2004	0.125
Current or former governor				
Haley Barbour	Mississippi	1947	2003	0.050
Jeb Bush	Florida	1953	1998 (could not run for reelection in 2006 because of term limits)	0.051
Charlie Crist	Florida	1956	2006	0.021
Mike Huckabee	Arkansas	1955	1998 (could not run for reelection in 2006 because of term limits)	0.101
Jon Huntsman	Utah	1960	2004 (resigned in 2009 to be ambassador to China)	0.032
Bobby Jindal	Louisiana	1971	2007	0.121
Gary Johnson	New Mexico	1953	1994 (could not run for reelection in 2002 because of term limits)	0.010
Sarah Palin	Alaska	1964	2006 (resigned in July 2009)	0.170
Tim Pawlenty	Minnesota	1960	2002	0.170

(Continued)

TABLE 11-3   Possible Candidates for the 2012 Republican Presidential
Nomination, as of September 20, 2009 *(continued)*

Candidate	Current state	Year of birth	Year of election to highest office	Subjective probability of winning nomination
Rick Perry	Texas	1950	2002	0.011
Mitt Romney	Massachusetts	1947	2002 (did not run for reelection in 2006)	0.280
Current or former members of the House				
Eric Cantor	Virginia	1963	2000	0.0300
Newt Gingrich	Georgia	1943	1978 (resigned in 1989)	0.110
John Kasich	Ohio	1952	1982 (Did not run for reelection in 2000)	0.025
Ron Paul	Texas	1935	1996	0.014
Mike Pence	Indiana	1959	2000	0.010
Paul Ryan	Wisconsin	1970	1998	0.006
Former mayor				
Rudy Giuliani	New York	1944	1993 (could not run for reelection in 2001 because of term limits)	0.020
No political office				
David Petraeus		1952		0.035

Source: Biographical data on potential candidates taken mainly from Chuck McCutcheon and Christina L. Lyons, eds., *CQ's Politics in America, 2010: The 111st Congress* (Washington, D.C.: CQ Press, 2009).

Note: The subjective probabilities of these potential candidates winning the Republican presidential nomination are based on the bid prices listed at www.intrade.com. Only potential candidates with a 0.005 probability or greater of winning are listed.

contest—becomes crucial. Also crucial are professionals who have the expertise to raise money using the new information technologies. The candidates who can recruit these experts and afford their services are likely to be heavily advantaged.[33]

PROSPECTS FOR A NEW POLITICAL PARTY

For 156 years, the Democrats and Republicans have held a duopoly in American politics. Ever since the election of Democrat Franklin Pierce in 1852, either a Republican or a Democrat has won the presidency. And in the thirty-seven elections between 1864 (when Abraham Lincoln was reelected) and 2008, in only six elections has a third-party or independent candidate won the vote of even a single state. Moreover, the Republicans and the Democrats have dominated Congress. The last Congress with more than ten members from a third party was the Fifty-fifth (1897–1899). Since the Seventy-ninth Congress (1945–1947), no House has had more than two members who were not affiliated with one of the major parties. In his study of twenty-seven democracies, Arend Lijphart classified the United States as having the lowest number of "effective parties" and the second lowest number of "effective parliamentary" parties.[34]

Third parties face many obstacles, the most important of which are the rules by which candidates win office. With the exception of Maine and Nebraska, all of the states and the District of Columbia have winner-take-all rules for allocating their presidential electors. To win the electoral votes of these states, a candidate (or, to be more precise, a slate of electors pledged to vote for a presidential and a vice presidential candidate) must win a plurality of the popular vote. Despite winning nearly a fifth of the popular vote in 1992, Ross Perot did not win a single electoral vote. The only third-party or independent candidates to win electoral votes since World War II were the States' Rights Democrats in 1948 and the American Independent Party in 1968, and all of their votes came from the states of the old Confederacy. Despite some regional variation in Perot's vote in 1992, he had no regional base, and there was very little regional variation in his support in 1996.

Third parties have a difficult time getting on the ballot, although court decisions have made it somewhat easier to gain ballot access than before George Wallace's 1968 campaign. Independents or third-party candidates also have financial problems, and the federal election law places limits on their ability to raise money. Democratic and Republican candidates are guaranteed federal funding, whereas third-party candidates can receive funding only if they win 5 percent of the vote, and then only after the election. In 1992 Ross Perot, who ran as an independent, spent $65 million of his own money on his campaign. In 1995 he announced that he would help fund efforts to create a new political party, the Reform Party. In 1996 Perot accepted $29 million in federal funding, to which he was entitled on the basis of his 1992 vote. Based on Perot's 1996 vote, the Reform Party was entitled to receive $12.6 million in federal funding in 2000, one of the reasons its nomination was attractive. And yet as Obama demonstrated in 2008, one can run a winning campaign without federal funding, although it seems unlikely that anyone other than a self-financed independent could raise the resources Obama generated in 2008.

Perot predicted that his new Reform Party would be "the largest political party in the country" and would replace either the Republican or the

Democratic Party.[35] But Perot's share of the popular vote fell from 18.9 percent to 8.4 percent in 1996. By the summer of 2000 the Reform Party was badly split. Two conventions were held, one nominating Pat Buchanan and the other selecting John Hagelin, who had run as the Natural Law candidate in 1992 and 1996. The Federal Election Commission funded Buchanan, but he won only 0.4 percent of the vote. The Green Party, with Ralph Nader as its candidate, was more successful, drawing 2.7 percent of the vote, but it fell short of its goal of winning 5 percent and therefore did not qualify for funding in 2004. In 2004 David Cobb, the Green Party candidate, won only 0.1 percent of the vote, and Nader, running as an independent, won 0.4 percent. The Reform Party did not field a candidate.[36]

In 2004 only the Democratic and Republican Parties qualified for federal funding. Although both George W. Bush and John Kerry had declined federal funding for the nomination contest, they both accepted funding for the general election; no minor party qualified. Both McCain and Obama had rejected federal funding for their nomination campaigns, and Obama announced he also would not accept federal funding for his general election funding. He therefore turned down $84 million, along with the restrictions the funding entailed. McCain did accept federal funding, but no other parties were eligible.[37]

One might question whether the Reform Party and the Green Party ever were political parties. In effect, the Reform Party was never much more than a vehicle for Perot's candidacy. The Green Party was willing to nominate Nader even though he was not a member of the party because it needed someone to give it visibility and credibility. But the party seemed ill-positioned to challenge the major parties. Environmentalist parties generally win only a small percentage of the vote, and so the plurality vote rules in American elections put them at a major disadvantage.[38]

As Joseph A. Schlesinger reminds us, in a democracy a political party is an attempt to gain political office by winning elections.[39] When the Republican Party emerged in 1854, it ran candidates at every level in the nonslave states. Politically ambitious Whigs, as well as members of the Free Soil Party and the Know-Nothing Party, could become Republicans and seek elections to state legislatures, Congress, and governorships. In the Thirty-fourth Congress, the first elected after the Republicans were formed, 108 of the 234 House members were Republicans. In other words, it was a real political party that gave many individuals the opportunity to win political office.[40]

Third parties face another fundamental problem: they find it difficult to recruit attractive presidential candidates, or even candidates for lower office. The very openness of the major-party nomination contests encourages strong candidates to seek either the Republican or the Democratic presidential nomination. There are no constraints on entering the primaries, and a major-party nomination will probably continue to attract more votes than it repels. Candidates who actually have a chance of winning the presidency are likely to seek one of the major-party nominations.[41]

PROSPECTS FOR CONTINUED ELECTORAL VOLATILITY

Although many scholars predicted a period of Republican dominance after the 2004 election, even before the 2006 election we thought there were solid reasons for predicting continued electoral volatility. Perot's success in 1992 is the main reason for this prediction. More than nineteen million Americans voted for Perot in 1992, even though he had a negligible chance of winning and even though Clinton's margin in the preelection polls was not high enough to inspire confidence that he would be elected. Even in 1996, Perot won eight million popular votes, and 10 percent of the electorate voted for Perot and other minor-party candidates. The 1992 and 1996 elections mark the first time since the Civil War that the two major parties failed to win more than 90 percent of the vote in two consecutive elections.

In both 1992 and 1996, Perot's success resulted partly from the weak party loyalties of the electorate. Party loyalties grew somewhat stronger in 2004, but they weakened again in 2008. In 2008, 32 percent of Americans were strong party identifiers according to ANES data, but in the GSS survey only 30 percent were, which is somewhat weaker than in the "steady-period" between 1952 and 1964 discussed by Philip E. Converse.[42] During the 1950s, about 75 percent of Americans identified as either a Republican or a Democrat.[43] In the 2008 ANES, only 60 percent did. Weak party loyalties increase the share of the vote that is likely to switch from election to election.

The relatively low turnout in the United States may also contribute to electoral volatility. Even though turnout has increased about five percentage points over the last two presidential elections, turnout in the United States is very low compared with that of other democracies. Even though Obama won by a margin of 9.6 million votes over McCain in 2008, the 81 million Americans who did not vote could easily have changed the outcome. Moreover, for scholars who hoped that the 2008 contest would be a realigning election, the slight increase in turnout is discouraging.

It is difficult to guess about the 2012 election. If Obama is relatively successful in dealing with the nation's economic and other problems, he may have an easy path to reelection. If the current economic problems persist, he may face a serious challenge. There are several qualified Republican candidates, but it is difficult to know whether the nomination process will produce a strong contender.

Our best guess is that American politics will be characterized by continued volatility, with the Democrats and Republicans retaining their duopoly on political power. The Democrats like to date their origins from Thomas Jefferson, although that seems a bit far-fetched. But the party's roots can clearly be traced back to Andrew Jackson's campaign to defeat John Quincy Adams in 1828. And the Republicans can trace their origins to 1854. This longevity, however, does not guarantee the parties' survival. The ability of the Democrats and Republicans to retain their duopoly depends on the abilities of their leaders to solve the nation's problems.

Appendix

TABLE A7-1   Evaluation of Government Performance on Most Important Problem and Major-Party Vote, 1972–2004

A. Evaluation of government performance on most important problem (percent)

Government performance	1972	1976	1980	1984	1988	1992	1996	2000	2004
Good job	12	8	4	16	8	2	7	10	60
Only fair job	58	46	35	46	37	28	44	44	
Poor job	30	46	61	39	56	69	48	47	40
Total	100	100	100	101	101	99	99	101	100
(N)	(993)	(2,156)[a]	(1,319)	(1,797)	(1,672)	(1,974)[a]	(752)[a]	(856)[a]	(1024)[a]

B. Percentage of major-party vote for incumbent party's nominee

	Nixon	Ford	Carter	Reagan	Bush	Bush	Clinton	Gore	Bush
Good job	85	72	81	89	82	70	93	70	76
(N)	(91)	(128)[a]	(43)	(214)	(93)	(27)[a]	(38)[a]	(58)[a]	(460)[a]
Only fair job	69	53	55	65	61	45	68	60	
(N)	(390)	(695)[a]	(289)	(579)	(429)	(352)[a]	(238)[a]	(239)[a]	
Poor job	46	39	33	37	44	39	44	37	11
(N)	(209)	(684)[a]	(505)	(494)	(631)	(841)[a]	(242)[a]	(230)[a]	(305)[a]

Source: Authors' analysis of ANES surveys.

Note: The numbers in parentheses are the totals on which the percentages are based. In 1972, 1996, 2000, and 2004, the questions were asked of a randomly selected half-sample. In 1972 respondents were asked whether the government was being (a) very helpful, (b) somewhat helpful, or (c) not helpful at all in solving this most important problem. In 2004 respondents were asked whether the government was doing (a) a very good job, (b) a good job, (c) a bad job, or (d) a very bad job. "Good job" includes both "very good" and "good job"; "poor job" includes both "bad" and "very bad."

[a] Number is weighted.

TABLE A7-2   Evaluation of Party Seen as Better on Most Important Problem and Major-Party Vote, 1972–2000 and 2008

Party better	1972	1976	1980	1984	1988	1992	1996	2000	2008
A. Distribution of responses on party better on most important problem (percent)									
Republican	28	14	43	32	22	13	22	23	27
No difference[b]	46	50	46	44	54	48	54	50	18
Democratic	26	37	11	25	24	39	24	27	55
Total	100	101	100	101	100	100	100	100	100
(N)	(931)	(2,054)[a]	(1,251)	(1,785)	(1,655)	(1,954)[a]	(746)[a]	(846)[a]	(1,932)[a]
B. Percentage of major-party voters who voted Democratic for president									
Republican	6	3	12	5	5	4	15	9	6
(N)	(207)	(231)[a]	(391)	(464)	(295)	(185)[a]	(137)[a]	(143)[a]	(429)[a]
No difference[b]	32	35	63	41	46	45	63	52	29
(N)	(275)	(673)[a]	(320)	(493)	(564)	(507)[a]	(250)[a]	(227)[a]	(237)[a]
Democratic	75	89	95	91	92	92	97	94	87
(N)	(180)	(565)[a]	(93)	(331)	(284)	(519)[a]	(133)[a]	(153)[a]	(800)[a]

Source: Authors' analysis of ANES surveys.

Note: The numbers in parentheses are the totals on which the percentages are based. Question wording, 1972–2000: "Thinking of the most important political problem facing the United States, which party do you think is best in dealing with it?" 2008: "Thinking of the most important political problem facing the United States, which party do you think is best in dealing with it?" In 1972, 1996, and 2000 the questions were asked of a randomly selected half-sample. In 1972 respondents were asked which party would be more likely to get the government to be helpful in solving the most important problem. This question was not asked in 2004.

[a] Number is weighted.

[b] In 2008 the middle response allowed was "other." Most of the respondents in the middle category volunteered no difference.

TABLE A8-1   Party Identification among Whites, 1952–1978 (percent)

Party identification[a]	1952	1954	1956	1958	1960	1962	1964	1966	1968	1970	1972	1974	1976	1978
Strong Democrat	21	22	20	26	20	22	24	17	16	17	12	15	13	12
Weak Democrat	25	25	23	22	25	23	25	27	25	22	25	20	23	24
Independent, leans Democratic	10	9	6	7	6	8	9	9	10	11	12	13	11	14
Independent, no partisan leaning	6	7	9	8	9	8	8	12	11	13	13	15	15	14
Independent, leans Republican	7	6	9	5	7	7	6	8	10	9	11	9	11	11
Weak Republican	14	15	14	17	14	17	14	16	16	16	14	15	16	14
Strong Republican	14	13	16	12	17	13	12	11	11	10	11	9	10	9
Apolitical	2	2	2	3	1	3	1	1	1	1	1	3	1	3
Total	99	99	99	100	99	101	99	101	100	99	99	99	100	101
(N)	(1,615)	(1,015)	(1,610)	(1,638)[b]	(1,739)[b]	(1,168)	(1,394)	(1,131)	(1,387)	(1,395)	(2,397)	(2,246)[b]	(2,490)[b]	(2,006)

Source: Authors' analysis of ANES surveys.

[a] The percentage supporting another party has not been presented; it usually totals less than 1 percent and never totals more than 1 percent.

[b] Number is weighted.

TABLE A8-2 Party Identification among Blacks, 1952–1978

Party Identification[a]	1952	1954	1956	1958	1960	1962	1964	1966	1968	1970	1972	1974	1976	1978
Strong Democrat	30	24	27	32	25	35	52	30	56	41	36	40	34	37
Weak Democrat	22	29	23	19	19	25	22	31	29	34	31	26	36	29
Independent, leans Democratic	10	6	5	7	7	4	8	11	7	7	8	15	14	15
Independent, no partisan leaning	4	5	7	4	16	6	6	14	3	12	12	12	8	9
Independent, leans Republican	4	6	1	4	4	2	1	2	1	1	3	b	1	2
Weak Republican	8	5	12	11	9	7	5	7	1	4	4	b	2	3
Strong Republican	5	11	7	7	7	6	2	2	1	0	4	3	2	3
Apolitical	17	15	18	16	14	15	4	3	3	1	2	4	1	2
Total	100	101	100	100	101	100	100	100	101	100	100	100	99	100
(N)	(171)	(101)	(146)	(161)c	(171)c	(110)	(156)	(132)	(149)	(157)	(267)	(224)c	(290)c	(230)

Source: Authors' analysis of ANES surveys.

[a] The percentage supporting another party has not been presented; it usually totals less than 1 percent and never totals more than 1 percent.

[b] Less than 1 percent.

[c] Number is weighted.

TABLE A8-3   Approval of Incumbent's Handling of Job, by Party Identification, 1972–2008 (percent)

Year	Strong Democrat	Weak Democrat	Independent, leans Democrat	Independent	Independent, leans Republican	Weak Republican	Strong Republican
2008	3	11	6	26	46	47	74
2004	6	26	23	39	78	89	98
2000	92	88	81	65	49	52	23
1996	98	89	85	66	45	49	18
1992	12	28	20	32	65	71	91
1988	24	43	37	70	82	83	94
1984	22	48	32	76	90	93	96
1980	73	54	44	35	19	19	9
1976	24	55	46	69	87	85	96
1972	38	65	52	73	87	92	94

Source: Authors' analysis of ANES surveys.

Note: To approximate the numbers on which these percentages are based, see Tables 8-2, 8-3, A8-1, and A8-2.

Notes

INTRODUCTION TO PART I

1. Adam Nagourney, "Obama: Racial Barrier Falls in Heavy Turnout," *New York Times*, November 5, 2008, 1.

2. "Signed, Sealed, Delivered," *The Economist*, November 6, 2008.

3. For an analysis of the strategies in this election, see John H. Kessel, *The Goldwater Coalition: Republican Strategies in 1964* (Indianapolis: Bobbs-Merrill, 1968).

4. See, for example, Benjamin Ginsberg and Martin Shefter, *Politics by Other Means: The Importance of Elections in America* (New York: Basic Books, 1990); and Matthew A. Crenson and Benjamin Ginsberg, *Downsizing Democracy: How America Sidelined Its Citizens and Privatized Its Public* (Baltimore: Johns Hopkins University Press, 2002).

5. See Paul R. Abramson et al., "Fear in the Voting Booth: The 2004 Presidential Election," *Political Behavior* 29 (June 2007): 197–220.

6. Polifact.com has compiled a list of more than five hundred promises that Obama made during the 2008 campaign and tracks whether he has fulfilled them.

7. Robert Pear, "Health Care's Early Pledges," *New York Times*, May 12, 2009, A1, A16; Robert Pear, "45 Centrist Democrats Protest Secrecy of Health Care Talks," *New York Times*, May 12, 2009, A16; Jonathan Weisman and Naftali Bendavid, "New Splits Emerge in Health-Plan Talks," *Wall Street Journal*, August 22, 2009, A4.

8. The final seat was decided on June 30, 2009, when Republican incumbent Norm Coleman of Minnesota ended his legal challenge to his Democratic challenger, Al Franken.

9. Lanny J. Davis, "The Obama Realignment," *Wall Street Journal*, November 6, 2008, A19.

10. Harold Meyerson, "A Real Realignment," *Washington Post*, November 7, 2008, A19.

11. James W. Ceaser, Andrew E. Busch, and John J. Pitney Jr., *Epic Journey: The 2008 Elections and American Politics* (Lanham, Md.: Rowman and Littlefield, 2009), 1. The issue of *Time* was published on November 24, 2008.

12. Kevin P. Phillips, *The Emerging Republican Majority* (New Rochelle, N.Y.: Arlington House, 1969).

13. Phil Gailey, "Republicans Start to Worry about Signs of Slippage," *New York Times,* August 25, 1988, E5.

14. The Democrats held control of the U.S. House from the Eighty-fourth Congress, elected in 1954, through the 103rd Congress, elected in 1992.

15. The Republicans had unexpectedly gained control of the U.S. Senate in the 1980 elections and held it until the 1986 midterm elections.

16. The GOP lost control during this period when Sen. James M. Jeffords of Vermont left the Republican Party to become an independent and voted with the Democrats on the organization of the Senate.

17. James W. Ceaser and Andrew E. Busch, *Red over Blue: The 2004 Elections and American Politics* (Lanham, Md.: Rowman and Littlefield, 2005), 2.

18. For a discussion of the history of this concept, see Theodore Rosenof, *Realignment: The Theory that Changed the Way We Think about American Politics* (Lanham, Md.: Rowman and Littlefield, 2003).

19. Ceaser and Bush, *Red over Blue,* 22.

20. Fred Barnes, "Realignment, Now More Than Ever: The Next Best Thing to a Permanent Majority," *Weekly Standard,* November 22, 2004. Even before the 2006 midterm elections in which the Democrats regained control of the House and the Senate, there were reasons to be skeptical about these claims. For our own views before the 2006 midterm elections, see Paul R. Abramson, John H. Aldrich, and David W. Rohde, "The 2004 Presidential Election: The Emergence of a Permanent Majority?" *Political Science Quarterly* 120 (Spring 2005): 33–57; and Paul R. Abramson, John H. Aldrich, and David W. Rohde, *Change and Continuity in the 2004 Elections* (Washington, D.C.: CQ Press, 2006), 266–278.

21. V. O. Key Jr., "A Theory of Critical Elections," *Journal of Politics* 17 (February 1955): 4.

22. V. O. Key Jr., "Secular Realignment and the Party System," *Journal of Politics* 21 (May 1959): 198.

23. These states were, and still are, the most heavily Democratic states. Both voted Republican in seventeen of the eighteen presidential elections between 1856 and 1924, voting Democratic only when the Republican Party was split in 1912 by Theodore Roosevelt's Progressive Party candidacy. For a discussion of partisan change in the New England states, see Chapter 3.

24. V. O. Key Jr., *Parties, Politics, and Pressure Groups,* 5th ed. (New York: Thomas Y. Crowell, 1964), 186.

25. James L. Sundquist, *Dynamics of the Party System: Alignment and Realignment of Political Parties in the United States,* rev. ed. (Washington, D.C.: Brookings, 1983), 4.

26. Lawrence G. McMichael and Richard J. Trilling, "The Structure and Meaning of Critical Realignment: The Case of Pennsylvania, 1928–1932," in *Realignment and American Politics: Toward a Theory,* ed. Bruce A. Campbell and Richard J. Trilling (Austin: University of Texas Press, 1980), 25.

27. Byron E. Shafer, ed., *The End of Realignment? Interpreting American Electoral Eras* (Madison: University of Wisconsin Press, 1991). See, for example, Joel H. Silbey, "Beyond Realignment and Realignment Theory," 3–23; Everett Carll Ladd, "Like Waiting for Godot: The Uselessness of 'Realignment' for Studying Change in Contemporary American Politics," 24–36; and Byron E. Shafer, "The Notion of an Electoral Order: The Structure of Electoral Politics at the Accession of George Bush," 37–84. Shafer's book also contains an excellent bibliographical essay: Harry F. Bass, "Background to Debate: Reader's Guide and Bibliography," 141–178.

28. David R. Mayhew, *Electoral Realignments: A Critique of an American Genre* (New Haven, Conn.: Yale University Press, 2002).

29. We maintain that during past realignments there have been increases in turnout and that new issues have divided the electorate. Mayhew writes that the thesis that turnout increases when there is a realignment is a basic claim of students of realignment (*Electoral Realignments,* 20). Regarding issues, he argues that "at least as regards the U.S. House, realigning elections hinge on national issues, nonrealigning elections on local ones" (24).

30. For recent evidence based on an analysis of congressional and presidential election results that supports this conclusion, see James E. Campbell, "Party Systems and Realignments in the United States: 1868–2004," *Social Science History* 30 (Fall 2006): 359–386.

31. See David W. Brady, *Critical Elections and Congressional Policy Making* (Stanford, Calif.: Stanford University Press, 1988), presents important evidence on changes during the 1890s. See also Peter F. Nardulli, "The Concept of a Critical Realignment, Electoral Behavior, and Political Change," *American Political Science Review* (March 1995): 10–22; and Gary Miller and Norman Schofield, "Activists and Partisan Realignment in the United States," *American Political Science Review* (May 2003): 245–260. In *Electoral Realignments,* Mayhew comments on Brady's and Nardulli's work. (The Miller and Schofield article appeared a year after Mayhew's book was published.) For a more extensive presentation of Nardulli's thesis, see his *Popular Efficacy in the Democratic Era: A Reexamination of Electoral Accountability in the United States, 1828–2000* (Princeton, N.J.: Princeton University Press, 2005).

32. In addition to the eleven states that formed the Confederacy (Alabama, Arkansas, Florida, Georgia, Louisiana, Mississippi, North Carolina, South Carolina, Tennessee, Texas, and Virginia), Delaware, Kentucky, Maryland, and Missouri were slave states. The fifteen free states in 1848 were Connecticut, Illinois, Indiana, Iowa, Maine, Massachusetts, Michigan, New Hampshire, New Jersey, New York, Ohio, Pennsylvania, Rhode Island, Vermont, and Wisconsin. By 1860

three additional free states—California, Minnesota, and Oregon—had been admitted to the Union.

33. As James M. McPherson writes, "Republicans did not even have a ticket in the ten southern states, where their speakers would have been greeted with a coat of tar and feathers—or worse—if they had dared to appear." *Battle Cry of Freedom: The Civil War Era* (New York: Oxford University Press, 1988), 223.

34. Ronald Inglehart and Avram Hochstein, "Alignment and Dealignment of the Electorate in France and the United States," *Comparative Political Studies* 5 (October 1972): 343–372.

35. Russell J. Dalton, Paul Allen Beck, and Scott C. Flanagan, "Electoral Change in Advanced Industrial Democracies," in *Electoral Change in Advanced Industrial Democracies: Realignment or Dealignment?* ed. Russell J. Dalton, Scott C. Flanagan, and Paul Allen Beck (Princeton, N.J.: Princeton University Press, 1984), 14.

36. Russell J. Dalton and Martin P. Wattenberg, "The Not So Simple Act of Voting," in *Political Science: The State of the Discipline II,* ed. Ada W. Finifter (Washington, D.C.: American Political Science Association, 1993), 202.

37. Note that Inglehart and Hochstein were comparing France and the United States.

38. Bo Särlvik and Ivor Crewe, *Decade of Dealignment: The Conservative Victory of 1979 and Electoral Trends in the 1970s* (Cambridge: Cambridge University Press, 1983).

39. Harold D. Clarke et al., *Absent Mandate: Canadian Electoral Politics in an Era of Restructuring* (Toronto: Gage Educational Publishing, 1966), 183.

40. Most of the respondents were interviewed before and after the election. Many of the questions we are interested in, such as whether people voted, how they voted for president, and how they voted for Congress, were asked in the survey conducted after the election. The postelection survey included 2,102 respondents.

41. The 2002 midterm survey was conducted by telephone. The ANES did not conduct a midterm survey in 2006.

42. For a brief nontechnical introduction to polling, see Herbert Asher, *Polling and the Public: What Every Citizen Should Know,* 7th ed. (Washington, D.C.: CQ Press, 2007). For a more advanced discussion, see Herbert F. Weisberg, *The Total Survey Error Approach: A Guide to the New Science of Survey Research* (Chicago: University of Chicago Press, 2005).

43. For a brief discussion of the procedures used by the Survey Research Center to carry out its sampling for in-person interviews, see Paul R. Abramson, *Political Attitudes in America: Formation and Change* (San Francisco: W. H. Freeman, 1983), 18–23. For a more detailed description, see Survey Research Center, *Interviewer's Manual,* rev. ed. (Ann Arbor: Institute for Social Research, 1976).

44. The magnitude of the sampling error is greatest for proportions near 50 percent and diminished somewhat for proportions above 70 percent or below 30

percent. The magnitude of the error diminishes markedly for proportions above 90 percent or below 10 percent.

45. The ANES pre-election poll was conducted from September 2, 2008, to November 3, 2008. During that period, at least forty-three other polls were conducted. They show Bush's approval ranging from a low of 20 percent to a high of 31 percent, with an average approval level of 26.6 percent.

46. For an excellent table that allows us to evaluate differences between two groups, see Leslie Kish, *Survey Sampling* (New York: Wiley, 1965), 580. Kish defines differences between two groups to be significant if the results are more than two standard errors apart.

47. For 2008—as well as for 1958, 1960, 1974, 1976, 1992, 1994, 1996, 1998, 2000, 2002, and 2004—a weighting procedure is necessary to obtain a representative result, and so we report the "weighted" number of cases. For 2008 we weight by v080101 when we are presenting results relying solely on the pre-election interview (for example, when we report the party identification of whites and of blacks or the relationship of presidential approval to party identification). When we report results that include any variable from the postelection interview (for example, whether people said they voted, how they voted for president, or how they voted for Congress), we weight by v080102.

48. Actually, the 2008 ANES survey includes a black supplement and a Latino supplement. The weighting factors we employ reduce the numbers of blacks and Latinos so that they represent the actual proportion of blacks and Latinos in the electorate. In the weighted pre-election survey, there are 1,839 whites, 279 blacks, and 211 Latinos. In the unweighted survey, which presents the actual numbers sampled, there are 1,442 whites, 583 blacks, and 509 Latinos. As of this writing, the ANES has not reported the appropriate procedures for analyzing the black supplement or the Latino supplement. Readers should recognize that in those parts of Chapters 4, 5, 8, and 11 analyses of race will somewhat overstate the number of whites and substantially understate the number of blacks and Latinos.

1. THE NOMINATION STRUGGLE

1. The Iowa Electronic Market (http://iemweb.biz.uiowa.edu) gives market-determined prices based on buying and selling shares in candidate fortunes. These imply an estimate of the likelihood of winning. On October 6, 2007, for example, the probability of Clinton winning the nomination was 0.67, with Obama at 0.17, John Edwards at 0.05, and the rest of the field at 0.10. Republicans were led by Giuliani with 0.33, followed by former Massachusetts governor Mitt Romney at 0.29, Thompson at 0.20, McCain at 0.08, and the rest of the field (including former Arkansas governor Mike Huckabee) at 0.10. Intrade.com (http://intrade.com) lists contract prices on the nomination contests. We used contract prices as of December 24, 2006, to predict potential

Democratic and Republican presidential candidates. See Paul R. Abramson, John H. Aldrich, and David W. Rohde, *Change and Continuity in the 2004 and 2006 Elections* (Washington, D.C.: CQ Press, 2007), 312–320.

2. See Joseph A. Schlesinger, *Ambition and Politics: Political Careers in the United States* (Chicago: Rand McNally, 1966); and Schlesinger, *Political Parties and the Winning of Office* (Ann Arbor: University of Michigan Press, 1991).

3. Since World War II, the U.S. Senate has been a major source of presidential candidates. However, until 2008 only two sitting senators had ever been elected president, Warren G. Harding in 1920 and John F. Kennedy in 1960. For a discussion of the factors that influence whether senators seek the presidency, see Paul R. Abramson, John H. Aldrich, and David W. Rohde, "Progressive Ambition among United States Senators: 1972–1988," *Journal of Politics* 49 (February 1987): 3–35.

4. This is sometimes referred to as the "Johnson rule," because Texas passed special legislation to allow Lyndon Johnson to run simultaneously for vice president and for reelection to the U.S. Senate in 1960.

5. The one exception was in 1836 when the Whigs ran three separate candidates to oppose the sitting vice president, Martin van Buren. The Republican Party has always used simple majority rule to select its nominees. The Democratic Party required that the nominee be selected by a two-thirds majority in every convention from its founding (except 1840) until 1936, when the requirement changed to a simple majority.

6. Because some states object to this feature, or object to registration with a party at all, any Democratic delegates so chosen would not be recognized as properly selected. Parties in those states use other procedures for choosing their delegates.

7. Louisiana and Maine began their delegate selection proceedings via caucus before February 5 (and Hawaii ran its first stage from January 25 to February 5), but they were not punished because they did not actually select delegates to the national convention until later. Nevada was also not punished because it was chosen by the national party to hold its caucus before the window opened.

8. The results are for the Democratic Party and do not include "superdelegates." The Republican versions look very similar. For more details, see John H. Aldrich, "The Invisible Primary and Its Effects on Democratic Choice," *PS: Political Science and Politics* 42 (January 2009): 33–38.

9. Theodore H. White, *The Making of the President, 1968* (New York: Pocket Books, 1970).

10. Quoted in ibid., 153.

11. He was helped in this effort by the fact that one-third of the delegates had been chosen in 1967, before Johnson's renomination faced serious opposition.

12. The Republican Party does not require that its delegates be bound. Many states (especially those that hold primaries and follow Democratic Party rules) do bind Republican delegates.

13. To be sure, there were calls from supporters of Clinton for her to maintain her candidacy, especially in light of the still unresolved situation about the delegates from Florida and Michigan. The Clinton campaign, however, chose to slowly wind down the level of competition and effectively accept defeat, without actually withdrawing formally until the convention itself. For a discussion of the importance of superdelegates in 1984, see Paul R. Abramson, John H. Aldrich, and David W. Rohde, *Change and Continuity in the 1984 Elections*, rev. ed. (Washington, D.C.: CQ Press, 1987), 25. For the best journalistic account of the 2008 nomination contest, including a discussion of the role played by superdelegates, see Dan Balz and Haynes Johnson, *The Battle for America 2008: The Story of an Extraordinary Election* (New York: Viking, 2009).

14. This account of the importance of pre-primary campaigning is developed in Phil Paolino, "Candidate Name Recognition and the Dynamics of the Pre-Primary Period of the Presidential Nomination Process" (PhD diss., Duke University, 1995).

15. See Aldrich, "Invisible Primary."

16. See Paul R. Abramson, John H. Aldrich, and David W. Rohde, *Change and Continuity in the 2000 and 2002 Elections* (Washington, D.C.: CQ Press, 2003), chap. 1, for more details on the nomination campaigns in 2000.

17. EMILY's List, a group that supports female candidates, draws its name from an acronym of this line.

18. The most important adaptation politicians have made to campaign finance requirements is the acquisition and use of "soft money"—that is, money that can be raised and spent without limit for party-building and turnout efforts. Soft money became controversial in 1996 because of the increasingly vast sums raised, the sources of the contributions, and alleged misuse of soft money for promoting the election of candidates. Soft money is not, however, a major factor in intraparty competition, including presidential nomination campaigns.

19. See, for example, Thomas E. Mann, "Money in the 2008 Elections: Bad News or Good?" www.brookings.edu/opinions/2008/0701_publicfinance_mann.aspx.

20. See, for example, Michael Muskal and Dan Morain, "Obama Raises $55 Million in February; Clinton Reports Surge in Funds," *Los Angeles Times*, March 7, 2008, http://articles.latimes.com/2008/mar/07/nation/na-money.

21. See John H. Aldrich, *Before the Convention: Strategies and Choices in Presidential Nomination Campaigns* (Chicago: University of Chicago Press, 1980). Larry M. Bartels, in *Presidential Primaries and the Dynamics of Public Choice* (Princeton, N.J.: Princeton University Press, 1988), examines the electoral process underlying these dynamics.

22. Actually, there was a potentially serious third candidate in 1980, California governor Jerry Brown. In this contest, he acquired the nickname "Governor Moonbeam" and so received very little support. Thus this case was reduced almost immediately to two major or serious candidates.

23. Jesse Jackson was also a candidate throughout the entire 1984 contest, but he was never likely to actually be the Democratic nominee. See Abramson, Aldrich, and Rohde, *Change and Continuity in the 1984 Elections,* chap. 1.

24. We use New Hampshire rather than Iowa because Iowa has varied from being less than a week before New Hampshire to being several weeks before and because the window of time available to other states opens only after the New Hampshire primary. The campaign is considered to have ended when a candidate has secured the commitment of a majority of delegates or when his or her last opponent or opponents announces their concession.

25. See Randall E. Adkins and Andrew J. Dowdle, "How Important Are Iowa and New Hampshire to Winning Post-Reform Presidential Nominations?" *Political Research Quarterly* 54 (June 2001): 431–444; and Wayne P. Steger, Andrew J. Dowdle, and Randall E. Adkins, "The New Hampshire Effect in Presidential Nominations," *Political Research Quarterly* 57 (September 2004): 375–390.

26. Barbara Norrander, "The End Game in Post-Reform Presidential Nominations," *Journal of Politics* 62 (November 2000): 999–1013.

27. They argue that southern candidates are advantaged because relatively few run. Moreover, they argue that since 1976 parties have often nominated southern candidates. The Democrats nominated southerners in 1976, 1980, 1992, 1996, and 2000, whereas the Republicans nominated southern candidates in 1988, 1992, 2000, and 2004.

28. For more details, see John H. Aldrich and Brian Pearson, "Understanding the 2008 Presidential Nomination Campaigns," unpublished paper, Duke University, 2008.

29. The presidential nominee may not, however, have a completely free hand in choosing his or her running mate. For example, McCain may have wanted to choose Joe Lieberman, an independent Democrat from Connecticut and Gore's running mate in 2000. But Lieberman is pro-choice, and by choosing him McCain risked being challenged by the delegates.

2. THE GENERAL ELECTION CAMPAIGN

1. The district system is not the only alternative to the statewide selection of presidential electors. For example, in 2004 a ballot proposal in Colorado would have allocated its electors according to proportional representation. For a discussion, see Paul R. Abramson, John H. Aldrich, and David W. Rohde, *Change and Continuity in the 2004 and 2006 Elections* (Washington, D.C.: CQ Press, 2007), 55.

2. Compare with ibid., 35–36.

3. The eight states were Hawaii, Massachusetts, Minnesota, New York, Oregon, Rhode Island, Washington, and Wisconsin. See Chapter 3 on long-term voting patterns.

4. California, Connecticut, Delaware, Illinois, Iowa, Maine, Maryland, Michigan, New Jersey, New Mexico, Pennsylvania, and Vermont.

5. For a discussion of electoral vote strategies in 1988–1996, see Daron R. Shaw, "The Methods behind the Madness: Presidential Electoral College Strategies, 1988–1996," *Journal of Politics* 61 (November 1999): 893–913. There were methodological mistakes in Shaw's analysis. After reanalyzing Shaw's data, Andrew Reeves, Lanhee Chen, and Tiffany Nagano conclude that none of Shaw's substantive conclusions are supported by their study; see "A Reassessment of 'The Methods behind the Madness: Presidential Electoral College Strategies, 1988–1996,'" *Journal of Politics* 66 (May 2004): 616–620. Shaw acknowledges errors in his analysis, but maintains that correcting for these errors leads to few changes in his conclusions. See "Erratum for 'The Methods behind the Madness: Presidential Electoral College Strategies, 1988–1996,'" *Journal of Politics* 66 (May 2004): 611–615. For a fuller development of Shaw's thesis, see Daron R. Shaw, *The Race to 270: The Electoral College and the Campaign Strategies of 2000 and 2004* (Chicago: University of Chicago Press, 2006).

6. McCain's success in securing his nomination earlier could have been an advantage, but he had difficulty getting media coverage in the face of the ongoing Democratic drama. See *Newsweek*, November 7, 2008, 76.

7. Unless otherwise indicated, the national poll results cited in this chapter were taken from realclearpolitics.com. This Web site collected data from national polls and averaged them over a period (usually about a week). This approach "smoothed" the variations across polls.

8. The polling data cited in this paragraph were taken from pollingreport .com.

9. Matthew Mosk, "In Money Race, Obama Has the Advantage," *Washington Post*, June 7, 2008, A1.

10. Michael Luo and Jeff Zeleny, "Reversing Stand, Obama Declines Public Financing," *New York Times*, June 20, 2008, A1.

11. See Emily Cadel and Alex Knott, "Former Bush Donors: Still Hesitant about Backing McCain," cqpolitics.com, June 10, 2008.

12. Fredreka Schouten, "McCain Totals His Highest Donations in June," *USA Today*, July 11, 2008, 4A.

13. Emily Cadel, "With Party Help, McCain Budgets for $400 Million," cqpolitics.com, July 10, 2008.

14. Emily Cadel, "Obama Outspending McCain, Big Time," cqpolitics. com, August 21, 2008; Matthew Mosk, "Obama Campaign Reports Raising $66 Million in August," *Washington Post*, September 15, 2008, A3.

15. Michael Luo, "Obama Led Opponent in Spending in August," *New York Times*, September 22, 2008, A19.

16. In all of these states Latinos constituted 10 percent or more of the eligible voters. See Larry Rother, "Obama and McCain Expand Courtship of Hispanics," *New York Times*, July 17, 2008, A16.

17. Kathy Kiely, "Latino Vote 'Up for Grabs,' Could Swing Election," *USA Today,* June 27, 2008, 8A. For a summary of the controversy about the Latino vote in 2004, see Abramson, Aldrich, and Rohde, *Change and Continuity in the 2004 and 2006 Elections,* 111.

18. See Perry Bacon Jr. and Juliet Eilperin, "Candidates Pushing Hard for the Latino Vote," *Washington Post,* July 14, 2008, A6.

19. *New York Times,* September 5, 2008, A1.

20. See Adam Nagourney and Jeff Zeleny, "Already, Obama and McCain Map Fall Strategies," nytimes.com, May 11, 2008.

21. John M. Broder, "Obama, Adopting Economic Theme, Criticizes McCain," *New York Times,* June 19, 2008, A19.

22. *Newsweek,* November 7, 2008, 97.

23. Michael D. Shear and Juliet Eilperin, "McCain Launches Verbal Sortie, Calls Obama's Record Flimsy," *Washington Post,* June 4, 2008, A1.

24. Ibid.

25. Patrick Healy and Michael Cooper, "Rival Tickets Are Redrawing Battlegrounds," nytimes.com, September 7, 2008.

26. *Newsweek,* November 7, 2008, 82.

27. Jill Lawrence, "Giuliani Attacks Democratic Ticket as Untested," *USA Today,* September 4, 2008, 2A.

28. David Jackson and Kathy Kiely, "Attacks Are Order of the Day," *USA Today,* August 1, 2008, 4A.

29. Alexis de Tocqueville, *Democracy in America,* trans. Harvey C. Mansfield and Delba Winthrop (Chicago: University of Chicago Press, 2000), 611.

30. *Newsweek,* November 7, 2008, 85.

31. Michael Cooper and Michael Powell, "McCain Camp Says Obama Plays 'Race Card,'" *New York Times,* August 1, 2008, A1.

32. Richard Wolf and Martha T. Moore, "Armey Predicts Obama Will Hit Blockade of 'Bubbas,'" *USA Today,* September 4, 2008, 8A.

33. *Newsweek,* November 7, 2008, 94.

34. See Bob Benenson and Tim Starks, "GOP Hopes Palin Resonates with Three Groups,"cqpolitics.com, September 4, 2008.

35. "The Power of Palin," *Newsweek,* September 22, 2008, 37.

36. The sixteen states were Colorado, Florida, Iowa, Michigan, Minnesota, Missouri, Nevada, New Hampshire, New Jersey, New Mexico, North Carolina, Ohio, Oregon, Pennsylvania, Virginia, and, Wisconsin. See *Washington Post,* June 8, 2008, A10.

37. The data are available at http://cnn.com/ELECTION/2008/map/candidate.visits. Of course, any measure like this is imperfect. CNN counted the number of times a state was visited. However, a brief stopover was treated the same as a full day with many appearances around the state.

38. The account in the remainder of this paragraph is taken from *Newsweek,* November 7, 2008, 98.

39. Ibid., 103.

40. Jill Lawrence, "Candidates' First Debate Bolsters Obama in Poll," *USA Today*, September 29, 2008, 1A.

41. E. J. Dionne Jr., "McCain's Dicey Gamble," *Washington Post*, October 3, 2008, A23.

42. Adam Nagourney, "Concerns about Palin's Readiness as a Big Test for Her Nears," *New York Times*, September 30, 2008, A16.

43. Robert Barnes and Juliet Eilperin, "Biden and Palin Square Off," *Washington Post*, October 3, 2008, A1.

44. See "Instant Polls Find Biden Wins," politicalwire.com, October 2, 2008.

45. Liz Sidoti, "McCain Campaign Writes Off Michigan, Turns to Indiana," *Durham Herald-Sun*, October 3, 2008, A3.

46. Adam Nagourney, "Campaigns Shift to Attack Mode on Eve of Debate," *New York Times*, October 7, 2008, A17.

47. See "CNN Poll: Obama Wins the Night," http://politicalticker.blogs.cnn.com, October 7, 2008.

48. *Newsweek*, November 7, 2008, 108.

49. Julie Kronholz, "Ready, Aim, Backfire: Nasty Political Ads Fall Flat," online.wsj.com, October 16, 2008.

50. Michael Cooper and Megan Thee, "Poll Says McCain Is Hurting His Bid by Using Attacks," *New York Times*, October 15, 2008, A1.

51. T. W. Farnam and Brad Haynes, "Democrats Far Outspend Republicans on Field Operations and Staff Expenditures," online.wsj.com, November 3, 2008.

52. *Newsweek*, November 7, 2008, 86.

53. Eli Saslow, "Democrats Registering in Record Numbers," *Washington Post*, April 28, 2008, A1.

54. Christopher Cooper and Susan Davis, "Obama Seeks to Add Black Voters," online.wsj.com, June 30, 2008.

55. Miriam Jordan, "Latino Voter-Registration Drive Likely to Aid Obama," online.wsj.com, September 25, 2008.

56. William M. Welch, "Study: Voter Interest High; Registrations Up 10 Million," *USA Today*, November 3, 2008, 9A.

57. *Rhodes Cook Letter*, October 2008, 9.

58. See Christopher Cooper and Susan Davis, "Obama Seeks to Add Black Voters," online.wsj.com, June 30, 2008.

59. Robert Barnes, "High Court Upholds Indiana Law on Voter ID," *Washington Post*, April 29, 2008, A1.

60. Mary Pat Flaherty and William Branigan, "Justices Rule against Ohio GOP on Voter Issue," *Washington Post*, October 18, 2008, A4.

61. Ibid.; Ian Urbina, "States' Purges of Voter Rolls Appear Illegal," *New York Times*, October 9, 2008, A1.

62. Lisa Lerer, "GOP Challenges to New Voters Set Back by Courts," news.yahoo.com, October 25, 2008.

63. Dan Frosh and Ian Urbina, "Colorado Agrees to Restore Voters to Rolls," *New York Times*, October 31, 2008, A21.

64. The data on early voting cited in this section were, unless otherwise indicated, taken from the Web site of Prof. Michael McDonald, George Mason University, http://elections.gmu.edu/Early_Voting_2008_Final.html.

65. *USA Today,* September 22, 2008, 1A.

66. Jonathan Weisman and Christopher Cooper, "Obama Seeks Advantage in Florida as Early Voting Starts," online.wsj.com, October 21, 2008.

67. Jon Cohen and Kyle Dropp, "Early Voters Breaking Records," *Washington Post,* October 30, 2008, A2.

68. The registration figures come from "Outsize Portion of Blacks Are Casting Early Ballots," online.wsj.com, October 22, 2008. The early voting percentages are from http://elections.gmu.edu/early_vote_2008.html.

69. See note 64.

70. The polling figures in this paragraph were taken from Michael Cooper and Dalia Sussman, "Growing Doubts on Palin Take a Toll, Poll Finds," *New York Times,* October 31, 2008, A1, A18.

71. Jeff Zeleny, "Donation Record as Colin Powell Endorses Obama," *New York Times,* October 20, 2008, A1, A22.

72. Fredreka Schouten, "Obama's Ad Buys Dwarf TV Presence of McCain," *USA Today,* October 28, 2008, 1A.

73. Bill Carter, "Infomercial for Obama Is Big Success in Ratings," *New York Times,* October 31, 2008, A19.

74. Ibid.

75. There has been a lot of interesting research in recent years on the impact of presidential campaigns on outcomes. See, for example, Thomas H. Holbrook, *Do Campaigns Matter?* (Thousand Oaks, Calif.: Sage Publications, 1996); James E. Campbell, *The American Campaign* (College Station: Texas A&M University Press, 2000); and Daron R. Shaw, "A Study of Presidential Campaign Effects from 1956 to 1992," *Journal of Politics* 61 (May 1999): 387–422. For his most extensive treatment, see Shaw, *Race to 270.*

76. All exit poll results reported in this section were taken from CNN, www.cnn.com/ELECTION/2008/results/polls/#val=USP00p1.

77. See, for example, Stuart Rothenberg, "Is 2008 a Realigning Election? Numbers Offer Some Clues," *Roll Call,* November 10, 2008, 7; and Robert G. Kaiser, "Pollsters Debate America's Political Realignment," *Washington Post,* November 23, 2008, A2.

78. On changing demographics and their political implications, see John B. Judis and Ruy Teixeira, *The Emerging Democratic Majority* (New York: Scribner's, 2002).

3. THE ELECTION RESULTS

1. http://pollingreport.com/wh08gen.htm.

2. See, for example, pollyvote.com, fivethirtyeight.com, realclearpolitics.com, pollster.com, and cqpolitics.com.

3. For a discussion of the relative predictive ability of the IEM and public opinion polls, see Robert S. Erikson and Christopher Wlezien, "Are Political Markets Really Superior to Polls as Election Predictors?" *Public Opinion Quarterly* 72 (Summer 2008): 190–215. (They conclude they are not.) For a discussion of Intrade.com, see Paul R. Abramson, "Using Intrade.com to Teach Campaign Strategies in the 2008 U.S. Presidential Election," *PS: Political Science and Politics* 43 (January 2010).

4. For example, in their projections for the 2008 presidential election, Michael S. Lewis-Beck and Charles Tien discuss the possibility of a Bradley effect, noting that there was no evidence of such an effect in the Democratic presidential primaries. See "The Job of the President and the Jobs Forecast Model," *PS: Political Science and Politics* 41 (October 2008): 687–690. Among the nine academic models presented in this issue, six predicted an Obama victory, two (including the Lewis-Beck and Tien model) a very close result, and one a McCain victory. These models, however, were based on data before the Wall Street meltdown in mid-September.

5. Polls also closed in Hawaii and Idaho, each with four electoral votes. Hawaii, a traditionally Democratic state as well as Obama's birthplace, was Obama's best state, whereas Idaho supported McCain.

6. "Transcript: McCain Concedes Presidency." www.cnn.com/POLITICS/11/04/mccaintranscript /index.html.

7. In his landslide victory in 1964, Democrat Lyndon Johnson won 61.1 percent, and in 1976 Jimmy Carter won 50.1 percent. The presidential election results we refer to throughout this chapter are based on *Presidential Elections, 1789–2008* (Washington, D.C.: CQ Press, 2009).

8. James W. Ceaser, Andrew E. Busch, and John J. Pitney Jr. present the margin of popular vote victories in all the presidential elections between 1896 and 2008 and conclude that the 2008 contest was "moderately competitive." They report that Obama's margin of victory ranked nineteenth among these twenty-nine elections. See Ceaser, Busch, and Pitney, *Epic Journey: The 2008 Elections and American Politics* (Lanham, Md.: Rowman and Littlefield, 2009), 1–5.

9. As we note in Chapter 2, in every election since 1972 Maine has used a system in which the plurality vote winner in the state receives two electoral votes and the plurality of each of its congressional districts receives that district's single electoral vote. Nebraska has used a similar system to allocate its votes since the 1992 election. In our previous books, we do not report these district-level results because these rules did not affect the outcome.

10. Kerry actually won only 251 electoral votes, because one Democratic elector in Minnesota voted for John Edwards, the Democratic vice presidential candidate.

11. We begin with the 1828 election because in 1824 state legislatures chose the presidential electors in six of the twenty-four states. It does seem very likely, however, that Andrew Jackson would have been the popular vote winner if all the

states had had popular vote elections in 1824. By 1828 in only two states were state legislatures choosing the electors.

12. In the disputed election of 1876, records suggest that Samuel J. Tilden, the Democrat, won 51.0 percent of the popular vote and that Rutherford B. Hayes, the Republican, won 48.0 percent. In 1888 Grover Cleveland, the incumbent Democratic president, won 48.6 percent of the vote, and Benjamin Harrison, the Republican, won 47.8 percent. In the disputed 2000 election, Gore won 48.4 percent of the vote, and Bush won 47.9 percent.

13. These fourteen winners were James K. Polk (Democrat) in 1844, with 49.5 percent of the popular vote; Zachary Taylor (Whig) in 1848, with 47.3 percent; James Buchanan (Democrat) in 1856, with 45.3 percent; Abraham Lincoln (Republican) in 1860 with 39.9 percent; James A. Garfield (Republican) in 1880, with 48.3 percent; Grover Cleveland (Democrat) in 1884, with 48.9 percent; Cleveland in 1892, with 46.0 percent; Woodrow Wilson (Democrat) in 1912, with 41.8 percent; Wilson in 1916, with 49.2 percent; Harry S. Truman (Democrat) in 1948, with 49.5 percent; John F. Kennedy (Democrat) in 1960, with 49.7 percent; Richard M. Nixon (Republican) in 1968, with 43.4 percent; Bill Clinton (Democrat) in 1992, with 43.0 percent; and Clinton in 1996, with 49.2 percent. The results for Kennedy can be questioned, however, mainly because voters in Alabama voted for individual electors, and one can argue that Nixon won more popular votes than Kennedy.

14. Britain provides an excellent example of the effects of plurality vote win systems on third parties. In Britain, as in the United States, candidates for the national legislature run in single-member districts, and in all British parliamentary districts the plurality vote winner is elected. In all seventeen general elections since World War II ended in Europe, the Liberal Party (and more recently the Alliance and the Liberal Democratic Parties) has received a smaller percentage of seats in the House of Commons than its percentage of the popular vote. For example, in the May 2005 election the Liberal Democrats won 22 percent of the popular vote, but won only 10 percent of the seats in the House of Commons.

15. The New England states are Connecticut, Maine, Massachusetts, New Hampshire, Rhode Island, and Vermont. Although the U.S. Census Bureau labels several border states and the District of Columbia as southern, we use an explicitly political definition—the eleven states that made up the old Confederacy, which are Alabama, Arkansas, Florida, Georgia, Louisiana, Mississippi, North Carolina, South Carolina, Tennessee, Texas, and Virginia.

16. These states are Arizona, Colorado, Idaho, Montana, Nevada, New Mexico, Utah, and Wyoming.

17. For a comparison of Wallace's regional strength in 1968, Anderson's regional strength in 1980, and Perot's regional strength in 1992, see Paul R. Abramson, John H. Aldrich, and David W. Rohde, *Change and Continuity in the 1992 Elections,* rev. ed. (Washington, D.C.: CQ Press, 1995), 73–76.

18. Although there are rare exceptions, presidential electors are pledged to support a presidential and a vice presidential candidate. Over eight thousand

pledged electors have been selected since 1944, and only eight have failed to vote for the presidential candidate they were pledged to support.

19. Third-party candidates are not always underrepresented in the Electoral College. In 1948 J. Strom Thurmond, the States' Rights Democrat, won only 2.4 percent of the popular vote but won 7.3 percent of the electoral vote. Thurmond won 55 percent of the popular votes in the four states he carried (Alabama, Louisiana, Mississippi, and South Carolina), all of which had low turnout. He received no popular vote at all in thirty-one of the forty-eight states.

20. Maurice Duverger, *Political Parties: Their Organization and Activity in the Modern State,* trans. Barbara North and Robert North (New York: Wiley, 1963), 217. In the original, Duverger's proposition is "le scrutin majoritaire à un seul tour tend au dualisme des partis." Duverger, *Les partis politiques* (Paris: Armand Colin, 1958), 247. For a discussion, see William H. Riker, "The Two-party System and Duverger's Law: An Essay on the History of Political Science," *American Political Science Review* 76 (December 1982): 753–766. For a more recent statement by Duverger, see "Duverger's Law Forty Years Later," in *Electoral Laws and Their Political Consequences,* ed. Bernard Grofman and Arend Lijphart (New York: Agathan Press, 1986), 69–84. For more general discussions of the effects of electoral laws, see Rein Taagepera and Matthew Shugart, *Seats and Votes: The Effects and Determinants of Electoral Systems* (New Haven, Conn.: Yale University Press, 1989); and Gary W. Cox, *Making Votes Count: Strategic Coordination of the World's Electoral Systems* (Cambridge, UK: Cambridge University Press, 1997).

21. Duverger's inclusion of "a single ballot" in his formulation is redundant because in a plurality vote win system there would be no need for second ballots unless needed to break ties. With a large electorate, ties will be extremely rare.

22. Duverger, *Political Parties,* 218.

23. William H. Riker, *The Art of Political Manipulation* (New Haven, Conn.: Yale University Press, 1986), 79.

24. For the most extensive evidence for the 1968, 1980, and 1992 elections, see Paul R. Abramson et al., "Third-Party and Independent Candidates in American Politics: Wallace, Anderson, and Perot," *Political Science Quarterly* 110 (Fall 1997): 349–367. For the 1996 and 2000 elections, see Paul R. Abramson, John H. Aldrich, and David W. Rohde, *Change and Continuity in the 1996 and 1998 Elections* (Washington, D.C.: CQ Press, 1999), 118–120; and Paul R. Abramson, John H. Aldrich, and David W. Rohde, *Change and Continuity in the 2000 and 2002 Elections* (Washington, D.C.: CQ Press, 2003), 124–126.

25. Paul R. Abramson, John H. Aldrich, and David W. Rohde, *Change and Continuity in the 2004 and 2006 Elections* (Washington, D.C.: CQ Press, 2007), 55.

26. Strategic voting can occur under other voting systems as well, including runoff elections and proportional representation. For evidence about Israel and the Netherlands, see Paul R. Abramson et al., "Strategic Abandonment or Sincerely Second Best? The 1999 Israeli Prime Ministerial Election," *Journal of*

Politics 66 (August 2004): 706–728; and Abramson et al., "Comparing Strategic Voting under FPTP and PR," *Comparative Political Studies* 43 (January 2010).

27. See George C. Edwards III, *Why the Electoral College Is Bad for America* (New Haven, Conn.: Yale University Press, 2004).

28. For the most extensive argument in favor of this reform, see John R. Koza et al., *Every Vote Equal: A State-Based Plan for Electing the President by National Popular Vote*, 2nd ed. (Los Altos, Calif.: National Popular Vote Press, 2008).

29. For a discussion of the interstate compact proposal, see Ceaser, Busch, and Pitney, *Epic Journey*, 190. Their main criticism is that the proposed compact lacks provisions for runoff elections.

30. The only other elections in which incumbent presidents were defeated in two straight elections were in 1888, when Benjamin Harrison defeated Grover Cleveland, and in 1892, when Cleveland defeated Harrison. As David R. Mayhew shows, between 1792 and 2004 in-office parties held the White House about two-thirds of the time when they ran the incumbent president, but have only won half the time when they did not run an incumbent. See David R. Mayhew, "Incumbency Advantage in U.S. Presidential Elections: The Historical Record," *Political Science Quarterly* 123 (Summer 2008): 201–228.

31. For two studies of the Whig Party, see Michael F. Holt, *The Rise and Fall of the Whig Party: Jacksonian Politics and the Onset of the Civil War* (New York: Oxford University Press, 1999); and Daniel Walker Howe, *The Political Culture of the American Whigs* (Chicago: University of Chicago Press, 1979).

32. Former Whigs founded the Constitutional Union Party in 1860. Its candidate, John Bell, won 12.6 percent of the popular vote and thirty-nine of the 303 electoral votes.

33. For a discussion of agenda-setting during this period, see William H. Riker, *Liberalism against Populism: A Confrontation between the Theory of Democracy and the Theory of Social Choice* (San Francisco: W. H. Freeman, 1982), 213–232; and John H. Aldrich, *Why Parties? The Origin and Transformation of Political Parties in America* (Chicago: University of Chicago Press, 1995), 126–156.

34. As we described in the introduction to Part I, not all scholars agree with this assessment. The most important dissent is found in David R. Mayhew, *Electoral Realignments: A Critique of an American Genre* (New Haven, Conn.: Yale University Press, 2002), 43–69.

35. Michael Nelson, "The Presidential Election," in *The Elections of 1988*, ed. Michael Nelson (Washington, D.C.: CQ Press, 1989), 195–196.

36. After the 2000 election, the Republicans and Democrats each had fifty senators, and the Republicans held control of the Senate by virtue of Vice President Dick Cheney's tie-breaking vote. When Sen. James M. Jeffords of Vermont left the Republican Party to become an independent and to vote with the Democrats on the organization of the Senate, the Democrats took control of the Senate from June 2001 until January 2003.

37. If one further takes into account that Maine and Nebraska use a district system to select their electors, there are actually fifty-six separate contests.

38. Since ratification of the Twenty-third Amendment in 1961, the District of Columbia has had three electoral votes, which it first cast in the 1964 election.

39. Abramson, Aldrich, and Rohde, *Change and Continuity in the 2000 and 2002 Elections*, 56.

40. Gerald M. Pomper, "The Presidential Election: Change Comes to America," in *The Elections of 2008*, ed. Michael Nelson (Washington, D.C.: CQ Press, 2009), 65. Pomper counts visits between September 8, 2008, after the two conventions, and election eve, November 3, 2008 (personal communication, May 6, 2009). The Florida contest did turn out to be close, with Obama winning by only 2.8 percentage points. In Virginia, Obama won by 6.3 percentage points, only slightly less than his 7.2-point national margin.

41. According to the U.S. Census Bureau, the West is made up of thirteen states: Alaska, Arizona, California, Colorado, Hawaii, Idaho, Montana, Nevada, New Mexico, Oregon, Utah, Washington, and Wyoming. But as Walter Dean Burnham points out, for presidential elections the ninety-sixth meridian of longitude provides a dividing line. See Burnham, "The 1980 Earthquake," in *The Hidden Election: Politics and Economics in the 1980 Presidential Campaign*, ed. Thomas Ferguson and Joel Rogers (New York: Pantheon, 1981), 111. In this chapter, we consider Kansas, Nebraska, North Dakota, Oklahoma, and South Dakota to be western as well. Even though most of Texas lies to the west of the ninety-sixth meridian, we classify it as southern, because it was a Confederate state.

42. U.S. Department of Commerce, *Statistical Abstract of the United States*, 101st ed. (Washington, D.C.: Government Printing Office, 1980), 514.

43. Ironically, the media designate Republican-won states as "red states" and Democratic-won states as "blue states." Red is the color often associated with revolution and socialism. For example, the song "The Red Flag," composed by James Connell in 1889, became the official song of the British Labour Party. As for flags themselves, red is one of the three colors of the French tricolor, adopted in 1794 during the Revolution, and, aside from the hammer and sickle, the flag of the Soviet Union was red.

44. See Andrew Gelman et al., *Red State, Blue State, Rich State, Poor State: Why Americans Vote the Way They Do* (Princeton, N.J.: Princeton University Press, 2008).

45. Alan I. Abramowitz, *The 2008 Elections* (New York: Longman, 2009), 37.

46. Joseph A. Schlesinger, *Political Parties and the Winning of Office* (Ann Arbor: University of Michigan Press, 1991).

47. Pomper also notes that the standard deviation among the states increased between 2004 and 2008. See Pomper, "Presidential Election," 71.

48. See Schlesinger, *Political Parties and the Winning of Office*, figure 5-1, 112. Schlesinger does not report the exact values, but he provided them to us in a personal communication. Including the District of Columbia, which has voted for president since 1964, increases the standard deviation because the District always votes more Democratic than the most Democratic state. We have reported Schlesinger's results for states, not for his alternative results that include D.C. Likewise, our updated results are for the fifty states.

49. After the 2010 census, Texas seems likely to gain four House seats, and Florida, Georgia, and South Carolina one each. Louisiana is likely to lose one seat. If these projections hold and if the election rules do not change, the South will have 159 electoral votes.

50. V. O. Key Jr., *Southern Politics in State and Nation* (New York: Knopf, 1949), 5.

51. There have been many excellent studies of the postwar South. For one that presents state-by-state results, see Alexander P. Lamis, *The Two-Party South*, 2nd exp. ed. (New York: Oxford University Press, 1990). For three other studies, see Earl Black and Merle Black, *Politics and Society in the Postwar South* (Cambridge, Mass.: Harvard University Press, 1987); Black and Black, *The Rise of Southern Republicans* (Cambridge, Mass.: Harvard University Press, 2002); and David Lublin, *The Republican South: Democratization and Partisan Change* (Princeton, N.J.: Princeton University Press, 2004).

52. Alabama, Georgia, Louisiana, Mississippi, and South Carolina are considered the five Deep South states. They are also the five states with the highest percentage of African Americans.

53. Earlier that month, southern Democrats suffered a defeat at the Democratic presidential nominating convention. Their attempts to weaken the civil rights platform were defeated. Meanwhile, Hubert Humphrey, then mayor of Minneapolis, argued that the platform was too weak and offered an amendment for a stronger statement. Humphrey's amendment passed by a vote of 651½–582½.

54. Kennedy made a symbolic gesture that may have helped him with African Americans. Three weeks before the election, Martin Luther King Jr. was arrested in Atlanta for taking part in a sit-in demonstration. Although all the other demonstrators were released, King was held on a technicality and sent to the Georgia State Penitentiary. Kennedy telephoned King's wife to express his concern, and his brother Robert F. Kennedy Jr., acting as a private citizen, made a direct appeal to a Georgia judge that led to King's release on bail. This incident received little notice in the press, but it had a great effect on the African American community. See Theodore H. White, *The Making of the President, 1960* (New York: Atheneum, 1961), 321–323.

55. Chuck Todd and Sheldon Gawiser, with Ana Maria Arumi and G. Evans Witt, *How Obama Won: A State-by-State Guide to the Historic 2008 Presidential Election* (New York: Vintage Books, 2009), 146–150, 160–164.

56. For a discussion of the reasons for this lack of attention, see Peter F. Galderisi and Michael S. Lyons, "Realignment: Past and Present," in *The Politics of Realignment: Party Change in the Mountain West*, ed. Peter F. Galderisi et al. (Boulder, Colo.: Westview Press, 1987), 34.

57. Arizona seems likely to gain two House seats after the 2010 census, while Nevada and Utah are likely to gain one apiece. If so, the mountain West would have forty-eight electoral votes.

58. Eric R. A. N. Smith and Peverill Squire, "State and National Politics in the Mountain West," in Galderisi et al., *Politics of Realignment*, 34.

59. Todd and Gawiser, *How Obama Won,* 141–145.

60. Arthur H. Miller, "Political Opinion and Regional Political Realignment," in Galderisi et al., *Politics of Realignment,* 98.

61. Ibid., 100.

62. This will drop slightly if, as expected, Massachusetts loses one House seat after the 2010 census.

63. Fred R. Shapiro, ed., *The Yale Book of Quotations* (New Haven, Conn.: Yale University Press, 2006), 251. Maine used to hold its statewide and congressional elections in September, and these races were sometimes seen as a bellwether for the national elections in November. This led to the expression "As Maine goes, so goes the nation." The Republicans did well in these early elections in 1936 (and Landon carried the state in its November presidential election). These Maine victories, as well as the *Literary Digest* poll predicting a Landon win, encouraged some Republicans.

64. At the beginning of the 111th Congress, ten of the twelve U.S. senators from New England were Democrats. All twenty-two members of the U.S. House of Representatives from New England were Democrats. For more discussion, see Chapter 9.

65. Nicol C. Rae, *The Decline and Fall of Liberal Republicans* (New York: Oxford University Press, 1989), 145.

66. California became a state in 1850 and is the only state to gain representation after every reapportionment. This distinction seems likely to end, however. Some projections suggest it might lose one seat after the 2010 census; others suggest it will retain its fifty-five seats. Our discussion is based on the assumption that it will have the same number of seats.

67. We count Nixon as a resident of California in 1968, even though he officially ran as a resident of New York.

68. If one includes only major-party voters in 1968, Nixon received 51.7 percent of the vote in California and 50.4 percent in the nation as a whole.

69. Mark Baldassare, *A California State of Mind: The Conflicted Voter in a Changing World* (Berkeley: University of California Press, 2002), 159.

70. "California Exit Polls—President," http://msnbc.com, 2004, www.msnbc.msn.com/id/5297147.

71. CNN Election Center '08, www.cnn.com/ELECTION/2008/results/polls.

72. Baldassare, *California State of Mind,* 224.

73. For a figure demonstrating the Republican dominance between 1972 and 1988, see Abramson, Aldrich, and Rohde, *Change and Continuity in the 1992 Elections,* rev. ed., 47.

74. Marjorie Randon Hershey, "The Campaign and the Media," in *The Election of 1988: Reports and Interpretations,* ed. Gerald M. Pomper (Chatham, N.J.: Chatham House, 1989), 74. Hershey did not claim that a Democratic presidential candidate could not win, but wrote that "another powerful environmental factor working for Bush was the so-called Republican lock on the electoral college."

75. James C. Garand and Wayne T. Parent, "Representation, Swing, and Bias in U.S. Presidential Elections, 1872–1988," *American Journal of Political Science* 35 (November 1991): 1000–1001.

76. Michael Nelson, "Constitutional Aspects of the Elections," in Nelson, *Elections of 1988,* 103–195; I. M. Destler, "The Myth of the 'Electoral Lock,'" *PS: Political Science and Politics* 29 (September 1996): 491–494.

77. Andrew Gelman, Jonathan N. Katz, and Gary King, "Empirically Evaluating the Electoral College," in *Rethinking the Vote: The Politics and Prospects of Electoral Reform,* ed. Ann N. Crigler, Marion R. Just, and Edward J. McCaffrey (New York: Oxford University Press, 2004), 75–88.

78. For the electoral vote balance after the 2004 election, see Abramson, Aldrich, and Rohde, *Change and Continuity in the 2004 and 2006 Elections,* 71–72.

79. Because South Carolina and Utah are each likely to gain one House seat, these thirteen Republican states should yield 102 votes in the 2012 election. Bear in mind that the Republican presidential candidate was a Texan in three of these five elections.

80. If, as expected, Arizona gains two House seats and Georgia gains one, these states will yield seventy electoral votes in 2012.

81. Florida will probably gain one House seat after the 2010 census. But because Louisiana and Missouri are each likely to lose a House seat, the overall number of electoral votes for these states will probably drop to eighty-five.

82. Six of these states are expected to lose one seat: Illinois, Massachusetts, Michigan, New Jersey, New York, and Pennsylvania. Oregon is the only consistently Democratic state that seems slated to gain a House seat. If these projections hold, these consistently Democratic states (and D.C.) would yield 242 electoral votes.

83. Iowa is expected to lose a House seat, reducing the total to fifteen.

84. Ohio is expected to lose two House seats, while Nevada is expected to gain one, reducing the total to twenty-four.

85. If the projections discussed here are correct, the states that have voted Republican most of the time will yield 257 electoral votes; the states (plus D.C.) that have voted Democratic most of the time will yield 281 electoral votes.

INTRODUCTION TO PART II

1. According to Michael P. McDonald, 212,720,027 Americans were eligible to vote. See McDonald, "2008 General Election Turnout Rates," http://elections.gmu.edu/Turnout_2008G.html. We say "on or before" November 4 because in 2008 about one-third of voters voted before election day.

2. For an excellent set of articles dealing with some of the major controversies, see Richard G. Niemi and Herbert F. Weisberg, eds., *Controversies in Voting Behavior,* 4th ed. (Washington, D.C.: CQ Press, 2001). For two excellent

summaries of research on voting behavior, see Russell J. Dalton and Martin P. Wattenberg, "The Not So Simple Act of Voting," in *Political Science: The State of the Discipline II*, ed. Ada W. Finifter (Washington, D.C.: American Political Science Association, 1993), 193–218; and Morris P. Fiorina, "Parties, Participation, and Representation in America: Old Theories Face New Realities," in *Political Science: The State of the Discipline*, ed. Ira Katznelson and Helen V. Milner (New York: Norton, 2002), 511–541.

3. For a more extensive discussion of our arguments, see Paul R. Abramson, John H. Aldrich, and David W. Rohde, "Studying American Elections," in *The Oxford Handbook of American Elections and Political Behavior*, ed. Jan E. Leighley (New York: Oxford University Press, 2010), 700–715.

4. Paul F. Lazarsfeld, Bernard R. Berelson, and Hazel Gaudet, *The People's Choice: How the Voter Makes Up His Mind in a Presidential Campaign* (New York: Duell, Sloan, and Pearce, 1944), 27. See also Bernard R. Berelson, Paul F. Lazarsfeld, and William McPhee, *Voting: A Study of Opinion Formation in a Presidential Campaign* (Chicago: University of Chicago Press, 1954). Their index was created for analyzing voting in Erie County, Ohio, a basically rural setting with little racial diversity.

5. See Robert R. Alford, *Party and Society: The Anglo-American Democracies* (Chicago: Rand McNally, 1963); Richard F. Hamilton, *Class and Politics in the United States* (New York: Wiley, 1972); and Seymour Martin Lipset, *Political Man: The Social Bases of Politics*, exp. ed. (Baltimore: Johns Hopkins University Press, 1981). For a more recent book using the perspective, see Jeff Manza and Clem Brooks, *Social Cleavages and Political Change: Voter Alignments in U.S. Party Coalitions* (Oxford, UK: Oxford University Press, 1999).

6. Angus Campbell et al., *The American Voter* (New York: Wiley, 1960). For a recent assessment of the contribution of *The American Voter*, see William G. Jacoby, "The American Voter," in Leighley, *Oxford Handbook of American Elections and Political Behavior*, 262–277.

7. For an excellent summary of research on political psychology, see Donald R. Kinder, "Opinion and Action in the Realm of Politics," in *The Handbook of Social Psychology*, 4th ed., Vol. 3, ed. Gilbert T. Sullivan, Susan T. Fiske, and Gardner Lindzey (Boston: McGraw Hill, 1998), 778–867. For an alternative approach to the study of political psychology, see Paul M. Sniderman, Richard A. Brody, and Philip E. Tetlock, with others, *Reasoning and Choice: Explorations in Political Psychology* (Cambridge, UK: Cambridge University Press, 1991). See also Paul M. Sniderman, "The New Look in Public Opinion Research," in Finifter, *Political Science: The State of the Discipline II*. For two other perspectives, see John R. Zaller, *The Nature and Origins of Mass Opinion* (Cambridge, UK: Cambridge University Press, 1992); and Richard R. Lau and David P. Redlawsk, *How Voters Decide: Information Processing during an Election Campaign* (Cambridge, UK: Cambridge University Press, 2006).

8. His single most important contribution is "The Nature of Belief Systems in Mass Publics," in *Ideology and Discontent*, ed. David E. Apter (New York: Free

Press, 1964), 206–261. For the best single summary of his views on voting behavior, see Philip E. Converse, "Public Opinion and Voting Behavior," in *Nongovernmental Politics*, ed. Fred I. Greenstein and Nelson W. Polsby, Vol. 4, *Handbook of Political Science* (Reading, Mass.: Addison-Wesley, 1975), 75–169. For more recent summaries, see Philip E. Converse, "Researching Electoral Politics," *American Political Science Review* 100 (November 2006): 605–612; and Philip E. Converse, "Perspectives on Mass Political Systems and Communications," in *The Oxford Handbook of Political Behavior,* ed. Russell J. Dalton and Hans-Dieter Klingemann (New York: Oxford University Press, 2007), 144–158.

9. Warren E. Miller and J. Merrill Shanks, *The New American Voter* (Cambridge, Mass.: Harvard University Press, 1996). Although re-emphasizing the importance of party identification, this book also demonstrates a shift away from the social-psychological tradition employed by Miller and his colleagues in *The American Voter.*

10. Michael S. Lewis-Beck et al., *The American Voter Revisited* (Ann Arbor: University of Michigan Press, 2008).

11. Anthony Downs, *An Economic Theory of Democracy* (New York: Harper and Row, 1957); William H. Riker, *A Theory of Political Coalitions* (New Haven, Conn.: Yale University Press, 1962).

12. See, for example, William H. Riker and Peter C. Ordeshook, "A Theory of the Calculus of Voting," *American Political Science Review* 62 (March 1968): 25–32; John A. Ferejohn and Morris P. Fiorina, "The Paradox of Not Voting: A Decision Theocratic Analysis," *American Political Science Review* 68 (June 1974): 525–536; and Morris P. Fiorina, *Retrospective Voting in American National Elections* (New Haven, Conn.: Yale University Press, 1981). For summaries of much of this research, see Melvin J. Hinich and Michael Munger, *Analytical Politics* (Cambridge, UK: Cambridge University Press, 1977); Kenneth A. Shepsle and Mark A. Boncheck, *Analyzing Politics: Rationality, Behavior, and Institutions* (New York: Norton, 1977); and John H. Aldrich and Arthur Lupia, "Formal Modeling and Strategic Behavior in the Study of American Elections," in Leighley, *Oxford Handbook of American Elections and Political Behavior,* 89–106. For an interesting perspective that combines rational choice and psychological approaches, see Samuel L. Popkin, *The Reasoning Voter: Communication and Persuasion in Political Campaigns* (Chicago: University of Chicago Press, 1991). For an excellent introduction to American voting behavior that relies on a rational choice perspective, see Rebecca B. Morton, *Analyzing Elections* (New York: Norton, 2006).

13. For a more extensive discussion of the merits and limitations of these approaches, see Abramson, Aldrich, and Rohde, "Studying American Elections."

14. The most important exception, at least in the study of elections, is Fiorina's *Retrospective Voting,* to which we refer extensively. The most widely known critique of the rational choice perspective is Donald P. Green and Ian Shapiro, *Pathologies of Rational Choice Theory: A Critique of Applications in*

Political Science (New Haven, Conn.: Yale University Press, 1994). For critiques of Green and Shapiro, see Jeffrey Friedman, ed., *The Rational Choice Contro- versy: Economic Models of Politics Reconsidered* (New Haven, Conn.: Yale Univer- sity Press, 1966).

15. Michael P. McDonald and Samuel L. Popkin, "The Myth of the Vanishing Voter," *American Political Science Review* 95 (December 2001): 963–974. For a link to McDonald's results for 2008, see note 1.

4. WHO VOTED?

1. Michael P. McDonald and Samuel L. Popkin argue that turnout should be measured by dividing the number of voters by the population eligible to vote. See McDonald and Popkin, "The Myth of the Vanishing Voter," *American Politi- cal Science Review* 95 (December 2001): 963–974. We would have preferred to present the U.S. results using turnout based on both the voting-age and the voter-eligible population. Unfortunately, although this method would have been feasible for midterm elections, it would be difficult to compute the percentage voting for the House in presidential elections. If we had used the measure preferred by McDonald and Popkin, turnout would be somewhat higher in the United States, but it would still rank well below that in Switzerland.

2. In Australia, nonvoters may be subject to a small fine. In Belgium, they may suffer from future disfranchisement.

3. In both countries, turnout tends to be lower in noncompetitive districts. See Paul R. Abramson, Abraham Diskin, and Dan S. Felsenthal, "Nonvoting and the Decisiveness of Electoral Outcomes," *Political Research Quarterly* 60 (September 2007): 500–515.

4. For a discussion of turnout in comparative perspective, see Mark N. Franklin, *Voter Turnout and the Dynamics of Electoral Competition in Established Democracies Since 1945* (Cambridge, UK: Cambridge University Press, 2004). Franklin shows turnout trends between 1945 and 1999 for all these countries except Portugal, Spain, and the United States (11). Russell J. Dalton presents turnout trends based on the voting-age population between the 1950s and 2000s in all these countries except Israel, Luxembourg, and Malta. See *Citizen Politics: Public Opinion and Political Parties in Advanced Industrial Democracies*, 5th ed. (Washington, D.C.: CQ Press, 2008), 37.

5. According to Michael P. McDonald, the voting-eligible population in 2008 was 212,720,027. McDonald, "2008 General Election Turnout Rates," http://elections.gmu.edu/Turnout_2008G.html. Using his numbers, we would conclude that 81,417,295 nonvoters could have been eligible to vote.

6. This chapter focuses on one form of political participation, voting. For an excellent study of other forms of political participation, see M. Margaret Conway, *Political Participation in the United States*, 3rd ed. (Washington, D.C.: CQ Press, 2000). For a major study of other forms of political participation, see Sidney

Verba, Kay Lehman Schlozman, and Henry E. Brady, *Voice and Equality: Civic Voluntarism in American Politics* (Cambridge, Mass.: Harvard University Press, 1995). For a collection of essays on voting as well as other forms of political participation, see Russell J. Dalton and Hans-Dieter Klingemann, eds., *The Oxford Handbook of Political Behavior* (New York: Oxford University Press, 2007).

7. For a useful summary of the history of turnout in the United States, see Michael P. McDonald, "American Voter Turnout in Historical Perspective," in *The Oxford Handbook of American Elections and Political Behavior*, ed. Jan E. Leighley (New York: Oxford University Press, 2010), 125–143.

8. It is difficult to calculate the total number of voters, but in most elections more people vote for president than for any other office.

9. See Martin J. Kousser, *The Shaping of Southern Politics: Suffrage Restrictions and the Establishment of the One-Party South, 1880–1910* (New Haven, Conn.: Yale University Press, 1974). For a more general discussion, see Paul Kleppner, *Who Voted? The Dynamics of Electoral Turnout, 1870–1980* (New York: Praeger, 1982), 55–82.

10. There has been a great deal of disagreement about the reasons for and the consequences of registration requirements. For some of the more interesting arguments, see Walter Dean Burnham, "The Changing Shape of the American Political Universe," *American Political Science Review* 59 (March 1965): 7–28; Philip E. Converse, "Change in the American Electorate," in *The Human Meaning of Social Change*, ed. Angus Campbell and Philip E. Converse (New York: Russell Sage, 1972), 266–301; Walter Dean Burnham, "Theory and Voting Research: Some Reflections on Converse's 'Change in the American Electorate,'" *American Political Science Review* 68 (September 1974): 1002–1023. For two other perspectives, see Frances Fox Piven and Richard A. Cloward, *Why Americans Still Don't Vote and Why Politicians Want It That Way* (Boston: Beacon Press, 2000); and Matthew A. Crenson and Benjamin Ginsberg, *Downsizing America: How America Sidelined Its Citizens and Privatized Its Public* (Baltimore: Johns Hopkins University Press, 2002).

11. For a rich source of information on the introduction of the Australian ballot and its effects, see Jerrold G. Rusk, "The Effect of the Australian Ballot on Split-Ticket Voting, 1876–1908," *American Political Science Review* 64 (December 1970): 1220–1238.

12. Burnham presents estimates of turnout among the politically eligible population between 1789 and 1984 in "The Turnout Problem," in *Elections American Style*, ed. James A. Reichley (Washington, D.C.: Brookings, 1987), 113–114. In a series of personal communications, Burnham provided us with estimates of turnout between 1988 and 2004: 52.7 percent in 1988, 56.9 percent in 1992, 50.8 percent in 1996, 54.9 percent in 2000, and 60.7 percent in 2004. McDonald and Popkin's estimates of turnout between 1948 and 2000 are available in Michael P. McDonald and Samuel L. Popkin, "The Myth of the Vanishing Voter," *American Political Science Review* 95 (December 2001): 996. McDonald's

estimates for the 2004 and 2008 elections are available on a Web site he maintains, http://elections.gmu.edu.

13. McDonald, "2008 General Election Turnout Rates," http://elections.gmu/edu/Turnout_2008G.html.

14. Thomas E. Patterson, *The Vanishing Voter: Public Involvement in an Age of Uncertainty* (New York: Knopf, 2002). See also Pippa Norris, *Democratic Participation Worldwide* (Cambridge, UK: Cambridge University Press, 2002).

15. See note 13.

16. As Table 4-3 shows, the 1960 election was not only a high turnout election but also one in which a very small share of the electorate voted for a third-party or independent candidate.

17. Burnham estimated turnout at 65.4 percent, and McDonald and Popkin estimated it at 63.8 percent. See Burnham, "Turnout Problem," 114; and McDonald and Popkin, "Myth of the Vanishing Voter," 966.

18. See Glenn Firebaugh and Kevin Chen, "Vote Turnout among Nineteenth Amendment Women: The Enduring Effects of Disfranchisement," *American Journal of Sociology* 100 (January 1995): 972–996.

19. For estimates of this reform on turnout, see Raymond E. Wolfinger and Jonathan Hoffman, "Registering and Voting with Motor Voter," *PS: Political Science and Politics* 34 (March 2001): 86–92. David Hill argues that while motor voter legislation has made the election rolls more representative, it has had little effect on turnout. See David Hill, *American Voter Turnout: An Institutional Perspective* (Boulder, Colo.: Westview Press, 2006), 49–52, 55.

20. United States Election Project, "2008 Current Population Survey Voting and Registration Supplement," http://elections.gmu/CPS_2008.html. The 2000 CPS was based on 80,667 respondents in each household studied. One person answers for all household members, and the survey provides information on about 132,812 respondents. We are grateful to McDonald for providing us with information on the number of respondents. As he points out, much of the information is not based on true self-reports (personal communication, May 22, 2009). The most important study to use the CPS remains Raymond E. Wolfinger and Steven J. Rosenstone, *Who Votes?* (New Haven, Conn.: Yale University Press, 1980).

21. As Wolfinger and Rosenstone demonstrate, about one-fifth of this decline resulted from the enfranchisement of eighteen-, nineteen-, and twenty-year-olds. Their nationwide enfranchisement stemmed from the 1971 ratification of the Twenty-sixth Amendment, which made it possible for more people to vote, but because these youth have low levels of voting, overall levels of turnout declined. See Wolfinger and Rosenstone, *Who Votes?* 58.

22. For our analysis of the reasons for the increase in turnout in 1992, see Paul R. Abramson, John H. Aldrich, and David W. Rohde, *Change and Continuity in the 1992 Elections,* rev. ed. (Washington, D.C.: CQ Press, 1995), 120–123. As we point out, it is difficult to demonstrate empirically that Perot's candidacy

made an important contribution to the increase in turnout. For additional analyses, see Stephen M. Nichols and Paul Allen Beck, "Reversing the Decline: Voter Turnout in 1992," in *Democracy's Feast: Elections in America,* ed. Herbert F. Weisberg (Chatham, N.J.: Chatham House, 1995), 62–65; and Steven J. Rosenstone, Roy L. Behr, and Edward H. Lazarus, *Third Parties in America: Citizen Response to Major-Party Failure,* 2nd ed. (Princeton, N.J.: Princeton University Press, 1996), 254–257.

23. In our analysis of the 1980, 1984, 1988, and 1992 elections, we also made extensive use of the Current Population Survey conducted by the U.S. Census Bureau. In 1996 only a preliminary report was available, but we used it wherever possible. In 2000 no report of the CPS was available at the time of our analysis. The Census Bureau published a detailed report of its 2004 survey in May 2005 and of its 2008 survey in July 2009. See U.S. Census Bureau, *Voting and Registration in the Election of November 2008,* http://www.census.gov/population/www/cps2008.html.

24. Half the respondents were asked:

In talking to people about elections, we often find that a lot of people were not able to vote because they weren't registered, they were sick, or they just didn't have time. Which of the following statements best describes you?
    One, I did not vote (in the election this November);
    Two, I thought about voting this time—but didn't;
    Three, I usually vote, but didn't this time;
    Four, I am sure I voted.

We classified respondents as voters if they were sure that they voted. The other half was asked a new version of the question:

In asking people about the elections, we often find that a lot of people were not able to vote because they weren't registered, they were sick, they didn't have time to vote, or something else happened to prevent them from voting.
    And sometimes, people who usually vote or who planned to vote forget that something unusual happened on Election Day one year that prevented them from voting that time. So please think carefully for a minute about the recent elections, and other past elections in which you may have voted and answer the following questions about your voting behavior.
    During the past 6 years did you USUALLY VOTE in national, state, and local elections, or did you USUALLY NOT VOTE?
    During the months leading up to the election, did you ever plan to vote, or didn't you plan to do that?
    Which of the following best describes what you did in the elections that were held November 4:

1. Definitely did not vote in the elections.
2. Definitely voted in person at a polling place on election day.
3. Definitely voted in person at a polling place before election day.
4. Definitely voted by mailing a ballot to election officials before election day.
5. Definitely voted some other way.
6. Not completely sure of whether you voted or not.

We classified respondents as voters if they were definitely sure they voted.

There was no significant difference in reported voting between respondents asked the first ("old") and the second ("new") version of the question. Among respondents who were asked the first version ($N = 1,053$), 77.3 percent said they voted for president; among those who were asked the second version ($N = 1,049$), 76.5 percent said they voted for president.

25. Most analyses that compare the results of reported voting with those measured by the validation studies suggest that *relative* levels of turnout among most social groups can be compared using reported turnout. However, these studies suggest that blacks are more likely to falsely claim to have voted than whites. As a result, racial differences are always greater when turnout is measured by the vote validation studies. For results for the 1964, 1976, 1978, 1980, 1984, 1986, and 1988 elections, see Paul R. Abramson and William Claggett, "Racial Differences in Self-Reported and Validated Voting in the 1988 Presidential Election," *Journal of Politics* 53 (February 1991): 186–187. For results for 1990, see Abramson, Aldrich, and Rohde, *Change and Continuity in the 1992 Elections*, 382. For a discussion of the factors that contribute to false reports of voting, see Brian D. Silver, Barbara A. Anderson, and Paul R. Abramson, "Who Overreports Voting?" *American Political Science Review* 80 (June 1986): 613–624. For a more recent study that argues that biases in reported turnout are more severe than Silver, Anderson, and Abramson claim, see Robert Bernstein, Anita Chadha, and Robert Montjoy, "Overreporting Voting: Why It Happens and Why It Matters," *Public Opinion Quarterly* 65 (Spring 2001): 22–44.

26. See Michael W. Traugott and John P. Katosh, "Response Validity in Surveys of Voting Behavior," *Public Opinion Quarterly* 43 (Fall 1979): 359–377; and Barbara A. Anderson, Brian D. Silver, and Paul R. Abramson, "The Effects of the Race of the Interviewer on Measures of Electoral Participation on Blacks in SRC National Election Surveys," *Public Opinion Quarterly* 52 (Spring 1988): 22–44.

27. In this analysis, we classify eleven respondents who said they voted but not for president as nonvoters.

28. Respondents were classified by the interviewer into one of the following categories: white; black/African American; white and black; other race; white and another race; black and another race; white, black, and another race. We classified only respondents who were white as whites; except for Asians, respondents in the other categories were classified as blacks.

29. See Warren E. Miller, Arthur H. Miller, and Edward J. Schneider, *American National Studies Data Sourcebook, 1952–1978* (Cambridge, Mass.: Harvard University Press, 1980), table 5.23, 317.

30. According to the 1964 ANES survey, whites were 14.7 percentage points more likely to report voting than blacks. See ibid.

31. See U.S. Census Bureau, *Voting and Registration in the Election of November 2004*, http://census.gov/prod/2006/p250.556.pdf, table B.

32. The results for 2004 are from "Election Results," CNN.com, www.cnn. com/ELECTION/2004/pages/results/state. The results for 2008 are from CNN Election Center '08, CNN.com, www/cnn/com/ELECTION/2008/results/polls.

33. Bear in mind that this tendency was found in all eight vote validation studies. The vote validation studies are not error-free, because some true voters may be classified as validated nonvoters if researchers cannot find a record that they registered or if the records inaccurately fail to show that they voted. The voting records in areas in which African Americans live are not as well maintained as those in areas in which whites are likely to live. Still, it seems unlikely that the finding that blacks are more likely to falsely report voting results from the poorer quality of black voting records. See Paul R. Abramson and William Claggett, "The Quality of Record-Keeping and Racial Differences in Validated Turnout," *Journal of Politics* 54 (August 1992): 871–880. See also Carol A. Cassel, "Voting Records and Validated Voting Studies," *Public Opinion Quarterly* 68 (Spring 2004): 102–108.

34. As we note in the introduction to Part I, there was a supplemental sample of blacks and Latinos, but we still do not have the information needed to analyze a representative version of this oversample.

35. As we explain in Chapter 3, we consider the South to include the eleven states of the old Confederacy. In our analysis of ANES surveys, however, we do not classify residents of Tennessee as southern because the University of Michigan Survey Research Center conducts samples in Tennessee to represent the border states. In this analysis, as well as analyses of ANES surveys later in this book, we classify the following ten states as southern: Alabama, Arkansas, Florida, Georgia, Louisiana, Mississippi, North Carolina, South Carolina, Texas, and Virginia.

36. U.S. Census Bureau, *Voting and Registration in the Election of November 2008*, table 3.

37. Ibid. The Census Bureau includes several border states in its definition of the South.

38. Miller, Miller, and Schneider, *American National Studies Data Sourcebook*, table 5.23, 317.

39. U.S. Census Bureau, *Current Population Survey, November 2006 and Earlier Reports*, www.census.gov/cps, table A-2.

40. U.S. Census Bureau, *Voting and Registration in the Election of November 2008*, table 2.

41. See Benjamin Highton and Raymond E. Wolfinger, "The First Seven Years of the Political Life Cycle," *American Journal of Political Science* 45 (January 2001): 202–209.

42. Our measure of family income is based on the respondents' estimates of their family income in 2007 before taxes. In those cases in which respondents refused to reveal family income or in which interviewers thought respondents were answering dishonestly, we relied on the interviewers' assessments.

43. Miller, Miller, and Schneider, *American National Studies Data Sourcebook*, table 5.23, 317.

44. U.S. Census Bureau, *Voting and Registration in the Election of November 2008*, table 7.

45. See Wolfinger and Rosenstone, *Who Votes?* 13–36.

46. Miller, Miller, and Schneider, *American National Studies Data Sourcebook*, table 5.23, 317.

47. The CPS has never measured religious preferences.

48. Miller, Miller, and Schneider, *American National Data Sourcebook*, table 5.23, 317. Between 1952 and 1976, Catholics were on average 8.0 percentage points more likely to vote in presidential elections, and between 1958 and 1988 they were 10.8 points more likely to vote in midterm elections.

49. Respondents were asked, "Would you call yourself a born-again Christian, that is, have you personally had a conversion experience related to Jesus Christ?"

50. Lyman A. Kellstedt, "An Agenda for Future Research," in *Rediscovering the Religious Factor in American Politics,* ed. David C. Leege and Lyman A. Kellstedt (Armonk, N.Y.: M. E. Sharpe, 1993), 293–299.

51. We are grateful to David C. Leege for providing us with the detailed information used to construct this measure. We constructed it as follows. Respondents who prayed several times a day received 2 points, those who prayed less often received a score of 1, and those who never prayed received 0 points. Those who attended religious services at least once a week received 2 points, those who attended less frequently received 1 point, and those who never attended received 0 points. Those who said religion provided "a great deal" of guidance in their lives received 2 points, those who said it provided "quite a bit" received 1 point, and those who said it provided "some" or no guidance received 0 points. Those who said the Bible was literally true or the "word of God" received 2 points, and those who said it "was written by men and is not the word of God" received 0 points. Respondents received a score of 1 for each ambiguous, "don't know," or "not ascertained" response, but respondents with more than two such responses were excluded from the analysis. Scores ranged from 0 to 8. In regrouping the scores into three categories, we classified respondents with 8 points as "very high," those with 6 or 7 points as "high," and those with a score below 6 as "medium or low" on religious commitment.

52. Kenneth D. Wald, *Religion and Politics in the United States,* 4th ed. (Lanham, Md.: Rowman and Littlefield, 2003), 161.

53. R. Stephen Warner, *New Wine in Old Wineskins: Evangelicals and Liberals in a Small-Town Church* (Berkeley: University of California Press, 1977), 173.

54. The branching questions used to classify respondents into specific denominational categories were changed in 2008, and therefore it is not possible to replicate our analyses of the 1992, 1996, 2000, and 2004 categories. In creating these new classifications, we relied largely on the Pew Forum on Religion and Public Life, *U.S. Religious Landscape Survey: Religious Affiliation, Diverse and Dynamic* (Washington, D.C.: Pew Forum on Religion and Public Life, 2008), 12. In addition, we were assisted by Corwin D. Smidt.

Our classification for 2008 used the following procedures. We used the variable v083185x in the 2008 ANES survey to determine the respondent's denomination. Codes 110, 150, 200, 229, 230, and 270 for this variable were classified as mainline; codes 120–149, 165– 200, 221, 223, and 250–269 were classified as evangelical.

55. See Miller, Miller, and Schneider, *American National Election Studies Data Sourcebook*, table 5-23, 317.

56. U.S. Census Bureau, *Voting and Registration in the Election of November 2008*, table 6.

57. Silver, Anderson, and Abramson's analysis of the 1964, 1968, and 1980 vote validation studies finds that Americans with high levels of education do have very high levels of turnout. However, their analysis also finds that persons with high levels of formal education who do not vote are more likely to claim falsely that they voted than nonvoters with lower levels of formal education. See Silver, Anderson, and Abramson, "Who Overreports Voting?" Our analysis shows a similar pattern for the 1978, 1984, 1986, 1988, and 1990 vote validation studies. We do not know if a similar pattern would be found in 2008, but, if it were, the results in Table 4-4 may somewhat exaggerate the relationship between age and formal education.

58. According to Jeff Manza and Christopher Uggen, 5.3 million Americans were disfranchised in 2004 because they were parolees or ex-felons or were in prison or in jail on election day. See Manza and Uggen, *Locked Out: Felon Disfranchisement and American Democracy* (New York: Oxford University Press, 2006), 76.

59. U.S. Census Bureau, *The 2009 Statistical Abstract of the United States* March 24, 2009, table 221, www.census.gov/compendia/statab/cats/education/educational_attainment/html.

60. Richard A. Brody, "The Puzzle of Political Participation in America," in *The New American Political System*, ed. Anthony King (Washington, D.C.: American Enterprise Institute, 1978), 287–324.

61. Walter Dean Burnham, "The 1976 Election: Has the Crisis Been Adjourned?" in *American Politics and Public Policy*, ed. Walter Dean Burnham and Martha Wagner Weinberg (Cambridge, Mass.: MIT Press, 1976), 24; Thomas E. Cavanagh, "Changes in American Voter Turnout, 1964–1976," *Political Science Quarterly* 96 (Spring 1981): 53–65.

62. Ruy A. Teixeira, *The Disappearing American Voter* (Washington, D.C.: American Enterprise Institute, 1992), 66–67. Teixeira is skeptical about our finding that the ANES surveys show that turnout did not decline among college graduates.

63. We assume that educational levels were the same in 2008 as they were in 1960, but that reported levels of turnout were the same as they were in the 2008 survey.

64. Teixeira, *Disappearing American Voter,* 47.

65. Steven J. Rosenstone and John Mark Hansen, *Mobilization, Participation, and Democracy in America* (New York: Macmillan, 1993), 214–215. For another discussion of changes in registration requirements, see Hill, *American Voter Turnout,* 33–57.

66. Teixeira, *Disappearing American Voter,* 47.

67. Rosenstone and Hansen, *Mobilization, Participation, and Democracy,* 215.

68. Warren E. Miller, "The Puzzle Transformed: Explaining Declining Turnout," *Political Behavior* 14, no. 1 (1992): 1–43. See also Warren E. Miller and J. Merrill Shanks, *The New American Voter* (Cambridge, Mass.: Harvard University Press, 1996), 95–114.

69. Robert D. Putnam, *Bowling Alone: The Collapse and Revival of American Community* (New York: Simon and Schuster, 2000), 265.

70. George I. Balch, "Multiple Indicators in Survey Research: The Concept 'Sense of Political Efficacy,'" *Political Methodology* 1 (Spring 1974): 1–43. For an extensive discussion of feelings of political efficacy, see Paul R. Abramson, *Political Attitudes in America: Formation and Change* (San Francisco: W. H. Freeman, 1983): 135–189. These are the same two fundamental attitudes that Teixeira studied in this first major analysis of the decline of turnout, and they are among the attitudes studied by Rosenstone and Hansen.

71. Ruy A. Teixeira, *Why Americans Don't Vote: Turnout Decline in the United States, 1960–1964* (New York: Greenwood Press, 1987). In his more recent study, *The Disappearing American Voter,* Teixeira develops a measure of party-related characteristics that includes strength of party identification, concern about the electoral outcome, perceived difference between the parties, and knowledge about the parties and the candidates. See also Rosenstone and Hansen, *Mobilization, Participation, and Democracy.*

72. Our first analysis studied the decline of turnout between 1960 and 1980. See Paul R. Abramson, John H. Aldrich, and David W. Rohde, *Change and Continuity in the 1980 Elections,* rev. ed. (Washington, D.C.: CQ Press, 1983), 85–87. For a more detailed analysis using probability procedures, see Paul R. Abramson and John H. Aldrich, "The Decline of Electoral Participation in America," *American Political Science Review* 76 (September 1982): 502–521.

73. See note 72 for our analyses through 1980. For our analyses from 1984 through 2004, see Paul R. Abramson, John H. Aldrich, and David W. Rohde, *Change and Continuity in the 1984 Elections,* rev. ed. (Washington, D.C.: CQ

Press, 1987), 115–118; Abramson, Aldrich, and Rohde, *Change and Continuity in the 1988 Elections,* rev. ed. (Washington, D.C.: CQ Press, 1991), 103–106; *Change and Continuity in the 1992 Elections,* 117–120; Abramson, Aldrich, and Rohde, *Change and Continuity in the 1996 and 1998 Elections* (Washington, D.C.: CQ Press, 1999), 81–84; Abramson, Aldrich, and Rohde, *Change and Continuity in the 2000 and 2002 Elections* (Washington, D.C.: CQ Press, 2003), 86–99; and Abramson, Aldrich, and Rohde, *Change and Continuity in the 2004 and 2006 Elections* (Washington, D.C.: CQ Press, 2007), 97–100.

74. The questions used to build the standard measure of party identification are as follows: "Generally speaking, do you usually think of yourself as a Republican, a Democrat, an Independent, or what?" Persons who call themselves Republicans are asked, "Would you call yourself a strong Republican or a not very strong Republican?" Those who call themselves Democrats are asked, "Would you call yourself a strong Democrat or a not very strong Democrat?" Those who called themselves independents, named another party, or who had no preference were asked, "Do you think of yourself as closer to the Republican party or to the Democratic party?" Respondents with no preference are usually classified as independents. They are classified as "apoliticals" only if they have low levels of political interest and political involvement.

In 2008 a question wording experiment was employed in which a randomly selected half-sample was initially asked, "Generally speaking, do you think of yourself as a Democrat, a Republican, an Independent, or what?"

The order in which the two major parties are named has little effect. When the standard question was asked, 59 percent of party identifiers ($N = 708$) were Democrats; when the experimental question was asked, 55 percent of the party identifiers ($N = 664$) were Democrats.

75. For the seminal discussion of turnout from the rational choice perspective, see Anthony Downs, *An Economic Theory of Democracy* (New York: Harper and Row, 1957), 260–276. For a more recent formulation, see John H. Aldrich, "Rational Choice and Turnout," *American Journal of Political Science* 37 (February 1993): 246–278. For a comment on Aldrich's essay, see Robert W. Jackman, "Rationality and Political Participation," *American Journal of Political Science* 37 (February 1993): 279–290.

76. Our measure is based on the responses to two statements: "Public officials don't care much what people like me think," and "People like me don't have any say about what the government does." Respondents who disagreed with both of these statements were scored as high in feelings of effectiveness; those who agreed with one statement and disagreed with the other were scored as medium; and those who agreed with both statements were scored as low. Respondents who scored "don't know" or "not ascertained" to one statement were scored high or low according to their answer on the other statement. Those with "don't know" or "not ascertained" responses to both statements were excluded from the analysis. In 1988, 1992, 1996, 2000, 2004, and 2008, respondents were asked whether they "strongly agreed," "agreed," "disagreed," or

"strongly disagreed" with the statements. In all six years, we classified respondents who "neither agreed nor disagreed" with both statements as medium on this measure. This decision has little effect on the results since only 3 percent of the respondents in 1988, 2 percent in 1992, 3 percent in 1996, 4 percent in 2000, 5 percent in 2004, and 5 percent in 2008 answered "neither agree nor disagree" to both statements. In 2008 this standard measure of feelings of "external" political efficacy was asked of only half of the sample.

77. These estimates are based on the assumption that each partisanship and strength of political efficacy category was the same size in 2008 as it was in 1960, but that the reported turnout for each category was the same as we observed in 2008. For an additional explanation of this procedure, see Abramson, *Political Attitudes in America*, 296.

78. We used an algebraic standardization procedure. To simplify our analysis, we combined whites with an eighth-grade education or less with whites who had not graduated from high school; we also combined weak partisans with independents who leaned toward a party.

79. This difference appears to result from the very low level of reported turnout among whites who had not graduated from high school. This group has a substantial effect on our estimates. In 1960, 47 percent of whites in the ANES survey had not graduated from high school; in 2008 this figure was down to 10 percent.

80. For a discussion of political trust, see Abramson, *Political Attitudes in America*, 193–238. For a more recent discussion, see Marc J. Hetherington, *Why Trust Matters: Declining Political Trust and the Demise of American Liberalism* (Princeton, N.J.: Princeton University Press, 2005).

Russell J. Dalton reports a decline in confidence in politicians and government in fifteen of sixteen democracies. Although many of the trends are not statistically significant, the overall decline is impressive. Dalton's report includes results from the ANES, where the trend toward declining confidence is unlikely to occur by chance on two of the three questions. See Dalton, *Democratic Challenges, Democratic Choices: The Erosion of Political Support in Advanced Industrial Democracies* (Oxford, UK: Oxford University Press, 2004), 28–32.

81. Respondents were asked, "How much of the time do you think you can trust the government in Washington to do what is right—just about always, most of the time, or only some of the time?"

82. This question was asked of a randomly selected half-sample in 2008.

83. Respondents were asked, "Would you say the government is pretty much run for a few big interests looking out for themselves or that it is run for the benefit of all the people?"

84. Respondents were asked, "The political parties try to talk to as many people as they can to get them to vote for their candidate. Did anyone from the political parties call or come around to talk with you about the campaign this year?"

85. As Paul R. Abramson and William Claggett show, the effects of contacting potential participants persist even when one takes into account that political elites are more likely to contact people who have participated in the past. See Paul R. Abramson and William Claggett, "Recruitment and Political Participation," *Political Research Quarterly* 54 (December 2001): 905–916.

86. Orley Ashenfelter and Stanley Kelley Jr., "Determinants of Participation in Presidential Elections," *Journal of Law and Economics* 18 (December 1975): 721.

87. James DeNardo, "Turnout and the Vote: The Joke's on the Democrats," *American Political Science Review* 74 (December 1980): 406–420.

88. Abramson, Aldrich, and Rohde, *Change and Continuity in the 1980 Elections,* 88–92; *Change and Continuity in the 1984 Elections,* 119–124; *Change and Continuity in the 1988 Elections,* 108–112.

89. Abramson, Aldrich, and Rohde, *Change and Continuity in the 1992 Elections,* 124–128.

90. Abramson, Aldrich, and Rohde, *Change and Continuity in the 1996 and 1998 Elections,* 86–89.

91. Gerald M. Pomper, "The Presidential Election," in *The Election of 2000: Reports and Interpretations,* ed. Gerald M. Pomper (New York: Chatham House, 2001), 114.

92. Paul R. Abramson, John H. Aldrich, and David W. Rohde, "The 2004 Presidential Election: The Emergence of a Permanent Majority," *Political Science Quarterly* 120 (Spring 2005): 43.

93. For our analysis of the impact of increased turnout in 2004, see Abramson, Aldrich, and Rohde, *Change and Continuity in the 2004 and 2006 Elections,* 100–105.

94. The results for 1980, 1984, and 1988 are based on an actual check of the voting and registration records to determine whether respondents voted. However, the Republican advantage was also found when we studied reported electoral participation.

95. The kind and number of issues used varied from election to election. We used only issues on which respondents were asked to state their own positions and where they thought the major-party candidates were located. See Table 6-4 for the number of issues used in each election between 1980 and 2004.

96. Abramson, Aldrich, and Rohde, *Change and Continuity in the 2000 and 2002 Elections,* 92–93, 143.

97. As part of a question-wording experiment, only the question about blacks was asked to the entire sample, whereas the remaining six were asked to a randomly chosen half-sample. As a result, the number of cases for the balance of issues measure is only half the number for party identification or for our measure of retrospective evaluations.

98. The 2004 measure was based on (1) an evaluation of Bush's performance as president; (2) an assessment of how good a job the government was doing solving the most important problem facing the country; and (3) the

respondent's assessment of which party would do a better job of dealing with the economy, terrorism, and keeping the United States out of war.

99. For the most influential statement of this argument, see Wolfinger and Rosenstone, *Who Votes?* 108–114.

100. Frances Fox Piven and Richard A. Cloward, *Why Americans Don't Vote* (New York: Pantheon Books, 1988), 21. See also Piven and Cloward, *Why Americans Still Don't Vote.*

101. Seymour Martin Lipset, *Political Man: The Social Bases of Politics,* enlarged ed. (Baltimore: Johns Hopkins University Press, 1981), 226–229. Lipset emphasized the dangers of sudden increases in political participation.

102. Gerald M. Pomper, "The Presidential Election," in *The Elections of 1980: Reports and Interpretations,* ed. Gerald M. Pomper (Chatham, N.J.: Chatham House, 1981), 86.

103. "When People Vote," *The Rhodes Cook Letter,* March 2005, 7. Clearly, Cook resorts to hyperbole when he refers to U.S. turnout as "sky high." U.S. turnout was not sky high by either cross-national standards (see Table 4-1) or by U.S. historical standards (Table 4-2).

5. SOCIAL FORCES AND THE VOTE

1. The social characteristics used in this chapter are the same as those used in Chapter 4. The variables are described in the notes to that chapter. For similar tables showing the results for elections between 1980 and 2004, see Paul R. Abramson, John H. Aldrich, and David W. Rohde, *Change and Continuity in the 1980 Elections,* rev. ed. (Washington, D.C.: CQ Press, 1983), 98–99; Abramson, Aldrich, and Rohde, *Change and Continuity in the 1984 Elections,* rev. ed. (Washington, D.C.: CQ Press, 1987), 136–137; Abramson, Aldrich, and Rohde, *Change and Continuity in the 1988 Elections,* rev. ed. (Washington, D.C.: CQ Press, 1991), 124–125; Abramson, Aldrich, and Rohde, *Change and Continuity in the 1992 Elections,* rev. ed. (Washington, D.C.: CQ Press, 1995), 133–135; Abramson, Aldrich, and Rohde, *Change and Continuity in the 1996 and 1998 Elections* (Washington, D.C.: CQ Press, 1999), 93–95; Abramson, Aldrich, and Rohde, *Change and Continuity in the 2000 and 2002 Elections* (Washington, D.C.: CQ Press, 2003), 98–100; and Abramson, Aldrich, and Rohde, *Change and Continuity in the 2004 and 2006 Elections* (Washington, D.C.: CQ Press, 2007), 109–110.

2. We frequently compare the 2008 results with those in 2004. In that year, the ANES survey was very small; it included only eight hundred self-reported voters.

3. For a discussion of our sources for these polls, see Abramson, Aldrich, and Rohde, *Change and Continuity in the 2004 and 2006 Elections,* 358n3. We present an analysis of these exit poll results in Paul R. Abramson, John H. Aldrich, and David W. Rohde, "The 2004 Presidential Election: The Making of a Permanent Majority?" *Political Science Quarterly* 120 (Spring 2005): 33–57.

Exit polls have three main advantages: (1) they are less expensive to conduct than the multistage probability samples conducted by the Survey Research Center of the University of Michigan; (2) because of their lower cost, a large number of people can be sampled; and (3) because persons are selected to be interviewed as they leave the polling stations, the vast majority of respondents have actually voted. But these surveys also have four disadvantages: (1) organizations that conduct exit polls must now take into account the growing number of voters who vote early—about a third of all voters in 2008; (2) the self-administered polls used for respondents leaving the polls must be relatively brief; (3) it is difficult to supervise the fieldwork to ensure that interviewers are using the proper procedures to select respondents; and (4) these studies are of relatively little use in studying turnout because persons who do not vote are not sampled. For a discussion of the procedures used to conduct exit polls and their limitations, see Albert H. Cantril, *The Opinion Connection: Polling, Politics, and the Press* (Washington, D.C.: CQ Press, 1991), 142–144, 216–218.

4. This brief discussion cannot do justice to the complexities of black electoral participation. For an important study based on the 1984 ANES survey of blacks, see Patricia Gurin, Shirley Hatchett, and James S. Jackson, *Hope and Independence: Blacks' Response to Electoral and Party Politics* (New York: Russell Sage Foundation, 1989). For two important studies that use this survey, see Michael C. Dawson, *Behind the Mule: Race and Class in African American Politics* (Princeton, N.J.: Princeton University Press, 1994); and Katherine Tate, *From Politics to Protest: The New Black Voter in American Elections* (Cambridge, Mass.: Harvard University Press, 1994). For a summary of recent research on race and politics, see Michael C. Dawson and Cathy Cohen, "Problems in the Politics of Race," in *Political Science: The State of the Discipline,* ed. Ira Katznelson and Helen V. Milner (New York: Norton, 2002), 488–510.

5. With the weighted data, only one black voted for McCain. If one examines the black supplement, only two black voters did. The pool poll compares black women with black men, but there was no meaningful difference between them. Ninety-six percent of black women voted for Obama; 95 percent of black men did.

6. For a summary of evidence about the Latino vote in 2004, see David L. Leal et al., "The Latino Vote in 2004," *PS: Political Science and Politics* 38 (January 2005).

7. For a review of research on Latinos as well as African Americans, see Paula McClain and John D. Garcia, "Expanding Disciplinary Boundaries: Black, Latino, and Racial Minority Groups in Political Science," in *Political Science: The State of the Discipline II,* ed. Ada W. Finifter (Washington, D.C.: American Political Science Association, 1993), 247–279. For analyses of Latino voting in the 1996 elections, see Rudolfo O. de la Garza and Louis DeSipio, eds., *Awash in the Mainstream: Latino Politics in the 1976 Election* (Boulder, Colo.: Westview Press, 1999). For a more recent review, see John D. Garcia, "Latinos and Political

Behavior: Defining Community to Examine Critical Complexities," in *The Oxford Handbook of American Elections and Political Behavior*, ed. Jan E. Leighley (New York: Oxford University Press, 2010), 397–414.

8. With the weighted sample, there are only thirteen Cuban American voters, seven of whom voted for Obama. Even with the Latino oversample, there are only twenty-two Cuban American voters.

9. For three reviews of research on women in politics, see Susan J. Carroll and Linda M. Zerelli, "Feminist Challenges to Political Science," in Finifter, *Political Science: The State of the Discipline II*, 55–76; Nancy Burns, "Gender: Public Opinion and Political Action," in Katznelson and Milner, *Political Science: The State of the Discipline*, 462–487; and Kira Sanbonmastu, "Organizing American Politics, Organizing Gender," in Leighley, *Oxford Handbook of American Elections and Political Behavior*, 415–432.

10. See Abramson, Aldrich, and Rohde, *Change and Continuity in the 1980 Elections*, 290.

11. The ANES survey reports six types of marital status: married, divorced, separated, widowed, never married, and partners who are not married. Here we compare the first two groups. Two different questions were used to measure marital status. Half the respondents were asked, "Are you married now, and living with your (husband/wife)—or are you widowed, divorced, separated, or have you never been married?" The other half were asked, "Are you married, divorced, separated, widowed, or have you never been married?" There was very little difference in the responses. Among respondents asked the standard version of the question ($N = 1,100$), 51.4 percent said they were married, and 24.8 percent said they had never been married. Among those asked the new question ($N = 993$), 48.6 percent said they were married, and 25.7 percent said they had never been married.

12. Exit polls ask voters to cast a "secret ballot" after they have left the polling station. They are handed a short form that records the respondent's behavior, political views, and demographic information. Use of this procedure reduces the pressure for the respondent to answer in a socially "acceptable" way.

13. Respondents were asked, "Do you consider yourself to be heterosexual or straight, homosexual or gay (lesbian), or bisexual?" This question was asked using an Audio Computer-Assisted Self-Interview (ACASI) in which the respondent enters his or her response into a personal computer.

14. The result in Table 5-1 is obviously wrong. If McCain had actually won 87 percent of the white vote in these states, he would have carried them by a very large margin.

15. Chuck Todd, Sheldon Gawiser, with Ana Maria Arumi and G. Evans Witt, *How Obama Won: A State-by-State Guide to the Historic 2008 Presidential Election* (New York: Vintage Books, 2009), 58, 81, 93. The surveys in all three states were sizable: 3,350 respondents in Florida, 2,814 in North Carolina, and 2,466 in Virginia.

16. Todd and Gawiser, *How Obama Won,* 31.

17. Abramson, Aldrich, and Rohde, *Change and Continuity in the 2004 and 2006 Elections,* 124–127. For cross-national evidence, see Ronald Inglehart, *Modernization and Postmodernization: Cultural, Economic, and Political Change in 43 Societies* (Princeton, N.J.: Princeton University Press, 1997), 255; and Russell J. Dalton, *Citizen Politics: Public Opinion and Political Parties in Advanced Industrial Democracies,* 5th ed. (Washington, D.C.: CQ Press, 2008), 145–152.

18. The *Los Angeles Times* sponsored a national exit poll of 5,154 voters as they left 136 polling stations throughout the United States. Sixty-five percent of the respondents were sampled as they left fifty voting places in California.

19. Jeffrey M. Stonecash, *Class and Party in American Politics* (Boulder, Colo.: Westview Press, 2000), 87–121; Larry M. Bartels, *Unequal Democracy: The Political Economy of the New Gilded Age* (New York: Russell Sage Foundation, 2008), 64–126.

20. See, for example, Walter Dean Burnham, *Critical Elections and the Mainsprings of American Politics* (New York: Norton, 1970); Everett Carll Ladd Jr., with Charles D. Hadley Jr., *Transformations of the American Party System: Political Coalitions from the New Deal to the 1970s,* 2nd ed. (New York: Norton, 1978).

21. "Election Results 2008," nytimes.com, http://elections.nytimes.com/2008 results/presidential/national_exit-polls,html. Although this site shows exit poll results from 1972 to 2008, not until the 1988 election does it provide a breakdown of results among voters with postgraduate education.

22. In both the ANES survey and the pool poll, union members were only somewhat more likely to vote for Obama than nonmembers who lived in a union household. Among white union members in the ANES survey ($N = 96$), 53 percent voted for Obama; among nonmembers who lived in a union household ($N = 71$), 49 percent did. In the pool poll, 60 percent of all union members voted for Obama; among nonmembers who lived in a union household, 57 percent did.

23. For the single best summary, see Kenneth D. Wald, *Religion and Politics in the United States,* 4th ed. (Lanham, Md.: Rowman and Littlefield, 2003). For a discussion of religion and politics in a comparative context, see Pippa Norris and Ronald Inglehart, *Sacred and Secular: Religion and Politics Worldwide* (Cambridge, UK: Cambridge University Press, 2004).

24. The question, which was asked to all Christians, was "Would you call yourself a born-again Christian, that is, have you personally had a conversion experience related to Jesus Christ?" This question was not asked in the 2004 ANES survey.

25. Lyman A. Kellstedt, "An Agenda for Future Research," in *Rediscovering the Religious Factor in American Politics,* ed. David C. Leege and Lyman A. Kellstedt (Armonk, N.Y.: M. E. Sharpe, 1993), 293–299.

26. Morris P. Fiorina, with Samuel J. Abrams and Jeremy C. Pope, *Culture War? The Myth of a Polarized America,* 2nd ed. (New York: Pearson/Longman, 2006), 134.

27. We do not report the results for church attendance because it is already included in our measure of religious commitment.

28. Robert Axelrod, "Where the Votes Come From: An Analysis of Electoral Coalitions, *American Political Science Review* 66 (March 1972): 11–20. Axelrod updates his results through the 1984 elections. For his most recent estimate, including results from 1952 to 1980, see Robert Axelrod, "Presidential Coalitions in 1984," *American Political Science Review* 80 (March 1986): 281–284. Using Axelrod's categories, Nelson W. Polsby estimates the social composition of the Democratic and Republican presidential coalitions between 1952 and 2000. See Nelson W. Polsby and Aaron Wildavsky, *Presidential Elections: Strategies and Structures of American Politics,* 11th ed. (Lanham, Md.: Rowman and Littlefield, 2004), 32. For an update through 2004, see Nelson W. Polsby, Aaron Wildavsky, with David A. Hopkins, *Presidential Elections: Strategies and Structures in American Politics,* 12th ed. (Lanham, Md.: Rowman and Littlefield, 2008), 28.

29. John R. Petrocik, *Party Coalitions: Realignment and the Decline of the New Deal Party System* (Chicago: University of Chicago Press, 1981).

30. Harold W. Stanley, William T. Bianco, and Richard G. Niemi, "Partisanship and Group Support over Time: A Multivariate Analysis," *American Political Science Review* 80 (September 1986): 969–976. Stanley and his colleagues assess the independent contribution that group membership makes toward Democratic loyalties after controls are introduced for membership in other pro-Democratic groups. For an update and an extension through 2004, see Harold W. Stanley and Richard G. Niemi, "Partisanship, Party Coalitions, and Group Support, 1952–2004," *Presidential Studies Quarterly* 36 (June 2006): 172–188. For an alternative approach, see Robert S. Erikson, Thomas D. Lancaster, and David W. Romero, "Group Components of the Presidential Vote, 1952–1984," *Journal of Politics* 51 (May 1989): 337–346.

31. For a discussion of the contribution of the working class to the Democratic presidential coalition, see Paul R. Abramson, *Generational Change in American Politics* (Lexington, Mass.: D. C. Heath, 1975).

32. See Axelrod, "Where the Votes Come From."

33. The NORC survey, based on 2,564 civilians, used a quota sample that does not follow the probability procedures used by the University of Michigan Survey Research Center. Following the procedures used at the time, southern blacks were not sampled. Because the NORC survey overrepresented upper-income groups and the middle and upper-middle classes, it cannot be used to estimate the contribution of social groups to the Democratic and Republican presidential coalitions.

34. Abramson, *Generational Change in American Politics,* 65–68.

35. As Figure 5-1 shows, Clinton did win a majority of the white major-party vote in 1992 and 1996.

36. Racial voting, as well as our other measures of social cleavage, is affected by including Wallace voters with Nixon voters in 1968, Anderson voters with Reagan voters in 1980, Perot voters with Bush voters in 1992, and Perot voters

with Dole voters in 1996. For the effects of including these independent or third-party candidates, see Abramson, Aldrich, and Rohde, *Change and Continuity in the 1996 and 1998 Elections,* 102, 104–106, 108, and 111.

37. The statements about low turnout in 1996 are true regardless of whether one measures turnout based on the voting-age population or the voting-eligible population. Turnout among the voting-eligible population fell about nine percentage points between 1960 and 1996.

38. As we explain in Chapter 3, we consider the South to include the eleven states of the old Confederacy, although in our analysis of ANES surveys we classify Tennessee as a border state. Because we cannot use this definition with either the 1944 NORC survey or the 1948 University of Michigan Survey Research Center survey, we have not included these years in our analysis of regional differences among the white electorate.

39. Of course, Bush lived in Texas, also a southern state.

40. Cheney had served as the U.S. representative from Wyoming from 1979 to 1989. When he became the chief executive officer of Halliburton in 1995, he established his residence in Texas. Being a resident of Texas would have complicated running on the same ticket as Bush because the Twelfth Amendment specifies that electors "vote by ballot for President and Vice-President, one of whom, at least, shall not be an inhabitant of the same state with themselves."

41. See, for example, Chapter 3 where we compare Kennedy's black support in the South in 1960 with Carter's in 1976.

42. Todd and Gawiser, *How Obama Won,* 58, 81, 93.

43. Officially known as the Labor-Management Relations Act, this legislation, passed in 1947, qualified or amended much of the National Labor Relations Act of 1935 (known as the Wagner Act). Union leaders argued that the Taft-Hartley Act placed unwarranted restrictions on organized labor. This act was passed by the Republican-controlled Eightieth Congress, vetoed by Truman, and passed over his veto.

44. According to the 2008 pool poll, Obama received 53 percent of the vote. Members of union households made up 21 percent of the electorate, and 50 percent voted for Obama. These numbers thus suggest that 23 percent of Obama's vote came from members of union households. Even if one takes into account that not all these union voters were white, these numbers suggest that about one in five of Obama's votes came from union households.

45. See Robert R. Alford, *Party and Society: The Anglo-American Democracies* (Chicago: Rand McNally, 1963); Seymour Martin Lipset, *Political Man: The Social Bases of Politics,* exp. ed. (Baltimore: Johns Hopkins University Press, 1981); and Inglehart, *Modernization and Postmodernization.*

46. The variation in class voting is smaller if one focuses on class differences in the congressional vote, but the data clearly show a decline in class voting between 1952 and 2004. See Dalton, *Citizen Politics,* 5th ed., 148.

47. Readers should bear in mind that in 2000 (and 2004) there was no measure of the head of household's occupation or of the spouse's occupation, but

our analysis of the 1996 data suggests that this limitation probably does not account for the negative level of class voting in the 2000 contest. Bartels discusses our attempts to maintain comparability in measuring social class in the face of changing survey measurement in *Unequal Democracy,* 70–71.

48. As we point out in *Change and Continuity in the 2000 and 2002 Elections,* when we define social class according to the respondent's own occupation, the overall size of the working class falls and the overall size of the middle class grows. Because the relatively small size of the working class in 2000 and 2004 results mainly from a redefinition of the way our measure of social class is constructed, we assumed that the sizes of the working and the middle class in 2000 and 2004 were the same as they were in the 1996 ANES. See Abramson, Aldrich, and Rohde, *Change and Continuity in the 2000 and 2002 Elections,* chap. 4, 313n26.

49. See Mark N. Franklin, "The Decline of Cleavage Politics," in *Electoral Change: Responses to Evolving Social and Attitudinal Structures in Western Countries,* ed. Mark N. Franklin, Thomas T. Mackie, and Henry Valen, with others (Cambridge, UK: Cambridge University Press, 1992), 383–405. See also Inglehart, *Modernization and Postmodernization,* 237–266.

50. Jeff Manza and Clem Brooks, *Social Cleavages and Political Change: Voter Alignments and U.S. Party Coalitions* (New York: Oxford University Press, 1999).

51. Exit polls conducted between 1972 and 2008 show the same pattern. In all ten elections, Jews have been more likely to vote Democratic than white Catholics, and white Catholics have been more likely to vote Democratic than white Protestants. See "Election Results 2008," nytimes.com.

52. For a discussion of the impact of religion on the 1960 election, see Philip E. Converse, "Religion and Politics: The 1960 Election," in *Elections and the Political Order,* ed. Angus Campbell et al. (New York: Wiley, 1967), 96–124.

53. According to the 2009 *Statistical Abstract of the United States,* as of 2007, 2.2 percent of the U.S. population was Jewish, and according to the Pew Forum on Religion and Public Life, only 1.7 percent was. The *Statistical Abstract* results are based mainly on information provided by Jewish organizations, whereas the Pew results are based on a representative survey of 35,000 Americans. The Pew survey is presented in Pew Forum on Religion and Public Life, *U.S. Religious Landscape Survey: Religious Affiliation, Diverse and Dynamic* (Washington, D.C.: Pew Forum on Religion and Public Life, 2008), 12. For the *Statistical Abstract,* see U.S. Census Bureau, *The 2009 Statistical Abstract of the United States: The National Data Book,* www.census/compedia/statab, table 76.

54. States are listed in descending order according to their estimated number of Jews.

55. Since 1860, the Democrats have won the presidency only twice without winning New York: 1916, when Woodrow Wilson narrowly defeated Charles Evans Hughes by a margin of twenty-three electoral votes, and 1948, when Harry Truman defeated Thomas Dewey. Dewey, the governor of New York, won 46.0

percent of the popular vote in his home state, and Truman won 45.0 percent. Henry A. Wallace, the Progressive candidate in 1948, won 8.2 percent of the New York vote, substantially better than his share in any other state.

56. Robert Huckfeldt and Carol Weitzel Kohfeld provide strong evidence that Democratic appeals to blacks weakened the party's support among working-class whites. See their *Race and the Decline of Class in American Politics* (Urbana: University of Illinois Press, 1989).

57. For evidence on this point, see Paul R. Abramson, *Political Attitudes in America: Formation and Change* (San Francisco: W. H. Freeman, 1983), 65–68.

58. Edward G. Carmines and James A. Stimson, *Issue Evolution: Race and the Transformation of American Politics* (Princeton, N.J.: Princeton University Press, 1999). For a critique of their thesis, see Alan I. Abramowitz, "Issue Evolution Reconsidered: Racial Attitudes and Partisanship among the American Electorate," *American Journal of Political Science* 38 (February 1994): 1–24.

59. This is not to argue that abortion is necessarily an issue that works against the Democrats. For example, in his study of the 1992 presidential election Alan Abramowitz argues that abortion was the most important issue influencing voters and that Clinton was the beneficiary. See Alan I. Abramowitz, "It's Abortion, Stupid: Policy Voting in the 1992 Presidential Election," *Journal of Politics* 57 (February 1995): 176–186.

60. James W. Ceaser and Andrew E. Busch, *Upside Down and Inside Out: The 1992 Elections and American Politics* (Lanham, Md.: Rowman and Littlefield, 1993), 168–171.

6. CANDIDATES, ISSUES, AND THE VOTE

1. This set of attitudes was first formulated and tested extensively in Angus Campbell et al., *The American Voter* (New York: Wiley, 1960), using data from what are now called the American National Election Studies (ANES) surveys. The authors based their conclusions primarily on data from a survey of the 1956 presidential election, a rematch between Democrat Adlai Stevenson and Republican (and this time the incumbent) Dwight Eisenhower. Recently, Michael S. Lewis-Beck, William G. Jacoby, Helmut Norpoth, and Herbert F. Weisberg applied similar methods to data from 2000 and 2004. See their *The American Voter Revisited* (Ann Arbor: University of Michigan Press, 2008).

2. See, for example, Wendy M. Rahn et al., "A Social-Cognitive Model of Candidate Appraisal," in *Information and Democratic Processes,* ed. John A. Ferejohn and James H. Kuklinski (Urbana: University of Illinois Press, 1990), 136–159, and sources cited therein.

3. For the most extensive explication of the theory and tests in various electoral settings, see Gary W. Cox, *Making Votes Count: Strategic Coordination in the World's Electoral Systems* (New York: Cambridge University Press, 1997). For an examination in the American context, see Paul R. Abramson et al., "Third-Party

and Independent Candidates in American Politics: Wallace, Anderson, and Perot," *Political Science Quarterly* 110 (Fall 1995): 349–367.

4. These elections are discussed in Paul R. Abramson, John H. Aldrich, and David W. Rohde, *Change and Continuity in the 1980 Elections*, rev. ed. (Washington, D.C.: CQ Press, 1983); Abramson, Aldrich, and Rohde, *Change and Continuity in the 1992 Elections*, rev. ed. (Washington, D.C.: CQ Press, 1995); Abramson, Aldrich, and Rohde, *Change and Continuity in the 1996 and 1998 Elections* (Washington, D.C.: CQ Press, 1999); and Abramson, Aldrich, and Rohde, *Change and Continuity in the 2000 and 2002 Elections* (Washington, D.C.: CQ Press, 2003).

5. We reproduce the feeling thermometer in Abramson, Aldrich, and Rohde, *Change and Continuity in the 1992 Elections*, rev. ed., 166; Abramson, Aldrich, and Rohde, *Change and Continuity in the 1996 and 1998 Elections*, 117; and Abramson, Aldrich, and Rohde, *Change and Continuity in the 2000 and 2002 Elections*, 123.

6. See Abramson et al., "Third-Party and Independent Candidates."

7. Abramson, Aldrich, and Rohde, *Change and Continuity in the 2000 and 2002 Elections*, table 6-1, 125–126.

8. The ANES survey also asks about respondents' emotional reactions to each candidate, specifically whether the candidate ever made them feel angry, proud, afraid, or hopeful. There is little difference between McCain and Obama on these measures, with respondents mostly reporting no. There is one exception for each candidate, however. A slight majority said that McCain made them feel proud (with choices, then, of rarely, occasionally, fairly often, or very often), and a majority said that Obama made them feel hopeful. These characterizations seem reasonable in view of McCain's hero status and Obama's strengths. All of these reactions are also clearly related to the vote, as one would expect.

9. For an analysis of how the candidates' campaign strategies in 1996, 2000, and 2004 shaped the voters' decisions, and in turn were shaped by the concerns of the voters, see John H. Aldrich and Thomas Weko, "The Presidency and the Election Campaign: Framing the Choice in 1996," in *The Presidency and the Political System*, 6th ed., ed. Michael Nelson (Washington, D.C.: CQ Press, 2000); John H. Aldrich and John D. Griffin, "The Presidency and the Campaign: Creating Voter Priorities in the 2000 Election," in *The Presidency and the Political System*, 7th ed., ed. Michael Nelson (Washington, D.C.: CQ Press, 2003); and John H. Aldrich, John D. Griffin, and Jill Rickershauser, "The Presidency and the Election Campaign: Altering Voters' Priorities in the 2004 Election," in *The Presidency and the Political System*, 8th ed., ed. Michael Nelson (Washington, D.C.: CQ Press, 2006).

10. If they named more than one problem, they were asked which problem was the most important. In 2004 respondents were asked, "What do you think has been the most important issue facing the United States over the last four years?"

11. These measures were first used in the ANES survey of the 1968 election. And they were used extensively in presidential election surveys beginning in 1972. The issue measures used in Chapter 7 were also used extensively beginning in the 1970s. Therefore in this and the next two chapters, we limit our attention to the last ten elections.

12. The 2008 ANES survey included two versions of most of these questions. Half of the sample was randomly selected to respond to these seven-point issue scales with the wording used in prior elections, and the other half was given questions about the same issues but with different wording. We base our analyses in this chapter (and subsequent chapters) on the questions with the traditional wording in order to make comparisons with earlier elections.

13. The median is based on the assumption that respondents can be ranked from most conservative to most liberal. The number of respondents who are more liberal than the median (or who see a candidate as more liberal than the median) is equal to the number who are more conservative (or see the candidate as more conservative) than the median. Because there are only seven points on these scales and because many respondents will choose any given point, the median is computed using a procedure that derives a median for grouped data. As we pointed out in note 12, we restrict our analyses to those respondents who received the traditional wording of the various issue scales. The aid to blacks scale was posed with traditional wording to the entire sample. With one exception, we use responses to this scale only from the random half-sample that received the traditional wording for all issue scales. The exception is in the calculation of the median placements on the aid to blacks scale. For this single set of calculations, we use the responses for the entire sample to provide the best information for estimating the median placements.

14. We draw self-placement as being at the left-most (or "1") scale position in Figure 6-2. Technically, the distribution of responses is so skewed to the left that the median placement as formally calculated is to the left of even that position. This degree of skewness reflects how much society had changed since that question was introduced in the 1970s, when responses were not that dramatically skewed to the liberal end of the scale. This sort of change is one of the reasons that the ANES began using new question wording for half the sample in 2008.

15. Morris P. Fiorina, with Samuel J. Abrams and Jeremy C. Pope, *Culture War? The Myth of a Polarized Electorate* (New York: Pearson, Longman, 2005).

16. Campbell et al., *American Voter,* 168–187.

17. In most years, including 2008, the ANES encouraged respondents to reveal the absence of an issue position. It did so by adding to the issue scale question the wording "or haven't you thought much about it?" This prompt is designed to remove feelings of social pressure to appear well informed, even if the respondent is not. However, the data show that it did not elicit much selection of the no opinion option. Recall that we employ the issues asked using the

traditional wording, so that the following analyses are restricted to the randomly selected half-sample that received the traditional wording.

18. Before 1996 the ANES interviewers did not ask those who failed to place themselves on an issue scale where they thought the candidates stood. Since then, they ask respondents who did not place themselves on an issue where the candidates stood. Therefore, before 1996 those who failed to meet the first criterion were not able to meet any of the remaining ones. Although some people who express no preference on an issue might know the positions of one or both candidates, it is difficult to see how they could vote based on those perceptions if they had no opinion of their own.

19. To maintain comparability with previous election surveys, for 1996, 2000, 2004, and 2008 we have excluded respondents who did not place themselves on an issue scale from columns II, III, and IV of Table 6-4. Because we do not know the preferences of these respondents on the issue, we have no way to measure the ways in which their issue preferences may have affected their votes.

20. For details, see Abramson, Aldrich, and Rohde, *Change and Continuity in the 1980 Elections,* table 6-3, 130; Abramson, Aldrich, and Rohde, *Change and Continuity in the 1984 Elections,* rev. ed. (Washington, D.C.: CQ Press, 1987), table 6-2, 174; and Abramson, Aldrich, and Rohde, *Change and Continuity in the 1988 Elections,* rev. ed. (Washington, D.C.: CQ Press, 1991), table 6-2, 165; Abramson, Aldrich, and Rohde, *Change and Continuity in the 1992 Elections,* table 6-6, 186; Abramson, Aldrich, and Rohde, *Change and Continuity in the 1996 and 1998 Elections,* table 6-6, 135; and Abramson, Aldrich, and Rohde, *Change and Continuity in the 2000 and 2002 Elections,* table 6-4, 137.

21. Although this is evidence that most people claim to have issue preferences, it does not demonstrate that they do. For example, evidence indicates that some use the midpoint of the scale (point 4) as a means of answering the question even if they have ill-formed preferences. See John H. Aldrich et al., "The Measurement of Public Opinion about Public Policy: A Report on Some New Issue Question Formats," *American Journal of Political Science* 26 (May 1982): 391–414.

22. Morris P. Fiorina, *Retrospective Voting in American National Elections* (New Haven, Conn.: Yale University Press, 1981).

23. We use "apparent issue voting" to emphasize several points. First, voting involves too many factors to infer that closeness to a candidate on any one issue was the cause of the voter's choice. The issue similarity may have been purely coincidental, or it may have been only one of many reasons the voter supported that candidate. Second, we use the median perception of the candidates' positions rather than the voter's own perception. Third, the relationship between issues and the vote may be caused by rationalization. Voters may have decided to support a candidate for other reasons and also may have altered their own issue preferences or misperceived the positions of the candidates to align themselves more closely with their already favored candidate. See Richard A. Brody and

Benjamin I. Page, "Comment: The Assessment of Policy Voting," *American Political Science Review* 66 (June 1972): 450–458.

24. Many individuals, of course, placed the candidates at different positions than did the public on average. The use of average perceptions, however, reduces the effect of individuals rationalizing their perceptions of candidates to be consistent with their own vote rather than voting for the candidate whose views are actually closer to their own.

25. They also received a score of 0 if they answered 5 (which was transposed to 3) on the government spending/services scale.

26. This procedure counts every issue as equal in importance. It also assumes that what matters is that the voter is closer to the candidate on an issue; it does not consider how much closer the voter is to one candidate or the other.

27. Scores of +5, +6, and +7 were designated strongly Republican, while similarly negative scores were designated strongly Democratic. Scores of +3 and +4 were designated moderately Republican, −3 and −4 moderately Democratic. Scores of +1 and +2 were slightly Republican, −1 and −2 slightly Democratic. A score of 0 was designated neutral. Three respondents who did not have an opinion on any of the seven issues were excluded from the analysis.

28. This is an oddity that appears to be attributable to the fact that our balance of issue measure counts only whether the respondent is closer to a candidate but does not consider by how much.

29. Note, however, that there are limits to the amount of projection given that so many respondents agreed on at least the ordinal location of the two candidates. "Persuasion," locating oneself close to where a favored candidate stands (especially when it is not "genuine" persuasion but simply rationalization of the vote choice), is another source of limits on the extent of prospective voting.

7. PRESIDENTIAL PERFORMANCE AND CANDIDATE CHOICE

1. By "war" we mean the wars in Afghanistan, Iraq, and against terrorism. For an analysis of the role of these issues in 2004, see Paul R. Abramson, John H. Aldrich, and David W. Rohde, *Change and Continuity in the 2004 and 2006 Elections* (Washington, D.C.: CQ Press, 2007), chap. 7.

2. See Paul R. Abramson, John H. Aldrich, and David W. Rohde, *Change and Continuity in the 2000 and 2002 Elections* (Washington, D.C.: CQ Press, 2003), chap. 7.

3. Bush became the first sitting vice president to be elected president since Democratic vice president Martin Van Buren was elected in 1836. As Nelson W. Polsby and Aaron Wildavsky point out, a sitting vice president may have many of the disadvantages of being an incumbent without the advantages of actually being president. See Polsby and Wildavsky, *Presidential Elections: Strategies and Structures of American Politics*, 11th ed. (Lanham, Md.: Rowman and Littlefield, 2002), 78–85.

4. See Paul R. Abramson, John H. Aldrich, and David W. Rohde *Change and Continuity in the 1992 Elections,* rev. ed. (Washington, D.C.: CQ Press, 1995), 203–208.

5. V. O. Key Jr., *Politics, Parties, and Pressure Groups,* 5th ed. (New York: Crowell, 1964), 568. Key's theory of retrospective voting is most fully developed in *The Responsible Electorate: Rationality in Presidential Voting, 1936–1960* (Cambridge, Mass.: Harvard University Press, 1966).

6. Anthony Downs, *An Economic Theory of Democracy* (New York: Harper and Row, 1957).

7. Morris P. Fiorina, *Retrospective Voting in American National Elections* (New Haven, Conn.: Yale University Press, 1981), 83. Two recent papers by Christopher H. Achen and Larry M. Bartels argue that the U.S. electorate is too ignorant to make informed decisions consistent with the assumptions of retrospective voting theorists. See Achen and Bartels, "Blind Retrospection: Electoral Responses to Drought, Flu, and Shark Attacks" (unpublished manuscript, Princeton University, January 2004); and Achen and Bartels, "Musical Chairs: Pocketbook Voting and the Limits of Democratic Accountability" (paper prepared for the annual meeting of the American Political Science Association, Chicago, September 1–5, 2004).

8. See Benjamin I. Page, *Choices and Echoes in Presidential Elections: Rational Man and Electoral Democracy* (Chicago: University of Chicago Press, 1978). He argues that "party cleavages" distinguish the party at the candidate and mass levels.

9. Arthur H. Miller and Martin P. Wattenberg, "Throwing the Rascals Out: Policy and Performance Evaluations of Presidential Candidates, 1952–1980," *American Political Science Review* 79 (June 1985): 359–372.

10. Note that this question differs from the one the ANES has asked in earlier elections. As we point out in Chapter 6 (note 12), respondents were asked a different question to determine what they thought the most important problem was.

11. Each respondent assesses government performance on the problem he or she considers the most important. In the seven surveys from 1976 to 2000, respondents were asked, "How good a job is the government doing in dealing with this problem—a good job, only fair, or a poor job?" In 1972 respondents were asked a different but related question (see the note to Table A7-1 in the appendix). In 2004 respondents were asked another question (see Chapter 6, note 10), and were given four options for assessing the government's performance: "very good job," "good job," "bad job," and "very bad job."

12. Negative evaluations are not surprising. After all, if one thinks the government has been doing a good job tackling the problem, then it probably would not be one's major concern. This reasoning seems to underlie the very low proportion of respondents in every survey who thought the government was doing a good job of addressing their most important concern. And yet an "issue" may not have the same connotations as a problem.

13. See Gerald H. Kramer, "Short-Term Fluctuations in U.S. Voting Behavior, 1896–1964," *American Political Science Review* 65 (March 1971): 131–143; Fiorina, *Retrospective Voting*; M. Stephen Weatherford, "Economic Conditions and Electoral Outcomes: Class Differences in the Political Response to Recession," *American Journal of Political Science* 22 (November 1978): 917–938; D. Roderick Kiewiet and Douglas Rivers, "A Retrospective on Retrospective Voting," *Political Behavior* 6, no. 4 (1984): 369–393; D. Roderick Kiewiet, *Macroeconomics and Micropolitics: The Electoral Effects of Economic Issues* (Chicago: University of Chicago Press, 1983); Michael S. Lewis-Beck, *Economics and Elections: The Major Western Democracies* (Ann Arbor: University of Michigan Press, 1988); Alberto Alesina, John Londregan, and Howard Rosenthal, *A Model of the Political Economy of the United States* (Cambridge, Mass.: National Bureau of Economic Research, 1991); Michael B. MacKuen, Robert S. Erikson, and James A. Stimson, "Peasants or Bankers? The American Electorate and the U.S. Economy," *American Political Science Review* 86 (September 1992): 597–611; and Robert S. Erikson, Michael B. MacKuen, and James A. Stimson, *The Macro Polity* (Cambridge, UK: Cambridge University Press, 2002).

14. John E. Mueller, *War, Presidents, and Public Opinion* (New York: Wiley, 1973); Edward R. Tufte, *Political Control of the Economy* (Princeton, N.J.: Princeton University Press, 1978). For a perceptive critique of the business cycle formulation, see James E. Alt and K. Alec Chrystal, *Political Economics* (Berkeley: University of California Press, 1983).

15. See Abramson, Aldrich, and Rohde, *Change and Continuity in the 2004 and 2006 Elections*, chap. 7, 172–176, esp. table 7-6, 174.

16. Fiorina, *Retrospective Voting*.

17. ANES first used the approval question in 1970. In the 1984 and 1988 surveys, this question was asked in both the pre-election and the postelection waves of the survey. Because attitudes held by the public before the election are what count in influencing its choices, we use the first question. In both surveys, approval of Reagan's performance was more positive in the postelection interview: 66 percent approved of his performance in 1984, and 68 percent approved in 1988.

18. A summary measure of retrospective evaluations could not be constructed using either the 1972 or the 2004 ANES data. We were able to construct an alternative measure for 2004. See Abramson, Aldrich, and Rohde, *Change and Continuity in the 2004 and 2006 Elections*, chap. 7, tables 7-9 and 7-10, 178–180, and 371n18. For procedures we used to construct this measure between 1976 and 2000, see Abramson, Aldrich, and Rohde, *Change and Continuity in the 2000 and 2002 Elections*, chap. 7, 328n13. A combined index of retrospective evaluations was created to allow an overall assessment of retrospective voting in 2008. To construct the summary measure of retrospective evaluations, we used the following procedures. First, we awarded respondents four points if they approved of the president's performance, two if they had no opinion, and zero if they disapproved. Second, respondents received four points if they thought the government had done a very good job in the last four years, three if they thought the

government had done a good job, one if they thought the government had done a bad job, zero if they said it had done a very bad job, and two if they had no opinion. Finally, respondents received four points if they thought Republicans would do a better job handling the most important problem, zero points if they thought the Democrats would do a better job, and two points if they thought there was no difference between the parties, neither party would do well, both parties would do the same, another party would do the better job, or they had no opinion. For all three questions, "don't know" and "not ascertained" responses were scored as two, but respondents with more than one such response were excluded from the analysis. Scores on our measure were the sum of the individual values for the three questions, and thus ranged from a low of zero (strongly against the incumbent's party) to twelve (strongly for the incumbent's party). These values were then grouped to create a seven-point scale corresponding to the seven categories in Table 7-9.

19. See Paul R. Abramson, John H. Aldrich, and David W. Rohde, *Change and Continuity in the 1996 and 1998 Elections* (Washington, D.C.: CQ Press, 1999), 158–159, for data on our (different) summary measure from 1972 to 1996, and see Abramson, Aldrich, and Rohde, *Change and Continuity in the 2000 and 2002 Elections,* 164–165, for this measure in the 2000 election.

20. The characterization of earlier elections is taken from Abramson, Aldrich, and Rohde, *Change and Continuity in the 2000 and 2002 Elections,* 164.

21. For data from the 1976 and 1980 elections, see Paul R. Abramson, John H. Aldrich, and David W. Rohde, *Change and Continuity in the 1980 Elections,* rev. ed. (Washington, D.C.: CQ Press, 1983), table 7-8, 155–157; from the 1984 election, see Abramson, Aldrich, and Rohde, *Change and Continuity in the 1984 Elections,* rev. ed. (Washington, D.C.: CQ Press, 1987), table 7-8, 203–204; from the 1988 election, see Abramson, Aldrich, and Rohde, *Change and Continuity in the 1988 Elections,* rev. ed. (Washington, D.C.: CQ Press, 1991), table 7-7, 195–198; from the 1996 election, see Abramson, Aldrich, and Rohde, *Change and Continuity in the 1996 and 1998 Elections,* 159–161; from the 2000 election, see Abramson, Aldrich, and Rohde, *Change and Continuity in the 2000 and 2002 Elections,* 165–166; and from the 2004 election, see Abramson, Aldrich, and Rohde, *Change and Continuity in the 2004 and 2006 Elections,* 178–180. The small number of seven-point issue scales included in the ANES survey precluded performing this analysis with 1992 data.

8. PARTY LOYALTIES, POLICY PREFERENCES, AND THE VOTE

1. Angus Campbell et al., *The American Voter* (New York: Wiley, 1960). For a recent statement of the "standard" view of party identification, see Warren E. Miller, "Party Identification, Realignment, and Party Voting: Back to the Basics," *American Political Science Review* 85 (June 1991): 557–568; and Warren E. Miller and J. Merrill Shanks, *The New American Voter* (Cambridge, Mass.: Harvard University Press, 1996), 117–183.

2. Campbell, *American Voter,* 121. See also Morris P. Fiorina, *Retrospective Voting in American National Elections* (New Haven, Conn.: Yale University Press, 1981), 85–86.

3. For the full wording of the party identification questions, see Chapter 4, note 74.

4. Most "apoliticals" in this period were African Americans living in the South. Because they were disenfranchised, questions about their party loyalties were essentially meaningless to them. For the most detailed discussion of how the American National Election Studies creates its summary measure of party identification, see Arthur H. Miller and Martin P. Wattenberg, "Measuring Party Identification: Independent or No Partisan Preference?" *American Journal of Political Science* 27 (February 1983): 106–121.

5. For evidence of the relatively high level of partisan stability among individuals from 1965 to 1982, see M. Kent Jennings and Gregory B. Markus, "Partisan Orientations over the Long Haul: Results from the Three-Wave Political Socialization Panel Study," *American Political Science Review* 78 (December 1984): 1000–1018. For analyses from 1965 to 1997, see Laura Stoker and M. Kent Jennings, "Of Time and the Development of Partisan Polarization," *American Journal of Political Science* 52 (July 2008): 619–635.

6. V. O. Key Jr., *The Responsible Electorate: Rationality in Presidential Voting, 1936–1960* (Cambridge, Mass.: Harvard University Press, 1966).

7. Morris P. Fiorina, "An Outline for a Model of Party Choice," *American Journal of Political Science* 21 (August 1977): 601–625; Fiorina, *Retrospective Voting,* 65–83.

8. Benjamin I. Page provides evidence of this. See Page, *Choices and Echoes in Presidential Elections: Rational Man and Electoral Democracy* (Chicago: University of Chicago Press, 1978). Anthony Downs, in *An Economic Theory of Democracy* (New York: Harper and Row, 1957), develops a theoretical logic for such consistency in party stances on issues and ideology over time. For more recent theoretical and empirical development, see John H. Aldrich, *Why Parties? The Origin and Transformation of Political Parties in America* (Chicago: University of Chicago Press, 1995).

9. Robert S. Erikson, Michael B. MacKuen, and James A. Stimson, *The Macro Polity* (Cambridge, UK: Cambridge University Press, 2002).

10. Donald Green, Bradley Palmquist, and Eric Schickler, *Partisan Hearts and Minds: Political Parties and the Social Identities of Voters* (New Haven, Conn.: Yale University Press, 2002).

11. See, for example, Donald Green, Bradley Palmquist, and Eric Schickler, "Macropartisanship: A Replication and Critique," *American Political Science Review* 92 (December 1998): 883–899; and Robert S. Erikson, Michael B. MacKuen, and James A. Stimson, "What Moves Macropartisanship? A Reply to Green, Palmquist, and Schickler," *American Political Science Review* 92 (December 1998): 901–912.

12. In Chapter 4 we noted that in 2008 the ANES survey included a question wording experiment. As we showed there, the experimental differences were sufficiently slight that we combine the two wordings to create a single measure of partisanship for the entire sample.

13. There is some controversy about how to classify these independent leaners. Some argue that they are mainly "hidden" partisans who should be considered identifiers. For the strongest statement of this position, see Bruce E. Keith et al., *The Myth of the Independent Voter* (Berkeley: University of California Press, 1992). In our view, however, the evidence on the proper classification of independent leaners is mixed. On balance, the evidence suggests that they are more partisan than independents with no partisan leanings, but less partisan than weak partisans. See Paul R. Abramson, *Political Attitudes in America: Formation and Change* (San Francisco: W. H. Freeman, 1983), 80–81, 95–96. For an excellent discussion of this question, see Herbert B. Asher, "Voting Behavior Research in the 1980s: An Examination of Some Old and New Problem Areas," in *Political Science: The State of the Discipline,* ed. Ada W. Finifter (Washington, D.C.: American Political Science Association, 1983), 357–360.

14. See, for example, Martin P. Wattenberg, *The Decline of American Political Parties, 1952–1996* (Cambridge, Mass.: Harvard University Press, 1998).

15. Gary C. Jacobson, "The 2008 Presidential and Congressional Elections: Anti-Bush Referendum and Prospects for a Democratic Majority," *Political Science Quarterly* 124 (Spring 2009): 1–20; and Jacobson, "The Effects of the George W. Bush Presidency on Partisan Attitudes," *Presidential Studies Quarterly* 39 (June 2009): 172–209.

16. See Paul R. Abramson and Charles W. Ostrom Jr., "Macropartisanship: An Empirical Reassessment," *American Political Science Review* 86 (March 1991): 181–192; and Abramson and Ostrom, "Question Wording and Partisanship: Change and Continuity in Party Loyalties During the 1992 Election Campaign," *Public Opinion Quarterly* 58 (Spring 1994): 21–48.

17. These surveys were conducted annually between 1972 and 1978, in 1980, annually between 1982 and 1991, in 1993, and in every even-numbered year between 1994 and 2008. The surveys conducted between 1972 and 2002 were conducted in February, March, and April. The 2004 survey was conducted from September through December, the 2006 survey from March through August, and the 2008 survey from April through November.

18. See "Latest *New York Times*/CBS News Poll," http://documents. nytimes.com/latest-new-york-times-cbs-news-poll#p-19. The most recent poll is based on 905 respondents. These polls do not measure the strength of party attachments among Republicans or Democrats, but they do ask independents to which party they feel closer. We are discussing the results reported on this Web site. Those results do not allow us to determine the "leanings" of independents.

19. See Paul R. Abramson, John H. Aldrich, and David W. Rohde, *Change and Continuity in the 2004 and 2006 Elections* (Washington, D.C.: CQ Press, 2007), 186–192.

20. The ANES did not conduct a congressional election survey in 2006.

21. For evidence on the decline of Republican Party loyalties among older blacks between 1962 and 1964, see Paul R. Abramson, *Generational Change in American Politics* (Lexington, Mass.: D. C. Heath, 1975), 65–69.

22. For the results of the white vote by party identification for the three leading candidates in 1968, 1980, 1992, and 1996, see Paul R. Abramson, John H. Aldrich, and David W. Rohde, *Change and Continuity in the 1996 and 1998 Elections* (Washington, D.C.: CQ Press, 1999), 186–187. Among blacks there is virtually no relationship between party identification and the vote. Even the small number of blacks who identify as Republicans usually either do not vote or vote for the Democratic presidential candidate.

23. In fact, among the 125 white pure independents who voted in 1992, 37 percent voted for Clinton, 41 percent for Ross Perot, and 22 percent for Bob Dole.

24. See also Larry M. Bartels, "Partisanship and Voting Behavior, 1952–1996," *American Journal of Political Science* 44 (January 2000): 35–50.

25. Bernard R. Berelson, Paul F. Lazarsfeld, and William N. McPhee, *Voting: A Study of Opinion Formation in a Presidential Campaign* (Chicago: University of Chicago Press, 1954), 215–233. The extent to which voters' perceptions were affected, however, varied from issue to issue.

26. See Richard A. Brody and Benjamin I. Page, "Comment: The Assessment of Policy Voting," *American Political Science Review* 66 (June 1972): 450–458; Page and Brody, "Policy Voting and the Electoral Process: The Vietnam War Issue," *American Political Science Review* 66 (September 1972): 979–995; and Fiorina, "Outline for a Model of Party Choice."

27. As we point out in Chapter 7, the ANES has asked the standard presidential approval question since 1970.

28. The question measuring approval of the president's handling of economic policy was not asked in ANES surveys before 1984. In our study of these earlier elections, an alternative measure of economic retrospective evaluations was created and shown to be almost as strongly related to party identification. See Paul R. Abramson, John H. Aldrich, and David W. Rohde, *Change and Continuity in the 1984 Elections,* rev. ed. (Washington, D.C.: CQ Press, 1987), table 8-6, 221. We also found nearly as strong a relationship between partisanship and perceptions of which party would better handle the economy in the data from 1972, 1976, and 1980 as from later surveys reported here. See Abramson, Aldrich, and Rohde, *Change and Continuity in the 1980 Elections,* rev. ed. (Washington, D.C.: CQ Press, 1983), 170, table 8-6, 173.

29. For a description of this measure, see Chapter 6. Because this measure uses the median placement of the candidates on the issue scales in the full

sample, much of the projection effect is eliminated. For the relationship between party identification and the balance of issues measure in 1972, see Abramson, Aldrich, and Rohde, *Change and Continuity in the 1980 Elections,* table 8-5, 171.

30. This earlier measure and its relationship with partisan identification are reported in Paul R. Abramson, John H. Aldrich, and David W. Rohde, *Change and Continuity in the 2000 and 2002 Elections* (Washington, D.C.: CQ Press, 2003), table 8-7, 185–186, discussed on 184–189, and in Abramson, Aldrich, and Rohde, *Change and Continuity in the 2004 and 2006 Elections,* table 8-7, 202, discussed on 201–203.

31. As we saw in Chapter 7, that conclusion applies to those individual components of the measure that are the same as in earlier surveys.

32. As in Chapter 7, we cannot directly compare the results for 2008 with those for earlier elections, except in very general terms. For an interpretation and the data over the previous seven elections, see Abramson, Aldrich, and Rohde, *Change and Continuity in the 2000 and 2002 Elections,* table 8-8, 187–188, discussed on 189; and Abramson, Aldrich, and Rohde, *Change and Continuity in the 2004 and 2006 Elections,* table 8-8, 203, discussed on 203–204.

33. See, for example, Aldrich, *Why Parties?*

34. Two important articles assess some of these relationships: Gregory B. Markus and Philip E. Converse, "A Dynamic Simultaneous Equation Model of Electoral Choice," *American Political Science Review* 73 (December 1979): 1055–1070; and Benjamin I. Page and Calvin C. Jones, "Reciprocal Effects of Policy Preferences, Party Loyalties and the Vote," *American Political Science Review* 73 (December 1979): 1071–1089. For a brief discussion of these articles, see Richard G. Niemi and Herbert F. Weisberg, *Controversies in Voting Behavior,* 2nd ed. (Washington, D.C.: CQ Press, 1984), 89–95. For an excellent discussion of complex models of voting behavior and the role of party identification in these models, see Asher, "Voting Behavior Research in the 1980s," 341–354. For another excellent introduction to some of these issues, see Richard G. Niemi and Herbert F. Weisberg, "Is Party Identification Stable?" in *Controversies in Voting Behavior,* 3rd ed., ed. Richard G. Niemi and Herbert F. Weisberg (Washington, D.C.: CQ Press, 1993), 268–283.

INTRODUCTION TO PART III

1. Between 1952 and 1988, seventeen states switched their gubernatorial elections from presidential election years to nonpresidential election years. Steven J. Rosenstone and John Mark Hansen estimate that in 1952 nearly half the electorate lived in states in which there was a competitive gubernatorial election. In the 1988 presidential election, according to their estimates, only 12 percent of the population lived in states in which there was a competitive gubernatorial

election. See Rosenstone and Hansen, *Mobilization, Participation, and Democracy in America* (New York: Macmillan, 1993), 183. In all eleven states that held gubernatorial elections in 2008, both major parties ran candidates, although in some of these contests there was relatively little competition between the two major parties. According to our estimates, 12 percent of the population lived in those states in 2008. Rosenstone and Hansen argue that this change in scheduling of elections is a major factor contributing to the decline in turnout in presidential elections.

2. For a discussion of state elections in 2008, see James W. Ceaser, Andrew E. Busch, and John J. Pitney Jr., *Epic Journey: The 2008 Elections and American Politics* (Lanham, Md.: Rowman and Littlefield, 2009), 181–183.

3. In September 2009, the governor of Massachusetts appointed Paul G. Kirk Jr. to fill Kennedy's seat until a special election could be held in January 2010.

4. In fact, the one exception was the 1934 midterm election in which the Democrats gained an additional nine seats.

5. The Republicans won control of the House in eight consecutive elections from 1894 to 1908, far short of the Democratic winning streak.

6. Although widely attributed to O'Neill, this statement actually appeared as early as July 1932. See Fred R. Shapiro, *The Yale Book of Quotations* (New Haven, Conn.: Yale University Press, 2006), 566.

7. As noted, in August 2009 the Democrats temporarily lost that sixty-vote advantage when Democratic senator Edward Kennedy died.

8. The American National Election Studies did not conduct a midterm survey in 2006.

9. Philip E. Converse, *The Dynamics of Party Support: Cohort-Analyzing Party Identification* (Beverley Hills, Calif.: Sage Publications, 1976), 43–63.

9. CANDIDATES AND OUTCOMES IN 2008

1. The last Democratic gain in the Senate was not confirmed until June 30, 2009, when the Minnesota Supreme Court unanimously ruled that Al Franken had defeated the incumbent Republican, Norm Coleman. Coleman had led by a slight margin in reported voting on election night, but during recounting over subsequent weeks Franken took a narrow lead. Coleman and his party fought the recount decisions in a series of lawsuits, but they were unsuccessful.

2. One independent is Bernard Sanders of Vermont, who was elected as an independent to the House from 1990 to 2004. Sanders had previously served as mayor of Burlington, Vermont, running as a socialist. However, throughout his House service he caucused with the Democrats, and he continued that course after his election to the Senate in 2006. The second independent is Joseph Lieberman of Connecticut. After being elected to three terms in the Senate as a Democrat, he was defeated in the Democratic primary in 2006. He then ran and won as an independent, but he continued to caucus with the Democrats (and

retained his committee chairmanship). For convenience in presenting results, we count both senators as Democrats throughout this chapter.

3. *Incumbents* is used here only for elected incumbents. This includes all members of the House because the only way to become a representative is by election. In the Senate, however, vacancies may be filled by appointment. We do not count appointed senators as incumbents. In 2008 the only appointed senators who ran for election were John Barasso of Wyoming and Roger Wicker of Mississippi. Barasso was appointed in June 2007 and Wicker in December 2007.

4. The scandal involved the House Bank in which many members deposited their paychecks. The bank had a policy of honoring the checks of members, even if they did not have sufficient funds in their accounts to cover them. During 1991, the public learned about this practice and that hundreds of members had written thousands of these "overdrafts." Many of the members who had written the most overdrafts retired or were defeated in the primary or the general election. For more details, see Gary C. Jacobson, *The Politics of Congressional Elections,* 7th ed. (New York: Addison Wesley Longman, 2009), 175–181.

5. The Republicans won control of the House in eight consecutive elections from 1894 to 1908, far short of the Democrats' series of successes.

6. The regional breakdowns used in this chapter are as follows: *East:* Connecticut, Delaware, Maine, Massachusetts, New Hampshire, New Jersey, New York, Pennsylvania, Rhode Island, and Vermont; *Midwest:* Illinois, Indiana, Iowa, Kansas, Michigan, Minnesota, Nebraska, North Dakota, Ohio, South Dakota, and Wisconsin; *West:* Alaska, Arizona, California, Colorado, Hawaii, Idaho, Montana, Nevada, New Mexico, Oregon, Utah, Washington, and Wyoming; *South:* Alabama, Arkansas, Florida, Georgia, Louisiana, Mississippi, North Carolina, South Carolina, Tennessee, Texas, and Virginia; *border:* Kentucky, Maryland, Missouri, Oklahoma, and West Virginia. This classification differs somewhat from the one used in earlier chapters (and in Chapter 10), but it is commonly used for congressional analysis.

7. Over the years, changes in the southern electorate have also made southern Democratic constituencies more like northern Democratic constituencies and less like Republican constituencies, North or South. These changes also appear to have enhanced the homogeneity of preferences within the partisan delegations in Congress. See David W. Rohde, "Electoral Forces, Political Agendas, and Partisanship in the House and Senate," in *The Postreform Congress,* ed. Roger H. Davidson (New York: St. Martin's Press, 1992), 27–47.

8. On the importance of party records electorally, see Gary W. Cox and Mathew D. McCubbins, *Legislative Leviathan: Party Government in the House* (Berkeley: University of California Press, 1993), 110–120.

9. Quoted in William Schneider, "The Toxic GOP Label," *National Journal,* May 24, 2008, 68.

10. Quoted in Ken Dilanian, "After Losses, Republicans Fear Public Has Lost Confidence in Party," *USA Today,* May 15, 2008, 6A.

11. Aaron Blake, "Republicans Look for New Message, No Sugar Coating after Latest Defeat," *The Hill,* May 15, 2008, 14.

12. Dilanian, "After Losses," 6A.

13. "GOP Looks for Ways to Regroup after Losses," cqpolitics.com, May 6, 2008.

14. See Brian Friel, "Spending Split," *National Journal,* May 31, 2008, 38–39.

15. Quoted in Adam Nagourney and Carl Hulse, "Election Losses for Republicans Stir Fall Fears," *New York Times,* May 15, 2008, A26.

16. "House G.O.P. Adopts Change Theme," thecaucusblogs.nytimes.com, May 12, 2008.

17. See Paul R. Abramson, John H. Aldrich, and David W. Rohde, *Change and Continuity in the 1996 and 1998 Elections* (Washington, D.C.: CQ Press, 1999), 207–212.

18. These polling data were taken from pollingreport.com, June 22, 2009.

19. For a discussion of the bigger role played by the national party organizations in congressional elections over the last three decades, see Paul S. Herrnson, *Congressional Elections,* 5th. ed. (Washington, D.C.: CQ Press, 2008), chap. 4.

20. Jared Allen, "House Chairmen Respond to Speaker Pelosi's Call for Cash," *The Hill,* October 22, 2008, 3.

21. See "PACs Put House Democrats on Top for First Time Since 1994," cqpolitics.com, November 18, 2008.

22. Raymond Hernandez, "National G.O.P. Ending Aid to Most New York Races," *New York Times,* October 31, 2008, A24.

23. *The Hill,* November 15, 2007, 15.

24. The ratings were taken from various issues of *The Cook Political Report.* Competitive races are those Cook classified as those only leaning toward the incumbent party, toss-ups, or those tilted toward the other party.

25. Richard F. Fenno Jr., *Home Style: House Members in Their Districts* (Boston: Little, Brown, 1978). For a discussion of how relationships between representatives and constituents have changed over time, see Fenno, *Congress at the Grassroots* (Chapel Hill: University of North Carolina Press, 2000).

26. For example, an analysis of Senate races in 1988 indicated that both the political quality of the previous office held and the challenger's political skills had an independent effect on the outcome of the race. See Peverill Squire, "Challenger Quality and Voting Behavior in U.S. Senate Elections," *Legislative Studies Quarterly* 17 (May 1992): 247–263. For systematic evidence on the impact of candidate quality in House races, see Gary C. Jacobson, *The Electoral Origins of Divided Government: Competition in U.S. House Elections, 1946–1988* (Boulder, Colo.: Westview Press, 1990), chap. 4.

27. Al Franken was an entertainment celebrity, which can bring some of the same electoral benefits to a candidate as previous office experience. See David T. Canon, *Actors, Athletes, and Astronauts: Political Amateurs in the United States Congress* (Chicago: University of Chicago Press, 1990).

28. Data on earlier years are taken from our studies of previous national elections.

29. The figures in this paragraph include races in which only one of the parties fielded a candidate as well as contests in which both did.

30. See Jacobson, *Electoral Origins of Divided Government*; Jon R. Bond, Cary Covington, and Richard Fleisher, "Explaining Challenger Quality in Congressional Elections," *Journal of Politics* 47 (May 1985): 510–529; and David W. Rohde, "Risk-Bearing and Progressive Ambition: The Case of Members of the U.S. House of Representatives," *American Journal of Political Science* 23 (February 1979): 1–26.

31. L. Sandy Maisel and Walter J. Stone, "Determinants of Candidate Emergence in U.S. House Elections: An Exploratory Study," *Legislative Studies Quarterly* 22 (February 1997): 79–96.

32. See Peverill Squire, "Preemptive Fund-raising and Challenger Profile in Senate Elections," *Journal of Politics* 53 (November 1991): 1150–1164; and Jay Goodliffe, "The Effect of War Chests on Challenger Entry in U.S. House Elections," *American Journal of Political Science* 45 (October 2001): 1087–1108.

33. Jeffrey S. Banks and D. Roderick Kiewiet, "Explaining Patterns of Candidate Competition in Congressional Elections," *American Journal of Political Science* 33 (November 1989): 997–1015.

34. Canon, *Actors, Athletes, and Astronauts.*

35. See Kenneth J. Cooper, "Riding High Name Recognition to Hill," *Washington Post,* December 24, 1992, A4.

36. See Thomas E. Mann and Raymond E. Wolfinger, "Candidates and Parties in Congressional Elections," *American Political Science Review* 74 (September 1980): 617–632.

37. See David R. Mayhew, "Congressional Elections: The Case of the Vanishing Marginals," *Polity* 6 (Spring 1974): 295–317; Robert S. Erikson, "Malapportionment, Gerrymandering, and Party Fortunes in Congressional Elections," *American Political Science Review* 66 (December 1972): 1234–1245; and Warren Lee Kostroski, "Party and Incumbency in Postwar Senate Elections: Trends, Patterns, and Models," *American Political Science Review* 67 (December 1973): 1213–1234.

38. Edward R. Tufte, "Communication," *American Political Science Review* 68 (March 1974): 211–213. The communication involved a discussion of Tufte's earlier article "The Relationship between Seats and Votes in Two-Party Systems," *American Political Science Review* 67 (June 1973): 540–554.

39. See John A. Ferejohn, "On the Decline of Competition in Congressional Elections," *American Political Science Review* 71 (March 1977): 166–176; Albert D. Cover, "One Good Term Deserves Another: The Advantage of Incumbency in Congressional Elections," *American Journal of Political Science* 21 (August 1977): 523–541; and Albert D. Cover and David R. Mayhew, "Congressional Dynamics and the Decline of Competition in Congressional

Elections," in *Congress Reconsidered,* 2nd ed., ed. Lawrence C. Dodd and Bruce I. Oppenheimer (Washington, D.C.: CQ Press, 1981), 62–82.

40. Morris P. Fiorina, *Congress: Keystone of the Washington Establishment,* 2nd ed. (New Haven, Conn.: Yale University Press, 1989), esp. chaps. 4–6.

41. See several conflicting arguments and conclusions in the following articles published in the *American Journal of Political Science* 25 (August 1981): John R. Johannes and John C. McAdams, "The Congressional Incumbency Effect: Is It Casework, Policy Compatibility, or Something Else? An Examination of the 1978 Election" (512–542); Morris P. Fiorina, "Some Problems in Studying the Effects of Resource Allocation in Congressional Elections" (543–567); Diana Evans Yiannakis, "The Grateful Electorate: Casework and Congressional Elections" (568–580); and McAdams and Johannes, "Does Casework Matter? A Reply to Professor Fiorina" (581–604). See also John R. Johannes, *To Serve the People: Congress and Constituency Service* (Lincoln: University of Nebraska Press, 1984), esp. chap. 8; and Albert D. Cover and Bruce S. Brumberg, "Baby Books and Ballots: The Impact of Congressional Mail on Constituent Opinion," *American Political Science Review* 76 (June 1982): 347–359. The evidence in Cover and Brumberg for a positive electoral effect is quite strong, but the result may be applicable only to limited circumstances.

42. Ferejohn, "On the Decline of Competition," 174.

43. Cover, "One Good Term," 535.

44. More recent research shows that the link between party identification and voting has strengthened again. See Larry M. Bartels, "Partisanship and Voting Behavior, 1952–1996," *American Journal of Political Science* 44 (January 2000): 35–50.

45. For an excellent analysis of the growth of and reasons for anti-Congress sentiment, see John R. Hibbing and Elizabeth Theiss-Morse, *Congress as Public Enemy* (New York: Cambridge University Press, 1995).

46. However, we note again that these results ignore races that do not have candidates from both major parties. There was a sharp increase in these races in 1998: ninety-four, compared with only seventeen in 1996 and fifty-two in 1994. The number was almost as large in 2000: eighty-one.

47. For an analysis that indicates that the variations in incumbents' vote percentages have few implications for incumbent safety, see Jeffrey M. Stonecash, *Reassessing the Incumbency Effect* (Cambridge, UK: Cambridge University Press, 2008).

48. The body of literature on this subject is now quite large. Some salient early examples, in addition to those cited later, are Gary C. Jacobson, *Money in Congressional Elections* (New Haven, Conn.: Yale University Press, 1980); Jacobson, "Parties and PACs in Congressional Elections," in *Congress Reconsidered,* 4th ed., ed. Lawrence C. Dodd and Bruce I. Oppenheimer (Washington, D.C.: CQ Press, 1989), 117–152; Jacobson and Samuel Kernell, *Strategy and Choice in Congressional Elections,* 2nd ed. (New Haven, Conn.: Yale University Press, 1983);

and John A. Ferejohn and Morris P. Fiorina, "Incumbency and Realignment in Congressional Elections," in *The New Direction in American Politics*, ed. John E. Chubb and Paul E. Peterson (Washington, D.C.: Brookings, 1985), 91–115.

49. See Jacobson, *Electoral Origins of Divided Government*, 63–65.

50. See Jacobson and Kernell, *Strategy and Choice in Congressional Elections*.

51. Evidence indicates that challenger spending strongly influences public visibility and that substantial amounts can significantly reduce the recognition gap between the challenger and the incumbent. See Jacobson, *Politics of Congressional Elections*, 134.

52. See Paul R. Abramson, John H. Aldrich, and David W. Rohde, *Change and Continuity in the 2004 and 2006 Elections* (Washington, D.C.: CQ Press, 2007), 229–241, and the earlier work cited there.

53. See Jacobson, *Electoral Origins of Divided Government*, 54–55, and the work cited in note 51.

54. Donald Philip Green and Jonathan S. Krasno, "Salvation for the Spendthrift Incumbent: Reestimating the Effects of Campaign Spending in House Elections," *American Journal of Political Science* 32 (November 1988): 884–907.

55. Gary C. Jacobson, "The Effects of Campaign Spending in House Elections: New Evidence for Old Arguments," *American Journal of Political Science* 34 (May 1990): 334–362. Green and Kranno's response can be found in the same issue on pages 363–372.

56. Alan I. Abramowitz, "Explaining Senate Election Outcomes," *American Political Science Review* 82 (June 1988): 385–403; Alan Gerber, "Estimating the Effect of Campaign Spending on Senate Election Outcomes Using Instrumental Variables," *American Political Science Review* 92 (June 1998): 401–411.

57. Gary C. Jacobson, "Campaign Spending and Voter Awareness of Congressional Candidates" (paper presented at the annual meeting of the Public Choice Society, New Orleans, May 11–13, 1977), 16.

58. Chuck McCutcheon and Christina L. Lyons, eds., *CQ's Politics in America 2010* (Washington, D.C.: CQ Press, 2009), 1167.

59. The exception was the defeat of Democratic representative William Jefferson of Louisiana, who was under indictment.

60. Challengers were categorized as having strong experience if they had been elected U.S. representative, to statewide office, to the state legislature, or to countywide or citywide office (for example, mayor, prosecutor, and so on).

61. Paul R. Abramson, John H. Aldrich, and David W. Rohde, *Change and Continuity in the 1980 Elections*, rev. ed. (Washington, D.C.: CQ Press, 1983), 202–203. See also Paul Gronke, *The Electorate, the Campaign, and the Office: A Unified Approach to Senate and House Elections* (Ann Arbor: University of Michigan Press, 2001).

62. Other Democratic Senate winners in 2000 who spent millions of their own money were Maria Cantwell of Washington and Mark Dayton of Minnesota.

63. Quoted in Angela Herrin, "Big Outside Money Backfired in GOP Loss of Senate to Dems," *Washington Post,* November 6, 1986, A46.

64. See David W. Rohde, *Parties and Leaders in the Postreform House* (Chicago: University of Chicago Press, 1991), esp. chap. 3; and Rohde, "Electoral Forces, Political Agendas, and Partisanship," 27–47.

65. For discussions of the ideological changes in the House and Senate over the last four decades, see John H. Aldrich and David W. Rohde, "The Logic of Conditional Party Government: Revisiting the Electoral Connection," in *Congress Reconsidered,* 7th ed., ed. Lawrence C. Dodd and Bruce I. Oppenheimer (Washington, D.C.: CQ Press, 2001), 269–292; Gary C. Jacobson, "The Congress: The Structural Basis of Republican Success," in *The Elections of 2004,* ed. Michael Nelson (Washington, D.C.: CQ Press, 2005), 163–186; and Sean Theriault, *Party Polarization in Congress* (Cambridge, UK: Cambridge University Press, 2008).

66. See Paul R. Abramson, John H. Aldrich, and David W. Rohde, *Change and Continuity in the 1992 Elections,* rev. ed. (Washington, D.C.: CQ Press, 1995), 339–342; and John H. Aldrich and David W. Rohde, "The Transition to Republican Rule in the House: Implications for Theories of Congressional Politics," *Political Science Quarterly* 112 (Winter 1997–1998): 541–567.

67. See John H. Aldrich and David W. Rohde, "Congressional Committees in a Continuing Partisan Era," in *Congress Reconsidered,* 9th ed., ed. Lawrence C. Dodd and Bruce I. Oppenheimer (Washington D.C.: CQ Press, 2009), 235.

68. Tory Newmyer and Paul Singer, "Dingell Waxman Brouhaha Awaits," *Roll Call,* November 6, 2008, 1.

69. John M. Broder, "Waxman Advances in Struggle to Wrest Energy Committee Reins from Dingell," *New York Times,* November 20, 2008, A24.

70. See Richard Cohen, "Pelosi's Shift," *National Journal,* June 6, 2009, 31–34.

71. Edward Epstein, "Pelosi's Action Plan for Party Unity," *CQ Weekly,* March 30, 2009, 706–707.

72. Greg Giroux, "Split Districts of '08 Key to GOP Rebound Hopes," *CQ Weekly,* March 23, 2009, 659.

73. For discussions of the role of filibusters in recent Congresses, see Barbara Sinclair, "The New World of U.S. Senators," in Dodd and Oppenheimer, *Congress Reconsidered,* 9th ed., 1–22; and Thomas E. Mann and Norman J. Ornstein, "Is Congress Still the Broken Branch?" in Dodd and Oppenheimer, *Congress Reconsidered,* 9th ed., 53–69.

74. Paul Cain and Shailagh Murray, "Democrats Allow Lieberman to Retain Key Chairmanship," washingtonpost.com, November 19, 2009.

75. "Less" is the operative word here. Despite its different rules, parties still can be consequential in the Senate. See Nathan W. Monroe, Jason M. Roberts, and David W. Rohde, eds., *Why Not Parties?* (Chicago: University of Chicago Press, 2008).

76. See *Roll Call,* November 20, 2008, 1.

77. http://caffertyfile.blogs.cnn.com/category/barack-obama/, January 19, 2009.

78. *The Hill,* January 21, 2009, 4.

79. Emily Pierce, "Reid Gets Spoils of 100th Day," *Roll Call,* April 29, 2009, 28.

80. See *New York Times,* April 16, 2009, A14.

81. Bart Jansen and Kathleen Hunter, "Sen. Specter Switches to Democratic Party," *CQ Weekly,* May 4, 2009, 1038.

82. See Carl Hulse and Adam Nagourney, "Specter Switches Parties; More Heft for Democrats," *New York Times,* April 29, 2009, A1.

83. The support of the GOP members came at a price, including reducing the amount of the stimulus plan by over $100 billion. See *Roll Call,* February 17, 2009, 1.

84. The Republican was Wayne Gilchrist and the Democrat was Albert Wynn.

85. *Roll Call,* April 29, 2009, 19.

86. Hulse and Nagourney, "Specter Switches Parties," A3.

87. The most recent line of research on these questions was launched by the publication of David R. Mayhew's *Divided We Govern* (New Haven, Conn.: Yale University Press, 1991). Mayhew contended that divided government was not less likely to produce major legislation. For a discussion of the research following on Mayhew's analysis, see David W. Rohde and Meredith Barthelemy, "The President and Congressional Parties in an Era of Polarization," in *Oxford Handbook of the American Presidency,* ed. George C. Edwards III and William G. Howell (New York: Oxford University Press, 2009), 289–310.

88. *New York Times,* November 24, 2009, A17.

89. *Washington Post,* January 24, 2009, A4; *New York Times,* January 28, 2009, A17.

90. Dana Milbank, "Agitated? Irritable? Hostile? Aggressive? Impulsive? Restless?" *Washington Post,* May 15, 2009, A3.

91. *The Hill,* March 25, 2009, 1.

92. *Roll Call,* April 6, 2009, 1; *New York Times,* March 31, 2009, A17.

93. David Clarke and Paul M. Krawzak, "Both Chambers Float Budget Plans," *CQ Weekly,* March 30, 2009, 725.

94. John Rogin, "Conferees Reach Deal on Supplemental," *CQ Weekly,* June 15, 2009, 1380.

95. *New York Times,* May 21, 2009, A16.

96. Eleven were signed by the president. The twelfth, the budget resolution, does not require a presidential signature.

97. Carl Hulse, "House Rebukes Wilson for Shouting 'You Lie,'" *New York Times,* September 15, 2009, www.nytimes.com/2000/09/16/us/politics/.

98. Earlier research indicated that for these purposes voters may tend to regard a president whose predecessor either died or resigned from office as a continuation of the first president's administration. Therefore, these data

are organized by term of administration rather than term of president. See Abramson, Aldrich, and Rohde, *Change and Continuity in the 1980 Elections*, rev. ed., 252–253.

99. Edward R. Tufte, "Determinants of the Outcomes of Midterm Congressional Elections," *American Political Science Review* 69 (September 1975): 812–826; Tufte, *Political Control of the Economy* (Princeton, N.J.: Princeton University Press, 1978); Jacobson and Kernell, *Strategy and Choice in Congressional Elections*.

100. The Jacobson-Kernell hypothesis was challenged by Richard Born in "Strategic Politicians and Unresponsive Voters," *American Political Science Review* 80 (June 1986): 599–612. Born argued that economic and approval data at the time of the election were more closely related to outcomes than were parallel data from earlier in the year. Jacobson, however, offered renewed support for the hypothesis in an analysis of both district-level and aggregate data. See Gary C. Jacobson, "Strategic Politicians and the Dynamics of House Elections, 1946–86," *American Political Science Review* 83 (September 1989): 773–793.

101. Alan I. Abramowitz, Albert D. Cover, and Helmut Norpoth, "The President's Party in Midterm Elections: Going from Bad to Worse," *American Journal of Political Science* 30 (August 1986): 562–576.

102. Bruce I. Oppenheimer, James A. Stimson, and Richard W. Waterman, "Interpreting U.S. Congressional Elections: The Exposure Thesis," *Legislative Studies Quarterly* 11 (May 1986): 228.

103. Robin F. Marra and Charles W. Ostrom Jr., "Explaining Seat Changes in the U.S. House of Representatives 1950–86," *American Journal of Political Science* 33 (August 1989): 541–569.

104. Brian Newman and Charles W. Ostrom Jr., "Explaining Seat Changes in the U.S. House of Representatives, 1950–1998," *Legislative Studies Quarterly* 28 (2002): 383–405.

105. This is why the president's party gained seats in the midterms of 1998 and 2002. In addition, evidence indicates that divided government may also reduce the vulnerability of the president's party in midterms. See Stephen P. Nicholson and Gary M. Segura, "Midterm Elections and Divided Government: An Information-Driven Theory of Electoral Volatility," *Political Research Quarterly* 52 (September 1999): 609–629.

106. These data were taken from pollingreport.com.

107. Ibid.

108. In eight states (Arizona, California, Hawaii, Idaho, Iowa, Maine, New Jersey, and Washington), congressional redistricting is not carried out by state legislatures, but is controlled or strongly influenced by independent bipartisan commissions. Seven other states (Alaska, Delaware, Montana, North Dakota, South Dakota, Vermont, and Wyoming) have only one House seat and so do not experience redistricting.

109. *The Rothenberg Political Report*, May 15, 2009.

110. The eleven are Florida, Georgia, Illinois, Massachusetts, Michigan, New York, North Carolina, Ohio, Pennsylvania, Texas, and Virginia.

111. *Roll Call,* April 28, 2009, 11.

112. Shira Toeplitz, "Ohio's Limits Tip Races," *Roll Call,* November 20, 2008, 13.

113. *USA Today,* May 4, 2009, 4A.

114. *Washington Post,* March 10, 2009, A2.

115. Damien Cave, "Ruling Prompts a Mixed Response," *New York Times,* June 23, 2009, A16.

116. Adam Liptak, "Case Could Overturn Rules on Campaign Spending," *New York Times,* June 30, 2009, A12.

117. *Washington Post,* May 14, 2009, A19.

118. *The Hill,* May 19, 2009, 6.

119. See "When People Stop Moving, So Do Congressional Seats," online.wsj. com, February 5, 2009.

10. THE CONGRESSIONAL ELECTORATE IN 2008

1. As we saw in Chapter 5, the 2008 ANES survey results show a very small overreport of the Democratic share of the presidential vote. There is, however, a small pro-Republican bias in the House vote. According to the 2008 ANES survey, the Democrats received 54 percent of the major-party vote; official results show that the Democrats received 55.5 percent of the actual national two-party vote. (The national results were taken from thegreenpapers.com/G08/House-VoteByParty.phtml.) To simplify presentation of the data, we have eliminated from consideration votes for minor-party candidates in all the tables in this chapter. Furthermore, to ensure that our study of choice is meaningful, in all tables except 10-1 and 10-2 we include only voters who lived in congressional districts in which both major parties ran candidates.

2. We confine our attention in this section to voting for the House because this group of voters is more directly comparable to the presidential electorate. We employ here the same definitions for social and demographic categories used in Chapters 4 and 5.

3. See Larry M. Bartels, "Partisanship and Voting Behavior, 1952–1996," *American Journal of Political Science* 44 (January 2000): 35–50.

4. Paul R. Abramson, John H. Aldrich, and David W. Rohde, *Change and Continuity in the 1980 Elections,* rev. ed. (Washington, D.C.: CQ Press, 1983), 213–216.

5. Among liberal voters who did not see the Democratic House candidate as more liberal than the Republican candidate ($N = 31$), 76 percent voted Democratic; among conservative voters who did not see the Republican candidate as more conservative than the Democratic candidate ($N = 53$), 35 percent voted Republican.

6. Alan I. Abramowitz, "Choices and Echoes in the 1978 U.S. Senate Elections: A Research Note," *American Journal of Political Science* 25 (February 1981): 112–118; and Abramowitz, "National Issues, Strategic Politicians, and Voting Behavior in the 1980 and 1982 Congressional Elections," *American Journal of Political Science* 28 (November 1984): 710–721.

7. Robert S. Erikson and Gerald C. Wright, "Voters, Candidates, and Issues in Congressional Elections," in *Congress Reconsidered,* 3rd ed., ed. Lawrence C. Dodd and Bruce I. Oppenheimer (Washington, D.C.: CQ Press, 1985), 91–116.

8. Robert S. Erikson and Gerald C. Wright, "Voters, Candidates, and Issues in Congressional Elections," in *Congress Reconsidered,* 6th ed., ed. Lawrence C. Dodd and Bruce I. Oppenheimer (Washington, D.C.: CQ Press, 1993), 148–150.

9. Robert S. Erikson and Gerald C. Wright, "Voters, Candidates, and Issues in Congressional Elections," in *Congress Reconsidered,* 9th ed., ed. Lawrence C. Dodd and Bruce I Oppenheimer (Washington, D.C.: CQ Press, 2009), 83–88.

10. Robert S. Erikson and Gerald C. Wright, "Voters, Candidates, and Issues in Congressional Elections," in *Congress Reconsidered,* 8th ed., ed. Lawrence C. Dodd and Bruce I Oppenheimer (Washington, D.C.: CQ Press, 2005), 93–95. See also Stephen Ansolabehere, James M. Snyder Jr., and Charles Stewart III, "Candidate Positioning in U.S. House Elections," *American Journal of Political Science* 45 (January 2001): 136–159.

11. For the wording of the ANES party identification questions, see Chapter 4, note 74.

12. Albert D. Cover, "One Good Term Deserves Another: The Advantage of Incumbency in Congressional Elections," *American Journal of Political Science* 21 (August 1977): 523–541. Cover includes in his analysis not only strong and weak partisans, but also independents with partisan leanings.

13. The 2008 ANES survey may contain biases that inflate the percentage that reports voting for House incumbents. For a discussion of this problem in earlier years, see Robert B. Eubank and David John Gow, "The Pro-Incumbent Bias in the 1978 and 1980 Election Studies," *American Journal of Political Science* 27 (February 1983): 122–139; and David John Gow and Robert B. Eubank, "The Pro-Incumbent Bias in the 1982 Election Study," *American Journal of Political Science* 28 (February 1984): 224–230.

14. Richard F. Fenno Jr., "If, as Ralph Nader Says, Congress Is 'The Broken Branch,' How Come We Love Our Congressmen So Much?" in *Congress in Change: Evolution and Reform,* ed. Norman J. Ornstein (New York: Praeger, 1975), 277–287. This theme is expanded and analyzed in Richard F. Fenno Jr., *Home Style: House Members in Their Districts* (Boston: Little, Brown, 1978).

15. Abramson, Aldrich, and Rohde, *Change and Continuity in the 1980 Elections,* 220–221.

16. Opinion on this last point is not unanimous, however. See Richard Born, "Reassessing the Decline of Presidential Coattails: U.S. House Elections from 1952–80," *Journal of Politics* 46 (February 1984): 60–79.

17. John A. Ferejohn and Randall L. Calvert, "Presidential Coattails in Historical Perspective," *American Journal of Political Science* 28 (February 1984): 127–146.

18. Randall L. Calvert and John A. Ferejohn, "Coattail Voting in Recent Presidential Elections," *American Political Science Review* 77 (June 1983): 407–419.

19. James E. Campbell and Joe A. Sumners, "Presidential Coattails in Senate Elections," *American Political Science Review* 84 (June 1990): 513–524.

INTRODUCTION TO PART IV

1. Some argue that the oracle did not have prophetic powers of her own, but that she did have the ability to pass on messages from Apollo. Christians suppressed the worship of pagan deities, and there is no longer an oracle to pass on messages.

2. Niccolò Machiavelli, *The Prince*, 2nd ed., trans. Harvey C. Mansfield Jr. (Chicago: University of Chicago Press, 1998), 98.

3. In Palm Beach County, the Gore-Lieberman ticket appeared as the second set of candidates on the left-hand side of the ballot, but the punch hole for the Democratic ticket was the third one down. The second punch was for the Buchanan-Foster Reform Party ticket. Not only did 3,400 voters punch the Reform Party ticket, but an additional 19,000 voters punched more than two holes, and these "overvotes" were invalid. For convincing evidence that Bush's 537-vote victory in Florida resulted from the butterfly ballot, see Jonathan N. Wand et al., "The Butterfly Did It: The Aberrant Vote for Buchanan in Palm Beach County, Florida," *American Political Science Review* 95 (December 2001): 793–810.

4. For an excellent discussion of American public opinion on these issues in light of the 9/11 terrorist attacks, see Darren W. Davis, *Negative Liberty: Public Opinion and the Terrorist Attacks on America* (New York: Russell Sage Foundation, 2007).

5. Paul R. Abramson et al., "Fear in the Voting Booth: The 2004 Presidential Election," *Political Behavior* 29 (June 2007): 197–220. See also Helmut Norpoth and Andrew H. Sidman, "Mission Accomplished: The Wartime Election of 2004," *Political Behavior* 29 (June 2007): 175–195; and Herbert F. Weisberg and Dino P. Christenson, "Changing Horses in Wartime? The 2004 Presidential Election," *Political Behavior* 29 (June 2007): 279–304.

6. *New York Times*/CBS News poll, September 9–13, 2005, www.nytimes.com/packages/khtml/2005/09/14/politics/2050915_POLL.html.

7. This number is from "The Iraq Body Count Data Base," www.iraqbodycount.net/database.

8. All these results were found at www.pollingreport.com/iraq/htm.

9. See Paul R. Abramson, John H. Aldrich, and David W. Rohde, *Change and Continuity in the 2004 and 2006 Elections* (Washington, D.C.: CQ Press,

2007), chap. 11. See also Gary C. Jacobson, "Referendum: The 2006 Midterm Congressional Elections," *Political Science Quarterly* 122 (Spring 2007): 1–24; and Gary C. Jacobson, *A Divider, Not a Uniter: George W. Bush and the American People, The 2006 Election and Beyond* (New York: Pearson Longman, 2008), 263–323.

10. Catherine Clifford, "CNN Foreclosures," http://money.cnn.com/2008/11/13.

11. Price History, PRES08_WTA, http://iemweb.biz,uiowa.edu/pricehistory/PriceHistory_GetData.cfm.

12. Of course, this is not the same as who will win the election, although in forty-two of forty-five contests between 1828 and 2004 the popular vote winner was elected.

13. Trading activity was not actually conducted every day during this period. In addition to the closing price for each day (regardless of whether there were trades), the IEM contract history shows the high and low prices for each day on which trading occurred. Even looking at these high and low daily prices, we noted that the Republicans were never favored.

14. Based on the daily low price for the Democrats and the daily high price for the Republicans.

15. James W. Ceaser, Andrew E. Busch, and John J. Pitney Jr., *Epic Journey: The 2008 Elections and American Politics* (Lanham, Md.: Rowman and Littlefield, 2009), 145–150.

16. One of these, Senate contender Al Franken, was not actually declared the winner by the Minnesota Supreme Court until June 30, 2009.

17. Neither the number of House seats nor the date of the election is constitutionally fixed. It seems unlikely that the date of the election (the first Tuesday after the first Monday in November) will be changed, but the number of House seats may increase marginally by 2010.

18. In addition to thirty-four races for a full six-year term, there will be races to fill the remaining four years of the term of Delaware's Joe Biden and the remaining two years of the term of New York's Hillary Clinton.

19. Even if Obama were to leave office, there would be no election to fill this presidency (see the Twenty-fifth Amendment for the rules for presidential succession). In France, a new election is held to select a new president for a full presidential term. This has happened twice—in 1969 when Charles de Gaulle resigned, and in 1974 when Georges Pompidou died in office.

20. Abraham Lincoln never considered postponing the 1864 election. As he explained, even if there were a constitutional way to cancel or to postpone them, "We cannot have free government without elections.... [I]f the rebellion could force us to forgo or to postpone a national election, it might fairly claim to have already conquered and ruined us." Quoted in David Herbert Donald, *Lincoln* (New York: Simon and Schuster, 1995), 539.

11. THE 2008 ELECTIONS AND THE FUTURE OF AMERICAN POLITICS

1. Maurice Duverger, *Political Parties: Their Organization and Activity in the Modern World,* trans. Barbara North and Robert North (New York: Wiley, 1963), 308–309. In this book, we use the term *majority* to mean more than half the vote. But it is clear that for Duverger the term *majorité* signifies a plurality of the vote—that is, more votes than any other party received.

2. Mapai is the Hebrew acronym for Mifleget Poa'alei Eretz Yisrael (Party of Eretz Yisrael [Land of Israel] Workers), which was founded in 1930. In 1968 Mapai merged with two smaller parties and became the Alignment. That coalition then fell apart. In 2009 Labor ran on its own.

Israel, Italy, Sweden, and Japan are the four countries discussed in *Uncommon Democracies: The One-Party Dominant Regimes,* ed. T. J. Pempel (Ithaca, N.Y.: Cornell University Press, 1990). Other democracies that might have been classified as having, or having had, a dominant party are Chile, Colombia, Denmark, Iceland, India, Norway, and Venezuela. See also Alan Arian and Samuel H. Barnes, "The Dominant Party System: A Neglected Model of Democratic Stability," *Journal of Politics* 36 (August 1974): 592–614.

3. Duverger, *Political Parties,* 312.

4. Duverger was vague about the reasons dominant parties tended to decline. He suggested that they become too bureaucratized to govern effectively and to respond to changing conditions. Although dominant parties clearly fell from power in Israel and Italy and have lost their dominance in Sweden and in Japan, a variety of reasons account for their decline.

5. Asher Arian, *Politics in Israel: The Second Republic,* 2nd ed. (Washington, D.C.: CQ Press, 2005), 124.

6. The election was held in February 2001, and there was no Knesset election. In March 2001, the Knesset abolished direct election of the prime minister.

7. For a discussion of the 2009 election, see Abraham Diskin, "The Likud," *Israel Affairs,* forthcoming.

8. For an analysis of the gradual decline of the DC, see Sidney Tarrow, "Maintaining Hegemony in Italy: 'The Softer They Rise, the Slower They Fall!'" in Pempel, *Uncommon Democracies,* 306–322. Tarrow could not foresee the rapid disintegration of the DC that would take place after Pempel's collection was published. For two more recent discussions, see Martin J. Bull and James L. Newell, *Italian Democracy: Adjustment under Duress* (Cambridge, UK: Polity Press, 2005); and Martin J. Bull and James L. Newell, "Italy," in *Political Parties in the World,* ed. Alan J. Day (London: John Harper, 2005), 330–341.

9. Martin J. Bull, personal communication, December 19, 2006.

10. Joseph A. LaPalombara, personal communication, December 9, 2006.

11. Martin J. Bull, personal communication, August 1, 2009.

12. "Sweden's Election: Reinfeldt Explained," *The Economist,* September 23, 2006, 60.

13. The next general election is scheduled for September 19, 2010. The Social Democrats are currently led by Mona Sahlin.

14. "The Vote That Changed Japan," *The Economist,* September 5, 2009, 13.

15. Maurice Duverger, *Les partis politiques,* 3rd ed. (Paris: Armand Colin, 1958). The English language translation we use appeared in 1963 (see note 1).

16. See, for example, Michael Nelson, "Constitutional Aspects of the Election," in *The Elections of 1988,* ed. Michael Nelson (Washington, D.C.: CQ Press, 1989), 161–201. See also Byron E. Shafer, "The Election of 2008 and the Structure of American Politics: Explaining a New Political Order," *Electoral Studies* 8 (April 1989): 5–21.

17. By 1828 every state except Maryland and South Carolina was choosing its electors by popular vote. The first incumbent to be elected after that was Andrew Jackson in 1832.

18. The only closer margin was in 1916 when Woodrow Wilson defeated Charles Evans Hughes by a twenty-three–vote margin.

19. Gary C. Jacobson, "The Congress: The Structural Basis of Republican Success," in *The Elections of 2004,* ed. Michael Nelson (Washington, D.C.: CQ Press, 2005), 166; and Gary C. Jacobson, "Polarized Politics and the 2004 Congressional and Presidential Elections," *Political Science Quarterly* 120 (Summer 2005): 199–218.

20. In April 2009, Republican senator Arlen Specter switched parties, and on June 30, 2009, the Minnesota Supreme Court awarded the Minnesota Senate seat to the Democratic challenger, Al Franken, over the Republican incumbent, Norm Coleman.

21. John B. Judis and Ruy Teixeira, *The Emerging Democratic Majority* (New York: Scribner's, 2002).

22. Ibid. Teixeira, along with William Galston and Stanley B. Greenberg, edits *The Democratic Strategist,* which publishes material for interpreting American politics with the goal of helping to elect Democratic candidates. See www.the democraticstrategist.org.

23. For poll results measuring opinions about Afghanistan, see http://pollingreport.com/afghan.htm.

24. Gary C. Jacobson, "The Effects of the George W. Bush Presidency on Partisan Attitudes," *Presidential Studies Quarterly* 39 (June 2009): 172–208.

25. NBC/*Wall Street Journal* Survey, Study #6095. The results are summarized in Laura Meckler, "Public Wary of Deficit, Economic Intervention," *Wall Street Journal,* June 18, 2009, A1, A14.

26. Ibid., A1.

27. Quoted in E. J. Dionne Jr., "Brand on the Run," *Washington Post,* May 16, 2008, A1.

28. *Bill Moyers Journal,* PBS, July 11, 2008, www.pbs.org/moyers/journal/07112008/transcript3.html.

29. The projections shown in Table 11-2 are for the entire resident population, although, obviously, it would be preferable to have projections for the voting-age population. Because the black and Hispanic populations are somewhat younger than the white population, the share of the white population may not decline as quickly as these projections predict, but not enough to make any substantive differences in our discussion.

30. We are highly skeptical of Samuel P. Huntington's widely discussed thesis that the growth of the Latino population poses a major threat to American "Anglo-Protestant" values. See Huntington, *Who Are We? The Challenges to America's National Identity* (New York: Simon and Schuster, 2004).

31. This was the same criterion used in identifying candidates for the 2008 presidential nominations. See Paul R. Abramson, John H. Aldrich, and David W. Rohde, *Change and Continuity in the 2004 and 2006 Elections* (Washington, D.C.: CQ Press, 2007), 312–320. Put differently, a subjective probability of 0.005 means that the candidate appears to have a one in two hundred chance of winning.

32. Linda Meckler and Deborah Solomon, "Governor's Move Highlights GOP Divide," *Wall Street Journal*, July 6, 2009, A3. Wendell Willkie was a forty-eight-year-old corporate lawyer who had never before run for public office.

33. See John H. Aldrich, "The Invisible Primary and Its Effect on Democratic Choice," *PS: Political Science and Politics* 42 (January 2009): 33–38.

34. Arend Lijphart, *Electoral Systems and Party Systems: A Study of Twenty-seven Democracies, 1945–1990* (Oxford, UK: Oxford University Press, 1994), 160–162.

35. "The Mouse That Roared," *The Economist*, September 30, 1995, 32.

36. A study that sent mail questionnaires to people who called Perot's toll-free telephone number between 1992 and 1996 concluded that Perot's 1992 candidacy had an important impact on the Republican Party by activating the electorate. See Ronald B. Rapoport and Walter J. Stone, *Three's a Crowd: The Dynamics of Third Parties, Ross Perot and Republican Resurgence* (Ann Arbor: University of Michigan Press, 2005).

37. In 2008 the total vote for minor candidates crept up to 1.4 percent.

38. Under proportional representation, an environmentalist party may be successful with a relatively small share of the vote. For example, in the 1988 German Bundestag election, the Green Party won only 6.7 percent of the votes and 7.0 percent of the seats, but it became part of the governing coalition. In 2002 the Greens won 6.6 percent of the vote and captured 9.1 percent of the seats, once again becoming part of the governing coalition. In the 2005 election, the Greens won 8.3 percent of the seats, but they did not become part of the governing coalition formed by the two largest parties.

39. Joseph A. Schlesinger, *Political Parties and the Winning of Office* (Ann Arbor: University of Michigan Press, 1991).

40. See John H. Aldrich, *Why Parties? The Origin and Transformation of Political Parties in America* (Chicago: University of Chicago Press, 1995), 126–162.

41. We are grateful to Joseph A. Schlesinger for this insight.

42. Philip E. Converse, *The Dynamics of Party Support: Cohort-Analyzing Party Identification* (Beverley Hills, Calif.: Sage Publications, 1976).

43. Angus Campbell et al., *The American Voter* (New York: Wiley, 1960), 125.

Suggested Readings

(Readings preceded by an asterisk include materials on the 2008 elections.)

Chapter 1: The Nomination Struggle

Abramson, Paul R., John H. Aldrich, Phil Paolino, and David W. Rohde. "'Sophisticated' Voting in the 1988 Presidential Primaries." *American Political Science Review* 86 (March 1992): 55–69.

Abramson, Paul R., John H. Aldrich, and David W. Rohde. "Progressive Ambition among United States Senators: 1972–1988." *Journal of Politics* 49 (February 1987): 3–35.

Aldrich, John H. *Before the Convention: Strategies and Choices in Presidential Nomination Campaigns.* Chicago: University of Chicago Press, 1980.

*———. "The Invisible Primary and Its Effects on Democratic Choice." *PS: Political Science and Politics* 42 (January 2009): 33–38.

*Balz, Dan, and Haynes Johnson. *The Battle for America: 2008, The Story of an Extraordinary Election.* New York: Viking, 2009.

Bartels, Larry M. *Presidential Primaries and the Dynamics of Public Choice.* Princeton, N.J.: Princeton University Press, 1988.

Brams, Steven J. *The Presidential Election Game.* New Haven, Conn.: Yale University Press, 1978, 1–79.

*Burden, Barry C. "The Nominations: Rules, Strategies, and Uncertainty." In *The Elections of 2008*, edited by Michael Nelson. Washington, D.C.: CQ Press, 2009, 22–44.

*Busch, Andrew E. "Assumptions and Realities of Presidential Primary Front-loading in 2008." In *Nominating the President: Evolution and Revolution in 2008 and Beyond*, edited by Jack Citrin and David Karol. Lanham, Md.: Rowman and Littlefield, 2009, 77–93.

*Ceaser, James W., Andrew E. Busch, and John J. Pitney Jr. *Epic Journey: The 2008 Elections and American Politics*. Lanham, Md.: Rowman and Littlefield, 2009, 53–129.

*Citrin, Jack, and David Karol. "Introduction." In *Nominating the President: Evolution and Revolution in 2008 and Beyond*, edited by Jack Citrin and David Karol. Lanham, Md.: Rowman and Littlefield, 2009, 1–25.

*Cohn, Marty, David Karol, Hans Noel, and John Zaller. *The Party Decides Presidential Nominations before and after Reform*. Chicago: University of Chicago Press, 2008.

Hasen, Richard L. "The Changing Nature of Campaign Financing for Primary Candidates." In *Nominating the President: Evolution and Revolution in 2008 and Beyond*, edited by Jack Citrin and David Karol. Lanham, Md.: Rowman and Littlefield, 2009, 27–45.

*Nelson, Michael. "The Setting: Diversifying the Presidential Talent Pool." In *The Elections of 2008*, edited by Michael Nelson. Washington, D.C.: CQ Press, 2009, 1–21.

*Norrander, Barbara. "Democratic Marathon, Republican Sprint: The 2008 Presidential Nominations." In *The American Elections of 2008*, edited by Janet M. Box-Steffensmeier and Steven E. Schier. Lanham, Md.: Rowman and Littlefield, 2009, 33–53.

Polsby, Nelson W., Aaron Wildavsky, with David A. Hopkins. *Presidential Elections: Strategies and Structures of American Politics*, 12th ed. Lanham, Md.: Rowman and Littlefield, 2008, 97–150.

*Reiter, Howard L. "The Nominating Process: Change, More Change, and Continuity." In *Winning the Presidency: 2008*, edited by William J. Crotty. Boulder, Colo.: Paradigm, 2009, 70–86.

*Sizemore, Justin. "Conventions: The Contemporary Significance of a Great American Institution." In *The Year of Obama: How Obama Won the White House*, edited by Larry J. Sabato. New York: Longman, 2010, 1–30.

*Thomas, Evan, and the staff of *Newsweek*. *"A Long Time Coming": The Inspiring, Combative 2008 Campaign and the Historic Election of Barack Obama*. New York: Public Affairs, 2009, 1–127.

*Wayne, Stephen J. "When Democracy Works: The 2008 Presidential Nomination." In *Winning the Presidency: 2008,* edited by William J. Crotty. Boulder, Colo.: Paradigm, 2009, 48–69.

Chapter 2: The General Election Campaign

Brams, Steven J. *The Presidential Election Game.* New Haven, Conn.: Yale University Press, 1978, 80–133.

*Ceaser, James W., Andrew E. Busch, and John J. Pitney Jr. *Epic Journey: The 2008 Elections and American Politics.* Lanham, Md.: Rowman and Littlefield, 2009, 131–162.

*Crotty, William J. "Electing Obama: The 2008 Presidential Campaign." In *Winning the Presidency: 2008,* edited by William J. Crotty. Boulder, Colo.: Paradigm, 2009, 20–47.

Geer, John G. *In Defense of Negativity: Attack Ads in Presidential Campaigns.* Chicago: University of Chicago Press, 2006.

*Hershey, Marjorie Randon. "The Media: Coloring the News." In *The Elections of 2008,* edited by Michael Nelson. Washington, D.C.: CQ Press, 2009, 122–144.

Iyengar, Shanto, and Donald Kinder. *News that Matters: Television and American Opinion.* Chicago: University of Chicago Press, 1987.

Johnson, Richard, Michael G. Hagen, and Kathleen Hall Jamieson. *The 2000 Presidential Election and the Foundations of Party Politics.* Cambridge, UK: Cambridge University Press, 2004.

*Owen, Diana. "The Campaign and the Media." In *The American Elections of 2008,* edited by Janet M. Box-Steffensmeier and Steven E. Schier. Lanham, Md.: Rowman and Littlefield, 2009, 9–31.

Polsby, Nelson W., Aaron Wildavsky, with David A. Hopkins. *Presidential Elections: Strategies and Structures of American Politics,* 12th ed. Lanham, Md.: Rowman and Littlefield, 2008, 151–218.

*Schier, Steven E., and Janet M. Box-Steffensmeier. "The General Election Campaign." In *The American Elections of 2008,* edited by Janet M. Box-Steffensmeier and Steven E. Schier. Lanham, Md.: Rowman and Littlefield, 2009, 55–78.

Shaw, Daron R. *The Race to 270: The Electoral College and the Campaign Strategies of 2000 and 2004.* Chicago: University of Chicago Press, 2006.

*Thomas, Evan, and the staff of *Newsweek.* "A Long Time Coming": The Inspiring, Combative 2008 Campaign and the Historic Election of Barack Obama.* New York: Public Affairs, 2009, 127–181.

Chapter 3: The Election Results

Abramson, Paul R., John H. Aldrich, Phil Paolino, and David W. Rohde. "Third-Party and Independent Candidates in American Politics: Wallace, Anderson, and Perot." *Political Science Quarterly* 110 (Fall 1995): 349–367.

Black, Earl, and Merle Black. *The Vital South: How Presidents Are Elected.* Cambridge, Mass.: Harvard University Press, 1992.

Burnham, Walter Dean. *Critical Elections and the Mainsprings of American Politics.* New York: Norton, 1970.

*Ceaser, James W., and Daniel DiSalvo. "The Magnitude of the 2008 Democratic Victory: By the Numbers." *The Forum* 6, no. 4 (2008): art. 8, www.bepress. com/forumvol6/iss4/art8.

*Ceaser, James W., Andrew E. Busch, and John J. Pitney Jr. *Epic Journey: The 2008 Elections and American Politics.* Lanham, Md.: Rowman and Littlefield, 2009, 1–34.

*Cook, Rhodes. "From Republican 'Lock' to Republican 'Lockout'?" In *The Year of Obama: How Barack Obama Won the White House,* edited by Larry J. Sabato. New York: Longman, 2010, 75–89.

Kelley, Stanley, Jr. *Interpreting Elections.* Princeton, N.J.: Princeton University Press, 1983.

Lamis, Alexander P. *The Two-Party South,* exp. ed. New York: Oxford University Press, 1990.

Mayhew, David R. *Electoral Realignments: A Critique of an American Genre.* New Haven, Conn.: Yale University Press, 2002.

———. "Incumbency Advantage in U.S. Presidential Elections: The Historical Record." *Political Science Quarterly* 123 (Summer 2008): 201–228.

*Mellow, Nicole. "Voting Behavior: A Blue Nation?" In *The Elections of 2008,* edited by Michael Nelson. Washington, D.C.: CQ Press, 2009, 145–162.

Miller, Gary, and Norman Schofield. "Activists and Partisan Realignment in the United States." *American Political Science Review* 97 (May 2003): 245–260.

Nardulli, Peter F. *Popular Efficacy in the Democratic Era: A Reexamination of Electoral Accountability in the United States, 1928–2000*. Princeton, N.J.: Princeton University Press, 2005.

*Pomper, Gerald M. "The Presidential Election: Change Comes to America." In *The Elections of 2008*, edited by Michael Nelson. Washington, D.C.: CQ Press, 2009, 45–73.

Presidential Elections, 1789–2008. Washington, D.C.: CQ Press, 2010.

Schlesinger, Joseph A. *Political Parties and the Winning of Office*. Ann Arbor: University of Michigan Press, 1991.

Sundquist, James L. *Dynamics of the Party System: Alignment and Realignment of Political Parties in the United States*, rev. ed. Washington, D.C.: Brookings, 1983.

*Todd, Chuck, and Sheldon Gawiser, with Ana Maria Arumi and G. Evans Witt. *How Obama Won: A State-by-State Guide to the Historic 2008 Presidential Election*. New York: Vintage Books, 2009.

Chapter 4: Who Voted?

Aldrich, John H. "Rational Choice and Turnout." *American Journal of Political Science* 37 (February 1993): 246–278.

Ansolabehere, Stephen, and Shanto Iyengar. *Going Negative: How Attack Ads Shrink and Polarize the Electorate*. New York: Free Press, 1996.

Burnham, Walter Dean. "The Turnout Problem." In *Elections American Style*, edited by James Reichley. Washington, D.C.: Brookings, 1987, 97–133.

Conway, M. Margaret. "The Scope of Participation in the 2008 Presidential Race: Voter Mobilization and Electoral Success." In *Winning the Presidency: 2008*. Boulder, Colo.: Paradigm, 2009, 110–122.

Crenson, Matthew A., and Benjamin Ginsberg. *Downsizing Democracy: How America Sidelined Its Citizens and Privatized Its Public*. Baltimore: Johns Hopkins University Press, 2002.

Highton, Benjamin. "Voter Registration and Turnout in the United States." *Perspectives on Politics* 2 (September 2004): 507–515.

Holbrook, Thomas M., and Scott D. McClurg. "The Mobilization of Core Supporters: Campaigns, Turnout, and Electoral Composition in United States Presidential Elections." *American Journal of Political Science* 49 (October 2005): 689–703.

Manza, Jeff, and Christopher Uggen. *Locked Out: Felon Disfranchisement and American Democracy.* New York: Oxford University Press, 2006.

Martinez, Michael D., and Jeff Gill. "The Effects of Turnout on Partisan Outcomes in U.S. Presidential Elections 1960–2000." *Journal of Politics* 67 (November 2005): 1248–1274.

*McDonald, Michael P. "The Return of the Voter: Voter Turnout in the 2008 Presidential Election." *The Forum* 6, no. 4 (2008): art. 4, www.bepress.com/forum/vol6/iss4art4.

*———. "2008 General Election Turnout Rates," http://elections.gmu.edu/Turnout_2008G.html.

McDonald, Michael P., and Samuel L. Popkin. "The Myth of the Vanishing Voter." *American Political Science Review* 95 (December 2001): 963–974.

Miller, Warren E., and J. Merrill Shanks. *The New American Voter.* Cambridge, Mass.: Harvard University Press, 1996, 95–114.

Patterson, Thomas E. *The Vanishing Voter: Public Involvement in an Age of Uncertainty.* New York: Knopf, 2002.

Piven, Frances Fox, and Richard A. Cloward. *Why Americans Still Don't Vote: And Why Politicians Want It That Way.* Boston: Beacon Press, 2000.

Putnam, Robert. *Bowling Alone: The Collapse and Revival of American Community.* New York: Simon and Schuster, 2000.

Rosenstone, Steven J., and John Mark Hansen. *Mobilization, Participation, and Democracy in America.* New York: Macmillan, 1993.

Teixeira, Ruy A. *The Disappearing American Voter.* Washington, D.C.: Brookings, 1992.

Wolfinger, Raymond E., and Steven J. Rosenstone. *Who Votes?* New Haven, Conn.: Yale University Press, 1980.

Chapter 5: Social Forces and the Vote

Alford, Robert R. *Party and Society: The Anglo-American Democracies.* Chicago: Rand McNally, 1963.

Axelrod, Robert. "Where the Votes Come From: An Analysis of Electoral Coalitions, 1952–1968." *American Political Science Review* 66 (March 1972): 11–20.

2025

Bartels, Larry M. *Unequal Democracy: The Political Economy of the New Gilded Age*. Princeton, N.J.: Princeton University Press, 2008.

Brewer, Mark D., and Jeffrey M. Stonecash. *Split: Class and Cultural Divides in American Politics*. Washington, D.C.: CQ Press, 2007.

Gelman, Andrew, et al. *Red States, Blue States, Rich States, Poor States: Why Americans Vote the Way They Do*. Princeton, N.J.: Princeton University Press, 2008.

*Guth, James L. "Religion in the 2008 Election." In *The American Elections of 2008*, edited by Janet M. Box-Steffensmeier and Steven E. Schier. Lanham, Md.: Rowman and Littlefield, 2009, 117–136.

Hamilton, Richard R. *Class and Politics in the United States*. New York: Wiley, 1972.

Huckfeldt, Robert, and Carol Weitzel Kohfeld. *Race and the Decline of Class in American Politics*. Urbana: University of Illinois Press, 1989.

*Klinker, Philip A., and Thomas Schaller. "LBJ's Revenge: The 2008 Election and the Rise of the Great Society Coalition." *The Forum* 6, no. 4 (2008): art. 9, www.bepress.com/forum/vol6/iss4/art9.

Lipset, Seymour Martin. *Political Man: The Social Bases of Politics*, exp. ed. Baltimore: Johns Hopkins University Press, 1981.

Manza, Jeff, and Clem Brooks. *Social Cleavages and Political Change: Voter Alignments and U.S. Party. Coalitions*. Oxford, UK: Oxford University Press, 1999.

Miller, Warren E., and J. Merrill Shanks. *The New American Voter*. Cambridge, Mass.: Harvard University Press, 1996, 212–282.

Stanley, Harold W., and Richard G. Niemi. "Partisanship, Party Coalitions, and Group Support, 1952–2004." *Presidential Studies Quarterly* 36 (June 2006): 172–188.

Tate, Katherine. *From Protest to Politics: The New Black Voters in American Elections*, enl. ed. Cambridge, Mass.: Harvard University Press, 1994.

Chapter 6: Candidates, Issues, and the Vote

Campbell, Angus, Philip E. Converse, Warren E. Miller, and Donald E. Stokes. *The American Voter*. New York: Wiley, 1960, 168–265.

*Campbell, David E. "Public Opinion and the 2008 Presidential Election." In *The American Elections of 2008*, edited by Janet M. Box-Steffensmeier and Steven E. Schier. Lanham, Md.: Rowman and Littlefield, 2009, 99–116.

Carmines, Edward G., and James A. Stimson. *Issue Evolution: Race and the Transformation of American Politics.* Princeton, N.J.: Princeton University Press, 1989.

Fiorina, Morris P., with Samuel J. Abrams and Jeremy C. Pope. *Culture War? The Myth of a Polarized America,* 2nd ed. New York: Pearson Longman, 2006.

Gerber, Elisabeth R., and John E. Jackson. "Endogenous Preferences and the Study of Institutions." *American Political Science Review* 87 (September 1993): 639–656.

Hillygus, D. Sunshine, and Todd G. Shields. *The Persuadable Voter: Wedge Issues in Presidential Campaigns.* Princeton, N.J.: Princeton University Press, 2008.

Lau, Richard R., and David P. Redlawsk. *How Voters Decide: Information Processing during Election Campaigns.* Cambridge, UK: Cambridge University Press, 2006.

Lau, Richard R., David J. Andersen, and David P. Redlawsk. "An Exploration of Correct Voting in Recent U.S. Presidential Elections." *American Journal of Political Science* 52 (April 2008): 395–411.

Lewis-Beck, Michael S., William G. Jacoby, Helmut Norpoth, and Herbert F. Weisberg. *The American Voter Revisited.* Ann Arbor: University of Michigan Press, 2008, 161–301.

Popkin, Samuel L. *The Reasoning Voter: Communication and Persuasion in Presidential Campaigns.* Chicago: University of Chicago Press, 1991.

Shafer, Byron E., and William J. M. Claggett. *The Two Majorities: The Issue Context of Modern American Politics.* Baltimore: Johns Hopkins University Press, 1995.

Chapter 7: Presidential Performance and Candidate Choice

*Ceaser, James W., Andrew E. Busch, and John J. Pitney Jr. *Epic Journey: The 2008 Elections and American Politics.* Lanham, Md.: Rowman and Littlefield, 2009, 35–52.

Dalton, Russell J. *Democratic Challenges, Democratic Choices: The Erosion of Political Support in Advanced Industrial Democracies.* Oxford, UK: Oxford University Press, 2004.

Downs, Anthony. *An Economic Theory of Democracy.* New York: Harper and Row, 1957.

Fiorina, Morris P. *Retrospective Voting in American National Elections.* New Haven, Conn.: Yale University Press, 1981.

Jacobson, Gary C. *A Divider, Not a Uniter: George W. Bush and the American People, The 2006 Election and Beyond.* New York: Pearson Longman, 2008.

Key, V. O., Jr. *The Responsible Electorate: Rationality in Presidential Voting, 1936–1960.* Cambridge, Mass.: Harvard University Press, 1966.

Kiewiet, D. Roderick. *Macroeconomics and Micropolitics: The Electoral Effects of Economic Issues.* Chicago: University of Chicago Press, 1983.

Lewis-Beck, Michael S. *Economics and Elections: The Major Western Democracies.* Ann Arbor: University of Michigan Press, 1988.

Riker, William H. *Liberalism against Populism: A Confrontation between the Theory of Democracy and the Theory of Social Choice.* San Francisco: W. H. Freeman, 1982.

Tufte, Edward R. *Political Control of the Economy.* Princeton, N.J.: Princeton University, 1978.

Chapter 8: Party Loyalties, Policy Preferences, and the Vote

Abramson, Paul R. *Political Attitudes in America: Formation and Change.* San Francisco: W. H. Freeman, 1983.

Aldrich, John H. *Why Parties? The Origin and Transformation of Political Parties in America.* Chicago: University of Chicago Press, 1995.

Bartels, Larry M. "Partisanship and Voting Behavior, 1952–1996," *American Journal of Political Science* 44 (January 2000): 35–50.

Campbell, Angus, Philip E. Converse, Warren E. Miller, and Donald E. Stokes. *The American Voter.* New York: Wiley, 1960, 120–167.

Fiorina, Morris P. "Parties, Participation, and Representation in America: Old Theories Face New Realities." In *Political Science: The State of the Discipline,* edited by Ira Katznelson and Helen V. Milner. New York: Norton, 2002, 511–541.

Green, Donald, Bradley Palmquist, and Eric Schickler. *Partisan Hearts and Minds: Political Parties and the Social Identities of Voters.* New Haven, Conn.: Yale University Press, 2002.

*Jacobson, Gary C. "The Effects of the George W. Bush Presidency on Partisan Attitudes." *Presidential Studies Quarterly* 39 (June 2009): 172–206.

Keith, Bruce E., David B. Magleby, Candice J. Nelson, Elizabeth Orr, Mark C. Westlye, and Raymond E. Wolfinger. *The Myth of the Independent Voter.* Berkeley: University of California Press, 1992.

Lewis-Beck, Michael S., William G. Jacoby, Helmut Norpoth, and Herbert F. Weisberg. *The American Voter Revisited.* Ann Arbor: University of Michigan Press, 2008, 111–160.

Miller, Warren E., and J. Merrill Shanks. *The New American Voter.* Cambridge, Mass.: Harvard University Press, 1996, 117–185.

Wattenberg, Martin P. *The Decline of American Political Parties, 1952–1996.* Cambridge, Mass.: Harvard University Press, 1998.

Chapter 9: Candidates and Outcomes in 2008

Abramowitz, Alan I., Brad Alexander, and Matthew Gunning. "Incumbency, Redistricting, and the Decline of Competition in U.S. House Elections." *Journal of Politics* 68 (February 2006): 75–88.

Aldrich, John H., Michael Brady, Scott de Marchi, Ian McDonald, Brendan Nyhan, David W. Rohde, and Michael Tofias. "Party and Constituency in the U.S. Senate, 1933–2004." In *Why Not Parties? Party Effects in the United States Senate,* edited by Nathan W. Monroe, Jason M. Roberts, and David W. Rohde. Chicago: University of Chicago Press, 2008, 39–51.

Brunell, Thomas L., and Bernard Grofman. "Explaining Divided U.S. Senate Delegations, 1788–1996: A Realignment Approach." *American Political Science Review* 92 (June 1998): 391–399.

Carson, Jamie, Erik J. Engstrom, and Jason M. Roberts. "Candidate Quality, the Personal Vote, and the Incumbency Advantage in Congress." *American Political Science Review* 101 (May 2007): 289–301.

*Ceaser, James W., Andrew E. Busch, and John J. Pitney Jr. *Epic Journey: The 2008 Elections and American Politics.* Lanham, Md.: Rowman and Littlefield, 2009, 163–181.

*Currinder, Marian. "Campaign Finance: Fundraising and Spending in the 2008 Elections." In *The Elections of 2008,* edited by Michael Nelson. Washington, D.C.: CQ Press, 2009, 163–186.

*Davidson, Roger H. "Partisan Surge and Decline in Congressional Elections: The Case of 2008. In *The American Elections of 2008*, edited by Janet M. Box-Steffensmeier and Steven E. Schier. Lanham, Md.: Rowman and Littlefield, 2009, 79–97.

Fenno, Richard F., Jr. *Home Style: House Members in Their Districts*. Boston: Little, Brown, 1978.

*Jacobson, Gary C. "Congress: The Second Democratic Wave." In *The Elections of 2008*, edited by Michael Nelson. Washington, D.C.: CQ Press, 2009, 100–121.

———. *The Politics of Congressional Elections*, 7th ed. New York: Pearson Longman, 2009, 1–105, 155–270.

*Larson, Bruce. "The Congressional and Gubernatorial Contests." In *The Year of Obama: How Barack Obama Won the White House*, edited by Larry J. Sabato. New York: Longman, 2010, 115–148.

Lau, Richard R., and Gerald M. Pomper. "Effectiveness of Negative Campaigning in U.S. Senate Elections," *American Journal of Political Science* 46 (January 2002): 47–66.

Rohde, David W. *Parties and Leaders in the Postreform House*. Chicago: University of Chicago Press, 1991.

Schlesinger, Joseph A. *Ambition and Politics: Political Careers in the United States*. Chicago: Rand McNally, 1966.

Stone, Walter J., and L. Sandy Maisel. "The Not-So-Simple Calculus of Winning: Potential U.S. House Candidates' Nomination and General Election Prospects." *Journal of Politics* 65 (November 2003): 951–977.

Stonecash, Jeffrey M. *Reassessing the Incumbency Effect*. Cambridge, UK: Cambridge University Press, 2008

Chapter 10: The Congressional Electorate in 2008

Abramowitz, Alan I., and Jeffrey A. Segal. *Senate Elections*. Ann Arbor: University of Michigan Press, 1992.

Beck, Paul Allen, Lawrence Baum, Aage R. Clausen, and Charles E. Smith Jr. "Patterns and Sources of Ticket Splitting in Subpresidential Voting." *American Political Science Review* 86 (December 1992): 916–928.

Burden, Barry C., and David C. Kimball. *Why Americans Split Their Tickets: Campaigns, Competition, and Divided Government.* Ann Arbor: University of Michigan Press, 2002.

Dalager, Jon K. "Voters, Issues, and Elections: Are the Candidates' Messages Getting Through?" *Journal of Politics* 58 (May 1996): 486–515.

Fenno, Richard F., Jr. "If, as Ralph Nader Says, Congress Is 'The Broken Branch,' Why Do We Love Our Congressmen So Much?" In *Congress in Change: Elections and Reform,* edited by Norman J. Ornstein. New York: Praeger, 1975, 277–287.

Jacobson, Gary C. *The Electoral Origins of Divided Government: Competition in U.S. House Elections, 1946–1988.* Boulder, Colo.: Westview Press, 1990.

—————. *The Politics of Congressional Elections,* 7th ed. New York: Pearson Longman, 2009, 113–153.

Sigelman, Lee, Paul J. Wahlbeck, and Emmett H. Buell Jr. "Vote Choice and the Preference for Divided Government: Lessons of 1992." *American Journal of Political Science* 41 (July 1997): 879–894.

Chapter 11: The 2008 Elections and the Future of American Politics

*Abramowitz, Alan I. "The 2008 Presidential Election: How Obama Won and What It Means." In *The Year of Obama: How Barack Obama Won the White House,* edited by Larry J. Sabato. New York: Longman, 2010, 91–114.

*Caraley, Demetrios James. "Eight Presidential Elections: Overview." In *Eight Presidential Elections, 1980–2008: Dealignments, Brittle Mandates, and Possible Majority Realignment,* edited by Demetrios James Caraley. New York: Academy of Political Science, 2009, 1–20.

*—————. "Three Trends over Eight Presidential Elections, 1980–2008: Toward the Emergence of a Democratic Majority Realignment?" *Political Science Quarterly* 124 (Fall 2009): 423–442.

*Ceaser, James W., Andrew E. Busch, and John J. Pitney Jr. *Epic Journey: The 2008 Elections and American Politics.* Lanham, Md.: Rowman and Littlefield, 2009, 189–210.

*Conley, Patricia. "A Mandate for Change? Decisive Victory in a Time of Crisis." In *Winning the Presidency: 2008,* edited by William J. Crotty. Boulder, Colo.: Paradigm, 2009, 169–184.

*Jacobson, Gary C. "The 2008 Presidential and Congressional Elections: Anti-Bush Referendum and Prospects for the Democratic Majority." *Political Research Quarterly* 124 (Spring 2009): 1–30.

*MacManus, Susan. "Presidential Election 2008: An Amazing Race, So What's Next? In *The Year of Obama: How Barack Obama Won the White House,* edited by Larry J. Sabato. New York: Longman, 2010, 261–296.

*Mayhew, David R. "The Meaning of the 2008 Elections." In *The Elections of 2008,* edited by Michael Nelson. Washington, D.C.: CQ Press, 2009, 187–204.

*Rae, Nicol C. "The Meaning of the 2008 Election." In *The American Elections of 2008,* edited by Janet M. Box-Steffensmeier and Steven E. Schier. Lanham, Md.: Rowman and Littlefield, 2009, 161–179.

*Sabato, Larry J. "The Election of Our Lifetimes." In *The Year of Obama: How Barack Obama Won the White House,* edited by Larry J. Sabato. New York, Longman, 2000, 33–74.

*White, John Kenneth. "A Transforming Election: How Barack Obama Changed American Politics." In *Winning the Presidency: 2008,* edited by William J. Crotty. Boulder, Colo.: Paradigm, 2009, 185–208.

Index

Tables, figures, and notes are indicated with t, f, and n/nn following the page number.